LIVESTOCK, SUGAR
AND SLAVERY

LIVESTOCK, SUGAR
AND SLAVERY

Contested Terrain in Colonial Jamaica

Verene A. Shepherd

Ian Randle Publishers

Kingston • Miami

First published in Jamaica, 2009 by
Ian Randle Publishers
11 Cunningham Avenue
Box 686
Kingston 6
www.ianrandlepublishers.com

© 2009, Verene A. Shepherd

National Library of Jamaica Cataloguing in Publication Data

Shepherd, Verene A.
      Livestock, sugar and slavery: contested terrain in colonial Jamaica/ Verene A.
Shepherd

      p. : ill., maps ; cm.

      Bibliography: p. Includes index

      ISBN 978-976-637-256-9 (pbk)

1. Land use – Jamaica – History 2. Livestock-Jamaica   3. Plantation life – Jamaica
4. Slavery – Economic aspects – Jamaica   5. Slavery – Social aspects – Jamaica
6. Slaves – Emancipation – Jamaica

I. Title

Cover image courtesy of the National Library taken from James Hakewill's A picturesque
tour of the island of Jamaica (A View of Cardiff Hall Pen, 1820)

Cover and book design by Ian Randle Publishers
Printed in the United States of America

For Bramwell, Deane and Duane

TABLE OF CONTENTS

List of Figures and Tables / **viii**

Preface / **xiii**

Introduction / **xvii**

Conventions and Abbreviations / **xxxviii**

1. Raising Livestock in the Pre-Plantation Era / **1**

2. The Interplay of Livestock and Cane: Contests over Land for Commodity Production / **14**

3. Trade and Exchange: Contesting the Classic Plantationist Trading Arrangement / **48**

4. The Pen-Keepers: Emergence, Demographic Profile and Economic Status / **77**

5. The Pen-Keepers: Socio-Political Status, Ideology, Relationships and the 'Ranking Game' / **100**

6. The Enslaved on Pens: Demographic Profile and Work Culture / **119**

7. Contesting Terrain: Negotiations for Freedom in a Slave System / **144**

8. Post-Slavery Adjustments / **175**

Conclusion / **217**

Notes / **222**

Bibliography / **254**

Index / **275**

LIST OF FIGURES AND TABLES

List of Figures

Figure 1.1
Jamaica's Parishes, 1845 / **9**

Figure 2.1
Dot Map Showing Distribution of Cattle in Jamaica, 1740 / **26**

Figure 2.2
Scatter Diagram Showing the Correlation between the Number of Sugar Works and the Number of Cattle used by Parish, 1740 / **27**

Figure 2.3
Scatter Diagram Showing the Correlation between the Number of Sugar Works and the Number of Cattle used by Parish, 1768 / **28**

Figure 2.4
Sugar Plantation Areas of Jamaica, 1793 / **44**

Figure 2.5
Social Areas, Kingston, 1745 / **47**

Figure 3.1
Livestock Trade, Cacoon Castle Pen, 1800 / **59**

Figure 3.2
Livestock Trade, Paradise Pen, 1800 / **60**

Figure 3.3
Livestock Trade, Farm Pen, 1800 / **60**

Figure 3.4
Percentage Costs of Imported Livestock by Type and Country of Origin, 1832 / **74**

Figure 3.5
Percentage Costs of Imported Livestock by Type and Country of Origin, 1845 / **74**

Figure 6.1
Representation of the Management Hierarchy on Pens / **129**

Figure 8.1
Plan of Lloyd's Pen, St David / **204**

Figure 8.2
Plan of Bonny Pen, St Mary 1843/44 / **205**

Figure 8.3
Plan of Malvern Park Pen, St Ann / **206**

List of Tables

Table 2.1
Distribution of Landholdings in Four Parishes, 1664 / **18**

Table 2.2
Ten Largest Landholders, 1754 / **19**

Table 2.3
Sugar Works and Cattle by Parish, 1740 and 1768 / **25**

Table 2.4
Distribution of Mills in Jamaica by Parish, 1763 / **29**

Table 2.5
Mill Types by Parish and County, 1804 / **31**

Table 2.6
Number of Pens, Sugar Estates and Plantations of Minor Staples, 1836 / **45**

Table 3.1
Breakdown of Livestock Sales by Type and Volume, 1780 / **58**

Table 3.2
The Internal Trade: Relative Value of Goods and Services from Selected Properties, 1820 / **61**

Table 3.3
Sample of Inter-Property Trade, 1820 / **64**

Table 3.4
Sources of Imported Livestock, 1815–25 / **72**

Table 4.1
Classification of the White Inhabitants of St James's Parish, 1773 / **79**

Table 4.2
Absentee Pen-Owners by Parish, 1820 / **84**

Table 4.3
Sexual Activities of Thomas Thistlewood, Vineyard Pen, 1750–51 / **89**

Table 4.4
Frequency of Thomas Thistlewood's Sexual Activites with Enslaved Females on Breadnut Island Pen, 1768 / **90**

Table 4.5
Value of the Possessions of Certain Pen-Keepers According to the Probate Inventories, 1739–1838 / **94**

Table 4.6
Valuation of the Properties Belonging to the Honourable John Tharp, Esq, 1792 / **95**

Table 4.7
Value of Enslaved People and Stock on John Tharp's Estates and Other Properties, 1792 / **97**

Table 4.8
Value of Household and Personal Effects of Selected Pen-Keepers, 1739–1838 / **98**

Table 4.9
Inventory of Thetford Estate, Fuller's Rest and Thetford Hall Pen, St John / **99**

Table 5.1
Number and Qualification of Freeholders Applying for the Vote in St Catherine at Five-Yearly Intervals, 1760–1840 / **113**

Table 6.1
Slave Demography, Pepper and Bonavista Pens, 1826–38 / **125**

Table 6.2
Demographic Characteristics of the Enslaved on Pens in Westmoreland, 1817 / **127**

Table 6.3
Age Profile on Selected Pens, Westmoreland, 1817 / **128**

Table 6.4
List of those Enslaved on St Jago and Paisley Pens,
January 1, 1827 / **134**

Table 6.5
The Division of Labour on Vineyard Pen, 1750 / **136**

Table 7.1
Summary of Runaways, Vineyard Pen / **157**

Table 7.2
Properties Attacked by Anti-Slavery Activities in the 1831/32
Emancipation War in Jamaica / **165**

Table 7.3
Losses Suffered by Enslavers in Hanover in the 1831/32
Emancipation War / **166**

Table 7.4
Summary of the Majority of Trials: 1831/32 Emancipation War / **167**

Table 7.5
Sample of Enslaved Pen Anti-Slavery Activists Punished for their Role
in the 1831/32 Emancipation War / **170**

Table 7.6
Punishment List, Parish of Manchester, 1831/32 / **172**

Table 8.1
Valuation of Pen Apprentices, January to June 1836 / **176**

Table 8.2
Return of the Number of Enslaved People and Estimated Value
Thereof, in Each Class, in Possession of Hamilton Brown, Owner on
the 1st Day of August, 1834 / **179**

Table 8.3
Accounts of Rents and Wages, Fort George Pen, 1843 / **195**

Table 8.4
Comparative Earnings on Selected Pens, 1840 and 1845 / **201**

Table 8.5
Accounts of Rents, 1840–45 / **207**

Table 8.6
Share of Exports of Major Products, 1883 / **208**

Table 8.7
Contribution of Major Staples to Total Agricultural Exports 1870–1900 / **212**

Table 8.8
Acres in Banana and Sugar Cane, 1891–1900 / **212**

PREFACE

It is now fairly well-established within Caribbean historiography that the history of Jamaica, like that of the wider colonized Caribbean and Atlantic World, has been one characterized by conflict over terrain, physical and ideological — border clashes — from the moment of the island's capture by the Spaniards, through the period of English and British socioeconomic and political domination and into the postcolonial period. A great deal of these conflicts developed between colonizers/imperialists and those they attempted to colonize. This is not surprising. The indigenous peoples and the enslaved, male and female, were not incorporated into the Atlantic World as citizens with equal rights, but as chattel enslaved and as the colonial 'Other'. Despite the dependence of the North Atlantic on the South Atlantic for labour and commodities, the cultural experiences and interaction of Africans and Europeans did not determine the creation of a Creole vision that ultimately became the symbol of an Atlantic identity. On the contrary, deep divisions, inequality and instability characterized the 'Atlantic World.' These divisions and lack of egalitarianism, especially in the slave relations of production, which were essentially relations of domination in the orthodox Marxist sense, made the Atlantic World deeply unstable. While the lack of equality was most pronounced in the relationships among Europeans, 'Free-Coloureds' and Africans, it was also manifested in the relationships between sugar planters and non-sugar proprietors as a result of the link between socio-political status and economic activity. The persistence of the colonial legacy of inequality in the region in the postmodern age has dictated that contests over rights and social, physical and ideological terrain are not confined to the historical past.

Livestock, Sugar and Slavery contributes to the ongoing discourses over the roots of conflict between the colonized and their oppressors in colonial Jamaica. But the book also engages with the contests over land use and commodity production brought on by the English (and British) colonizers' attempts to establish sugar monoculture in the island. In this regard, the book broadens the discussion to include the non-sugar producers, mostly European and mixed-race farmers. Its empirical examples relate specifically to those called pen-keepers who used to raise livestock on southern savannah lands in the pre-sugar era but who had to relocate to more interior lands because of the land needs of the more dominant sugar barons after 1740. The book examines the issue of diversification even in the age of sugar, rehearses the evolution and expansion of livestock farming (one of the chief challenges to the sugar industry), and looks at the role and status of the pen-keepers, and the experiences of enslaved labourers on the pens. Above all, the book argues that the relationship between those whose livelihood depended on raising livestock and those who predominantly raised cane, while symbiotic in one sense, was conflict-ridden in another. Pens, though emerging in the pre-sugar era when they had their own independent economic dynamic, had developed into virtual appendages of the sugar industry by the late eighteenth and nineteenth centuries, leading to contests over land, boundaries, trade, prices of animals, enslaved labourers and the social and political status of their owners and managers. Importantly though, by their establishment and local trading activities (plus the creole origin of many of their owners), the pens dictated that Jamaica departed from the strict application of the plantation economy model and maintained an enduring diversified economy.

The book also engages with the 'ranking game', a central feature of all multi-ethnic societies in which there is no essential egalitarianism among the constituent classes and ethnic groups. Within the current Jamaican context, 'ranking' represents the linguistic, oral and literary aspects of social culture that are manifested in the ritualized and politicized codes and consciousness of difference. It is the engine that drives Jamaica's political sociology. But the 'ranking game' has deep historical roots, as this study will demonstrate, and led to social hierarchizing and the maintenance of boundaries among the island's different ethnicities and classes. For some, situating difference established the boundaries of belonging; for others, situating difference was a way of signifying the opposite tendency of 'unbelonging.' This tension between 'belonging' and 'unbelonging' was a fundamental characteristic of the 'ranking game', a ritual that was invested with all the social and political capital available to the society. Ranking was understood historically within the colonial formation in terms of access to restricted status, as manifested primarily in signs and symbols that with social consensus offered respect and respectability. The book does not deny the presence of consensus in Jamaican history and society, but has deliberately chosen to highlight the historic root factors which have caused divisons and instability.

The book was compiled with the help of many people and I owe a debt of gratitude to those who assisted in its preparation. First of all, I am grateful to my family for supporting me and creating an extra-university environment more conducive to creative work. I thank Betty Wood of the Faculty of History, University of Cambridge, for her guidance and inspiration long after her role as academic supervisor ended. I also thank Barry Higman, former Chair of the Mona History Department and currently at the Australian National University; and Stanley Engerman, of the University of Rochester, who read and critiqued various versions of the manuscript and gave insightful comments. Barry influenced my choice of topic for this work and encouraged me to take the topic further. Not surprisingly, his influence on the book is clear.

I extend appreciation to the librarians and archivists in Jamaica and the United Kingdom who went beyond the limits of their duty to assist me in the location of documents. Many of the archivists in the County Archives in Britain sent back such detailed replies to my letters enquiring about their holdings, that I was often spared the expense of a 'wild goose chase'.

For assistance with tables, figures, the bibliography, proofreading and word processing at various stages of the work, I thank Dalea Bean, Valerie Bedward, Nadine Hunt, Grace Juttan, Veta Rowe, Duane Shepherd, and Carol Thompson.

A sabbatical year from the University of the West Indies, a Research Fellowship at the Institute of Commonwealth Studies, University of London, a Fellowship granted by the York/UNESCO Nigerian Hinterland Project (which involved my serving as one of the Network Professors for the academic year 2000–01), and the peaceful writing spaces in London provided by Karen Porteous; Annette, Janice and Phillip Brade and Angella and Jason Lazarus over several summers, provided me with the necessary time, space and resources to complete this long-overdue project, and I extend heartfelt thanks to all the facilitators involved. Finally, I am grateful to my supportive 'sisters' — Annette Brade, Sonia Fennell, Elfreda Hedger, Lena Cay Mullings, Hilrett Owusu, and Sandra Touzalin, whose friendship and company (including 'retail therapy' and extended telephone chat sessions during some of my writing breaks), helped to make the task a little easier.

Verene A. Shepherd

INTRODUCTION

One of the significant features of Jamaica's post-independence history is the emergence and maintenance of spaces called 'garrisons' and the control of such barricaded and often politicized spaces by men dubbed 'dons', some non-aligned, others of various political persuasions. This 'donmanship' phenomenon has been known to create conflicts in Kingston and St Andrew, St Catherine and other parts of the island. The border clashes, gangsterism and party politics that have so polarized the island physically, economically and ideologically, have their roots deeply embedded in the historical past. Indeed, a constant feature of Jamaica's colonial history has been the struggle waged over land as well as over political, economic and ideological terrain. This contest over 'terrain' (or turf) was manifested in several ways historically; and here 'terrain' is used in the metaphorical sense of colonized space/sphere of influence and power, hegemonic territory, as well as physical land. An overview of the island's history from Taino occupation to the period of decolonization will demonstrate the long existence of the trend.

The first contest over Jamaican terrain was manifested in the struggles between indigenous Ciboney and later settlers, Tainos. The Ciboney, referred to by archaeologists as a 'meso-Indian' nomadic shell culture migrated to the island either southward from Florida and The Bahamas or northwards from South America, perhaps not as one ethnic group but as waves of different migrants over an extensive period of time from pre-farming cultures. As hunter-gatherers, the Ciboney developed no village life around agriculture and artisan technologies; so that their contest with the Tainos was not so much over land for economic use, but over 'territorial space' over which they had prior, hegemonic claim.

Research indicates that the more numerous and technologically developed Tainos dominated and enslaved the Ciboney as the latter were not organized for military activity. These 'neo-Indian' Tainos from the Arawakan language group (a reason they have been called 'Arawaks'), originated in the Americas, migrating northwards from the Guianas and Venezuela, settling various islands in the Caribbean chain before reaching Jamaica and the Greater Antilles. The Tainos are believed to have settled Jamaica somewhere between AD 600 and 900, with settlements stretching along the island's north coast from Priestman's River in the east to Negril in the west. They also established themselves on the south coast at Savanna-la-Mar, Bluefields, Cow Bay, White Marl (near Spanish Town), continuing to Morant Point. The Tainos thus effectively occupied the entire island ahead of the Spanish invasion in 1494. The fifteenth century Spanish colonizers, therefore, found no empty space; nor did they find uncivilized people, despite their racist justification for subjugating these indigenous peoples and appropriating their land, suppressing their brave resistance in the process.[1]

Far from being 'uncivilized', the Tainos were a highly developed sedentary civilization with standards of industrial technology in textiles and ceramics that were on par with what obtained in the rural communities of Asia and Europe. They lived by fishing, hunting and conuco agriculture. The social organization of the Tainos dictated that they lived in loosely structured family groups, each with its own ruler or chief. The Tainos had their own religious beliefs, social structure and political organization. They were ruled by their local Cacique who in turn came under the jurisdiction of a regional Cacique. Taino theological ideas were distinct and expressed through complex rituals and ceremonies. At the core of their religious belief was the recognition of a spiritually structured world in which both humans and gods were classified and ranked. They believed in a Supreme Being, Creator of the world, and worshipped deities called 'Zemis'. They believed, like many people today, in immortality and life after death. They enjoyed recreational activities like the ball game *batos*. It is usual to describe the Tainos as 'peaceful'; but the Tainos fought enemies to protect their space when the need arose. They had to defend themselves, for example, from other indigenous Caribbeans (most notably the Kalinagos) looking to expand their settlement and hegemony in the region. Europeans stereotyped the Tainos as 'peaceful' because they wanted to distinguish them from the Kalinagos, who because they tried to prevent the North-West Europeans from capturing their space, stereotyped them as 'fierce cannibals'. The Windward Islands of the Eastern Caribbean rather than Jamaica, however, became the centre of Kalinago occupation and struggle with the European colonizers.[2]

The next phase of contested terrain in Jamaica occurred after Columbus and his crew, operating under the Spanish flag, invaded the island on May 5, 1494, landing off the north coast near the Taino village of Maima near Seville, located in the parish of St Ann. Conquest disrupted the lives of the indigenous people severely. Above all, Columbus imposed hegemony over Jamaica, seizing ownership from the Tainos. Columbus returned nine years later and was shipwrecked and marooned on the island for just over a year with his base at Santa Gloria. During this extended stay conflicts developed between indigenous people and the Spaniards. The Tainos were subjected to forced labour, sexual exploitation and other abuses that contributed to their misery. By the time Columbus was rescued in 1504, the Taino population, which stood at about 50,000-60,000 at the time of conquest in 1494 had been severely depleted.

Columbus's departure in June 1504 did not end the Spanish colonization of Jamaica as Spanish hegemony continued, under new rulers, until 1655. 'Ownership' of the island fluctuated between Columbus and his heirs, and the Spanish Crown. Regardless of who was actually in charge, between 1504 and 1655 the Tainos' economic, social and political life was disrupted severely. Their chain of command changed from the local Cacique whose power diminished, to that of Spanish conquistador or Crown. Their system of worship was deemed 'pagan' and the Spanish tried to convert them to Christianity. Some accepted Spanish rule, others resisted. They were made to produce a surplus of food to feed the Spanish and had to provide forced labour in agricultural fields and ranches under the *encomienda* and *repartimiento* systems of labour organization. By 1600 the Taino population had been virtually wiped out, though their heritage survived in the Maroons and in the artefacts they left behind. The causes of decline were varied and included suicide, infanticide, overwork, lack of immunity to diseases and outright murder at the hands of Spanish settlers. To more effectively resist Spanish occupation and hegemony, the Tainos established hideouts in such areas as the Blue Mountains (where runaway Africans later joined them and established Maroon communities), Carpenter's Mountain and the Dry Harbour Mountains.

Spanish occupation did not proceed unproblematically. They faced resistance from the Tainos, Maroons and enslaved Africans. In the contest for terrain between the Tainos and the Spaniards, however, the latter were the victors, leading to the Spanish occupation from 1494–1655 when they were forced to yield to the English invaders. As the island lacked mineral wealth, the Spanish settlers developed its agricultural potential beyond the conocu economy of the Tainos. They established many *hatos* (cattle ranches, later called pens by the English) on the southern plains, planting some sugar cane for the production of sugar for domestic use, and growing tobacco, indigo, pimento, hardwoods, cotton, foodcrops and a variety of fruits and vegetables. They thus succeeded in changing the landscape from what it was under Taino sovereignty.[3]

Once the Spaniards had subdued internal resistance, they concentrated on staving off rival European threats to the island. They were put to the test in 1655 when the island was seized by the English under an expedition led by Admiral William Penn and General Robert Venables. By then, the Spanish population had declined so considerably that under 200 men defended Fort Caguaya, making conquest easy for the English; for disappointed at Jamaica's mineral poverty, many settlers had left the island for other richer sections of the Spanish–American empire. England, (like other European states) jealous of Spanish expansion in the Caribbean and the increasing mineral wealth that the Spanish Indies (though excluding Jamaica) generated, had embarked on a campaign to diminish Spanish hegemony in the Caribbean. This expedition, which intended initially to invade and capture Hispaniola, was repelled and so captured Jamaica as a lesser prize. The English had not been the first to attempt to capture Jamaica from the Spaniards, the Dutch and French having tried before. The Spaniards, with some help from some of their labourers, resisted and held out as best they could but eventually had to surrender to the English expeditionary force. By 1663, the island had established civil government.

The early English invaders were essentially soldiers and reluctant settlers who, realizing Jamaica's mineral poverty, wanted to relocate. England, however, realized Jamaica's strategic location, and first Cromwell, then

Charles II insisted on permanent colonization after the Restoration. The number of settlers increased later as non-military colonizers emigrated to the island. The English continued to pursue a diversified economy for close to a century, but by 1740 had virtually changed the rural agricultural landscape by cultivating sugar as the dominant export crop. The switch to sugar resulted in conflicts over terrain. The plains were the early location for provision farmers and pen-keepers; but these activities were pursued on lands eminently suited for cane cultivation. The small-settler food producers and ranchers were forced to relocate to the interior as the more powerful sugar planters increasingly won the battle over land for the cane. Other crops were thus facilitated only if there was no contest over land between sugar barons and non-sugar producers. Thus coffee became significant in the hilly regions of St Andrew and livestock-farming proceeded in interior sections of St Ann. Livestock was also raised in other parishes like St Elizabeth and St Catherine on lands less suitable for the cane. Thus, English colonialism did not succeed completely in introducing structural discontinuities by appropriating the land resources of the region for its monopolistic sugar plantation designs. By 1782 there were 300 'pens' in the island.[4] By 1832, the island had 176 coffee plantations employing 22,562 enslaved people and 15 pimento plantations employing 1,287 enslaved workers. By that date, sugar had 49.5 per cent of the enslaved population, coffee, 14.4 per cent and livestock farms (pens) 12.8 per cent.[5] The non-sugar producers, while fairly influential in the pre-sugar era, soon lost their political power to the sugar barons. Nevertheless, the contest over space and socioeconomic and political influence and status continued to characterize the relationship between sugar barons and non-sugar producers as the book will demonstrate later.

The indentureship of marginalized Europeans and the enslavement of Africans ushered in another period of conflict and contestation over terrain in colonial Jamaica. Unlike the Spanish settlers before them, the English found no indigenous peoples to exploit as servile labourers; and as most of the colonizers had no intention of performing manual labour themselves, they turned to importing their own countrymen and women as indentured servants. Some indentured servants volunteered for service in the Caribbean, but others were convicts and vagrants forcefully transported to various parts of the English empire in exchange for a prison term in England. At the end of their term of service, indentured servants received a 'freedom due' in land. As land became important for the expansion of the sugar economy, however, the land incentive became less and less usual, a factor leading to the decrease in English and Irish servant labour migration or relocation to the colonial Caribbean. The continuation of the subjugation of fellow Europeans also became incompatible in a slave system that relied on assumptions and assertions of a white supremacist ideology. The battle for social and political dominance between Europeans and Africans required some semblance of European solidarity, another factor contributing to the ending of English and Irish indentured servitude. Above all, Europeans resisted attempts to be reduced to conditions of quasi-slavery.[6]

As the sugar industry expanded and the number of plantations increased, and as the flow of English and Irish labourers decreased, the English colonizers turned to Africa for a labour supply. Comparatively few Africans were enslaved in Jamaica under the Spaniards (who nevertheless pioneered the use of enslaved Africans in Jamaica); for the Spaniards never developed the Jamaican economy to the point where large-scale slavery was considered essential. It was under the English that this brutal and inhumane system of labour exploitation expanded.[7] Enslaved Africans were used in every sector of the economy, including rural and urban regimes. Those enslaved also sought to carve out an economic niche for themselves, establishing the right to cultivate provision grounds and time to market their surplus. They had to struggle to maintain their right to grounds and market, a factor that set them in conflict with the enslavers.

The slave system established by the English was racist and sexist. Their elite controlled the government, marginalizing working-class people. While the system of government was labelled 'The Old Representative System', the restricted franchise (based on property), effectively resulted in a rather unrepresentative system of government. They constructed a social hierarchy, placing the English elite at the apex of the social ladder, people of mixed race in-between and African people at the bottom. Mixed-race people invented their own internal hierarchy in which the less black their skin, the higher up on the social ladder they were. The tyranny of skin shade and its racist implications predictably generated conflicts between the English and free mixed-race people, who, as creoles, claimed greater 'rights' to the island. The military and other forms of control established by the ruling class to keep the society stable also generated conflicts. Indeed, during slavery, the subalterns, or enslaved Africans and other racially marginalized groups, demanded room for themselves. Thus, the society influenced by the slave system in Jamaica was highly unstable despite the military force maintained by the colonizers to 'keep order' among the colonized. Enslaved Africans used every opportunity to resist slavery, with Maroons like Cudjoe, Nanny, Queen Cubah and Tacky waging wars against British domination. The Maroons were successful in their struggle, winning Treaty Rights against the English. Many other armed revolts also erupted across the island and involved rural enslaved peoples on sugar as well as non-sugar properties and the urban workers. Enslaved women, like men, joined in all revolts and resistance strategies in a concerted effort to end the tyranny of enslavement and, possibly, drive out the enslavers. The resistance of these enslaved persons combined with internal and external economic, political and social forces eventually ended, first the trade in Africans (1807-08) and then slavery itself.[8]

The Emancipation Act was passed in 1833 and took effect in August 1834. The enslaved did not win outright freedom in 1834, however. The British introduced a system of neo-slavery euphemistically called the 'Apprenticeship System', designed to last from 1834–38 for non-field labourers (non-praedials) and from 1834–40 for those located in field jobs (praedials). Anti-slavery/anti-Apprenticeship forces, including the protest of the apprentices, especially women, brought down the entire system in 1838. The protestors' view was that former owners tried to recreate slave relations of production and found every chance to abuse the so-called Apprenticeship system. The freed people argued that the aims of Apprenticeship were ludicrous: they had no need for a transition period to full freedom. Immediate freedom was what they wanted.

The abolition of slavery and Apprenticeship did not end systems of domination and exploitation in Jamaica; for this reason, the contest over terrain continued in the post-slavery period. Intent on maintaining the plantation system in the face of freed people's refusal to continue in a capital-labour relationship with employers who used coercive labour tactics, the landholding class imported indentured labourers from Europe, Asia, North America and Africa (once again) to provide a labour force. They imported more than they needed in order to build up a surplus labour supply and keep wages low. They believed that with wages low, African-Jamaicans would have little choice but to return to the estates to work, no matter how low the wages. While the African–Jamaican participation in the agricultural labour force continued to be significant, the possibilities of peasant development defeated the landholders' wishes. Jamaica was larger than most of the other British-colonized Caribbean territories, and, like colonial Guyana, had land on which freed people could squat, rent or purchase for peasant development. The planter-class was generally unwilling to dispose of land if that meant African-Jamaican economic independence; but their opposition could not prevent entirely the expansion of the peasantry. The contest over land between the Jamaican labouring class and the traditional landholding class was, however, a recurring theme in the island's post-slavery history.

Despite the landholders' belief that imported labourers would be more controllable than the African-Jamaican workers, many resisted their status as exploited labourers using some of the same strategies as enslaved Africans. Relations between indentured labourers and the landholding class was thus conflict-ridden. The attempt to transform indentured labour migration into settler colonization made land once more a central issue, a land colonization bounty initially being offered in lieu of state-financed repatriation. The poor physical terrain offered to Indians was a central aspect of the conflicts.

The post-Apprenticeship period in Jamaica was politically unstable as the battle over terrain continued. One reason for political instability was the continuation of the system of government that had operated under slavery. Admittedly, the franchise was gradually lowered to enable more people to have the right to vote, but women and non-propertied men (most of whom were black-skinned) continued to be disenfranchised; and those in power still engaged in unfair governing practices, ignoring most of the economic, social and political claims of the African-Jamaican majority. In 1865, for example, there was less than one in every 200 Jamaicans with the right to vote, and all but a handful comprised British persons. This and other factors determined that mass protest characterized the post-slavery period as it did the previous centuries.[9]

One such mass protest broke out in Morant Bay in St Thomas-in-the-East (now simply St Thomas), in 1865. There were several causes for the

'Morant Bay Rebellion'. The limited franchise was one. Another factor was agrarian distress, compounded by the economic impact of the American Civil war. Rural economic hardship was made worse by an absence of broad-based democracy and local accountability by those in power. The planter class did not do enough to facilitate freed people's land hunger. As squatting became more commonplace, so did the pace of evictions. In 1865, a group of African-Jamaican labourers from the parish of St Ann went as far as to petition Queen Victoria directly, asking to rent vacant Crown lands. The Queen probably never read the letter; nevertheless, the reply attributed to her urged the petitioners to work harder on the planters' estates. This 'Queen's Advice' only served to further discontent among the rural poor and localized protests increased in the depressed mid-1860s. Paul Bogle of Stony Gut, one of George William Gordon's black deacons in the Baptist church, led the Morant Bay Rebellion. Gordon was a member of the Assembly, a planter of mixed-race heritage and businessman who championed the cause of the masses. On October 11, 1865, Bogle, after unsuccessful attempts to get redress for the suffering of the people, led his followers in the town, seized weapons, and marched on the Morant Bay courthouse. A protest broke out, several demonstrators were shot by the militia, the courthouse was torched and a handful of British persons were killed. Protest spread to other parts of the parish and several plantations were attacked. The rebellion was severely put down by the governor, Edward Eyre, a former lieutenant-governor of New Zealand and a former governor of St Vincent. He had prior experience in dealing with indigenous peoples in Australia and New Zealand and with Indian indentured workers in St Vincent and developed a harsh policy of dealing with black-skinned people in Jamaica. He was clearly hostile to African-Jamaicans and represented the reactionary and unyielding ruling elite. At his direction Paul Bogle, allegedly caught by Maroons in a cane-piece, was hanged from the Morant Bay courthouse; so was George William Gordon, who had always been critical of government's policies and attitudes towards the poor and who was accused of being intimately involved in the protest. Almost 600 people were killed and as many flogged. As part of the retribution, many women who were suspected of hiding male rebels, were raped or had their heads shaved. Over 1,000 houses were burned. A Commission of Enquiry was sent out. It concluded that the system of government in Jamaica was unworkable. Eyre was recalled and the legislature was given a choice: give more people the right to vote or surrender the government to the Crown. They chose to surrender their political power rather than give African-Jamaicans more access to power. The Old Representative System of government thus gave way to what was called 'Crown Colony' rule.[10]

The terrible events at Morant Bay as well as the abolition of representative government ushered in a further period of discontent and, predictably, an outright movement for decolonization. The decolonization movement gathered momentum despite several modifications to Crown Colony government itself, for example, some unofficial members were nominated to the legislative councils. Provision was later made for a number of elective seats, until eventually elected members outnumbered nominated members in both the executive and the legislative councils. As governors became increasingly obligated to accept advice from elected legislatures, the Crown Colony system gradually evolved into responsible government. The Jamaican people demanded even more constitutional changes, however; for the modest changes did not satisfy the desire of Jamaican people to govern themselves without external interference.

The pan-Africanist, Marcus Mosiah Garvey — 1887–1940 — (himself influenced by Robert Love, the Bahamian anti-colonialist), influenced the decolonization movement in Jamaica. His Black Power ideology radicalized many people, influencing them to protest their colonial status, and continued European domination of Jamaican terrain. The labour protests of the late 1930s represented another step in the direction of self-rule as workers demanded the right to unionization and proper representation in a land in which they were being increasingly marginalized. Garvey once said: 'It is an axiom that other things being equal, the majority must rule and we shall see that other things are equal'.[11] Thus modifications to Crown Colony government did not end the discussion on the best form of political structure for Jamaica. Some wanted outright and full independence; others wanted the Caribbean to form itself into a close and unified political structure through federation.

After an unsuccessful attempt to federate the West Indies, Jamaica took the path to political independence. Political parties, some emerging out of trade unions, spearheaded the movement toward independence which was finally achieved in August 1962. The failure of independence to bring about economic power and social justice for the masses caused some African-Caribbean intellectuals to side with the poor, the youth and the unemployed to take the struggle to another level. Intellectuals such as Walter Rodney and other members of the New World Group — which had branches in Guyana, Trinidad and Tobago, and Jamaica — criticized the continuation of colonial structures even after independence. Influenced by Garveyism, Rastafarianism, the writings of Franz Fanon (a Martinican psychiatrist who emphasized the destructive effects of racism on the minds of colonized peoples) and pan-Africanism, these intellectuals were a part of the Black Power movement of the 1960s and 1970s. In the post-independence period also, Rastafarianism developed an appeal as a social doctrine proclaiming the dignity of African people. Many intellectuals embraced this doctrine and its outward trappings such as dreadlocks. While the Black Power movement, which saw protest in Trinidad and Tobago, and Jamaica in the 1960s and 1970s, raised the consciousness of Africans in the Diaspora, the various governments of the region were not all sympathetic and many radicals were persecuted in this contest for ideological terrain. The struggle for rights and social justice continues into the present era, with the ideological terrain still being highly contested.[12]

It is within this context of contested terrain in colonial Jamaica that this book is inserted. Its central focus, though, is on the contest over land for commodity production between sugar planters and dedicated livestock farmers, styled pen-keepers, in Jamaica, and the results/implications of that contest. The book also examines the contest over socio-political status between sugar and non-sugar producers within the context of a social system that constructed a hierarchy among land users, direct involvement in the sugar industry being equated with high status, and political office dictated by level of economic wealth. Despite the fact that pen-keepers and sugar planters were obliged by economic necessity to maintain a symbiotic relationship through the trade in livestock and related pen products and services, they existed as antagonistic sections — British and mixed-race people, creole born and metropolitan born, small entrepreneurs and larger, more profitable proprietors — among whom there were few common social goals outside of the context of their similar aspirations to the socioeconomic status of the sugar barons. Those pen-keepers who could afford it invested in the sugar economy as soon as they had built up the capital to do so; and they showed little cultural affinity with 'Creole Society' as defined by Kamau Brathwaite.[13] Indeed, they helped to reinforce the dichotomy of separate cultures that was a pervasive characteristic of Caribbean societies during slavery and engaged in the 'ranking game.'[14]

Ranking is understood historically within the colonial formation in terms of access to restricted status, as manifested primarily in signs and symbols that with social consensus offer respect and respectability. This ranking game was not only a feature of postcolonial Jamaica but was intensely engaged in during the age of modernity. It was manifested in the complex interaction of sugar planters and livestock farmers. Pen-keepers, some mixed-race and free and most resident in the island, were ascribed a social position below that of the sugar barons. One reason was that in the eighteenth and nineteenth centuries, being born in Jamaica was sufficient reason for low ranking within the context of a society where top ranking went to those who were British, metropolitan born, the owners of large sugar plantations, able to live as absentee proprietors, or, if in the island, as members of the elite class of British people who controlled the socioeconomic and political life of the island and lived grandly in great houses staffed by a large army of enslaved domestics. Land use was a further complication; for during slavery, land use was an important factor that ascribed social position; and status mobility was, therefore, fundamentally related to the type of economic activities in which settlers and colonizers engaged. It was within this context that sugar planters were ranked above those involved in other economic enterprises and, on the basis of the higher status of sugar planters, the primarily creole pen-keepers struggled to acquire the trappings to enable them to become a part of the British elite. The book raises several questions in an attempt to understand the role of the pen-keepers in Jamaica's socioeconomic and political history. Did they contribute to the development of Creole Society 'in every way' as Barry Higman has argued? [15] In contrast to the sugar plantation that has been associated with Caribbean underdevelopment, did the pens represent a contribution to Jamaican development through their generation of internal linkages and their contribution to the growth of something recognizable even during slavery as a domestic economy? Did pen-keepers represent simply an economic interest group, uniting around narrow economic self-interests or did their participation in the 'Jamaican'/creole economy imply a creole consciousness and a commitment to the development of Creole Society? Was their greater local resident status due to choice or economic circumstances? Finally, were they clearly ideologically differentiated from the sugar planter class?

While property holders were involved in their contests over space and status, enslaved peoples were waging their own battle for liberation and 'room to be' in colonial Jamaica. Black-skinned and mixed-race people born in the island launched their own fight for a stake (territorial hegemony) in the island. These contests reflected the lack of egalitarianism in the 'Atlantic World'. Despite the dependence of the North Atlantic on the South Atlantic for labour and commodities, the cultural experiences and interaction of Africans and Europeans did not determine the creation of a Creole vision that ultimately became the symbol of an Atlantic identity. On the contrary, deep division, inequality and instability characterized the 'Atlantic World.' These divisions and lack of egalitarianism, especially in the slave relations of production, which were essentially relations of domination in the orthodox Marxist sense, made the Atlantic World deeply unstable. The enslaved, male and female, were responsible for a great deal of the instability that characterized the Atlantic World. They were not incorporated into the Atlantic World as citizens with equal rights, but as chattel enslaved and as the inferior 'Other'.

Certain generalizations will be obvious from this book. First, some of the battles over economic, social and political space were successful for those contesting monoculture. The contest over land for commodity production resulted in a diversified economy in Jamaica — more diversified than the economies of the Eastern Caribbean. Economic diversification in turn resulted in the ethnic, class, colour and gender heterogeneity of the enslaver class and in the diversity in the economic and social experiences of the enslaved Africans. The enslaver class, for example, was neither all male, nor all European elite but comprised Europeans and mixed-race free women and a significant number of free mixed-race men, many of whom were pen-keepers. The livestock industry in Jamaica provided an alternative route for property ownership and capital accumulation for some non-elite free men and women. There were also quite wealthy coffee farmers in the island during slavery. Second, diversity in property ownership and in occupations dictated that many of the enslaved lived their lives off the sugar cane fields as domestics in rural and urban households, as hired artisans or as labourers on non-sugar agricultural units. This evidence of diversification, therefore, must temper the wholescale application of the plantation economy model, which stresses the role of the sugar plantation complex in structuring Caribbean society along the lines of a rigid enslaver-enslaved dichotomy — to Jamaica.[16]

Indeed, few Caribbean colonies were truly monocultural. Despite the switch to sugar and the dominance of the sugar planters in many territories by the late eighteenth century, all Caribbean economies continued to produce some non-sugar crops, with some colonies producing no exportable quantities of sugar at all. Belize, the Cayman Islands, the Turks and Caicos Islands, The Bahamas, Barbuda, Anguilla, the Dutch 'ABC' islands of Aruba, Bonaire and Curaçao, St Eustatius and most of the Virgin Islands never became dominated by the sugar industry, exploiting instead a variety of forest, maritime and non-sugar agricultural resources. For Belize, the extraction of timber remained the economic *raison d'être* up to and after 1789, when it became a British colony, and labour organization and work processes for the extraction of timber differed greatly from those of the sugar plantation.[17] Similarly, The Bahamas never developed as a sugar plantation society. The inhabitants were occupied principally in maritime activities, woodcutting, cotton cultivation and subsistence agriculture.

Even the so-called 'classic plantation colonies' of the Eastern Caribbean produced other commodities on land unsuitable for cane. St Kitts, Antigua and Barbados, prototypical plantation economies, exported small quantities of cotton;[18] and even at the height of the sugar economy, Cuba, Puerto Rico, St Domingue, Martinique and Guadeloupe grew varying quantities of coffee, tobacco, indigo and produced animals and timber. Before the Haitian Revolution of 1791, St Domingue produced most of the coffee exported from the Caribbean. In the late 1830s, Cuba's coffee plantations numbered just over 2,000 and employed some 50,000 enslaved Africans, roughly the same number as there were on the sugar estates; and another 100,000 enslaved peoples were engaged in other rural agricultural pursuits and in urban/non-agricultural tasks.[19] It is also well-known that tobacco cultivation has played an important role in Cuban agricultural history even in the age of sugar.[20] Similarly, while sugar was very important to Brazil's economy, other economic activities were pursued. B.J. Barickman, in *A Bahian Counterpoint* and Stephen Bell, in *Campanha Ga'cha* illustrate the ways in which tobacco and cassava cultivation, and ranching, interrupted the traditional monocultural interpretation of Brazilian economic history.[21] The relative dominance of the sugar plantation as a system of production, however, must be recognized. Only differences in the price and quality of land created variations in the extent to which intensive monoculture came to dominate the economies of particular territories. Barry Higman's quantitative analysis of 960 properties returned in the Accounts Produce for Jamaica in 1832 showed that sugar and its by-products accounted for 76 per cent of total receipts; and these properties had 53.6 per cent of the enslaved population.[22] The dominance of the sugar economy was greater in Barbados where sugar and its by-products accounted for 97 per cent of the island's exports, and over 75 per cent of the enslaved population laboured on sugar estates, compared to less than 50 per cent in Jamaica.[23]

Despite this evidence of diversification, for years Caribbean socioeconomic history displayed a rather totalizing tendency, with historians focusing on the sugar sector and virtually ignoring other agricultural sectors. In this tradition of scholarship, non-sugar producing units represented a divergent pattern of socioeconomic development and were largely under-researched. Similarly, though enslaved peoples were located outside of the physical context of the sugar plantation, within the context of Caribbean history, slavery became synonymous with sugar plantation society. Enquiry into class and race dynamics outside of the sugar plantation per se has been confined to a position of secondary importance by students of rural history. In addition, the historiography of colonial life in Caribbean societies conceptualized developments in terms of a hegemonic (and male), rural enterprise, with insufficient scholarly investigation of urban régimes.

Recent research indicates that Caribbean socioeconomic history needs to be reproblematized and its history of diversity explored in greater detail. The call for attention to diversity has been strongest among those who study Caribbean slavery. There is growing awareness of the need to acknowledge the internal diversities and contrasting conditions of slavery within the Caribbean, since one can no longer assume spatial and other homogeneity in the enslaver systems of the region. The efforts to identify and classify variation, certainly for the British-colonized Caribbean, took on new dimension with the publication of Barry Higman's *Slave Population and Economy in Jamaica, 1807–1834* and *Slave Population of the British*

Caribbean. Higman essentially provided a demographic framework for a comparative analysis of British Caribbean enslaved populations, taking on board the issue of diversity in commodity production and the occupations of the enslaved — which in large measure determined enslaved people's demographic experiences. His 1989 analysis of the internal economic features of Jamaica's pens does much to illuminate the complex nature of Caribbean economy in the eighteenth and nineteenth centuries and the ways in which these units contributed to the variation in the lives of the enslaved. Yu Wu's detailed 1995 quantitative study of Jamaica's trading links in the seventeenth and eighteenth centuries also reinforces the extent of the island's economic diversification,[24] although its lack of property differentiation in the origin and destination of goods traded reduces its usefulness for this present study.

Demographic work has also been undertaken by other historians, including Michael Craton and Gail Saunders for The Bahamas; Humphrey Lamur for the Dutch colonies; Meredith John for Trinidad and Jack Eblen for Cuba.[25] But there is still need to go beyond the quantitative demographic studies to explore in greater detail the daily and annual cycles of enslaved life in rural non-plantation and urban settings. Issues such as the differences in the gender division of labour, method of labour organization, the degree of autonomy achieved by the enslaved, control and patterns of resistance in sugar and non-sugar settings also need to be explored. There is also the need to expand the study of slavery outside of the context of sugar to take in places in the Circum-Caribbean region and the so-called 'marginal colonies', as well as the experiences of male and female enslavers not engaged directly in the sugar culture. Indeed, the study of the experiences of property owners who were not members of the sugar-planting elite is among the most under-researched areas of Caribbean history.

The livestock industry, which is the focus of this study, predated the large-scale cultivation of sugar cane in Jamaica and continued after the shift to sugar. The properties (outside of the sugar estates) devoted to large-scale cattle-raising were styled 'pens' in Jamaica. 'Pens' used in this sense apparently stems from the Old English word 'pennian' meaning 'to shut up' to 'to enclose', but which was first seen in literal use around the fourteenth century.[26] By the post-medieval period, 'pen' was generally accepted as the generic British term for a stock enclosure.[27] This usage was observed all over British North America and the Caribbean from the seventeenth century onwards. The other pens that became residential estates in St Andrew and elsewhere fall outside of this definition. Apparently the term was commonly applied to the residential units in Kingston and St Andrew, or to country estates, 'not specifically a sugar, banana or coconut property, but a gentleman's estate or park'.[28] Anthony Trollope observed in 1860 that 'the fact is that hardly any Europeans, or even White Creoles, live in the town. They have country seats, pens as they call them, at some little distance'.[29] Units styled 'pens' but which actually designated relatively small properties producing a variety of minor crops (that is, polincks/settlements) are also excluded from this study.[30] Although the various types of 'pens' may have produced some livestock, as long as stock-raising was only of minimal value, this study excludes such units.

The pens under discussion supplied crucial plantation inputs in the form of grass and working animals and services such as wainage and pasturage; and these farms also supplied meat to a mostly British consumer market. They helped in the establishment and maintenance of inter-property links through the internal commodity trade and generally supported the sugar industry. The majority were owned by proprietors who called themselves 'pen-keepers'. The word 'pen-keeper' appeared frequently in the eighteenth-century literature, and carried three different meanings. First, enslaved men in charge of temporary or permanent cattle enclosures on estates or pens were usually styled 'pen-keepers'. There were the 'head pen-keeper' and several assistants. This job was strictly allocated along gender lines, and only male slaves held this designation.[31] Second, the overseer or manager of a grazing farm was sometimes referred to as the 'pen-keeper'. Thus, Thomas Thistlewood noted in his diary that Florentinus Vassal, proprietor of Vineyard Pen, appointed him as pen-keeper in 1750.[32] Third, the proprietors of pens were classified as 'pen-keepers'.[33] This was the accepted usage in the island — as is underscored by Benjamin M'Mahon — which will be used in this context throughout this study. He stressed: 'let it be understood that pen-keepers in Jamaica mean graziers ... who generally reside on their pens after purchasing them'.[34] This clarification is extremely important; for there were people in the island who owned pens, but were not called 'pen-keepers'. These were sugar planters who, because of the need for efficiency and accessible plantation supplies, established their own livestock farms to supply their estates with working stock. Such planters did not, however, refer to themselves as pen-keepers; neither were they regarded as such by the larger society. Unlike the independent pen-keepers, they did not rely on livestock husbandry for the greater part of their income and did not reside on their pens.[35]

The history of the pen-keeping industry demonstrates the way in which Jamaica's economic history deviated from the strict Plantation Economy Model [PEM]. Classic plantation economies are supposed to be monocultural enclaves, lacking economic links with other sectors of the economy, without a domestic sector or significant internal trade, and with plantation inputs being largely imported and outputs exported. Further, the plantation economy model stresses the limited possibilities for internal capital accumulation because of the monopolistic control of trade and the absentee nature of the proprietors. In classic plantation economies, in addition, the life of enslaved people were dictated by the regimen of the plantation as an economic unit (be it sugar or another staple).[36]

The book makes it clear, however, that the concept of a single type of plantation complex modelled on sugar can no longer be applied sweepingly to the colonial Caribbean. It provides confirmation that the institution of slavery possessed complex and diverse aspects and that plantation economy based on involuntary servitude was capable of subtle adaptations. It is also clear that conditions of enslaved labour varied according to the nature of the agricultural/economic enterprise. The pen regime, as on coffee and cotton plantations, indigo farms and the urban milieu, offered those enslaved a less-arduous régime, unlike the sugar estates where life for the enslaved was described as nasty, brutish and short. In sum, the main characteristics of life outside of the sugar estates were a more individualized labour régime; an absence or lower incidence of gang labour; less close supervision by the British; lower mortality; higher fertility; a higher incidence of natural increase; an absence of the brutal work schedule during crop time; little night work; and a tendency to task over day labour, with the enslaved getting more time to work on their grounds. Of course, similarities also existed, particularly in the layout of large coffee and sugar estates; the use of gang labour on large properties; the allocation of provision grounds to the enslaved; internal marketing by the enslaved; the gender division of labour; the (s)exploitation of enslaved women by owners; and slave resistance. It has been demonstrated that there were significant implications in the co-existence of sugar and non-sugar units within the same territory, for this facilitated inter-property trade, variation in the occupation of the enslaved, internal capital accumulation, and the local provision of some plantation inputs. Clearly, the sugar plantation economy model that conceptualized plantations as enclaves importing all inputs and exporting all outputs is, along with slavery being defined by the sugar industry, now outdated.

Finally, despite the differences in régimes on sugar estates and in non-sugar plantation settings, the self-liberation ethos was no less developed among enslaved people who lived outside of the physical context of the large sugar plantation. Indeed, as has been shown elsewhere, non-sugar units like pens were considered by planters to be oases of social instability and those enslaved on pens were engaged in a variety of non-violent and violent resistance strategies.[37] The revelations in the detailed journals of Thomas Thistlewood,[38] which have now propelled the study of livestock farms and enslaved women's experiences to a prominent position, provide testimony enough of the violence (among which sexual violence can be counted)[39] perpetuated against enslaved peoples whether on sugar or non-sugar properties; and the exploitation of their sexuality faced by enslaved urban domestics was cause enough for the enslaved to try and win their freedom. Logically, every form of subjugation and domination generates an opposing struggle for liberation.

The book relies heavily on contemporary secondary books, manuscripts, newspapers and official publications. The Accounts Produce and the Accounts Current, deposited in the Jamaica Archives, form two of the main manuscript sources. The former are volumes containing accounts of 'all rents, issues, profits, proceeds and produce' on properties belonging to absentee proprietors. They were made in accordance with 'An Act for preventing frauds and breaches of trust by attorneys or agents of persons absent from the island,' and start in 1740. They are crucial for the analysis of the internal commodity trade as they detail all internal movement of goods. The Accounts Current which begin in 1806, shed light on the ways in which properties accumulated capital internally, as well as on their items of expenditure. Though they also relate to absentee proprietors, they explain vital inter-property links which developed between the units owned by absentees and local pen-keepers. These have been supplemented by the probate inventories, vestry minutes, wills, Moravian church records, various journals and plantation papers and the triennial returns of the registration of slaves which are so important for the study of the demographic characteristics of the slave population.

Organizationally, the book is divided into eight chapters. Chapter one provides a historical overview of the rise of the livestock industry in Jamaica, from Taino settlement to the early seventeenth century. Chapter two examines the factors that created a need for the continued existence of the pens even after the change to sugar. It also takes on board the early contests over land for livestock and land for cane. Chapter three reinforces the contests between livestock and cane, using the issue of trade as a focal point of the discussion. That chapter admits that the Atlantic was the centre of the international economy during slavery and that the output of the Caribbean was destined more for markets external than internal to the region. But it also shows that not all commodities produced in the colonies were destined for the extra-regional markets in Europe, though the making of an integrated market culture in the Atlantic has overshadowed the study of intra-Caribbean trading links before and after the conquest. But intra-Caribbean links, which predate conquest, though not as developed, were not complete casualties of colonization and the monopolistic tendencies of empire. In other words, regional interconnectedness was not lost in the 'making of the Atlantic World'; and an understanding of the emergence of the larger Atlantic World must take greater cognizance of intra-American labour mobilization and resource exchange that operated within the panoramic context of what Immanuel Wallerstein has described as the world system.[40] Slavery and the plantation system had a catalytic function in the linking of the disparate Caribbbean territories as they did the linking of properties within the islands.

Chapter four rehearses the process by which a pen-keeping sector evolved in Jamaica, offers a demographic profile of the group and sheds light on their economic status. Chapter five continues the discussion of the pen-keepers, this time looking at their ideological location in a plantation society, discussing the impact of the 'ranking game' and exploring the socioeconomic and political conflicts between the sugar and pen sectors. Chapter six examines the internal world of the enslaved on Jamaica's pens and Chapter seven takes the contests from the level of the proprietors to the level of the enslaved trapped within the confines of the pens. Chapter eight, the final chapter, is offered by way of conclusion in an attempt to follow both freed people and pen-keepers into the post-slavery period.

CONVENTIONS AND ABBREVIATIONS

Conventions

Monetary values are stated in Jamaican currency unless otherwise stated. In the eighteenth century, £1 sterling was equivalent to £1 8s. currency and 1s. sterling was equivalent to 8½d. currency. In the nineteenth century, £1 sterling was equal to £1 4s. currency.

Abbreviations

AC	Accounts Current
Add. MS(S)	Additional Manuscript
AP	Accounts Produce
BBJ	Blue Book of Jamaica
CO	Colonial Office
Fol.(s)	Folios
HBJ	Handbook of Jamaica
IRO	Island Record Office
JA	Jamaica Archives
JAR	Jamaica Annual Report
JEP	Jamaica Estate Papers (Vanneck Manuscripts)
JHAJ	Jamaica House of Assembly Journals
JHAV	Jamaica House of Assembly Votes
NLJ	National Library of Jamaica
PP	Parliamentary Papers
PRO	Public Record Office (Kew, London)
	[now known as National Archives]
RRS	Returns of the Registration of Slaves
USA	United States of America
UWI	University of the West Indies
WIC	West Indies Collection

I

RAISING LIVESTOCK IN THE PRE-PLANTATION ERA

Despite the widespread application of the (sugar) plantation economy model to colonial Jamaica, sugar did not dominate the island's physical landscape immediately upon colonization. Before the rise and expansion of the large sugar plantation complex, the island sustained a diversified economy in which early settlers grew tobacco, ginger, pimento, cotton, indigo, cocoa, food provisions, and planted a variety of fruits and vegetables. Livestock husbandry and buccaneering activities also generated significant incomes to the early English colonizers that many later ploughed into the sugar industry. The island sustained a diversified economy even before the English colonization. For example, the Ciboney, Taino and Spanish settlers never developed a plantation economy in the island, concentrating instead on diversified agriculture, fishing, hunting and, beginning with the Spaniards, ranching. When the English captured the island from Spain, the ranching was one that they continued, after their initial rampage.

Livestock husbandry typically played an important role in rural economies. This was as true for England and Continental Europe in the sixteenth, seventeenth and eighteenth centuries as it was for the colonies they established in the Americas. Of England's Caribbean colonies, it was Jamaica that developed the most significant livestock industry and which became closely associated with the 'pen-keeping' industry. It is usual to attribute the rise of 'pen-keeping' in Jamaica to the English, who are said to have caught and enclosed in 'cowpens', the cattle that the former Spanish colonists had let loose. In *Lady Nugent's Journal*, it was explained that 'the use of the word 'penn' or 'pen' in Jamaica to mean a farm or property with livestock dates from the seventeenth century, when the first English settlers found the cattle left by the Spaniards running wild.[1] The enclosing of livestock in pens was not, however, an English innovation. The livestock industry in Jamaica really had its origins during the Spanish occupation of the island from 1494 – 1655, at which time the island's economy replicated that of the other Greater Antillean Hispanic territories. Along with soldiers, priests and gold miners, the ships of Columbus had brought to Hispaniola in 1494, war-horses, beasts of burden and poultry. In 1495 the jennets, mares, cattle, pigs and domesticated animals followed.[2] From there, these were introduced to Jamaica, and multiplied so considerably that by 1657 it was estimated that the island contained over 40,000 head of livestock.[3] According to the planter-historian, Edward Long, (sections of whose work are extremely racist) these cattle and 'horsekind' abounded on the southern savannah lands (formerly Taino *conucos*) and some were reared in *hatos* or stockfarms, which the English later termed 'penns'.[4]

Despite their involvement in subsistence agriculture, under the Spaniards, it was livestock husbandry that emerged as the most important economic activity. This was linked to demographic factors. Cattle rearing required fewer labourers than plantation agriculture and so was suited to an island with an inadequate population to effectively settle it and develop its economy. In 1655, for example, Jamaica is said to have had a Spanish and African population of about 1,500;[5] for the absence of wealth measured according to the bullionist theory of the age had caused a drift of population to more lucrative areas of the Spanish 'New World' empire. The declining Taino labour force and an initially small enslaved population also combined to determine that the economic activities of Spanish Jamaica were not labour intensive, but commensurate with the size of its population.

The animals kept in *hatos* were principally used for their hides. This product soon emerged as the dominant export. Less emphasis was placed on meat, though some smoked beef and pork were exported to Havana, Cuba. The importance of hides as an export commodity — even later in the century was stressed by D. Mason who noted that 'their only exports were hides which they obtained by hunting wild cattle'.[6] The principal importers of hides from Spanish Jamaica were Cuba and Spain.[7] Indeed, wherever the absence of mineral wealth threatened the economic viability of Spanish colonies in the Indies, livestock rearing was undertaken. Thus, livestock husbandry was important also to Puerto Rico, Santo Domingo and Cuba. This great demand for cowhides in Spain some of which were re-exported to places like Italy, France, and the Low Countries, was attributed to the late medieval shift of the peninsular tanning and leather traders from goat and sheepskins to the tougher, if less workable, cowhide.

In addition to livestock rearing, Spanish colonists grew provisions and pimento. Some sugar was also grown; and there were a few sugar works as early as 1655.[8] Noel Deerr noted the existence of about 30 sugar works in the island during the Spanish occupation.[9] However, according to Sir Hans Sloane, who accompanied the Duke of Albermarle as his physician in 1687, when the Duke was appointed governor of Jamaica, there was really only one significant sugar plantation in Spanish Jamaica. This was owned by a rich widow in Liguanea. Even she concentrated more on livestock than on cane, ranging, according to contemporary writers, a dubious 40,000 head 'in the adjacent savannas'.[10] This has given rise to the debate as to whether the Spanish period can correctly be included in any discussion of the 'pre-sugar era'. Nevertheless, sugar at this time was grown essentially for local consumption and was not cultivated on a scale comparable to the sugar plantation era. Unlike the period which followed, therefore, Spanish Jamaica relied not on sugar for export, but on the export of hides and minor staples, and the provisioning of passing ships. Jamaica's location was strategic to Spanish trade with the Indies, located on the route from Cartagena to Havana which was taken by the treasure fleets on their homeward trip. In exchange for Jamaican provisions, ships left supplies of clothing, wine, oil, wheat flour and a few luxury items.[11]

This thriving Spanish livestock industry was not, however, in evidence at the time of the English capture of Jamaica in 1655. It is true that the English found large herds of animals in the island; but no systematic livestock husbandry was being undertaken, the once thriving industry having been already in a state of decline. This decline in the livestock industry is said to have dated back to about 1611, by which time Jamaica as a Spanish colony had seemingly settled into 'tropical stupour'. Apparently, the Spaniards were much too shorthanded to pen their stock. When the Abbott of Jamaica wrote to the King in July 1611, he stated that there were many hunting grounds of horned stock 'in which the colonists have their shares similar to

3

the ranches, (*hatos*) they formerly had stocked with tame cattle from which have sprung those that are now wild in these grounds'.[12] On the eve of the English capture of Jamaica, an account of the island by one Sederno, a Spanish resident, confirmed the decline of Spanish Jamaica and the depletion of its population. Sederno noted that 'this island had formerly a large population of Spaniards, so much so that there were seven towns.... Only St. Jago de la Vega now remains'.[13] His explanation for this decline in population was related to the dying out of the Tainos, 'whereupon the Spaniards left for new conquests and settlements'.[14] This helped the English to capture the island because in 1655, according to Sederno, there were '... a little over three hundred colonists (not counting blacks) — mostly poor people. Nearly four hundred and fifty men bear arms including the hunters and country folks, all of whom are labouring people ... [but] lacking in military discipline'.[15]

This decline in the livestock industry by 1655 had far-reaching consequences for the later history of the island. By the time the English arrived, not only had the Spaniards let loose their domestic animals, but previously domesticated cattle had reverted to a wild state. It was left to the English to revive the pen-keeping industry.

Livestock husbandry did not, however, immediately attract the attention of the Cromwellian soldiery. Their first concern was to find mineral wealth; for it had been rumoured that all Spanish colonies were mineral rich. The capture of Jamaica had, after all, been made two years after Oliver Cromwell had accomplished the erection of his nominal Protectorate, by which time his aim of obtaining Spanish wealth had become well known.[16] Spanish opposition to the English capture was too ineffective to have been successful and by 1670 both countries had signed the Anglo-Spanish Treaty.[17]

Instead of reviving the livestock industry immediately, William Gardner notes that 'the infatuated soldiery ... ruthlessly destroyed vast numbers of the herds of cattle which a little before had covered the plains around Spanish Town and that on the edge of which Kingston now stands'.[18] Gardner, influenced by Long, further wrote that 'twenty thousand cattle had been killed and the rest driven so wild that it was almost impossible to catch them'; that horses, 'once accounted as the vermin of the country', had become so scarce by the end of the seventeenth century, 'ships had to be sent to New England to fetch some from thence'.[19]

Long confirmed the destruction of the livestock industry by the English and the difficulty of finding horses locally for the troops: 'at their first arrival here, horses were in such abundance, as to be called the vermin of the country; but so scare are they now grown that among all the regiments they cannot mount one hundred men'.[20] Regarding cattle, Long observed that 'for the cattle, such of them as they were in any degree tame, have all been killed; few or none are left'.[21]

The explanations for the action of the soldiers are varied, but an overriding reason seems to have been that they were disappointed at finding such a poor colony and were anxious to move on to more wealthy sections of the Spanish-American empire. They supposedly resented Cromwell's efforts to keep Jamaica and turn them into colonizers, and adopted a mutinous attitude. Not only did they destroy livestock and existing crops, but for a long time, refused to grow their own food. According to Long, 'these early settlers all had a dislike against settling and planting in this part of the world and made no effort to do so'.[22] By such mutinous attitude, adopted also by the principal officers, they hoped to force Cromwell to relinquish the island. They however did not succeed and the result of their actions was almost disastrous, as starvation soon threatened the existence of the English settlers.

By 1657, conditions in Jamaica had become so precarious that the soldiers were forced to rethink their position. Food supplies from England were irregular, and soon there was no alternative to starvation but to turn to farming and livestock husbandry. It was at this time that serious attempts were made to establish pens and tame wild cattle. Like their Spanish predecessors, the early English settlers in Jamaica were not totally unfamiliar with livestock husbandry. Pastoral economies existed in parts of England, Scotland, Wales and Ireland, at times as alternate husbandry in a mixed farming economy. In England, there were four main pastoral regions, namely, (1) in the mountains and moorlands of Northern England and on the moorlands of the SouthWest where cattle and sheep were reared, (2) in the vales of the West Midlands and in other areas where the heavy soils lay under permanent grass and which specialized in dairying, rearing and fattening, (3) the forest areas where horsebreeding and pig fattening played an important role, alongside stockkeeping, and (4) in the fenlands of eastern England and the Somerset Level, where stock enterprises were mixed. The rearing and fattening of cattle and sheep had been particularly important in the Kesteven fen in Lincolnshire (the homeland of the Jamaican pen-keeper, Thomas Thistlewood) and in Staffordshire. Indeed, the Crown looked to Staffordshire in the seventeenth century to supply oxen and wethers for royal use. The country was celebrated for its fine oxen the black longhorned cattle of the northern counties. Graziers from as far away as Buckinghamshire came to Staffordshire to buy oxen.[23]

The English efforts to revive the livestock industry were not without obstacles. Lowland animals had already been wantonly destroyed so that densely forested areas had to be searched for stock for these units. Hunting parties were organized and, not surprisingly, the value of horses in such ventures was quickly appreciated. In fact, some of these 'horse-catchers' became quite well off and later used their resources to invest in the sugar economy. A good example is Peter Beckford, the founding member of one of the richest planter families in Jamaica. Described as 'a young man of good family but of no fortune',[24] Peter went out to Jamaica in 1660 to better his circumstances. He lacked the capital to immediately invest in the sugar industry, so like many others, he launched the family business by catching horses which he sold to pen-keepers and others. As horses were difficult to ship and were in short supply in the island, a successful horse catcher could expect to prosper.

This hunting stage of the livestock economy coincided with the pioneer or subsistence stage of Jamaica's economic evolution as outlined by Richard Sheridan. In this stage, hunting, land clearance and the beginnings of the cultivation of food crops were undertaken. According to Sheridan, the early English colonists generally possessed little capital; they cleared small tracts of land, hunted or raised their own food. They also experimented with crops that could be marketed in Europe. Lacking knowledge of the country and having few resources to develop it, they practised a subsistence economy that was supplemented at intervals by the exchange of crude tropical commodities for supplies to Europe.[25] It was in this period that animals began to be herded for their hides; and hides in early English Jamaica, as in Spanish Jamaica, continued to be important articles for export. By 1768, Jamaica was exporting 2,287 hides to North America alone.[26] This figure rose to 8,636 in 1774 and hides continued to be exported throughout the nineteenth century.[27]

The earlier wanton destruction of livestock caused a shortage of animals in English Jamaica to provide meat and hides, however, and soon importation of stock was being undertaken to help alleviate the situation. At the same time, the prospects of breeding were quickly realized as a means of capitalizing on the local demand for meat. This demand increased as through encouragement by Cromwell and the incentives of generous land grants, the island's population slowly increased. The penning and breeding of cattle were thus embarked upon with enthusiasm; and even though no thought was as yet given to rearing cattle for plantation use, laws were passed to protect the nascent industry. For example, Charles Leslie makes mention of the fact that in order to protect the livestock industry from further decline, a law was passed to make it illegal to 'kill any cattle, horse, mare or Assenigo under penalty' of a fine. Livestock were also to be penned and grazing farms fenced.[28]

Among those who engaged in pen-keeping in the seventeenth century and invested the profits in the sugar industry was Francis Price. He seemed to have been one of the members of the Cromwellian army, recruited either in Barbados or the Leeward Islands. Price was one of the first patentees of land in Jamaica, and by 1663 had established himself as a substantial land owner in the vale of Guanaboa. In 1670, he patented 840 acres of land at Lluidas Vale in the parish of St John. The property formed here was named Worthy Park. Lacking the capital needed to turn this land into a sugar estate, Price, like other early settlers, became a hunter of wild cattle, horses and boars. He probably sold the horses in Spanish Town but also penned, domesticated and bred livestock on Worthy Park.[29] By 1660, Gardner noted that 'small herds of cattle and sheep [are] now to be seen in the pastures'.[30]

Long stressed the fact that Lluidas Vale, and, indeed, St John parish, was devoted to cattle before the sugar revolution. According to him

> before sugarworks were formed here, it contained only breeding penns, whose pastures were so rich that the cattle were remarkably fat and their flesh of an exquisite flavour. These pen keepers used to supply the market at Spanish Town with veal which Sir Hans Sloane, I think, extols very highly.[31]

Interest in livestock continued after the establishment of civil government which followed the Restoration of 1660 and accompanied what Sheridan describes as the diversified production stage of Jamaica's economic development. In this stage, preceding the 1680s, the island's agricultural economy was characterized by the diversified production of exportable staples, provisions, and livestock. Generally speaking, the subsistence stage was shortlived, for settlers quickly understood that cash crops could be grown at a profit. European merchants were encouraged by this discovery to grant trade credit, thus enabling settlers to obtain capital and labour for the production of these commodities for export. In the shift to commercial agriculture, small staples such as tobacco, indigo, cotton, cocoa, and ginger generally took precedence over the sugar cane which some settlers had begun to plant by 1670.

The low labour and capital requirements and the adaptability of minor staples even to small units further encouraged their expansion. Mercantile credit and reinvested profits further facilitated this expansion. At the same time, the uncertainty of trade and commerce made it imperative to continue the provision and livestock economies to supply the food needs of local consumers. During this diversified stage, a few planters accumulated sufficient capital to shift from minor staples to the more profitable sugar cane. However, it was not economical to produce sugar on small farms because a considerable amount of fixed capital was needed for a sugar work. In many cases, a type of transitional economy was practised with some lands devoted to the cane, and some to provisions, minor staples and cattle. This effectively reduced the heavy debt burden that would otherwise be incurred.

Independent pen-keeping also expanded in this stage of Jamaica's economic evolution. Increasingly, attention was paid to the excellent quality of the pasturage, and, according to a contemporary observer, 'cattle soon received a proper share of attention from the ... settlers'.[32] By the time of Sir Hans Sloane's visit to the island, pens had been established in all of the southern parishes. The north and west were as yet, uncultivated. By 1687, the wild cattle mentioned in earlier reports of English Jamaica 'had been reclaimed and the Savanna pens were so abundantly stored with neat kine that one single settlement counted 40,000 head'.[33] Such wild cattle as still existed, were confined to the unsettled northside and the remote districts of St James.[34] The main emphasis of these pens continued to be on the production of meat and hides.

A factor which assisted the expansion of both pen-keeping and planting before the sugar revolution was the successful, if slow, growth of the settler population. For decades, Jamaica had struggled with the problem of attracting settlers. Beginning in 1656 with the immigration of 1,000 men from Scotland

Figure 1.1
Jamaica's Parishes, 1845

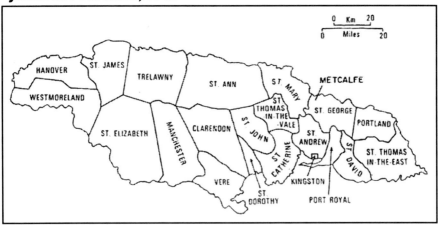

Note: By Law, 20 of 1867 the Parishes were reduced to the present 14. Those absorbed into other Parishes were St John, St Dorothy, St Thomas-in-the-Vale, Metcalfe, Vere, Port Royal, St George and St David.

under Lieutenant General Brayne and 1,500 settlers from Nevis, the island's settler population began a slow increase. Additional population was also obtained from New England, Bermuda, and Ireland. This influx combined with the new land policy of the late 1650s of distributing land in 30-acre lots to soldiers and settlers gave a new fillip to agriculture. In the next few years, according to Edward Long, the activities of the officers had changed from one of indolence and negativism to that of 'redhot planters'.[35] Among them was Colonel Francis Barrington, who, along with his whole regiment formed several plantations of provisions and tobacco.[36] However, not all of them were this successful. A large proportion of the Nevis planters who had settled in Morant Bay had died.

This success in agriculture resulted in the fact that by 1660, products from Jamaica began to find their way to the North American market. Provision farmers continued to conduct a thriving internal trade. The demand for provisions was especially great at Port Royal. According to Long, 'the great consumption of provisions of all sorts in that town, and for the outfit of so many privateers, created a very large demand for cattle, sheep, hogs, poultry, corn, and every other similar supply furnished by the planters and settlers.'[37]

While this diversified production stage lasted, cocoa emerged as the leading export staple. Sir Thomas Modyford observed in 1668 that this crop was 'the best commodity of the island; neither sugars nor indigo will turn to account so well'.[38] Modyford himself is said to have had the best cocoa walk in the island, and stressed the merits of cocoa growing in order to encourage others to participate in this agricultural activity. The fact that the staple enjoyed growing popularity as a beverage in Europe, and that the Spaniards had successfully cultivated cocoa trees in the island encouraged its production. Above all, its cultivation required a small capital and labour outlay.[39] In 1670, the 47 cocoa walks produced 188,000 pounds of nuts, compared to 49 indigo works producing 49,000 weight of indigo per annum.

Encouraged by the possibility of profits from cocoa, and by the example set by Modyford, a leading merchant, Cary Helyar, also ploughed his profits into cocoa plantations. In 1669, he began to acquire land, slaves and equipment with a view to setting up a cocoawalk.[40] In this, he was helped by Modyford who granted him a sizeable tract of land, later given the name of 'Bybrook' plantation.[41] By November 1670, Helyar had 12 enslaved Africans, one white servant and about six acres planted in cocoa trees. The cost of the undertaking amounted to $1346. 5s. 6d., and was partly met by Squire William, his partner. The cocoa boom proved to be short-lived. In the summer of 1670 a blight set in which by the following year had rapidly destroyed the trees.

The failure of cocoa led some ex cocoa planters to begin to establish sugar estates. However, the sugar revolution was to be further delayed because of the flourishing buccaneering and privateering activities centred on Port Royal. The prospects of quick fortunes from the contraband trade lured many would-be planters to Port Royal. This has been amply demonstrated by Nuala Zahedieh in her study of the role of privateering capital in financing Jamaica's sugar revolution.[42] The men who turned to privateering, says Long, lacked, 'that sufficient degree of patience, steadiness and decorum so essential to the establishment of new plantations'.[43] Consequently, the business of planting in Jamaica did not proceed 'with that rapidity so conspicuous in other islands'.[44] Indeed, to such men, 'the privateering trade at length opened a channel by which these disorderly spirits were driven into an occupation perfectly suited to them the acquisition of [easy] wealth to themselves which they dissipated in riot and debauchery'.[45]

By 1680, however, buccaneering activities had declined. When Sir Thomas Lynch succeeded Modyford as governor, he was instructed to suppress piracy and privateering and to pardon all buccaneers who 'submitted to His Majesty'. Furthermore, all buccaneers who seemed willing to engage in agriculture would be assisted by grants of land. Some buccaneers did exhibit the desire to embark on sugar, among them, the notorious Henry Morgan. Thus, the decline of buccaneering, the effects of the cocoa blight of 1670, and the willingness of ex-buccaneers to plough the profits of their 'ill-gotten gains' into the sugar industry at last paved the way for Jamaica to embark upon its sugar revolution. In addition, ex-cocoa planters and pen-keepers had also accumulated profits which would enable them to invest in the sugar industry.

Finally, Jamaica's development in the pre-sugar era must be placed in its hemispheric context. It will be seen from a comparative look at other plantation colonies in the region that the island's economic history in the period was unique because of the dominant role played by livestock husbandry in the economy. Indeed, the rearing of cattle, horses and mules seemed to have been important in the pre-sugar era only in places formerly settled by Spain. Thus, Jamaica displayed similar features to Cuba, Hispaniola and Puerto Rico, rather than to Barbados, St Kitts and Antigua. Barbados was generally typical of the pure plantation colonies in the pre-sugar era. The island was remote from Spanish possessions in the New World and south of the main track of the galleons which plied between Spain and her colonies. When the English founded the colony in the 1620s, however, they did not find any large herds of livestock comparable to those found in Jamaica in 1655. Indeed, Richard Dunn records that few species of wild animals were to be found in Barbados at the time of its settlement by the English. He noted that 'the island was full of wild hogs ... which the planters were slaughtering at a terrific rate'.[46] Apart from small stock for meat, however, there were no cattle and horses which might have formed the basis of an early pen-keeping industry.[47] As in Brazil, livestock husbandry in Barbados developed as an adjunct to the sugar industry. Tobacco, fustic, cotton, a variety of fruits and dye woods rather than livestock husbandry, thus formed the basis of Barbados's pre-sugar economy.[48]

Similarly, the Windward Islands of Grenada, Dominica, and St Vincent, and the island of Trinidad, had no early thriving livestock industry. Tobacco was the basis of Trinidad's economy in the sixteenth and seventeenth centuries.[49] Though a Spanish colony for much of its history, lack of mineral wealth and distance from the Spanish Main had led to its neglect by Spain. In the early eighteenth century, cocoa formed the basis of Trinidad's economy. Livestock was more important in Tobago where by 1790 there were 5,356 acres in pasture. Even here, pigs, sheep and goat, rather than cattle and horses dominated the livestock industry. Working stock did not become important in these colonies until after the sugar revolution. In the Windward Islands, plantations of minor staples dominated the landscape of the pre-sugar era. Mountainous terrain, after all, did not facilitate the development of pasture land, and the flatlands were devoted to these plantations of minor staple.

Like the Spanish Caribbean, native agriculture in the American South before the arrival of the Europeans does not seem to have incorporated much livestock apart from turkeys, wild hens, and other poultry.[50] Horses, mules, cattle, sheep and pigs were all introduced by the Spanish, French and English colonizers, either directly from Europe or from already settled Caribbean islands. At the time of the English settlement, for example, Virginia had no livestock. The first livestock of the Jamestown settlement were brought in with the first English expedition. The rapid multiplication of the stock brought in soon decreased the need for further importation. Despite the history of the importation of stock into the American South, however, it is undeniable that in the pre plantation era, livestock husbandry was of considerable importance. According to Lewis Gray, in many newly settled districts the herding industry preceded the development of systematic agriculture. A transition stage then followed in which the keeping of large numbers of stock by semi-herding methods was combined with the production of crops. The open range method of grazing rather than enclosed pens, however, generally characterized such husbandry. Later, when the range became scarce, the raising of stock in general farming districts developed the characteristics of systematic animal husbandry. Systematic livestock husbandry, did not seem to have been combined with arable farming, however, but was confined to non-farming districts; because in the plantation districts the raising of stock became secondary to the production of staples, being carried on largely for domestic consumption.[51]

Before the concentration on export staples such as tobacco, rice, cotton and sugar, however, some southern colonies derived their incomes from the exportation of barrelled beef and pork to the West Indies. Before the development of the Caribbean market, livestock was kept for domestic supply of meat, milk and cheese. From the last half of the seventeenth century, however, first Barbados and then other Caribbean colonies which did not have a local livestock industry provided ample markets for beef and pork from Maryland, Virginia and the Carolinas. Of these states only South Carolina developed similar early 'cowpens' like Jamaica.[52]

As the next chapter will show, like many other sections of the Atlantic World, the evolution of staple crops, an active domestic or international market demand for such staples and the general agricultural upswing which resulted, had a negative impact on the survival of the livestock industry; and in the case of Jamaica started a competition for terrain between sugar barons and pen-keepers. As Peter Kriedte has shown for eighteenth century Europe, stock-raising gave way to agricultural crops because of an upswing in agriculture, partly attributable to population growth, protoindustrialization, and the slowly improving price and cost positions of agricultural production. In England and Western Europe, as a consequence, grassland was taken under the plough and stock-raising gave way to agriculture.[53] This process was replicated in the Southern United States and in the sugar plantation complex in the Caribbean and Brazil as these regions experienced the 'sugar plantation revolution'. During the period of bouyancy in the sugar industry in Brazil, for example, stock rearing was exiled into the interior and away from the coast, eminently suitable for sugar cultivation. Similarly, in the Eastern Caribbean, which later developed into classic plantation economies, sugar cane cultivation was given primacy over stock raising or other forms of competing agricultural activities. In Hispanic America, the process was repeated, except that the switch to plantation agriculture developed later and thus the livestock industry had a longer lifespan. Thus, the intensification of sugar production (or grain, cotton and tobacco production in some areas) resulted in changes in the agrarian pattern which were predictable in conditions of agricultural upswings. Of note, however, is that stock-raising only lagged behind crop production in cases where pasture lands could support agricultural crops. This fact underscores Jamaica's separate development in the period of slavery in contrast to the experiences of islands in the rest of the English-colonized Caribbean.

2

THE INTERPLAY OF LIVESTOCK AND CANE: CONTESTS OVER LAND FOR COMMODITY PRODUCTION

Although Jamaica's economy showed diversity after the introduction of sugar with tobacco, ginger, cocoa, indigo, dyewoods and livestock still being produced, sugar quickly became the leading colonial export. From its arrival on the European market, it yielded a far higher and steadier profit than any other American cash crop. Sugar marginalized other agricultural and economic activities and gave rise to levels of wealth and conspicuous consumption that eventually elevated the sugar planting elite above other sectors in the island. This chapter will explore the processes by which Jamaica made the switch to sugar and examine how the pen-keeping industry fared after this change was effected. It will be seen that far from declining in importance and giving way to the great staple, the pen-keeping industry experienced marked growth and expansion after Jamaica's version of the 'sugar revolution'. Indeed, the rise of sugar facilitated the expansion of pen-keeping. However, of significance for the thesis of this book is that, unlike the case of coffee (that was grown in locations that could not support the cane), there was competition initially between pens and plantations for the most suitable land for production. The contest over terrain later extended to markets and lines of trade, as chapter three will show.

By the end of the seventeenth century, there were still well below 100 pens in the island. As the livestock industry struggled to recover from its decline in the later years of Spanish, and the first years of English colonization, marked expansion was not experienced until well into the eighteenth century. The principal factor in the phenomenal increase in the number of pens in Jamaica in the eighteenth century was the process usually described as the 'sugar revolution'. From a mere 73 pens in 1684,[1] located primarily in the southern parishes, the island had over 300 pens by 1782.[2] By the latter date, however, pens were not confined to southern parishes, but had spread to western, central and northeastern parishes, in particular, to St Ann, St Elizabeth and Westmoreland.

There is some dispute over the precise date of this so-called 'sugar revolution' — the change from hide-hunting, buccaneering and plantations of minor staples utilizing limited capital, a small labour force and relatively small landholdings — to the extensive cultivation of the sugar cane with its attendant changes in capital, labour and land. Noel Deerr has attributed the 'sugar revolution' in Jamaica to the period of Governor Modyford's tenure between 1664 and 1670. According to Deerr, Modyford, with Barbadian immigrants and his own wide knowledge of sugar technology derived from his prior sugar interests in Barbados, encouraged sugar cultivation in the island 'and from this time on their produce grew in esteem in the British market'.[3]

Both Richard Dunn and Richard Sheridan have challenged Deerr's claim that Modyford quickly transformed Jamaica into an island of great sugar estates. Sheridan, for example, argues that Jamaica in the age of Modyford was still only an island of 'many hopeful plantations',[4] and that indigo and cocoa were more prominent than sugar. Indeed, this is confirmed by the 1670 census that enumerated only 57 sugar works in contrast to 96 plantations of 'minor' staples.[5] Dunn, while acknowledging Modyford's efforts to make land grants and encourage the sugar industry, still admits that Modyford was as responsible as anyone for the colony's peculiar dual development in the late seventeenth century; for he simultaneously promoted agricultural settlement and filibustering attacks upon the Spaniards.[6] This continuation of buccaneering activities, in fact, delayed Jamaica's 'sugar revolution'.

After Modyford left the island, however, a more concerted effort was made to outlaw privateering. No significant success was achieved until the 1680s, and it is around this time, according to Dunn, that sugar became the island's leading staple export.[7] Even then, the low state of the sugar market, lack of an adequate labour and settler population, and the concentration of the industry in southern parishes, caused the island to experience a rather slow growth in the sugar industry during the next 60 years. The removal of these 'impediments' by 1740, however, had the effect of bringing about a great expansion in the island's sugar economy, and from this point onwards, Jamaica became Britain's leading sugar exporting colony. As the changes in Jamaica occurred over a longer period of time and were gradual rather than swift, the term 'sugar revolution' might be less applicable. Also, when the changes did occur, their impact was less revolutionary in that sugar cultivation did not result in a total change from diversification to sugar monoculture; and the sugar plantation did not define the landscape in the way it did in Barbados.

A brief discussion of the major changes in the island's landholdings, population, and capital investment between the latter part of the seventeenth century and the mid-eighteenth century will serve to explain the process of change from a 'pre-sugar era' to that of extensive sugar monoculture. These factors of production were, after all, essential to the transformation to a dominant sugar economy.

To better understand the relationship between these factors and the switch to large-scale sugar production, it might be useful to examine Sheridan's estimate of a medium-sized plantation around 1774. His calculation, based on the Probate Inventories in the Jamaica Archives, revealed that at least £19,027 sterling was needed to settle an average estate in the island.[8] Bryan Edwards's estimate of the cost of establishing a successful sugar estate around 1793 was somewhat higher. According to him, 'a sugar plantation consists of three parts: the Lands, the Buildings and the Stock. It requires a capital of no less than £30,000 sterling to embark in this employment with a fair prospect of advantage'.[9] He further explained that an average sugar plantation should consist of 600–900 acres of land, 250 enslaved workers and 140 working animals.[10]

Land requirement for a successful sugar plantation necessitated major changes in the system of land allocation and ownership. Initially, land was issued only to the resident officers of the Cromwellian army in 30-acre allotments. In 1656, a council of 12 officers resolved that in an attempt to encourage more planting, similar allotments should be made to private soldiers.[11] This move was initially opposed by those officers who simply wanted the privates to perform the role of servants. However, the position ascribed to them had so infuriated the low-ranking soldiers that they had protested. Governor D'Oyley thus sought to implement and reinforce the resolution of the Council of Officers.[12] Starting in 1661, successive seventeenth-century governors were enjoined to extend the granting of 30-acre lots to indentured servants at the end of their four year contract, and to all others who settled as planters in Jamaica.[13] On such comparatively small allotments, however, only provision growing and the cultivation of minor staples were possible.

Provision farmers had been particularly numerous around the centres of population with ready access to markets. Writing of provision growing in the eighteenth century, Long remarked that

> it is owing to this cause, that we find such a prodigious number of
> these settlements grouped together in all the environs of St Jago de
> la Vega, and in the maritime parts not far from Port Royal Harbour
> ... all subsisting well by their traffic with that town.[14]

This pattern of small landowners cultivating subsistence crops or minor staples on the southern plain changed with the introduction of the sugar plantation.

Beginning around 1660, and accelerating thereafter, a large number of the 30-acre lots were bought by the more opulent planters and merchants and consolidated into single properties.[15] During his governorship, Modyford facilitated this process by issuing approximately 1,800 land patents totalling over 300,000 acres. By the late 1680s, the finest sugar lands in the parishes of St Andrew, St Catherine, St John and Clarendon on the south-central coast were already laid out, much of them in large plots. Modyford and his eldest son, Thomas, patented 9,042 acres. Charles, a younger son, patented 6,330 acres. In total, the Modyford clan held 22 parcels of land in eight parishes.[16] Soon, there was a territorial expansion of the plantations from the eastern and south central parts of the island to the western and northern sections.

The change in the pattern of landholdings can best be illustrated by three land surveys. The first, done in 1664 at the beginning of Modyford's governorship revealed that the majority of landowners held less than 500 acres of land. In the parish of St Thomas-in-the-East, for example, only four persons held land of 1,000 or more acres. In St David, three persons held over 1,000 acres, the largest allotment of 1,338.75 acres being owned by Lieutenant Colonel Robert Freeman. Seventy-three persons in the parish owned less than 500 acres of land.[17] As table 2.1 illustrates, a similar pattern characterized the four other parishes included in the survey report. By 1670, according to the census returns, the island total of those owning over 1,000 acres was 47, and the total patented was 209,020.50 acres. This was held by 11,898 persons.[18] A return of landholders in 1754 (table 2.2) confirms the change in the pattern of land ownership accompanying the change to large-scale sugar production. According to that return, 827 people owned less than 500 acres of land, 296 owned between 500 and 999 acres, 252 held between 1,000 and 1,999 acres and 205 owned upwards of 2,000 acres. Thirty-two of those owning over 2,000 acres held between 5,000 and 7,000 acres, 16 owned between 7,000 and 10,000 acres, eight owned between 10,000 and 20,000 and one man, William Beckford, owned over 20,000 acres of land.[19] Table 2.2 compiled from the return shows that the largest ten landowners in Jamaica had appropriated a total of 140,509 acres.

Table 2.1
Distribution of Landholdings in Four Parishes, 1664

Acreages	Parishes				
	St Andrew	St Catherine	St John	Clarendon	Total
Below 100 acres	146	63	30	60	299
100–500	29	63	39	65	196
500–1000	14	16	11	8	49
Over 1000	5	16	3	10	34
Total Landholders	194	158	83	143	578

Note: The northern parishes were, for the most part, unsettled and unpatented by the conquerors and difficult to survey. In 1664, only about 1,500 settlers lived in this part of the island owning approximately 20,000 acres of land.

Source: A list of landholders in Jamaica, 1754, CO 142/31.

Table 2.2
Ten Largest Landholders, 1754

No.	Name	Acres
1	William Beckford	22,021
2	Saddler Hals	18,885
3	Henry Gale	16,510
4	James Dawkins	14,294
5	Charles Price	13,651
6	Andrew Arcedeckne	12,711
7	Isaac Gale	11,838
8	Collin Campbell	11,293
9	Henry Gale (a minor)	10,065
10	Richard Gale	9,241
Total		**140,509**

Source: A list of landholders in Jamaica, 1754, CO 142/31.

A large labour force was crucial to the full utilization of such huge parcels of land. Also crucial to Jamaica's development was an increase in the number of settlers who would extend cultivation to remote parts of the island. Both aspects of the population problem were solved by 1740. With respect to the labour force, planters in Jamaica were successful by 1740, in securing enslaved Africans for their plantations. The lack of an adequate labour force in the early years of English settlement had been particularly problematic for the struggling colony. Long records that the early soldiers were an inadequate labour force and, moreover, had been 'reduced to a life of too much labour', [20] for their superior officers felt manual labour to be beneath their status, and so ... 'were apt to impose the same kind of work upon them as what the Negro labourers were afterwards employed in'. The protector had thus been prevailed upon to encourage indentured servants and enslaved Africans for Jamaican plantations. Long mistakenly believed that such labourers would be better treated by plantation owners as 'their masters having by this means an interest in their servants, and would be more careful of them, and work them more moderately, by which many lives would be saved and the plantations more forwarded'. The high mortality rate of enslaved Africans, especially before 1808 when the trade in captives was abolished, attest to how wrong Long was.

Despite the inducements to indentured servants, however, planters were unable to secure them in sufficient numbers. Between 1662 and 1686, for example, only 468 English indentured servants emigrated to the island and by the 1770s Jamaica had virtually ceased to import indentured servants. Planters thus increasingly resorted to enslaving Africans. After 1658, there had been a marked increase in the enslaved population of the island.[21] In that year Long had estimated that the population of Jamaica consisted of 4,500 English persons and 1,400 Africans. By 1673, the number of Africans reached 9,504, surpassing the English population by 1,736. By 1722, there were 80,000 African people in the island.[22]

Contributing to this phenomenal increase in the labouring population was the addition facilitated by the formation of the Royal African Company in 1672. Between 1673 and 1689, the company's annual deliveries of African people to Jamaica averaged 4,010 or a total of 22,900.[23] Britain's negotiation of the *asiento* from Spain at the Treaty of Utrecht in 1713, also had a limited influence. The *asiento* was the license granted to the English to supply the Spanish colonies with 4,800 enslaved Africans per annum.[24] Though more enslaved Africans were re-exported than were retained in Jamaica during the operation of this license, nevertheless, it did cause an increase in the enslaved population. In 1739, the loss of the *asiento* halted the expansion of enslaving centres on the African coast and caused a consequent decrease in the number of captives imported to the English-colonized Caribbean. During the seven-year war (1756–63), however, Britain captured Goree and Senegal, both of which supplied African labourers. England subsequently expanded its trading centres in Africa so that by the 1740s and 1780s it had forged ahead of the Iberians and the Dutch to become the foremost participant in the Trans-Atlantic trade in enslaved Africans. This greatly facilitated the expansion of the sugar industry.

The increase in the free settler population also contributed to the slow shift to a sugar-dominated economy. Measures to encourage immigration had met with positive response, especially from planters from the Lesser Antilles and by young men from Scotland. As an active land market developed, a growing proportion of captured Taino land was either cultivated by new patentees or sold to immigrants at a speculative profit. Though widespread absenteeism of the entrepreneurial class later characterized

Jamaica's plantation society, up to 1740, the resident proprietors were in the majority and gave much needed attention to the new plantations. The Accounts Produce of 1740, for example, contained 175 returns pertaining to the properties of absentee proprietors. Of this number, 85 were sugar estates.[25] This means that in 1740, resident sugar planters comprised 75 per cent of the island total.[26]

Finally, the lack of capital had also delayed Jamaica's version of the 'sugar revolution'; for there were no initial large investors in the colony. The switch to large-scale sugar production could not occur until sufficient capital had been accumulated to finance the costs involved in establishing sugar works. Such internal capital generation came mainly from buccaneering, the contraband trade and plantations of minor staples, with pen-keeping playing only a minor role. As Sheridan, Michael Craton and more recently, Nuala Zahedieh, have pointed out, this conflicts with Adam Smith's view that it was the wealth of Britain that had financed the sugar revolution in the island. Richard Sheridan has cited the case of the Englishman, Cary Helyar, who initially carved plantations out of the 'wildwoods' of Jamaica, as the prototype of an entrepreneur who ploughed his profits into the sugar revolution in 1671. Like Modyford, Helyar had first invested in cocoa, but later shifted to cane. Similarly, Zahadieh, who has shown conclusively that a large part of the capital used to finance the sugar revolution in Jamaica came from privateering, observed that Adam Smith was wrong. The prosperity of Jamaica was not 'owing to the great riches of England of which a part had overflowed'. He cites the case of the notorious Henry Morgan who later became a sugar planter. Later on, of course, merchants were to become heavily involved as financiers in the sugar industry.[27]

Of the four factors of production discussed above, Carlyle Batie gives primacy to population (labourers and planters) in determining the switch to sugar cane as the staple crop. This demographic determinism is tied to the staple thesis that relates population changes to the profitability of cultivating export staples.[28] Batie, therefore, argues that the extent to which marketable commodities were produced in the Caribbean in the seventeenth century, depended not only on the current demand and price on the European market, but on the availability of people to cultivate them.[29] Thus, plantations of minor staples and livestock farming, rather than a sugar industry, were profitable in the early period of settlement. Thereafter, the Trans-Atlantic trade in enslaved African captives and the influx of Europeans to the Caribbean provided the population necessary to produce such a labour-intensive commodity. It was not lack of interest or knowledge that had stifled the early sugar industry in the Spanish Caribbean, therefore, but lack of population. By 1680, in the English-colonized Caribbean, demographic changes and the availability of capital to invest in large landholdings facilitated the dominance of the sugar economy.

Sugar had thus emerged as the most profitable crop in Jamaica by the last quarter of the seventeenth century. By 1740, the island was firmly established as the major producer in the British Empire. From a mere 57 sugar plantations in 1670, the island had 246 sugar estates in 1685 and 340 established sugar works by 1740, with Clarendon alone having 66 units.[30] For most of the eighteenth century, Jamaica was Britain's leading sugar exporter and in the 1770s surpassed all other British colonies combined. Production more than quadrupled between the 1720s and 1770s and aggregate levels of capital investment increased markedly.[31]

The development of a plantation economy dominated by the production of sugar for export, created an extraordinary demand in Jamaica for livestock. This was because before the development of chemical fertilizers and until draft animals were largely displaced by motor transport, sugar estates relied heavily on animals for a variety of draft and other purposes. The need was greatest in the sugar parishes of St Thomas-in-the-East, Trelawny, Hanover, St James, St Mary, Westmoreland, Clarendon, St Thomas-in-the-Vale and Vere that, together in 1789, accounted for 542 or 76.34 per cent of the 710 sugar estates in the island.[32]

The types of animals most in demand on sugar estates are clearly indicated by the Accounts Produce. These were steers (oxen), mules and heifers. Steers and spayed heifers were often referred to in the Accounts as 'planters' stock'. Though the pens sold a considerable number of horses, these were used for the racehorse industry and for riding by the free supervisory class, rather than as work animals.[33] Mules were used primarily for draft purposes. They were used to take off the crop from the fields and to transport sugar to the wharf.[34] Up to 12 mules at a time were also frequently used to transport coffee to the wharf.[35] In the early years of the sugar industry, mules were also used along with cattle to turn the rollers that ground the juice out of the canes at the mill. By the nineteenth century, however, they were largely displaced by steers and spayed heifers.

A partial indication of this change is supplied by the data on pens returned in the Accounts Produce. In 1740, for example, the working stock sold by the 20 pens represented in the Accounts included 19 steers, eight heifers and seven mules. In 1760, 144 steers, 54 mules and 12 heifers were sold; and in 1780, 278 steers, 181 mules and 19 heifers were disposed of to estates. By 1820, however, 3,162 steers, 1,162 spayed heifers and only 511 mules were sold through the internal trade. By 1840, the number of mules sold by the pens represented in the Accounts had fallen to 283, compared to 2,461 steers and 1,006 heifers.[36]

Cattle were important sources of manure for sugar estates. They were also used as draft animals, but predominated as mill animals. This presumably influenced the use of the term 'cattle mills' to refer to even those powered by a few mules. Up to 1740, animal mills were almost exclusively used on sugar estates, though other forms of power were being explored. As Charles Leslie records, in that year, 'the mills that are most in use here are cattle mills, but lately, some substantial Planters have One or Two Windmills, and some Three'. Windmills were at this stage regarded as curiosities, however, and according to Leslie, 'the late President Ayscough erected One at his Plantation to Windward, which is a very curious Piece of mechanism'.[37]

As sugar plantations proliferated after 1680, the demand for livestock to provide all of the above functions increased. After all, as Franklin Knight observed in the case of Cuba, 'sugar depended as much on cattle as it did on slave labour';[38] consequently, writes Knight 'the livestock is the second element of an ingenio which comes after the Negroes'. This was applicable to eighteenth-century Jamaica as it was to nineteenth-century Cuba. In Jamaica, therefore, as the demand for cattle, horses and mules grew, so did the efforts to establish local breeding farms. It was for this reason that pens increased and, moreover, that their role in Jamaica's colonial economy was assured.

An anonymous writer in *Jamaica Pamphlets* in 1890 later underscored the relationship between the establishment of pens and the use of animals as working stock, noting that, 'the universal use of bullocks for the heavy draught on plantations and elsewhere demands a large supply of stock, independent of what is required for food purposes, and these are bred on the large cattle estates called locally, "pens".[39]

The direct relationship between the expansion of the livestock industry in Jamaica and the evolution and growth of the sugar industry was, perhaps, best established by Edward Long. After discussing the 'sugar revolution' with its creation of land monopolies by those who bought out the 30-acre farmers to create larger sugar estates, he explained that, 'to sustain these sugar estates, large breeding farms were requisite'.[40] Pens, as a result, did not suffer the fate of coastal provision farms and plantations of 'minor' staples for whereas the increasing dominance of sugar in Jamaica in the eighteenth century stifled the production of competing staples other than coffee, the growing demand for livestock on sugar estates was met by an increasing number of pens. Far from giving way to sugar, therefore, by 1740, pens along with sugar estates had swallowed up by degrees all the little settlements around; which from their contiguity, and being already cleared for canes or pasturage, the lordly planters found convenient to be purchased, and added to their territories. This process, according to Long, was similar to the building up of large farms in Britain.

As further indication that pens were not sacrificed at the expense of sugar cultivation, Edward Long explained that

> some have imagined, that the sugar estates have increased at the expense of sacrificing many of the farms or penns; but that this has not been the case is manifest from the great increase in the number of Negroes; which would not have happened if the settlers had done no more than remove their Negroes from penns to sugar estates .... It is more probable, that the augmentation of sugar estates has been the means of increasing the number of penns, by enlarging the demand for pasturage and stock.[41]

By the outbreak of the American War of Independence, in 1776 therefore, Jamaica was being described as an island of large sugar plantations and cattle farms.[42] The island had 400 pens at the time of emancipation which represented an increase from approximately 80 pens in 1740; and in 1844, the census revealed an island total of 378 pens.[43] Pen-keeping thus developed both as an aid to diversification and a prop for the sugar economy, helping to reinforce its dominance.

Table 2.3
Sugar Works and Cattle by Parish, 1740 and 1768

Parish	1740		1768	
	Cattle	Sugar Works	Cattle	Sugar Works
St. Catherine	8,581	3	10,402	?
St. Dorothy	5,468	8	4,661	12
St. John	2,837	28	2,726	21
St. Thomas-in-the-Vale	4,813	48	5,782	41
Clarendon	12,299	?	14,276	70
Vere	8,580	7	7,462	19
St. Mary	2,972	19	7,996	49
St. Ann	2,342	20	6,207	22
St. Andrew	5,244	34	4,626	?
Kingston	607	None	923	None
Port Royal	158	None	170	1
St. Thomas-in-the-East	5,256	44	9,007	66
St. David		No Figures Available		
Portland	178	3	1,651	29
St. George	1,024	4	3,421	12
St. Elizabeth	9,695	32	16,947	31
Westmoreland	8,921	32	13,750	69
Hanover	2,631	39	8,942	71
St. James	1,204	19	15,137	95
Trelawny	Still Part Of St James		8,130	4
All Island Total	82,810	340	142,216	612

Note: ? = Not stated. Totals given are thus incomplete.
Source: E. Long, History of Jamaica, II, Add. MS 12,405, fols. 39-192.

The number of cattle in Jamaica from year to year and the extensive use of cattle mills on sugar estates throughout the island in the period of slavery, help to indicate the extent to which livestock was vital to the plantation economy. In 1734, Jamaica had 74,846 head of cattle.[44] Six years later, Jamaica's colonial agent, James Knight, compiled a table of the number of enslaved Africans and cattle in each parish based on the returns of a tax of 12 pence per head on the enslaved and three pence on cattle. The total was 99,239 enslaved and 84,313 cattle.[45] Figure 2.1 and table 2.3, compiled from Long's *History of Jamaica*, show that Knight's figure

Figure 2.1
Dot Map Showing Distribution of Cattle in Jamaica, 1740

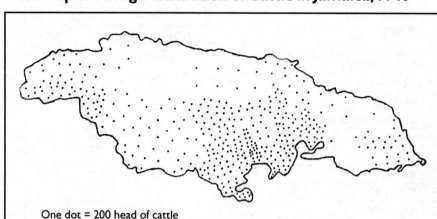

One dot = 200 head of cattle

Source: Compiled from data in E. Long, *History of Jamaica*, II, Add. MS 12,405, fols. 39-192.

for cattle is somewhat higher than Long's calculations, but the difference might be explained by the absence of figures in the table for St David, an essentially pen/coffee parish. There is also some discrepancy in the figures for cattle for 1768, by which year, according to calculations from the poll tax roll authorized in that year, cattle had increased to 135,773 head, 6,443 lower than Long's calculations of 142,216 head of cattle in the 20 parishes. However, this confusion could have resulted from the difference between taxable and working stock in the island. The latter did not attract a tax and would not have been represented on the poll tax roll relating to sugar estates.

To test the general impression conveyed by Long and others that cattle increased as the number of sugar estates grew, a mathematical base was used. Both Figures 2.2 and 2.3 indeed support these views; for they indicate a high and positive correlation between the number of cattle demanded. In 1768, for example, the result, 0.72 establishes a positive correlation between the two variables.

In 1768 also, there were said to have been 648 sugar estates in the island (three fewer than Long's estimate of 651) of which 369 had cattle mills, 235 had water mills and 44 had windmills.[46] This means that the number of cattle mills in the island in 1768 was 13 less than the number in 1763 (see table 2.4).

Figure 2.2
Scatter Diagram Showing the Correlation between the
Number of Sugar Works and Number of Cattle used by
Parish, 1740

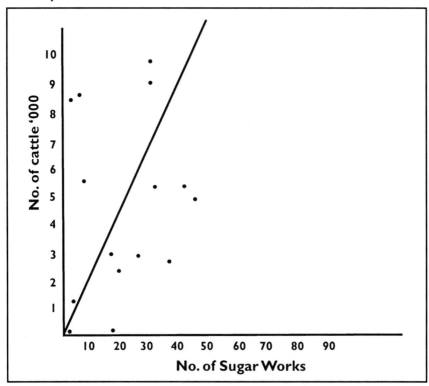

On the other hand, the number of water and windmills had increased since 1763, showing a gradual shift away from cattle mills. Even though rivers, topography and wind currents determined the selection of windmills, watermills and tidemills in the Caribbean, most planters in Jamaica still kept a cattle mill or two in cases of emergencies as they were considered more reliable. To illustrate, the case of St Jago estate can be cited. Throughout 1822, the attorney for the Mitchells' estate in Jamaica complained to the proprietors about the severe drought in the island, especially in St Catherine. This had affected the use of the watermill on St Jago estate, thus forcing the estate to revert to the cattle mills. According to the attorney, 'St Jago is now getting on as fast as they can with the Old Cattle Mills the water having entirely failed and is not likely to return now before the May season.'[47] The rains did come in May, but by

Figure 2.3
Scatter Diagram Showing the Correlation between the Number of Sugar Works and Number of Cattle used by Parish, 1768

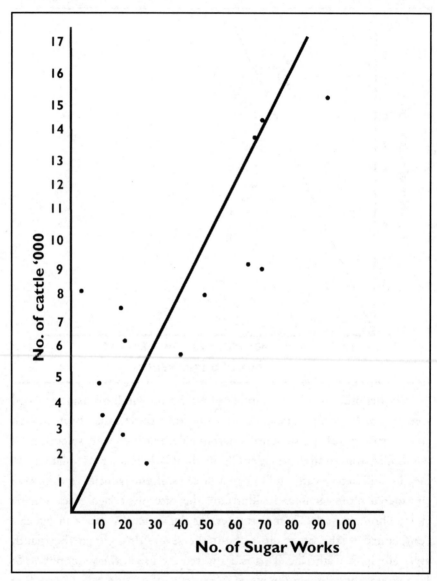

Table 2.4
Distribution of Mills in Jamaica by Parish, 1763

Parish	Mills		
	Cattle	Water	Wind
St. Thomas-in-the-East	34	17	2
Portland	21	5	-
St. David	2	5	-
Port Royal	1	1	-
St. George	10	4	1
St. Andrew	23	5	-
St. Catherine	3	-	-
St. John	25	2	1
St. Thomas-in-the-Vale	35	7	5
St. Mary	33	15	7
St. Ann	4	12	1
Clarendon	21	38	2
Vere	14	-	3
St. James	38	7	2
St. Elizabeth	18	10	1
Hanover	50	-	8
Westmoreland	42	22	1
St .Dorothy	8	-	-
Total	382	150	34

Source: Simpson and Craskill, Map of Jamaica c. 1763, CO 700/16.

December, St Catherine was again in the grip of drought forcing the attorney to write that 'St Jago has lost the use of the ... water again and will be obliged to go on with the cattle mills'.[48]

An indication that despite technological changes in power, cattle mills were dominant in Jamaica's sugar economy even in the nineteenth century is Robertson's map of Jamaica. Table 2.5, compiled from this map, indicates that the island had 656 cattle mills in 1804, compared to 88 windmills and 333 watermills. Furthermore, as there were 830 estates in Jamaica in 1804, this further strengthens the argument that even where alternative forms of power were utilized, cattle mills were maintained for emergencies, for there were 1,077 mills in all. Parishes that were susceptible to drought were especially careful to maintain cattle mills in addition to their water mills. Clarendon is a good example. Of 59 estates in Clarendon, only 17 or 28.8 per cent did not have a water mill; for the proximity of the Rio Minho or its tributaries to most estates made water a natural choice of power. Nevertheless, estates such as Danks, Clarendon Park and St Toolies also had cattle mills.[49] Thus, the need for animal standby mills differed from place to place according to the reliability of water supply.

This continued dominance of animal mills indicates the extent to which mill type was dictated not by efficiency, but by the state of available technology and by topographical and locational factors. Mills varied in efficiency by up to 50 per cent according to their power source. As Craton observed, watermills turned fastest, most continuously and most reliably, and were the cheapest to run once installed; but not every estate had access to rivers or ponds or could afford to have aqueducts built for the diversion of water from distant sources. Wind power was cheap but capricious as the wind itself and windmills were most useful on windward estates though in Hanover a few were noted. Estates in the vales of St John, for example, had no use for windmills. Animal power, it was true, turned mills slowly and was relatively expensive as there was a constant necessity to replace the animals. Animal mills were, nevertheless, efficient as to juice extraction. They were also reliable and were not subject to changes on account of climatic forces. Thus, even in dry Antigua, unsuitable for water mills but where nearly every planter had a windmill, plantations also had at least one cattle mill to use when the northeast trades failed.

Barbados, largely streamless, could not use water mills. However, the trade winds were reliable, so that some estates had as many as three windmills.[50] There were very few cattle mills in Barbados, however, as planters did not generally put into pasture land suitable for sugar cane. Indeed, unlike most other Caribbean islands, Barbados has a very high percentage of arable land. Its coral limestone soil is thin but fertile. Its annual rainfall, however, averages only 60 inches; but because the whole island is windswept, wind mills were more general.[51] A census of Barbados of 1710–12 returned 1,309 plantations. Of this number, 485 were sugar estates. Of them 409 used windmills and 76 cattle mills. A detailed map of Barbados in 1750 failed to indicate any cattle mills. However, in 1773, the island is shown as having had only 14 cattle mills, a ratio of about 40 windmills to every cattle mill. In Barbados, the shortage of cattle, attributed

Table 2.5
Mill Types by Parish and County, 1804

	Mill Type			Total No. of	
	Wind	Water	Cattle	Mills	Estates
County of Cornwall					
1. Hanover	13	15	88	116	85
2. St James	4	29	84	117	89
3. Trelawny	21	14	100	135	95
4. Westmoreland	0	24	59	83	70
5. St Elizabeth	0	16	12	28	26
Total	**38**	**98**	**343**	**479**	**365**
County of Middlesex					
6. St Catherine	0	1	4	5	4
7. St Dorothy	0	6	13	19	15
8. St John	2	8	17	27	19
9. St Thomas-in-the-Vale	4	13	27	44	34
10. Vere	7	1	35	43	30
11. St Ann	1	40	25	66	59
12. Clarendon	2	23	27	52	46
13. St Mary	14	41	54	109	68
Total	**30**	**133**	**202**	**365**	**275**
County of Surrey					
14. St Andrew	0	6	20	26	24
15. Kingston	0	0	0	0	0
16. St George	1	19	7	27	26
17. St David	0	12	5	17	15
18. Portland	3	11	21	35	32
19. St Thomas-in-the-East	16	51	57	124	89
20. Port Royal	0	3	1	4	4
Total	**20**	**102**	**111**	**233**	**190**
Grand Total (All Counties)	88	333	656	1,077	830

Note: Manchester and Metcalfe were not yet formed.
Source: J. Robertson, Maps of the Counties of Cornwall, Middlesex and Surrey (Jamaica, 184), NLJ.

to the shortage of pastureland and the high cost of imported cattle, determined that this form of power was not widespread.[52] In Jamaica, with its vast acreages suitable for pastures and with the continuous demand for livestock on estates, constantly expanding in the early eighteenth century, the future prospects of pen-keeping seemed bright.

Spring Plantation: A Case Study

The case of Spring Sugar Plantation in the parish of St Andrew demonstrates vividly the ways in which pens quickly became essential to the sugar industry, particularly in cases where plantations lacked adequate pasturage facilities, satellite pens, or the financial ability to import cattle.

Spring Sugar Plantation was situated between Constant Spring and Norbrook estates. The earliest plans of the estate in the manuscript collection in the National Library of Jamaica indicate that this land, containing 600 acres, had been granted to John Lewis, by Charles II, in 1665. Several parties seem to have owned shares in Spring. One moiety of Lewis's land had passed to Joseph Hunt around 1666. When Hunt died intestate c.1678, his moiety passed to Michael Hunt, his eldest brother. Michael's share was left in his will to his wife, Judith, and his seven children. These shares were later bought by George Freeman and Mary, John and Rebecca, three members of the Elbridge family of Bristol.[53] Freeman's share passed to Thomas French, and after French's death, to Thomas Rothley and Richard Stratton, whose interests passed to A.P. Collings around 1804.

Aldworth Elbridge, according to an undated plan, also held shares in Spring Plantation. It is not established how he came into this land, but it is quite possible that he bought Lewis's moiety. When Aldworth Elbridge died in 1703, he left his share in Spring Estate jointly to his daughters Mary and Rebecca. Rebecca sold her share to her uncle, John, and Mary, hers to her uncle, Robert. Robert bequeathed his share to Mary, his wife, for life, then to John and Thomas, his brothers, and Mary and Rebecca, his nieces, in equal proportions. John divided his shares equally to Rebecca, his niece, and Thomas, his nephew. Rebecca's share eventually came to Elizabeth Woolnough, her daughter, and so to John Hugh Smyth, Elizabeth's husband. Thomas Elbridge and his wife, Ann, both died in 1743, leaving no heir. Letters of Administration for Ann were taken out by Mrs Ann Hort, her mother, who claimed one-half of John Elbridge's estate and so became a co-heir with John Smyth.

While Freeman, French, Aldworth, and Mary Elbridge seem to have resided in Jamaica, the other subsequent shareholders were primarily absentee owners who left the management of the estate to a succession of attorneys. This necessitated frequent, often copious, correspondence between owners and attorneys. Detailed information from the other shareholders about Spring's affairs have not been seen. The Elbridge Family Papers, deposited in the Bristol archives office, however, provide a wealth of information about the family's Jamaican affairs up to 1804. This account of Spring Sugar Plantation, therefore, relies heavily on these papers.

According to the Elbridge Papers, in 1761, Spring sugar plantation consisted of approximately 900 acres of land. One hundred and fifty acres of this land were planted in cane, a few acres were devoted to the sugar works and the remainder consisted of mountain land, with only a few acres in pastureland. A plan of 1784 showed a reduction in the land planted in cane to 121 acres and nine perches, with about 37 acres in pasture. The remaining acres were devoted to the sugar works, 'negro grounds', waste land and ruinate.

The size of the estate itself conformed to Bryan Edwards's idea of what the size of an average estate should be. Its land use, labour supply, livestock and output did not, however, meet Edwards's criteria of what these should be on an average estate. Edwards took the average estate as one making 200 tons of muscovado sugar along with 14,300 gallons of rum. To produce this quantity of sugar and rum, he estimated a total acreage of 900 divided one-third in cane, one-third in pasture and provisions, and one-third in forest for the supply of fuel and timber. With regard to stock, Edwards observed that 'the stock on a plantation of this magnitude cannot prudently consist of less than 250 negroes, 80 steers and 60 mules'. Furthermore, £1,300 was estimated to be the annual expenditure on an average estate for the replacement/renewal of working stock.[54] Spring plantation, however, spent £1,437 4s. 6d. to replace cattle in 1784 alone.[55] In 1817, according to the Returns of the Registration of Slaves, its enslaved labour force numbered 124,[56] and throughout its history, it produced under 100 hogsheads of sugar. Indeed, its highest production of sugar was 84 hogsheads in 1800; by 1832 this had again dropped to 70 hogsheads.[57] In addition, its supply of livestock continued to be inadequate.

From the correspondence between the estate's attorneys, agents and overseers, it becomes clear that poor economic performance and a lack of animals because of poor pasturage were inextricably linked. In 1749, for example, Messrs Watson & Company informed Rebecca Woolnough that:

the Estate hath made this year 56 hhds. of sugar and will make about 75 or so next year, but we must be obliged to put on 20 steers and 10 mules more next year or otherwise the stock which they have on the estate, which is but 15 mules and 10 steers, will not be sufficient to take off the crop.[58]

In 1757, the complaint was specifically related to the poor pasturage 'which seldome is sufficient for the support of all the stock', and which led to a high degree of mortality among cattle on the estate. Although by 1761 the estate's stock had increased to 38 mules, 20 steers, three bulls, ten cows and followers, the attorneys still continued to urge that the number of working stock be increased by at least ten more steers. This suggestion seems to have been implemented, as the annual accounts indicate an annual expenditure on the purchase of mules and steers. These had to be procured from distant pens, primarily from Chief Justice George Ellis's pen, Agualta Vale, in St Mary, which later passed to the merchant, Thomas Hibbert. By 1784, the estate's supply of stock had increased to 97 head. In that year alone, £192 was spent on the purchase of six young steers at £132 per head, and £267 4s. 6d. for the purchase of eight mules.

In an attempt to solve its dual problem of poor pasturage and insufficient working stock for the needs of the estate, Spring, like other St Andrew estates, tried to lessen its dependence on cattle mills by turning to water mills. This would also obviate the need to purchase cattle from distant parishes. Water was diverted from rivers via aqueducts. According to the attorneys, in 1767, 'the advantages of a water work over a cattle mill are considerably great in every part of the island but especially in Liguanea where there is so little pasturage for cattle, the want of which for the Spring this year occasioned great expence and loss'.[59] Second, the estate rented pasturage from nearby Delacree pen. A disagreement between the pen-keeper and Spring's overseer, however, caused the discontinuation of this agreement. This was lamented by the attorneys who, anticipating an increase in pasturage rates, wrote that 'we fear the pasturage will not come so cheap in the future'.[60] Rates did increase in some parishes in the nineteenth century, moving from between 7s. 6d. 10 s per head to as much as 15s. per head of livestock in Kingston and St Catherine.[61]

The disruption in the existing arrangements for providing extra pasturage for the estate's stock on a nearby pen led the estate to seek other alternatives. For one thing, its stock seemed to have been subsequently pastured miles away at the Ferry Pen on the St Catherine border and at several pens in St Catherine, including Farm, Salt Pond and Ellis's Crawle.

Ultimately, however, Spring Plantation hoped to establish or lease a 'satellite' pen to satisfy its needs for grass and pasturage; for not only were pasturage fees increasing, but the long distances over poor roads travelled by the animals to rented pastures, was taking its toll on them. It has already been seen that cattle were brought from St Mary and even up to 1784, from St Ann. In that year's annual account, it was recorded that James Betty, the overseer, was paid £16 6s. 8d. for 'going to and returning from St Annes to buy cattle with 6 negroes'.[62] The decision to 'hire a pen; if to be got'[63] was taken as early as 1757. Several advantages were anticipated from this decision. According to the attorneys, one advantage would be that such a pen 'can fatten up the Old Cattle, of which the Estate has many, the produce of these will purchase younger ones fitter for service'.[64]

This suggestion does not seem to have been acted upon until 1768. In that year, Hibbert and Jackson reported that:

> the mortality of cattle and mules last year was great and by reason of dry weather and want of pasturage, unavoidable; to obviate the like Evils in future, we have agreed with Mr. French [shareholder in the estate] to hire a pen in the neighbourhood with about 30 negroes, consisting above 200 acres of land whereby to keep the plantation cattle and stock and by breeding, to be no more under the necessity of purchasing steers.[65]

The pen rented was Unity Park Pen, the property of a Mr Barton. The annual rent charged was £1,320.

The result of this attempt to solve the problem of cattle for the estate does not seem to have been entirely satisfactory, because the lease for the pen was terminated around 1785. Indeed, there had been complaints about the unsatisfactory nature of the pen since 1775. Hibbert and Company wrote thus to Smyth in 1775:

> a most capital inconvenience attending the spring and which raises greatly the amount of contingent charges is the total want of ground for pasturage, which has obliged us to lease the Pen called Unity Park Pen, for which we pay £1320 per annum, and at the same time that it is known to be impossible to do without some such place, it must be confessed that this is a most Capital Drawback

from the Proceeds of so small a Property. It would be some satisfaction if by the assistance of this pen it was possible to avoid the frequent purchases we are obliged to make of cattle, but its being subject as well as every part of Liguanea to such frequent drought renders breeding upon it out of the question.[66]

The decision was therefore taken to get rid of the pen, and the estate continued its practice of renting pasturage from pens in St Catherine, buying mules and steers, and buying grass. The estate also sought to extend its own pastureland. A major development, the recovery of part of the Spring's land from the adjoining estate, contributed greatly to this effort. It had long been suspected by the attorneys that Norbrook Estate had encroached on Spring's lands and for this reason, a re-survey had been commissioned to ascertain the true boundaries of the estate. This revealed that the Spring Plantation was indeed entitled to more land. When this land was recovered, a new possibility was opened up for solving the problem of the supply of pasturage and livestock for the estate's needs. A part of the land thus recovered was planted in cane, but the greater part was devoted to pasture, 'by which', according to the attorneys, 'we shall, in maturity, avoid the Expence and losses hitherto incurred by sending the cattle to distant parts of the Country'.[67] In addition, 30 acres of the estate's mountain lands were turned into pasture land. Since this area was elevated, it was hoped that it would experience more frequent rainfall.

The extension of pasture on its own lands did not solve Spring's problems. Inadequate rainfall, poor grass for grazing, declining production and the great expense incurred in the replacement of livestock from rural parishes, continued to pose obstacles to the economic development of this estate.[68]

Contested Terrain: The Interplay of Livestock and Cane

Finally, what were the dynamics that affected the location of sugar estates and the location of pens and to what extent were physical environmental factors of paramount significance in the spatial distribution of land use types in the island? Were 'behavioural' factors significant? The rest of this chapter will explore these issues.

Several factors explain the spatial variations in agricultural activity in eighteenth- and nineteenth-century Jamaica. The differences in these determinants make it impossible to utilize exclusively any one of the developed theoretical models of agricultural geography employed in the analysis of land use patterns. Traditional explanations have been located within the context of geographical determinism, which assumes that the physical environment acts in a deterministic manner and controls agricultural decision-making.[69] Increasingly, this model is being rejected by scholars who hold to the theory of economic determinism. Recently, some agricultural geographers have deviated from these two models in order to stress the primacy of what is called the 'behavioural model'. The conceptual assumption of this model is that social conditions and human motives are crucial to agricultural activity.

B. Ilbery, for example, opines that

> there are few, if any, situations where physical factors are either all important or of no account in the distribution of agricultural practices. Rather, it is the interaction of physical and human factors which determines patterns of agricultural land use.[70]

The dynamic nature of agriculture, which often leads to an imbalance between the environmental and the economic factors, makes the issue more complex; for although the physical environment may remain relatively stable over long periods of time, the economic environment can be very unstable and fluctuates according to changes in such basic factors as demand, supply, commodity prices and government policy.

Conversely, changes in the physical environment can result in changes in land utilization. Making the use of a single-factor theory even more difficult is the idea of demographic determinism — that is, that population changes play an important part in agricultural activity. In tracing the history of the location of pens in Jamaica, therefore, a multi-factor approach will be employed. This will involve an examination of the role of soil, topography and climate, the crucial interplay of livestock and cane, and the important factor of economic determinism. Behavioural factors such as the role of culture and status aspirations of agriculturalists must also be recognized.

In deciding where sugar estates were to be located, proprietors had to consider the differential fertility of the land. However, when these early settlers began to cultivate, they did not possess total knowledge of the island variations in soil fertility and so chose land accessible to the coast and therefore, the ports for marketing. Access to urban markets had also been uppermost in the minds of those engaged in livestock husbandry; so that the first pens were located near the main centres of population. For this reason, up to 1740, sugar estates and pens competed for space on the island's southern coast. This explains why in the Accounts Produce of that year, St Catherine emerged as the foremost pen parish in the island, followed by the other south coast parishes of St Andrew, Clarendon, Vere and St Dorothy.[71] St Catherine was still the front-runner in 1760, but by 1780 had lost its supremacy to St Ann. Thereafter, the stage of the 'sugar revolution' in each parish determined the extent to which either pens or estates predominated.

Between 1740 and 1790, sugar plantations spread rapidly along the north coast and on to the western plains in response to the buoyancy of the sugar market and the availability of enslaved labour. By 1804, plantations were as dense in the northern and western coastal plains as on the more extensive southern lowlands on which estates had rapidly pushed out pens. Between 1800 and 1820, specialized agricultural areas had developed. Though pens were still widely distributed, they became generally restricted to St Ann, St Elizabeth, Westmoreland, St Catherine, and Clarendon by 1800. A similar pattern was observed in 1820 and 1840, but with one important development: parishes which were regarded as sugar areas, that is, St Mary, Hanover, St Thomas-in-the-East and Trelawny, had by then, also established pens.

According to the Accounts Produce returns there were 13 pens in St Mary in 1820 compared to only one in 1780. This phenomenon is explained by the fact that to increase efficiency and reduce their dependence on independent pen-keepers, sugar planters were establishing their own 'satellite' (or related) holdings as close as possible to the estates. By 1800 too, specialized coffee zones had also developed and were concentrated in the mountainous parts of parishes such as (upper) St Andrew.[72]

An independent check in the In-givings of 1815 confirms this zoning of agricultural activity with the principal pen areas emerging as St Ann, St Elizabeth, Westmoreland, Clarendon, St Catherine, and St Dorothy. There were few pens in St John, St Thomas-in-the-Vale, Vere, Port Royal, St Andrew, Kingston, St Thomas-in-the East, St David, St James, St George and Portland. Some sugar parishes like St Mary, continued to show a significant number of 'satellite' holdings.[73]

This pattern of regional specialization that had emerged by 1820 is explained by physical environmental and economic factors. First of all, as in other plantation colonies of the 'New World', settlers in Jamaica had by the mid-eighteenth century come to accept that sugar was the preferred export staple. The great demand for sugar on the international market led to the expansion of this industry to the detriment of other competing staples. Thus, as long as the land could support cane, and despite its suitability for pasture, the livestock industry was not encouraged at the expense of sugar. Sugar planters realized early the comparative advantage of planting cane instead of breeding stock, the latter being imported from external sources best suited to cattle rearing. This economic choice was not confined to the English-colonized territories. Cuba and Brazil also experienced this phenomenon of the interplay of cattle and cane at some stage of their economic development.

Cuba, in the pre-sugar era, had been dominated by cattle ranches and tobacco farms. After the sugar revolution, cattle rearing was confined to the lands unsuitable for cane. In Brazil, as in Jamaica, the livestock industry first developed on coastal flatlands. In the third quarter of the sixteenth century, the sugar plantations and the livestock ranches occupied much of the same territory. As the sugar industry expanded, the Portuguese government moved to forbid livestock husbandry within ten leagues of the coast. This effectively exiled the cattle industry into the interior.[74]

Despite the function of economic factors in the decision to plant cane, ultimately, soil, topography and climate had to be considered.[75] Thus, contemporary writers and modern historians have tended to point to the development of the sugar industry in parishes where these factors were ideal. Bryan Edwards felt that the best soil for the cane was a fine 'brick-mold'.[76] Douglas Hall and Barry Higman recorded that because of the fertility of this soil in certain areas sugar dominated the lower part of St Andrew, lying in the Liguanea Plain, the fertile interior valleys such as Lluidas Vale, St John, Queen of Spain's Valley on the St James-Trelawny border, the entire parish of St Thomas-in-the-Vale, the entire length of the flat north coast, the alluvial plains of St Thomas-in-the-East and the Plantain Garden River area of that parish; on the plains of Westmoreland,

Vere and Hanover, and the interior basins of the upper Black River of St Elizabeth and the Rio Minho of Clarendon.[77]

At times, soil fertility, adequacy of rainfall and other physical geographical factors had to be sacrificed because of the friction factor. The friction of distance is basically the cost in time and money required to overcome distance.[78] Sugar had to be transported to the coast by mule or horse-drawn carts. Long distances would obviously take a high toll of stock thus eventually pushing up production costs. Distance from the coast and the modes of transportation available effectively confined sugar estates to coastal or flatland areas.

The distribution of pens by parish according to physical environmental determinants has been particularly well-documented by Edward Long. From his account, it seems clear that the Pedro Distict located between St Ann and Clarendon, was an ideal pen area. This district was neither flat nor lowland, but was said to contain 'an infinite number of little round hills whose surface is covered with a loose limestone, or honeycomb rock'. It was these 'dales' or 'cockpits' which 'meander between these hummocks (hills)' which contained the soil so suitable for guinea grass on which cattle thrive.[79] According to Thomas Coke, 'the introduction of this grass soon increased the number of breeding farms on spots where the hand of cultivation had rarely laboured before'.[80] Long reported that the grass here was so good that 'the mules and cattle bred here are larger and finer than in most other parts of the island'.[81] St Ann's suitability for guinea grass and livestock-pens in comparison to parishes like St Thomas-in-the-East, was corroborated by Simon Taylor, attorney and planter, in 1790. He pointed out that:

> St Ann is a very different soil for Guinea Grass than] St Thomas-in-the-East is. They have large Glades of level lands between their Hills, their Hills are all rocky which gives them stone for fences and their dews are so heavy that the cattle seldom or never drink, but in exceeding dry years.[82]

St Ann had three distinct agricultural zones. The areas between the hills and the coast were devoted to sugar cane. The hills had few estates: pimento, however, thrived. The savannas were full of ferns and were of no use for agriculture, but the eastern area behind the range of hills and mountains was ideally suited for pens. These pens flourished as the sugar area was subjected to drought, making water mills unusuable and cattle mills indispensable. By 1833, over 25 per cent of the enslaved population in the parish were attached to pens.[83]

The main topographical zones supporting pens in St Catherine were the dry southside region and the midland mountains and lowlands, where mountain running grass or 'sour grass' was common. Apparently, when green, cattle rejected this grass, but when cut, dried and cured, it made good hay, which they ate. The latter area was also suitable for cane growing, but, as Long observed, 'because the rainy season has been uncertain for many years' grass, rather than sugar cane, was cultivated there. In places of extreme dryness, however, cattle did not thrive so that in such areas, grass pens rather than breeding pens developed to provide pasturage for estates' cattle. The area of the salt-pan land was also devoted to pens.

St Dorothy was similar to St Catherine in soil type and topography and was also subjected to periodic drought. It was slow to be planted in sugar, and in 1740, had only eight sugar estates. The southern flatlands were, however, suitable for pasture. The in-givings of 1815 list ten sugar estates compared to 20 pens — a significant increase over 1740.

Clarendon and Vere (in the precinct of Clarendon) though dominated by sugar plantations, also had pens in the areas unsuitable for the cane. Clarendon was one of the largest, healthiest and best settled parishes in the island. The lower part of the parish consisted chiefly of savanna land 'about six miles in length, here and there interspersed with rocky hills of no great height'.[84] In fact, there were few hills steep enough to be a deterrent to cultivation. Its many rivers made the vales between the hills fertile and well-watered. The vales were enriched by fine cane lands. Long records that 'the conveniency of having water mills and the firmness of the roads in general has encouraged the inhabitants to carry their sugar plantations much further inland than in any other district of the island'.[85] On the savanna, however, some pens were established.

The pens in Vere were located on the level tract of land that ran from the sea to the mountains of Clarendon. Around 1773, this area was about 16 miles long and 14 miles wide in the broadest part. Wherever sugar estates were not established in this tract, pens were usual.

The only other significant pen parishes were located in the county of Cornwall. These were Hanover, Westmoreland, and St Elizabeth. Of the three, St Elizabeth was the most important. The topography of St Elizabeth was diverse, ranging from the savannas of the eastern district, for example, the Pedro Plains, to the mountainous areas of Santa Cruz and Burnt Savanna mountains. In the eastern savanna area, few sugar estates were established. In this area, however, Long recorded that 'a great number of very fine pens for breeding horned cattle, horses, mules, sheep and goats as well as poultry of all kinds' existed. The area around the Black River was not drained, and so remained largely wasteland. The soil of Middle Quarters mountains in the south-west was stony and unsuitable for both cane and pens, and the plains of Luana was too sandy and was mainly taken up by palmetto trees, 'a sure sign of its poverty', according to Long.

Westmoreland was formed in 1703 out of part of St Elizabeth, so it is not surprising that this parish also contained some fine breeding pens. However, these pens competed with sugar estates for land on the plains; for Westmoreland was first and foremost a sugar parish, said by Long to have been 'so congenial to the sugar-cane that a long and uninterrupted culture seems not in the least to have exhausted or even impaired its fertility'. Even Long, who was an ardent supporter of the establishment of local breeding pens, felt that as every part of Westmoreland was eminently suitable for the sugar cane, the lowland pens should be relocated — perhaps in the north-east mountains. Yet, mountainous land is not exactly the most ideal for rearing livestock. The result was a continued competition for land for pens and a failure of the pen-keeping industry to develop to its maximum in this parish in the period of slavery.

The pens of Hanover were near the Westmoreland border. This was not surprising as this parish was formed out of Westmoreland in 1723. Among the largest Hanover pens were Ramble, Shettlewood, Knockalva, Haughton Grove, Burnt Ground, and Cacoon Castle.[86] More land in Hanover could have supported the livestock industry, but here again, the need to expand the sugar industry caused planters to increase at the expense of pen-keepers.

Pens were scarce in the mountainous parishes. Upper St Andrew and upper St David were unsuitable for pasture. Lower St David was, however, dry and as it could not support estates, was turned over to pasture. Kingston and Port Royal were primarily commercial or residential areas, and supported little agricultural activity. Of the other parishes, only St George and Manchester had a few significant pens, the others being geographically unsuitable for this enterprise. Of the two, Manchester had the larger number. Coffee was, however, the principal crop grown in this parish because of the area of rocky limestone hills centred there.[87] Towards the St Elizabeth border a few pens were, however, established. In addition, crop combinations developed and Manchester thus had a large number of pen/coffee units. The supply of livestock from such units was, however, smaller than from monocultural farms.

By contrast, most of St George, like St Mary and Portland, lay in the north-east rain belt area. This made it heavily forested and large areas were consequently unsuitable for any type of agriculture. Favourable rains did, however, make sugar cultivatable but the soils were heavy and difficult to work. Furthermore, as marginal backlands and relatively infertile hilly areas — usually devoted to pens in other parishes — were limited in these areas, pens were few and livestock were purchased from parishes, which specialized in its production.

Crop specialization by geographical zones and parishes was fairly well established by the 1830s. Figure 2.4, generalized by P.P. Courtenay from Edwards's *History of the West Indies* illustrates the areas of sugar cultivation by the late eighteenth century. Table 2.6, based on stipendiary magistrates' returns, gives a partial idea of the number of each of the main units in the island in 1836.

The eastern coffee areas remained fairly constant over the period under review, being too steep for either sugar or livestock. In the other major coffee region — Manchester — the area devoted to coffee underwent changes depending on the competition for land for livestock-raising. This parish, indeed was a prime example of crop combination (pens and coffee). Areas devoted to sugar estates and pens changed more frequently. The change in the spatial distribution of these units was a function of the dynamic nature of agriculture and related to changes in soil fertility and climatic conditions as well as in the decision of some pen-keepers to shift to the higher status estates. These factors affected sugar estates, but with one exception, it worked in favour of the distribution of pens.

Sugar estates did not always practise mixed rotational farming methods. Added to this were the inadequate sources of manure. As a result, soil fertility became quickly exhausted. This, in turn, led to the abandonment of sugar estates and the establishment of pens on these former sugar lands.[88] Whereas estates had expanded at the expense of pens in the early eighteenth century, therefore, the reverse was true by the end of the century, with

43

Figure 2.4
Sugar Plantation Areas of Jamaica, 1793

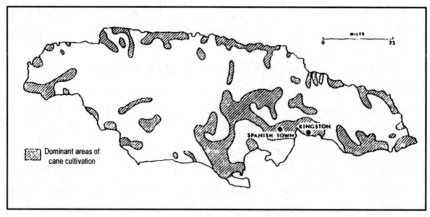

Generalized from Edwards's *History of the West Indies*
Source: P.P. Courtenay, *Plantation Agriculture* (London, 1965), 19.

estates such as Pepper and Barton Isles being later turned into pens.[89]

Additionally, climatic changes led to the further contraction of sugar lands. The forested areas found by the English settlers in 1655 had been quickly cleared and planted. Such deforestation affected rainfall. By the eighteenth century certain sections of the island became too dry to support sugar estates and planters frequently complained of the 'failure of the seasons'. This was particularly true of the south side from Liguanea to Vere. This is evident from the following extract from Charles Leslie's account of Jamaica. According to him:

> In the plantations on the south side the seasons have much failed. Liguanea is quite dry, and fine sugar works that used to produce many hundred hogsheads are now carried into Cattle penns. This is likewise the fate of the fine parishes of St Katherine's, St Dorothy and Vere which once were the choicest and richest spots in the whole island, but are now good for little but to graze cattle. They are dry for almost nine months, at Pt. Royal where scarce fall Forty showers in a year.[90]

What Leslie failed to point out, however, was that the pens which replaced estates in these dry southern plains were little more than grass

Table 2.6
Number of Pens, Sugar Estates and Plantations of Minor Staples, 1836

Parishes	Sugar Estates	Coffee Plantations	Pen	Pimento Plantations	Ginger Plantations	Pen/ Coffee
1. St Mary	60	16	24	8	-	-
2. Manchester	-	102	5	-	-	32
3. St Thomas-in-the East	73	18	14	-	-	-
4. St Ann	32	8	54	74	-	-
5. St Catherine	5	-	31	-	-	-
6. Vere	29	-	4	-	-	-
7. St James	89	1	27	12	3	-
8. Westmoreland	48	2	32	-	-	-
9. Trelawny	84	5	20	5	-	-
10. St Elizabeth	37	16	46	2	3	-
11. St George	30	33	4	2	1	-
12. Port Royal	3	51	4	-	-	-
13. St. Thomas-in-the-Vale	28	31	4	3	-	-
14. St. Andrew	14	22	-	7	-	-
15. St. Dorothy	14	-	8	-	-	-
16. Kingston	No Return Made					
17. Clarendon	41	24	15	1	-	-
18. Hanover	59	-	5	2	4	-
19. Portland	16	-	4	2	1	-
20. St John	9	3	2	3	-	-
21. St David	9	21	2	-	-	-
Total	680	353	305	121	12	32

Note: This Return was incomplete. It was based on the returns submitted by the stipendiary magistrates. Only 57 of them sent in returns. Nevertheless, the return gives a fairly accurate idea of the geographical distribution of pens in Jamaica.
Source: Governor Sligo to Lord Glenelg, Despatch 331, February.13, 1836, (PRO) CO 137/209.

pens; for the lack of water equally hampered the breeding of livestock. St Catherine became primarily noted for its grass pens by 1820, and pen-keepers in this parish sold hundreds of bundles of grass to Kingston and Spanish Town. In addition, livestock from these properties were pastured on the grass pens for a fee. As St Catherine had very few sugar estates, however, grass pens combined with the few real breeding establishments in the parish, were adequate to serve the needs of the planters there. Pens in nearby parishes could also be tapped, but on the island level climatic factors which facilitated grass pens, militated against the further extension of breeding pens and contributed to the inadequate number of local units producing livestock.

The situation in Liguanea was somewhat different. Indeed, St Andrew was confronted with a paradox: an apparent abundance of 'pens' and a shortage of working stock. Thus, on the one hand, Colin Clarke noted that the dry, lower part of Liguanea Plain was, by 1763, devoted to cattle farms or pens, there being 50 of these in that year.[91] Seeming to confirm Clarke's claim are the St Andrew Estate maps that detail approximately 62 pens in the early nineteenth century. On the other hand, there were the frequent complaints about the lack of pasturage for cattle in Liguanea, from the planters and attorneys in the parish, as the case study of spring plantation has so effectively demonstrated.[92] Despite the proliferation of pens in St Andrew, however, figure 2.5 shows that these were primarily the residential units of the Kingston merchants. They had the highest rating value for tax purposes.[93] Of the 62 pens mentioned above, for example, only about 26 contained over 100 acres of land. Most of them were located in the dry, lower part of the plain, just beyond the peripheral lower settlements of free pastureland.

Additionally, the role of behavioural factors must not be underestimated. In eighteenth-century Jamaica, it was more socially acceptable to be a sugar planter. Pen-keepers were often considered marginal to the White elite planter class. One way of changing status was to invest the earnings from pens into sugar estates. This did not necessarily imply the total abandonment of the pen in all cases, but the diversification into sugar resulted in upward social mobility for pen-keepers.[94]

It is clear from the preceding account of the economic and agricultural geography of pens that cultural, climatic and physical environmental factors restricted their expansion in the period of slavery. The competition for land between plantations and pens meant that areas eminently suitable for pasture were often under sugar cultivation. Although climatic changes forced the abandonment of sugar plantations and facilitated the establishment of pens on such lands, these units were forced to be small enterprises, devoted primarily to grass; for access to water supplies was as much a matter of importance to pens as it was for sugar estates. In southern St Catherine and the dry Liguanea Plain, the lack of sufficient breeding pens forced planters to import livestock or obtain animals from other

Figure 2.5
Social Areas, Kingston 1745

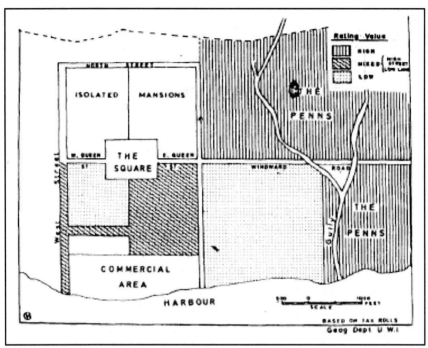

Source: W. Bailey, 'Kingston, 1692-1845', p. 150.

parishes. The history of Spring Plantation further underscores the causal relationship between economic performance and adequate plantation working stock. Where greater access was realized in meeting the demand for livestock, and where other factors of production were favourable, performance was usually better. Thus, other St Andrew estates, some smaller than Spring, though faced with the same problem of inadequate pens in the parish, were more successful in their attempts to overcome the problem. Mona, Constant Spring, Papine and Norbrook consequently fared better economically than did the Spring.

3

TRADE AND EXCHANGE:
CONTESTING THE CLASSIC PLANTATIONIST TRADING ARRANGEMENT

Slavery transformed the Atlantic into a complex trading area, turning it into the centre of the international economy especially during the eighteenth and nineteenth centuries, with goods from the Caribbean destined more for external than for local and regional markets. The making of an integrated market culture in the Atlantic has, predictably, overshadowed the study of intra-island and intra-regional trading links. Yet such links, though not as lucrative as the links between the colonies and the metropoles, were not complete casualties of colonization and the monopolistic tendencies of empire. In other words, local and regional interconnectedness was not lost in the making of the Atlantic World; and an understanding of the emergence of the larger 'Atlantic World' must take greater cognizance of the intra-American labour mobilization and resource exchange that operated within the panoramic context of the world system. This chapter will show that slavery and the plantation system had a catalytic function in the linking of disparate Caribbbean territories as they did the linking of different economic sectors within individual islands. Jamaica presented a case in point, its internal markets and links with regional markets conflicting with the classic plantation model.

In classic plantation systems in the eighteenth and nineteenth-century Atlantic World, the trading network conformed, at least in theory, to the mercantilist model established by the colonial powers. For the British-colonized territories, this meant that, initially, all inputs were expected to be imported from, and all outputs exported to, Britain. For pragmatic reasons, the trading network in the British-colonized Atlantic World was allowed to depart from this model, with trade among colonies eventually allowed. Because of economic necessity, trade through free ports with 'foreign powers' was also allowed by the nineteenth century. Some colonies like Jamaica departed in other significant ways from the mercantilist model, developing an internal network of trade and exchange. The pens played a large role in the internal commodity trade in Jamaica. The trade conducted by the pens, therefore, signalled a failure on the part of the pen-keepers to adhere to the dictates of the plantation system and their efforts to contest the monopolistic trading tendencies of the plantation system. In other words, they carved out their own trading terrain, going against the wishes of the sugar barons in some cases.

Goods and Lines of Trade

The production and disposal of goods in formal/informal markets were as integral to the operation of the pens in Jamaica as these activities were for the sugar estates. The pens engaged in three levels of exchange. One was the export of commodities, primarily 'minor staples', and various woods; the other was the domestic trade in provisions and livestock; and yet another was a type of informal, non-monetary exchange of commodities with other properties.

The Export Dimension

The early history of livestock farming in Jamaica indicates that the export dimension of trade was highly developed in the seventeenth century. In that period, the farms had an independent economic dynamic, exporting hides, lard and dried, cured meat to the Spanish Indies and Spain. By 1740, however, the majority of the livestock farms disposed of their output on the domestic market, principally the sugar estates. Quantitative data on the disposal of pen output are not abundant, especially for those units which had resident owners. The available trade statistics provided by the Accounts Produce from 1740 relate primarily to the properties of absentees; nevertheless, they can be used effectively to demonstrate some broad trends in the extent of pen participation in the export and internal trade.

The Accounts Produce show quite clearly that pens participated only minimally in the direct export trade and, further, that where goods were produced for export, their value did not generally exceed the proceeds from local transaction. Before 1800, the commodities exported were ginger, pimento, cotton, dyewoods and hardwood (logwood, fustic, mahogany). These products could be related clearly to specific parishes. Ginger was sold from the pens in St Andrew; pimento from St Ann and Trelawny, but mostly from the former; dyewoods, fustic and cotton from St Elizabeth, with some cotton also from the pens in St Catherine.

Two distinct patterns of trade seemed to have existed. One method was to ship the commodity to Britain, presumably to an agent who handled the sale there. The most frequently observed practice, however — and one which was in direct contrast to the usual method of disposing of sugar — was to sell the product to merchants in Kingston, who then arranged the sale.

Evidence of the participation of pens in the export trade was most available from the 1770s. Accounts for the earlier period were scanty, perhaps because of the greater residency of the pen-keepers then. In 1740, for example, whereas it was evident that estates were exporting minor staples in addition to sugar, (such crops also being exported from plantations of minor staples) only two of the 18 pens for which returns were seen exported any commodity, in this case, cotton. In this period, most of the pens were located on the south side, particularly St Catherine, and supplied primarily grass and provisions to the urban markets.[1] Forty years later, of the 21 returns relating to livestock farms, only five participated in the export trade. One hundred and eighteen bags of pimento valued at £256 17s. 1d. were shipped from Dornoch, Riverhead and Gordon Valley pens in St Ann. Several other bags valued at £161 0s. 4d. were sold in Kingston, presumably for later export. In all then, pimento sales totalled £417 17s. 4d. but this represented just over 11 per cent of the total earnings of the pen which amounted to £3,858 7s. 7d.[2]

Taking the period 1776–85 together, it is evident that the pens continued to export ginger, pimento, fustic, mahogany, logwood and cotton. A similar commodity-parish relationship existed as in 1740.[3] The just over 40 returns seen (representing 25 pens), showed a mere seven pens active in the export market. In all cases, the value of exports fell far below the receipts from internal transactions. The best example in this period is from Luana Pen in St Elizabeth which had eight separate returns in the period under review. Between 1776 and 1785, Luana exported 58 tons of fustic (£340 16s. 9d.), 65 tons of logwood (£325. 0.0.) and 995 pounds of cotton (£87 1s. 3d.) — totalling £752 18s. 0d; but over the same period, receipts from livestock sales and pen services totalled £3,156 12s. 0d. Exports represented just under 20 per cent of total earnings of £3,909 10s. 0d.[4] In the other accounts, the percentage represented by exports was lower.

Accounts for 1800 and 1820 — the other years sampled — also replicated these earlier trends with respect to commodities produced, parishes which produced, patterns of trade and comparative receipts from sales, with one important exception, the addition of coffee to the list of exports. In 1800, coffee was shipped from pens in St Ann, Clarendon, and St James. Cotton, logwood and fustic continued to be produced in St Elizabeth, and Westmoreland, by this time an important exporter of logwood. One pen in St Dorothy shipped a quantity of lignum vitae wood and pimento continued to be associated with the St Ann pens.[5]

Unlike in the preceding period, the value of exports from the pens in 1800 and 1820 at times exceeded earnings from internal transactions. Two notable examples were firstly Bellemont Pen, which in 1800 exported coffee valued at £1,117 6s. 8d. — 67 per cent of total receipts for that year. The second case was Patherton Pen whose coffee exports formed 82 per cent of total earnings. As not all the accounts contained the volume and value of the commodities and as it is not at all times safe to assign current prices to the crops (if sold in Jamaica, for example, commodities fetched a different price from those exported directly to Great Britain), it is impossible to ascertain the extent to which Patherton and Bellemont typified the situation with the pens in 1800 with respect to value of exports versus internal trade. A further complication limiting generalization about the trend is that it would seem that it is those pen/coffee combined units, mostly in Manchester, which showed an increase of exports over internal sales. Pens like Luana which were primarily devoted to livestock rearing, continued to show an excess of internal transactions over exports. In 1800, Luana earned 32 per cent from export sales, for example. Indeed, of the eight complete accounts seen for this year, six recorded that sales from internal transactions exceeded those from exports. It should also be added that of 73 returns of pens in 1800, 21 (29 per cent) participated in the external trade — a significant enough improvement over previous years in numbers, though not necessarily in percentage. This improvement seemed attributable to the increase of pens producing and exporting coffee.

In 1820, 153 returns of pens were recorded. Of this number, 43 or 28 per cent participated in the direct export trade. The products exported were coffee, pimento, fustic, lignum vitae, logwood and hides. One pen, Castille Fort, provided ballast for outgoing ships. Most pens exported only one commodity. Only a minority exported two. The usual combination was pimento and coffee (four pens) or logwood and fustic (two pens). One pen exported both pimento and fustic. St Ann's pens continued to be over-represented in the export of pimento. The combined pen/coffee units in Manchester most likely dominated the export of coffee, but because of the high residency among the coffee farmers, were under-represented in the Accounts Produce. In the 1820 returns, it is the St Ann pens which seemed to be exporting most of the coffee.

Most of the products were recorded as having been 'sent to Kingston'. Again, as not all commodity prices were included, only tentative statements can be made about the value of the products sold abroad. What seems clear is that of the 18 pens which had detailed information on prices and volume of goods, only three seemed to have earned more from exports than from internal transactions, the percentage from exports ranging from 59–71 per cent. The others earned between 0.2 per cent and 39 per cent from external trade. The limited quantitative data, therefore, serve to reinforce the impression from qualitative sources that unlike the sugar estates, pens catered essentially to the domestic market in the island.

The Domestic Dimension

In contrast to this relatively minimal involvement in the direct export trade, Jamaican pens participated actively in the domestic system of exchange. According to Barry Higman, around the time of emancipation, the flow of goods and labour from one unit to another resulted in approximately 17 per cent of the total production of sugar estates and coffee plantations remaining in Jamaica.[6] Thus, pens were not the only units which disposed of commodities locally, but it is safe to say that pens dominated the inter-property trade, most marked in the trade between such farms and the sugar estates.

While such inter-property links were unique to Jamaica among the British-colonized Caribbean territories, such economic relations developed in other diversified economies, notably Cuba and Brazil. Both these countries had local livestock farms and ranches, which supported other sectors.[7]

The volume and value of goods and services (including labour) between properties in Jamaica can best be studied by reference to the Accounts Produce, sampled 20-yearly for this purpose. A variety of goods were involved in the internal system of exchange between Jamaican properties. The primary product was livestock, comprising working steers, spayed heifers, breeding cows, mules, horses, bulls, calves, asses, fat cattle, old, worn out estate cattle and small stock. Other goods included food provisions (mainly corn and plantains), grass, milk, bricks, white lime, shingles, fresh beef, fish, timber, staves, sugar, rum, coffee and miscellaneous items. Most of these goods were sold by the pens. Those sold or exchanged by estates were sugar, rum and old working cattle. Where pen/coffee units or monocultural coffee units were involved in the trade, they sold coffee and livestock in the case of the former.

The principal services provided by pens were jobbing, pasturage and wainage (cartage). Sugar estates rented excess land, at times in exchange for more pastureland from nearby properties. They also jobbed their tradesmen. Jobbing was, however, probably dominated by pens and specialized, independent jobbing gangs.

Of the goods listed above, the trade in livestock was the most lucrative for pens. According to Bryan Edwards, an eighteenth-century estate spent a minimum of £300 per annum to replace stock.[8] The majority, indeed, spent far more. In 1782, Simon Taylor, the attorney for Golden Grove estate in St Thomas-in-the-East, reported that the estate needed 100 working steers annually.[9] At around £30 each in 1820, this would cost this estate £3,000 per annum. As estates also bought mules and spayed heifers annually, pens stood to gain considerably from the trade in working stock, especially around 1820 when the price of a mule was £40 and for a young, spayed heifer, £22 10s. to £26 each. J.B. Moreton recorded that an estate with even 100 acres of cane needed to buy 40 mules annually and maintain 100 always on the estate in the late eighteenth century.[10] Horses, proof asses and fat stock sold to the butchers also fetched considerable sums.

Of the services provided by pens, jobbing was the most financially rewarding. Jobbing consisted chiefly of digging cane holes and planting the spring canes on estates. In 1834, the cost of digging cane holes was £8 per acre. In this and previous years, some pens profited considerably from this service provided by their hired, as opposed to resident, workers. Stoneyfield Pen in St Ann, for example, earned £660 1s. 6d. in 1820 for jobbing done on Fellowship Hall estate. This represented 52.54 per cent of its total earnings from internal transactions.[11]

Pasturage, particularly for St Catherine's pens, was also quite lucrative. In the eighteenth century, the typical rates charged for this service were 15 shillings per month for each horse or mule, and ten shillings per month for each head of cattle.[12] If pastured by the score, rates were slightly lower. For example, 7s. 6d. for each animal was charged where cattle were pastured in batches of 20 or more. Rates increased in the nineteenth century to a maximum of 20 shillings for each horse.

For sugar estates, the sale of their old, meagre or fat cattle after the crop to pens or butchers gave them handsome returns on their initial investment in young working stock. James Stevenson, the attorney for the Scarlett's estates in Jamaica, noted in 1800 that fat cattle from the estates sold at around £40 each. He stressed that formerly, old, fat cattle sold at between £18 and £25 each, but now fetched almost as much as for young cattle. Even though estates then had to buy fresh beef from such stock, at 1s. to 1s. 8d. a pound, he felt they still made a profit in the sale of fat stock.[13] The army used a substantial proportion of the fresh beef sold by pens.[14]

The internal sale of rum also provided estates with money to help with local contingencies. As most of this product would have eventually been re-exported by Kingston merchants this was, perhaps, not a true part of the domestic trade. However, sugar estates still participated in local transactions by providing for the sugar and rum needs of non-sugar-producing units.

The availability of goods and services provided by Jamaican pens was made known to potential customers in one of three ways. First, the sale of livestock was advertised in the various newspapers. One hundred and twenty pens advertised the sale of animals in various newspapers sampled between 1780 and 1834.[15] Second, pen-keepers or overseers, utilizing the services of enslaved couriers, sent letters to sugar planters or their representatives and butchers indicating the availability of planters' stock and fat cattle respectively. Thistlewood noted in 1751, for example, that he 'sent Julius to Mr. Markham with a letter to let him know what fat cattle we have'.[16] Third, pen-keepers or pen overseers themselves visited estates to enquire about the availability of livestock for sale. Over time, estates developed a relationship with particular pens, getting to know their routine and approximate selling time for young steers, heifers and mules.

In the majority of cases, the enslaved men on pens supplied the orders sent in by sugar estates for livestock. The driving of cattle and horsekind to and from estates provided the enslaved involved with a great deal of mobility. On July 27, 1750, for example, Charles Guy and Julius left Vineyard Pen with 15 steers, 2 young horses, 10 heifers and 2 mules for a property in Westmoreland. They did not all return until August 2. Their explanation was that they had been delayed unduly because several people asked them to collect and deliver letters.[17] Enslaved pen workers often covered longer distances than were involved in the case of Vineyard Pen's labourers. Some of the enslaved from Agualta Vale Pen in St Mary, for example, drove animals to Spring Estate in St Andrew — approximately 34 miles away.[18] Enslaved people from other properties, or those belonging to individual butchers, also went to the pens to collect goods for their enslavers. Mr Markham, for example, 'sent his negroes for one dozen crabs caught by Titus and a he-lamb'.[19] Markham similarly sent enslaved workers to purchase fat cattle from Vineyard Pen. According to overseer Thomas Thistlewood, however, his 'hands' were inadequate to manage the nine cows and calves; so that Charles and Cuffie had to help with them as far as Black River.[20] In some cases, the butchers, or estate overseers, visited the pen personally to make arrangements for purchase.[21]

In addition to driving livestock to markets, pen workers fetched animals bought for the pen or to be pastured on its lands. In 1807, for example, the overseer of Thetford Hall Pen in St John, sent labourers from that property to Mile Gully in Clarendon for a bull purchased from that pen.[22] Similarly, Thistlewood sent Dick, Guy, Charles, Julius and Simon to Mr. Allen's pen to fetch the mares for pasturage.[23] Where pen workers themselves delivered livestock to markets, or fetched and returned animals for fattening or pasturage, an extra cost was added.

The method used to dispose of other pen products seemed less systematic. On Vineyard and Breadnut Island pens, for example, no letters were exchanged respecting the sale of vegetables and food crops. Also, no advertisements appeared in the newspapers relating to the sale of products other than large stock and its by-products. Products such as capons, crabs, poultry, eggs, fruits, sheep, goats and vegetables were sent to market in Westmoreland or Black River each week. These were clearly not marketed by the enslaved people on their own account as such sales were not usually made on Saturdays or Sundays. On some Saturdays, however, products were prepared for sale the following week. In addition to these products, Phibbah, Thistlewood's 'housekeeper', frequently sold cloth (usually 'check') in Westmoreland.

Few pens returned in the Accounts Produce established butcheries in the period under review. Those that did also developed significant links with properties and individuals within and outside of the area of their location. The best example of the scale of transactions in fresh beef from a pen, is provided by Batchelor's Hall Pen's accounts. In 1833, this pen earned £2,120 2s. 11d. from its sale of fresh beef to estates, individuals, the troops and ships. This represented 57.63 per cent of its total earnings for that year.[24]

The participation of the various units in the internal commodity trade varied in extent, volume and value from year to year. In 1740, when the Accounts Produce returns begin, 175 accounts were sent in by overseers. These represented 85 sugar estates, 20 pens, five plantations of minor staples, 19 jobbing gangs, 19 multiple crop combinations and 27 returns relating to merchants' earnings or house rents collected. Eighteen of the 20 pens, 20 of the 85 estates and the plantations of minor staples participated in the internal trade. Unfortunately, there is no detailed account of the buyers involved, so that the extent of economic links for 1740 cannot be measured.

The returns for 1760 indicate that inter-property transactions remained essentially the same as for 1740 in terms of the total number of properties involved. Sugar estates had, however, improved their participation moving from 23.52 per cent in 1740 to 35.68 per cent in 1760. Pens basically remained at the same level, but the participation by plantations had declined. By 1780, 120 properties of the 266 returned were involved in local transactions. The number of properties involved continued to increase along with the increase in the number of returns. These indications are for units owned by absentees, but resident proprietors also participated in the trade, though the extent of their involvement cannot be ascertained. In the post-slavery period, however, the nature of transactions underwent slight changes. While the sale of livestock continued between pens and estates, there was a drastic reduction in the jobbing of pen labourers on the estates. Indeed, only five such cases were noted in the 152 returns of pens in 1840, compared to 64 of the 145 such units in the 1820 return.

The extent of trade is clearer in the nineteenth-century returns. The majority of estates relied either on pens or local butchers to buy their old stock. Pens dominated this trade, however, as they were better placed than the butchers to fatten such animals prior to their being killed for fresh beef. Only five of the pens returned in 1820 had their own butcheries, and the supply of beef — a form of final demand linkage — was probably in the hands of urban butchers and independent pens not returned.

The volume of livestock being sold in the island can be partially ascertained from the Accounts Produce. In the first return when pens were not as numerous as later on, these units supplied only 34 head of working stock to estates. In that year, few pens were monocultural livestock units, and St Catherine's units, in particular, sold more sheep and small stock than cattle and mules. By 1780, 21 out of the 266 returns were pens. The latter were involved in the sale of livestock to the number of 942. This represented 50.7 per cent of the 1,881 sold by the 120 units involved in local trading.[25] Table 3.1 showing the specific breakdown of the numbers traded, indicates the relative importance of each type of livestock in the eighteenth century. It is clear that in the late eighteenth century, heifers and mules were over-represented in terms of working animals. The mule, indeed, was recognizedly unsurpassed in its hardiness as a work animal. The horse, on the other hand, and the 'steers' were under-represented as work animals, the former being more important for transportation and the horse-racing industry. This was in contrast to the trend in England where by 1850, English farmers, with some regional variations, had virtually dispersed with the working of cattle in favour of the use of horses. This was because after the Napoleonic Wars, more favourable price conditions and the increasing efficiency of horses in farming caused the emphasis in cattle husbandry to shift to beef production.[26] In Jamaica, however, competition from horse-racing and the expensiveness of procuring and maintaining horses determined their unattractiveness as draught animals.

Table 3.1
Breakdown of Livestock Sales by Type and Volume, 1780

All Properties		Pens Only	Percentage
Working steers	278	137	49.28
Heifers	19	15	78.95
Cows	30	24	80.00
Calves	56	38	67.86
Horses	*123	91	73.98
Old/fat/cattle	1,039	407	39.17
Bulls	3	-	-
Sheep	140	95	67.86
Mules	181	131	72.38
Asses	12	4	33.33
Total	**1,881**	**942**	**50.08**

*Including six mill horses.
Source: JA, AP, 1780, 1B/11/4/9.

The table reinforces qualitative statements about the lucrative nature of the sale of old stock from the estates and the dominance of pens in the trade in working stock. By 1820, when the total number of livestock traded internally was 14,134 head, pens were responsible for 8,267 or 54.49 per cent, an improvement over their 1780 level. In the former year, the returns included 145 pens and 470 sugar estates. As in previous years, sugar estates dominated the sale of old meagre stock, while pens controlled the sale of working animals. Pens acted as 'middlemen' in the trade in the old stock which could not be sold straight to the butcher. These were fattened on the pens' pastures prior to sale to urban butchers, enabling them to make a profit on their purchases from the estates.

By the mid-nineteenth century, however, mules had largely been displaced by steers and spayed heifers. A partial indication of this shift is that by 1820, and in contrast to 1780, an estimated 3,162 steers, 1,162 spayed heifers and only 511 mules were sold or exchanged internally. By 1840, the number of mules sold by the pens represented in the Accounts Produce had fallen to 283 compared to 2,461 steers and 1,006 heifers.[27]

Contemporary sources provide no explanations for this shift, but one can speculate that the dual income yielded by oxen was attractive to both planters and pen-keepers. Unlike the oxen, mules realized little of a return on initial investment at the end of their working life.

As a result of the trade in livestock, therefore, a significant degree of economic links developed among the island's main economic units. An indication of the extensive links formed by some units is demonstrated in figures 3.1, 3.2 and 3.3. These links typified the relations between estates and pens throughout the island. The relative value of each type of good and service to properties involved in the internal trade is demonstrated by table 3.2. Examples are drawn from the 1820 Accounts Produce which is far more detailed than previous samples returned. In 1740, for example, though 35 units indicated earnings from the domestic trade, the purchasers of these goods and services were rarely given. Generally values were equally absent, making calculations based on known price rates, virtually impossible.

Figure 3.1
Livestock Trade, Cacoon Castle Pen, 1800

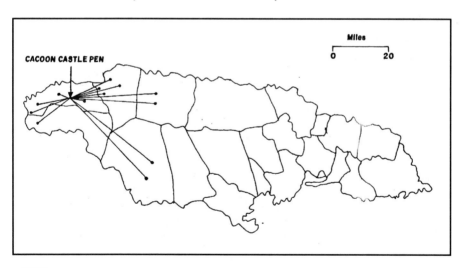

KEY
• Location of properties buying livestock.
———— General direction of trade.
Note: The volume of livestock sold was 135 head valued at £9,665 19s 9d.
Source: JA1B/11/4/27-8, AP, 1800.

Figure 3.2
Livestock Trade, Paradise Pen, 1800

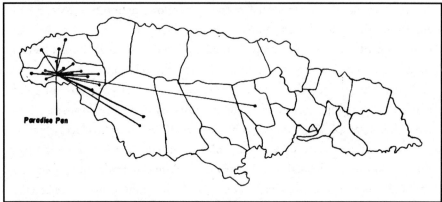

KEY
• Location of properties buying livestock
——— General direction of trade
Note: Transactions involved livestock and provisions to 20 estates.
Source: JA1B/11/4/27-8 1800.

Figure 3.3
Livestock Trade, Farm Pen, 1800

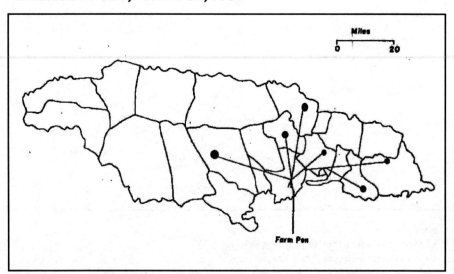

KEY
——— General direction of trade.
Note: This pen served 25 properties in 7 parishes.
Source: JA1B/11/4/54-6 1820.

Table 3.2
The Internal Trade: Relative Value of Goods and Services from Selected Properties, 1820

Property	Livestock			Jobbing			Pasturage			Wainage		
	£	s.	d.	£	s.	d.	£	s.	d.	£	s.	d.
1. Forest Pen	4,027	16	8	75	0	0	-			-		
2. Maverly Estate	137	0	0	-			-			-		
3. Lyndhurst Plantation	620	0	0	-			-			-		
4. Pindar's River Estate	124	0	0	-			-			20	0	0
5. Phantilland's Pen	356	13	4	746	16	8	45	6	8	-		
6. Chudleigh Plantation	1,326	10	0	-			-			-		
7. Brazellitta Estate	174	0	0	294	0	9½	-			40	0	0
8. Crescent Park Pen	787	0	0	20	0	0	-			-		
9. Batchelor's Hall Pen	1,304	0	0	-			-			84	0	0
10. Petersville Estate	1,655	10	0	-			-			-		
11. Monymusk Estate	-			60	0	0	-			-		
12. Spring Garden Pen	1,740	13	0	-			18	10	0	-		
13. Worthy Park Estate	225	0	0	-			-			-		
14. Aboukir Plantation	72	10	0	-			-			97	0	0
15. Paynestown Pen	640	0	0	1	5	0	-			3	0	0
16. New Forest Pen	219	16	0	47	10	0	207	2	6	263	13	4
17. Chesterfield Estate	220	0	0	-			-			10	0	0
18. Crawle Pen	2,379	0	8	211	7	9	446	5	10	393	3	8½
19. Lower Works Pen	1,049	0	0½	-			375	0	0½	-		
20. Palmyra Pen	167	6	8	662	0	0	-			50	18	9
21. Rosehall Estate	148	0	0	50	10	0	-			5	6	8
22. Cherry Gardens Estate	52	0	0	-			-			-		
23. Holland Estate	400	0	0	-			-			-		
24. Sevens Plantation	300	0	0	-			-			-		
25. Santa Cruz Park Pen	924	0	0	72	0	0	-			-		
26. Ramble Pen	1,450	0	0	-			-			105	5	0
27. St. Faith's Pen	1,386	7	0	99	14	10½	6	18	4	-		
28. Ardoch Pen	574	10	0	190	9	7½	20	8	0	-		
29. Bryan's Pen	980	7	8	476	0	0	-			368	0	0
30. New Ground Estate	108	0	0	-			-			38	0	0
31. Dunbarton Estate	-			80	0	0	-			-		
32. Phoenix Park Pen	2,028	6	8	-			-			-		
33. Prospect Estate	368	8	0	-			-			-		
34. Roaring River Estate	32	0	0	-			-			-		
35. Williamsfield Estate	12	10	0	85	0	0	-			-		

Table 3.2 (Cont.)

Property	Provisions			Wood, staves, shingles			Misc. Rents, etc.		
	£	s.	d.	£	s.	d.	£	s.	d.
1. Forest Pen		-			-			-	
2. Maverly Estate		-		363	7	6	134	4	11
3. Lyndhurst Plantation		-		554	7	7		-	
4. Pindar's River Estate		-			-		150	0	0
5. Phantilland's Pen		-			-		122	4	5
6. Chudleigh Plantation		-			-			-	
7. Brazellitta Estate		-			-		37	3	4
8. Crescent Park Pen		-			-			-	
9. Batchelor's Hall Pen	2,272	3	9		-			-	
10. Petersville Estate		-			-			-	
11. Monymusk Estate		-			-		45	0	0
12. Spring Garden Pen		-			-		16	5	0
13. Worthy Park Estate		-			-			-	
14. Aboukir Plantation	38	1	3	70	16	0		-	
15. Paynestown Pen		-			-			-	
16. New Forest Pen	39	0	0		-			-	
17. Chesterfield Estate	32	8	4		-		25	0	0
18. Crawle Pen		-			-			-	
19. Lower Works Pen		-			-			-	
20. Palmyra Pen		-			-			-	
21. Rosehall Estate		-			-			-	
22. Cherry Gardens Estate		-			-			-	
23. Holland Estate		-			-			-	
24. Sevens Plantation	88	5	0		-				
25. Santa Cruz Park Pen		-		10	0	0		-	
26. Ramble Pen	78	0	0	427	15	0	155	0	0
27. St. Faith's Pen		-		403	1	6		-	
28. Ardoch Pen		-		16	0	0		-	
29. Bryan's Pen	115	0	0		-		78	17	6
30. New Ground Estate		-			-			-	
31. Dunbarton Estate	522	0	2		-			-	
32. Phoenix Park Pen		-			-			-	
33. Prospect Estate	88	8	0	202	0	0	47	0	0
34. Roaring River Estate	58	4	6		-			-	
35. Williamsfield Estate		-			-			-	

It should be stressed that not all transactions involved money, but all could be reduced to monetary value. Where goods were exchanged for other goods or services, however, a money value was not given. Flamstead Estate in St James, for example, bartered 110 gallons of rum for stock in 1780.[28] Unlike in other Caribbean territories, however, the products of the island were not made legal tender after 1751, despite an attempt to get the Assembly to sanction this. Where it occurred, it was more custom than law. Indeed, Edward Long confirmed that 'money is the chief agent for carrying on any trade'.[29] Increased draining of money from the island by American and Spanish merchants, however, not only made bartering common, but according to Long, 'credit became a part of Commerce'.[30] Although pens diversified their activities to a greater extent after the abolition of slavery, up to 1840, earnings from the livestock trade still accounted for the largest share of their income. A sample of 24 per cent of the pens returned in 1820 (representing 9–10 per cent of the estimated island total) reveals earnings of £25,990 5s. 8½d. from livestock sales to estates (table 3.2). These pens earned more from such sales (69 per cent) than from other important income-generating activities such as jobbing, wainage, pasturage, the sale of food (ground provisions and fresh beef) and wood. These other sales and services combined yielded £11,974 19s. 0d. or 31 per cent of the total earnings of £37,965. Taken singly, jobbing represented eight per cent, pasturage three per cent, wainage four per cent, provisions nine per cent and miscellaneous items (rents, shingles, wood, staves) seven per cent. These percentages varied, of course, from pen to pen. Forest Pen, for example, earned only two per cent from non-livestock sources.

On the whole, estates and pens were unequal partners in the internal trade. In the majority of cases, as table 3.3 illustrates, estates accumulated less from their internal transactions with pens than they did from other sources such as the sale of rum to Kingston merchants and fat cattle to butchers. On the other hand, pens relied on the estates for the greater portion of their earnings. Additionally, the estates' gains from the internal trade represented an insignificant part of their total earnings from the domestic export trade. For example, Prospect Estate in Hanover earned £12,650 18s. 0d. from the sale of sugar and rum and only £183 10s. 0d. from internal transactions. Of the money accumulated locally, £128 10s.

Table 3.3
Sample of Inter-Property Trade, 1820

Property	Type	Parish	Total earnings from the internal trade			Proportion earned from dealings with estates/pens			%
			£	s.	d.	£	s.	d.	
1. Golden Grove	Sugar estate	Hanover	2,405	2	0	840	0	0	3.5
2. Silver Grove	Sugar estate	Hanover	1,923	14	0	157	2	0	8.2
3. Steelfield	Sugar estate	Trelawny	1,318	10	6	135	0	0	10.2
4. Unity Hall	Sugar estate	St James	2,300	16	6	179	0	0	7.8
5. Seven Rivers	Sugar estate	St James	267	3	0	267	3	0	100.0
6. Old Montpelier	Sugar estate	St James	3,896	18	0	219	0	0	5.6
7. Grange	Sugar estate	Hanover	1,540	15	8	115	0	0	7.5
8. Fontabelle	Sugar estate	Westmoreland	695	9	4	622	0	0	89.4
9. Frome	Sugar estate	Westmoreland	178	15	7	82	4	7	46.2
10. Spring Garden	Sugar estate	Westmoreland	186	0	0	128	0	0	68.8
11. Silver Grove	Sugar estate	Trelawny	169	10	0	136	0	0	80.2
12. Golden Grove	Sugar estate	Trelawny	134	10	0	119	10	0	88.8
13. Harding Hall	Sugar estate	Hanover	1,348	5	8	108	0	0	8.0
14. Old Shafston	Pen	Westmoreland	1,321	0	6	204	0	0	15.4
15. Carysfort	Pen	Westmoreland	3,998	19	3½	3,396	19	3½	84.9
16. Midgham	Pen	Westmoreland	1,451	12	11	1,251	15	0	86.2
17. Paradise	Pen	Westmoreland	790	6	8	218	18	0	27.7
18. Mount Edgecombe	Pen	Westmoreland	2,120	13	0½	1,350	8	10½	63.7
19. Hamstead	Pen	St Mary	428	8	0	428	8	0	100.0

Source: JA, AP, 1B/11/4/54-6.

0d. resulted from trade with pens. Similarly, Mint estate in Westmoreland earned £7,818 17s. 0d. from the export of sugar and rum and £420 14s. 0d. from the domestic trade.[31]

The Import Dimension

Finally, despite their efforts, the pen-keepers and planter/pen-owners were never able to supply the total livestock needs of the island in the period under review and sugar planters had to resort to importation. At first the level of importation of livestock was low. For example, only three horses and 19 mules were imported in 1691. In 1709, four horses and ten mules were imported. By 1729, however, the figures had increased to 688 horses and 1,104 mules; and the Naval Office Shipping Lists showed 1,036 mules, 76 asses, 721 cattle and 260 horses in 1762/63. In 1820, when 145 pens and 470 estates were returned in the Accounts Produce, only 8,050 head of working stock, or an average of 55.51 per pen, were sold from these livestock farms. On the all-island level, there were 562 estates and c. 400 pens in 1820.[32] Taking 55.51 as the average, and assuming that contemporary writers are correct in their claim that a typical estate needed 100 working steers annually in addition to mules and steers, an estate would need over 56,200 instead of the 22,204 per annum produced by pens. This lack of self-sufficiency in plantation animals encouraged the development and maintenance of a vibrant import trade in livestock, particularly from Spanish America.

This trade may seem surprising in an age of mercantilism and during the existence of the English Navigation Acts. According to the tenets of mercantilism, colonies were primarily sources of supply for the metropole. In turn, colonies were expected to import their necessities from the 'Mother Country'.[33] National self-sufficiency was the goal desired by this mutual commerce and thus such valuable possessions required strict commercial control, one which would effectively exclude foreign trade. The Navigation Acts of 1660 sought to impose such control. By these Acts, the staple produce from the West Indian colonies — sugar, rum, molasses, indigo, pimento, ginger and coffee — were to be carried in English ships. Ships were to be manned by a majority of English crewmen and goods consigned solely to English ports.[34] Such policies under the Restoration, contrasted with the virtual free trade of Cromwell's day during which the Spanish trade to Jamaica had developed and not surprisingly, such laws were virtually ignored.

The importance of the Spanish trade to Jamaica had, however, been long recognized and moves had been made to legalize it. Spain had consistently refused to sanction any such freedom of trade. Nevertheless, successive governors from the time of Modyford encouraged a clandestine Anglo-Spanish trade, granting licences to traders to sell enslaved captives and commodities to Spanish America and to import livestock.[35] Spain did not reciprocate by granting similar licences. On the contrary, the illegal nature of the trade was emphasized in the Anglo-Spanish Treaty of Madrid in 1670. Article 8 of that treaty stated that:

> Subjects of the King of Great Britain shall on no account direct their commerce or undertake navigation to the ports or places which the Catholic King holds in the said Indies, nor trade with them. Reciprocally, the subjects of the King of Spain shall not said to or trade in the places that are possessed there by the King of Great Britain.[36]

However, articles 9, 10, and 11 opened up certain loopholes which were fully exploited and facilitated the continuation of the contraband trade. These provided that if for any reasons — whether pirate attacks, storm, or revictualling — ships of either nations found it necessary to enter the other's ports, such ships should be allowed.[37] Furthermore, it was stated that if in the future 'either king shall deem it convenient to grant any general or special licence or any privileges to the subjects of the other for navigating and trading ... the said navigation and commerce shall be practiced and maintained'.[38]

The passing of the Free Port Act of 1766 had further opened up Spanish trading to Jamaica. This Act sanctioned a branch of colonial trade which had hitherto been conducted in a clandestine manner. It facilitated the importation and exportation of certain types of goods at certain ports in the British West Indies by small vessels from neighbouring foreign colonies. This did not, however, represent a departure from the Navigation Acts which still attempted to control the trade of staple commodities and English manufacturers. The Free Port Act was designed to allow only trade in goods which did not compete with the products of Britain and her colonies.[39] The trade in enslaved people, North American supplies and the carrying trade between Britain and her colonies remained firmly in British hands. In Jamaica, Lucea, Savanna-la-mar, Kingston and Montego Bay were declared Free Ports in 1776 and with the passing of the Act and the opening up of ports other than Kingston, the Spanish trade with Jamaica was revived.

The existence of the Spanish trade was a controversial issue in eighteenth- and nineteenth-century Jamaica. The opponents of the trade blamed it for the failure of a larger number of small settlers to engage in the pen-keeping industry. The proponents argued that its continuation was vital to the better regulation of the price of beef and plantation stock, that is cattle, mules and horses. At first the level of importation was low, but had increased by 1729. Between 1729 and 1739, 124 horned cattle, 1,500 horses, 4,285 mules, 243 asses, 129 hogs and 825 sheep, or an annual average of 826 animals were imported.[40] A total of 14,456 animals were imported in the following decade and averaged £11,000 per annum. The same level of importation in 1773 was estimated at £16,000. By 1825, the annual number imported increased to 11,836.[41] The largest share of the total expenditure on imported livestock in the eighteenth century was spent on mules. Between 1729 and 1749, a total of 10,477 mules were imported. In 1774, when 745 mules were brought in, the cost to the island was £11,175 sterling.[42]

To illustrate the extent of the island's dependence upon external supplies of livestock, Long used the example of mules which were in such great demand on plantations in the eighteenth century. In 1768, it was estimated that a minimum of 3,900 mules were needed for Jamaica's 651 sugar estates. In this year, the estimated number of breeding pens in the island was 200. Even if each pen supplied an average of 12 mules per annum, there would still remain a shortfall of 1,500. At £28 per head, planters needed to spend £109,200 each year to fill their total demand of mules. Next in demand on sugar estates were horned cattle, but this demand, like that for mules, could not be locally filled. Thus, according to Long, 'there is likewise a considerable importation of horned cattle from the Spanish coast, for the markets as well as for labour and breeding'. He again stressed that such a situation was on account of the lack of sufficient pens in the island.

Long also elaborated on two of the reasons that necessitated the importation of mules, asses, horses, and cattle, and emphasized that once these were removed, the trade would end. The first obstacle to Jamaican self-sufficiency was a lack of 'a sufficient stock of industrious inhabitants to have been employed in breeding the number of these animals proportioned to the annual consumption'.[43] The second was the absence of

> the patriotic endeavours and subsidies of the Assembly, as well as
> for encouraging such breeding farms, as for making good roads in
> every district, at the public charge, whereby the internal parts of
> the country must have been settled and improved with greater facility
> and the waste of cattle in great measure prevented.[44]

Long believed that £10,000 per annum was the sum needed for the latter purpose, a sum which would have easily been recovered 'by rendering the importation from foreigners inexpedient'.[45]

One of the reasons put forward for the failure of more settlers to engage in pen-keeping was the fear of overproduction and a consequent price fall. Long records that

> many persons have been deterred from engaging their time and
> capitals in this way; imagining that a glut would be the consequence
> and the price of cattle and mules would be lowered because the
> Spanish breed are imported and sold at a cheaper rate than they
> can afford and make a suitable profit.[46]

Long disagreed with this reasoning, believing instead that local breeds, by being hardier than imported stock, would be in great demand as plantation working animals. A far more plausible reason in his view was that 'most men have a prejudice in favour of foreign articles, despising their own far superior in value'.[47] Thus as some sugar planters exhibited a preference for imported mules and cattle, this acted as a disincentive for the greater expansion of pen-keeping.

The pen-keepers themselves echoed Long's sentiments. In a petition to the governor in 1790, the pen-keepers in the St Ann vestry complained of

> the distressing Prospect arising in the Community in general ...
> and this Parish

... in Particular of the trade carried on between the Spaniards of Cuba and a few of the trading or commercial Persons of this country from the vicinity of the coasts which facilitates the impolitic Intercourse.

Like Edward Long, they stressed that the trade posed an obstacle to the expansion of the pen-keeping industry

which is being partly discontinued by the Introduction of Spanish Horses, mules, mares, and neat cattle, subject to no Impost or Duty whatever, and that at a time when we are paying Taxes towards the support of Government from the time of sale.[49]

As the Spaniards were underselling local producers, Spanish cattle, horses, and mules were generally about one-third to one-half cheaper than local breeds. Spanish American horses could fetch as low as £10 sterling each, for example. Local breeds cost much more. A further request was that livestock be removed as an allowed article of trade under the Free Port Act.[50] This was particularly crucial at a time when, according to them, the local supply of stock exceeded current demand.[51] In their defence, planters complained that the form of payment demanded by pen-keepers was at variance with the existing method. Pen-keepers required immediate payment in cash upon delivery of their livestock to sugar or coffee estates whereas importers gave credit and demanded payment at the end of 12 months, charging six per cent interest[52] However, the scale of operation of importers was far greater than that of pen-keepers who could not afford to wait a year for payment.

The drain of capital occasioned by the import trade from Spanish America was a matter of concern towards the end of the eighteenth century. According to Long, 'vast amounts of our small hammered silver rials [ryalls] and pistorins are constantly exported together with dollars for purchasing mules and cattle'.[53] Planters even sold some of their rum internally in order to obtain cash to purchase Spanish stock. This 'in every respect', said Long, 'seems to be a traffick extremely pernicious to the island and it is from this consideration probably that it has been more connived at by the Spaniards than any other'.[54] He urged that active and immediate steps be taken to end this 'pernicious' trade. Two solutions were, first, for the Assembly to impose a tax on imported stock and second, for local pen-keepers to begin to give credit — say six or nine months credit — so as to enable the poorer planter to defray the cost of his purchase out of his rent or succeeding crop.[55]

Up to 1816, however, neither solution seems to have been adopted. The matter of taxation was especially problematic and Long's call for a tax to be imposed on foreign stock was echoed by pen-keepers all over the island. In 1816, for example, the pen-keepers of St Elizabeth and Manchester petitioned the House of Assembly to impose a tax on imported stock on account of the hardships they suffered from the allowance of foreign imports.[56] The St Elizabeth graziers complained that

> from late large importation of horned or neat cattle, mules and horses, the stock of the native breeder and grazier has become almost unsaleable, more particularly in respect of mules, there having been scarcely a spell of mules disposed of this season in the whole pen] district .[57]

The pen-keepers of Manchester echoed these sentiments. They protested that

> the petitioners are sorely aggrieved by constant importations into this Island, of horses, mules, asses and neat cattle from the Spanish Main and other parts, to the great loss and injury of the greater part of the petitioners; and that such importations enable the importers very considerably to undersell the breeders of the island.[58]

The complaints of the pen-keepers were referred to a committee of the House of Assembly and in 1817 'An Act for laying a duty on all horses, mares, geldings, mules, and horned cattle, imported into this island, except from Great Britain and the United States of America',[59] was effected. The duty initially levied on each head of cattle was £11,[60] but this was increased to £12 in the 1830s after repeated agitation by the pen-keepers that the stock duties be raised.[61] By 1843, the duties seemed to have been lowered and were as follows:

> Asses - £0 10s. 0d. per head
> Neat cattle - £1 0s. 0d. per head
> Horses, Mares, Geldings - £2 0s. 0d. per head
> Mules - £1 10s. 0d. per head

Swine - £0 4s. 0d. per head

Sheep - £0 2s. 0d. per head

Source: BBJ, 1843, London, PRO CO 142/57.

Livestock duty continued to be an issue throughout the nineteenth century. In 1837, for example, the House of Assembly resolved itself into a committee to debate the horned cattle bill. The proposition was that the import duty ought to be 40 shillings per head. Hamilton Brown, the member for St Ann, felt that this sum was too low, and that unless a more realistic duty was imposed, pen-keepers would be unable to compete with the importers of Spanish cattle. He suggested that 80 shillings should be the charge levied.[62] The planters were unsupportive of this, and the duty was eventually set at 24 shillings per head.[63]

Members of the House of Assembly continued to disagree over the cattle duty and even towards the end of the century, the matter was still not satisfactorily settled.[64] The other solution suggested by Long pertaining to periods of credit to be extended to planters, was adopted by some pens in the 1820s. This is indicated by their crop accounts which detail methods of payment. In the 1820 account for Paradise Pen in Westmoreland, for example, some estates were given a year to pay for livestock they bought.[65] This credit system continued into the 1840s. In its 1840 account, for example, credit facilities were extended to Beans, Woodchurch, Spring Garden, Retreat, Moreland, Blue Castle and Mint estates.[66]

Despite these proposed solutions, the lucrative Spanish trade, noted from the early eighteenth century, continued well into the nineteenth century, as is indicated by trade statistics contained in the Naval Office Shipping Lists, *Blue Books*, *Votes of the House of Assembly* and information relating to this trade reported in the *Royal Gazette*. It appears that the import trade in livestock was more numerically significant in the eighteenth century. Then, more estates were using cattle mills; and the number of pens established in the eighteenth century was inadequate to meet the estates' demand for livestock. After 1800, the trade is said to have declined as more estates shifted to wind and water power and the number of pens increased to meet local demand.[67]

In the absence of complete eighteenth-century trade figures, however, it is impossible to substantiate quantitatively Gardner's claim that

Table 3.4
Sources of Imported Livestock, 1815–25

Countries	Horses	Mules	Asses	Cattle	Total
Great Britain and Ireland	0	0	0	0	0
British Plantations	541	2	0	154	697
United States	570	54	0	157	781
Spanish Main Islands in the Tropics	12,189	21,947	5,032	18,536	57,704
Foreign Ports in Europe	0	0	0	0	0
Total	13,300	22,003	5,032	18,847	59,182

Sources: JA, Naval Officer's Returns, 1815–25, JHAV, 1815–25; BBJ 1822–25, CO 142/34-8.

importation of cattle and mules decreased after 1800. Furthermore, the available statistics for the nineteenth century do not show a declining trend. The level of importation may simply have been determined by demand at a particular time — especially when local supply was affected by natural disasters such as drought or hurricane. Level of importation could also be affected by war-time conditions. Thus, in times of war, importation would be low and in times of peace, more favourable to trade, importation would increase. We do know, however, that the substantial importation of livestock to the island started around 1729. As for the nineteenth century, mules dominated the eighteenth century trade, followed by cattle and horses. Whereas 2,453 horses were imported between 1691 and 1762, the number of mules was 4,212. Table 3.4 indicates the level of trade as well as the dominance of this trade by Spanish America between 1815 and 1825.

The Naval Office Shipping Lists, *Blue Books* and the *Votes* do not generally indicate the specific areas of Spanish America from which livestock were imported. The Shipping Lists indicate that the 'Spanish Main' and 'Spanish Coast' were primary sources of livestock, but hardly identify the individual countries. These lists do indicate that Cuba and Curaçao (especially between 1719–48) supplied some livestock to Jamaica in the eighteenth century. The more detailed information on country origin is, however, supplied by the *Royal Gazette* which regularly advertised the arrival for sale of imported livestock. From these advertisements, which were closely examined from 1794 to 1845, it becomes clear that the principal areas of origin were Chagres, Rio de la Hacha, Coro and Santo Domingo.[68]

Modern authors also indicate that Puerto Rico participated in this trade along with other 'Spanish Main' ports.[69] As Zahadieh has pointed out, the Spaniards were not noted for their economic efficiency.[70] What factors then explained their ability to undersell Jamaican livestock farmers? The answer seems to lie in their unlimited pasture land, large ranches and low labour costs. The plantation system developed late in the Spanish islands and, in Santo Domingo, for example, the most widespread and profitable business prior to 1870 was livestock-raising. Thus, as Scarano points out:

> the independent cultivators and the ranchers of the Spanish islands fulfilled an important role as suppliers of the sugar islands where specialization in export crops virtually precluded their self-sufficiency in foodstuffs, timber and draft animals. The Spanish islands, prevented by lack of capital and a restrictive imperial trade policy from trading along the plantation course, participated in an intra-Caribbean division of labour which promoted highly sophisticated export economies in some islands.[71]

Only occasionally were livestock imported from Britain and other European countries because of the high cost involved and the high level of mortality of the animals. Figures 3.4 and 3.5 based on *Blue Book's* statistics, indicate, however, that the greater portion of the money spent on imported stock was paid out to 'foreign states'. In 1832, of £16,383 3s. 0d. expended, Spanish America earned £16,069 11s. 0d. This was in contrast to the pre-1750 period when North America, Ireland and England were more significant suppliers. Yu Wu indicates that in 1688, 38.46 per cent of mules and horses imported by Jamaica came from North America. In 1691 and 1709, this had shot up to 100 per cent. By 1729, this percentage had declined to 50.59 per cent and by 1769 to 13.30 per cent (although there were occasional fluctuations). By this latter date also 0.00 per cent came from European ports and 53 per cent from the Caribbean area (including the circum-Caribbean region).[72] The percentage contribution from the Caribbean and Spanish Coast/Main increased thereafter, also with the usual fluctuations depending on the stability of the political climate.

Figure 3.4
Percentage Costs of Imported Livestock by Type and Country of Orgin, 1832

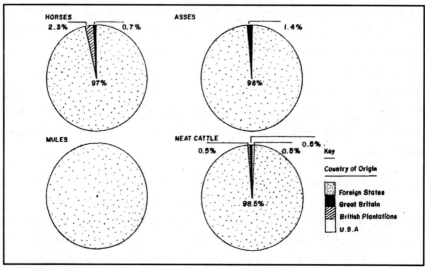

Source: BBJ, 1832.

Figure 3.5
Percentage Costs of Imported Livestock by Type and Country of Orgin, 1845

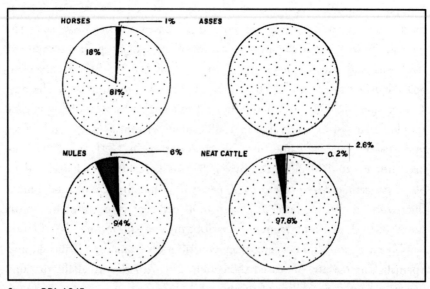

Source: BBJ, 1845.

The *Blue Books* do not identify individual foreign states, but there is every reason to believe that these were Spanish countries within the tropics. In addition, there was a small trade from British plantations, usually a re-export of animals from Free Ports in the British Caribbean territories.

From the planters' perspective, so vital to Jamaica's plantation economy was the trade with the Spaniards, that any interruption in it was tantamount to an economic crisis. When war with Spain in 1776–83 endangered this trade, there were repeated requests to the king to suspend this war so that trade with the Spanish islands could continue. A report from a committee of the House of Assembly appointed to enquire into the state of the island in 1799 and transmitted to the Duke of Portland found that a great cause of Jamaica's distress was the cessation of the livestock trade with Spanish America. According to the committee:

> the foreign trade carried on in this island under the authority of the freeport act, in foreign vessels in peaceable times, afforded very considerable advantages, particularly by the importation of cattle and mules; the interruption of which, occasioned chiefly by war with Spain, has been the cause of a very great rise in the prices, by which the article of fresh beef has risen to more than double what it formerly was: the same rise has taken place in the price of mules, which are essentially necessary for the carrying on of the plantations.[73]

Representations were consequently made to the king to suspend his war with Spain. This was done and the Spaniards were allowed to trade in their own ships. For the encouragement and protection of this trade, the commander-in-chief, by direction from the British government, granted certificates or passports to Spaniards under which they arrived from time to time in the free ports of the island. Unfortunately, in the nineteenth century, Spain confined its trade to bullion, cochineal, indigo and cotton and the exportation of manufactures imported from Great Britain which it then supplied to the Spanish colonies. Though Jamaicans welcomed the inflow of specie from this trade, they lamented the fact that 'since the late protection afforded them, the Spaniards have not imported any considerable number of cattle and mules. This trade has of late been considerably declined as the Spanish government has directed that it be curtailed'.[74]

The Committee thus recommended that greater efforts be made to settle 'small whites' in the interior of the island to establish pens and thereby expand the pen-keeping industry to meet the great demand for livestock on the island. Nevertheless, up until 1845, Jamaica's pens had not expanded sufficiently to satisfy this demand. Figure 3.5 indicates that in this year though the US and British plantations increased their share of this trade, foreign states continued to dominate it. The only significant change was the shift in the monopoly of trade from the supply of mules to the supply of asses. These were presumably imported to improve breeds of horsekind in the island.

4

THE PEN-KEEPERS:
EMERGENCE, DEMOGRAPHIC PROFILE AND ECONOMIC STATUS

Jamaican pen-keepers, though classified as 'small settlers' to distinguish them from the larger sugar barons, nevertheless, along with the coffee farmers, formed a non-sugar elite within the dominant socioeconomic sugar-based structure. They had no counterpart in the rest of the British-colonized Caribbean. In Barbados, St Kitts, and Montserrat, there were small farmers or 'cotton men' who constituted a sub-group within the planter class.[1] As a non-sugar base or interest, this sub-group perhaps corresponded in theory, but not in size, to the Jamaican pen-keepers. As this and the subsequent chapter will illustrate, a study of the pen-keepers should result in the revision of traditionally held views of the ruling class in plantation societies particularly in terms of its structural composition, diverse economic interests, but unified political and socio-cultural interest

Several questions have to be answered in any attempt to understand the role and status of the pen-keepers in Jamaica's socioeconomic and political history. Did they contribute to the development of Creole Society? In contrast to the sugar planters who have been associated with Caribbean underdevelopment, did the pen-keepers make a greater contribution to Jamaican development through their generation of internal linkages and their contribution to the growth of something recognizable even during slavery as a domestic economy? Did pen-keepers represent simply an economic interest group, uniting around narrow economic self-interests or did their participation in the 'Jamaican'/creole economy imply a creole consciousness and a commitment to the development of Creole Society? What dictated their overwhelming resident status? Finally, were they clearly ideologically differentiated from the sugar planter-class? The next two chapters wrestle with these questions, seeking to provide even partial answers, with the evidence available; but this chapter rehearses the emergence of the pen-keepers and discusses their internal diversities and routes to capital formation.

Becoming a Pen-Keeper: The 17th–19th Century

How did one become a pen-keeper in colonial Jamaica? The Spaniards were the first dedicated livestock farmers in Jamaica; but the earliest settlers who were described as 'pen-keepers' were among the soldier-settlers of the Cromwellian expeditionary force of 1655. Their contribution to the settlement of inland districts attracted the attention of contemporary writers. Some of the earliest interior pen-keepers, for example, were those in the Pedro's Cockpit area of the parish of St Ann. They were singled out by Edward Long to indicate the success of resident small entrepreneurs. Writing in the 1770s, he observed that 'not many years ago this district was without a single European settlement'.[2] Graziers or pen-keepers, however, established themselves there and were soon conducting a thriving trade with the lowland estates. The first settler had patented 300 acres of land in that area. He set out to build 'a defensible house upon a rising ground, and formed pastures'.[3] His success attracted others to the district and by the end of 1774, there were 34 settlers there. These had even pooled together to build a road to facilitate the marketing of their livestock.[4]

The St Ann Vestry extolled the contributions of these settlers. They were lauded not only because they were necessary suppliers of plantation work animals but because their pens had 'turned the dreary mountainous parts, that were the Resort of runaway and rebellious negroes, into fruitful Fields ... and adds to the increase of commerce, population and security'.[5]

By 1820, the initial character of those who established pens had changed. In the early stages, pen-keepers comprised settlers who were building up capital to invest in sugar through the sale of meat, hides and horses. After the start of the large-scale production of sugar, ex-provision planters who were forced to give way to sugar planters on the coast, made up the bulk of this group. As the switch to sugar did not force small settlers to emigrate but presented them with new opportunities, Jamaica was often referred to as 'the best poor man's country in the world'.[6] A survey of the inhabitants of St James parish taken in 1773, for example,

Table 4.1
Classification of the White Inhabitants of St James's Parish, 1773

Occupation	No.
Sugar Plantation	73
Pen-Keepers	8
Coffee Planters	1
Jobbeis	14
Millwrights	4
Carpenters	4
Pimento Walk Proprietors	1
Coffee and Pimento Proprietors	1
Pen/Jobbing Proprietors	1
Overseers and Jobbers	10
Surveyors and Jobbers	10
Doctor and Jobbers	1
Merchant	1
Total	**136**

Source: Add. MS 12,435, Long MSS fols. 3-4.

revealed that in addition to the 73 sugar planters, there were 63 people engaged in other agricultural and skilled jobs (see table 4.1).[7]

The existence of a vibrant sugar industry soon created a new group of pen-keepers. The industry had resulted in the development of about 6,000 wealthy sugar planters, merchants and their families.[8] These formed the 'upper class' of Jamaican plantation society. Their great wealth enabled them to reside in comparative ease in England — the 'Mother Country'.[9] Their abseenteeism necessitated the employment of bookkeepers, supervisors, overseers, skilled artisans and attorneys to attend to the affairs of their estates. Members of this group used the money generated by their jobs to invest in pens and join the ranks of the pen-keepers. This is supported by Benjamin M'Mahon, a former pen overseer, who observed in the early nineteenth century that the graziers in Jamaica were usually old attorneys or overseers 'who made their fortunes while in charge of properties belonging to their absentee proprietors'.[10] Once established, the sugar industry fostered their growth.

M'Mahon was extremely critical of the ways in which attorneys and overseers became pen-keepers. He described them as greedy and dishonest, building up their wealth at the expense of their employers. For example, he outlined in detail what he considered to have been the fraudulent actions of James Betty, a trustee of Amity Hall Pen who also happened to be a pen-keeper. Betty was the executor of the late owner, Mr Ratigan, and guardian to his mixed-race children to whom he had left the pen. M'Mahon worked for Betty as overseer on Amity Hall. One of his first tasks was to select 24 head of cattle to be sent to the fattening pasture for later sale to Prosper Hall Pen. The latter pen was also under the attorneyship of James Betty, who received a certain percentage for each head of cattle he sold there. Not knowing at first of this connection, M'Mahon discussed the sale of fat cattle from Amity Hall with another pen that offered to buy them at £18 a head. On learning of this, Betty simply told M'Mahon not to interfere with his existing style of management. When the cattle were eventually sold to Prosper Pen, they fetched only £5 a head.[11]

Similarly, attorneys, in collusion with other pen-keepers, allegedly defrauded the planters and built up their own capital. It was the job of the attorney to purchase all the livestock needed for the sugar estate. He used his prerogative to acquire livestock that he himself needed for his own enterprise in the following manner: the attorney would first go to the pen-keeper and select the horses and mules that suited him. He then proposed to take a large number of horned stock on consideration of his being allowed to take his own at a sum far below their real value. It was ultimately arranged 'that the whole stock of horses, mules and cattle be reckoned to the estate at so much per head — a sum which in all probability exceeded their real value by £2–£3 a head'.[12] According to M'Mahon, 'by this plan the attorney always gets bargains from pen-keepers; but they are bargains which are purchased at a heavy expense to the estate'.[13]

Overseers who were allowed to handle this transaction were equally accused of being dishonest. Many added a butchery to their own pens after their establishment. A further network of underhand dealings allegedly took place between pen-keeper/butcher and the estate attorney. This functioned in the following manner: the pen-keeper/butcher arranged to sell about 40–60 pounds of fresh beef to the attorney each week, according to the number of servants on the estate under his care. The attorney in return, undertook to sell the estate's annual supply of old, meagre stock to the same pen-keeper at a much-reduced cost. The attorney also contracted to buy from the same pen-keeper, the estate's annual requirement of working stock, and arranged for the pen-keeper to add £2–£3 extra to their cost. By this system of 'hand go hand come', the attorney obtained fine animals for his own use at the same price as the common mules for the estate'.[14] These he later resold at a profit of sometimes as much as 300 per cent. 'By this piece of policy', said M'Mahon, 'he makes fully £500 a year out of the pen-keeper'.[15] Furthermore, the attorney (or overseer) who also owned a pen and a butchery, made sure that he provided the beef supply for the properties under his management. In the same way, he arranged for all the estate's working stock to be bought from his pen. In many cases, he sent to the estate twice the amount of beef required 'knowing that the overseers of the properties dare not grumble, either at quantity or quality'.[16]

M'Mahon's charges may seem exaggerated, but were later supported by John Cooper who compiled detailed reports on the estates of Simon Taylor in 1835. In his report on Haughton Court estate in Hanover, Cooper stated that this property needed 20 oxen per annum. Although the estate had a related pen, Haughton Grove, this demand was being met from Old Hope Pen. Furthermore, the livestock supplied by Old Hope were regarded by Cooper as inferior to those available on Haughton Grove. The reasons for this situation were rather revealing. In the first place, Cooper found that

> it appears that it is the practice of the larger attorneys to equally
> distribute their good and bad stock from their pens upon the
> Estates, charging the *same price* for bad ones as for good ones,
> thus making the pens of good stock assist the pens of *bad stock*.[17]

Second, Cooper found out that Miller, the attorney for Haughton Court, was also the overseer and receiver for Old Hope which had been put before the Chancery Court. In this case, Miller usually earned over and above the five per cent usual on such transactions. For example, when half-fat stock from Haughton Grove Pen were sold to Old Hope at low prices, fattened at the latter property and resold in a fortnight, the attorney got ten per cent on them 'to the injury of both properties'.[18]

To test the claim that by the nineteenth century the more successful attorneys were also the richest pen-keepers, the Returns of the Registration of Slaves, for St Ann in 1817, generally sent in by attorneys, were examined.

This revealed that Alexander Kidston, James Betty, Hamilton Brown, David Finlay, James Kelly, Hay Haggart, and Benjamin Scott-Moncrieffe, who were among the most prominent pen-keepers in the parish, were also the attorneys for several estates and pens.[19] This finding was generally replicated in the returns for other properties, and in the Accounts Produce sent in by overseers.

Despite the reports of M'Mahon and Cooper, there is some evidence to indicate that less fraudulent methods were used in the formation of the pen-keeping group. John Lamond, for example, was at first a small holder who eventually established a pen. He could not afford to buy one outright. He started off by renting Castile Fort Pen for £220 per year. He purchased all the stock on the property for several hundred pounds, and from the profits of the pen, may later have bought it.[20]

George Forbes started off neither as an attorney nor as an overseer. When his uncle, Mungo Forbes, died, he left Thatchfield Pen to his niece, Elizabeth. George either bought or leased the pen from his sister and came to Jamaica to run it. He lived on the pen, gradually building up his resources through the sale of cattle.[21] The Barclay brothers, John and Alexander of Walthamstow, Essex, became the owners of Unity Valley Pen on account of a debt owed to them by the former owner.

Perhaps the best documented case of the method by which an overseer acquired the capital needed to invest in pen-keeping is that of Thomas Thistlewood who was born in Tupholme, Lincolnshire in 1720. After his father died, he moved to York to be educated. By 1739, he was back in Lincoln learning agriculture and taking care of the farm at Tupholme. He obtained practical experience in livestock husbandry from one Mr Robson on whose farm he had also worked.[22] He noted in his diary, that he bought and sold livestock, sold wool, and attended livestock fairs and hay markets. Finally, in 1750 he came to Jamaica and very fittingly, was employed by Florentinus Vassal as his 'pen-keeper' on Vineyard Pen in St Elizabeth.[23] There is nothing in his extremely detailed journals to suggest that he earned money dishonestly (according to the dictates of the times) or that Vassal, who monitored his activities closely, ever accused him of fraudulent practices. After one year at Vineyard Pen he moved to Egypt sugar estate as overseer for a Mr Dorril.[24] He also supervised activities on Paradise Pen, a related property. With his wages, Thistlewood gradually bought enslaved Africans and by 1766 had acquired 23 of them. He built up his capital further by hiring out enslaved people as jobbers on Egypt and Masemure estates. By 1768, he was ready to launch out on his own as proprietor of Breadnut Island Pen. For some years he struggled to establish his pen, at first selling small stock and vegetables until the main aspect of the pen was fully developed.[25]

Demographic Composition: Internal Diversity

Despite their unified economic interests, pen-keepers displayed internal demographic diversities. Several factors accounted for this diversity among these proprietors, some of which distinguished them clearly from the sugar planter class. Unlike the latter, for example, the majority of pen-keepers were resident proprietors. According to John Bigelow, pens were categorized as moderate-sized farms and 'it would not be worthwhile for a non-resident to keep up the supervision of a moderate-sized farm 3,000 miles from home'.[26] He explained that

> nothing less than the profits of a very large estate could compensate ... for the trouble and expenses of keeping up a force of attorneys, agents, and bookkeepers, and for the absence of that personal devotion to its management which none but a proprietor ever feels.[27]

The residency of pen-keepers was also stressed by M'Mahon[28] and is borne out by the Accounts Produce. In the first return of properties in 1740, only 18 pens were owned by absentees.[29] Forty years later, 24 were so owned, and by the time of the abolition of slavery, 140 pens had absentee proprietors.[30] When expressed as a percentage of total returns and the total number of pen-keepers in the island, these figures become even more significant. In 1740, only 11 per cent of absentees owned pens. In 1780 the proportion fell to 7.14 per cent and was still only 15.02 per cent by 1820.[31] This increased to 16.80 per cent in 1840. Thereafter, a gradual decline was observed. These percentages become higher if one calculates them based on the total number of pens in the island. At the time of emancipation, for example, when there were around 400 pens, 35 per cent belonged to absentee proprietors.[32] However, if one bears in mind that most of these were owned by sugar planters, then the high degree of residency among independent pen-keepers becomes apparent.

The level of residency among the pen-keepers was surpassed only by that among the coffee farmers. In 1799, of a total of 519 coffee plantations, at least

Table 4.2
Absentee Pen Owners by Parish, 1820

Parish	Number	Parish	Number
• St. Ann	29	• St Thomas-in-the-Vale	5
• St. Mary	13	• St Thomas-in-the-East	6
• St. James	1	• St David	1
• Trelawny	5	• Kingston	0
• Westmoreland	13	• St Andrew	1
• St. Elizabeth	19	• Port Royal	1
• Hanover	5	• St George	4
• St. John	2	• Portland	0
• Vere	2	• Clarendon	12
• St. Dorothy	8	• Manchester	5
• St. Catherine	13		
		Total	**145**

Source: JA, AP, 1820, 1B/11/4/54-6. This 145 represented 15.02 per cent of the 965 proprietors returned in that year.

467, representing 90 per cent, were owned by resident farmers and 46 were owned by absentees.[33] While the level of absenteeism within the industry had risen by 1808, the number of properties owned by resident proprietors was still high. In that year, out of a total of 607 properties, 478, or nearly 80 per cent, were owned by residents. This pattern of ownership only underwent change in the 1830s and 1840s when the industry was in decline and creditors foreclosed on properties, resulting in a higher level of absentee ownership within the sector.[34]

Pen-keepers also showed certain variations in colour, place of birth, gender, educational level, marital status and social, economic, political and ideological positions. Though it is generally accepted that Europeans dominated plantation society economically and politically, there is ample evidence that some mixed-race persons managed to build up quite substantial wealth. This was despite the severe restrictions placed on their economic opportunities in the society.[35] What is less well-known is that a significant number of those who made it economically were pen-keepers. This resulted from the fact that planters sometimes left property to their mixed-race children or to their mixed-race mistresses. Alarmed at the rapid economic growth among mixed-race people that such inheritance engendered, the Assembly in 1761 enacted a law forbidding planters to leave property worth more than £1,200 sterling to their mixed-race children or mistresses.[36]

Until 1830 when it was lifted, this law effectively crippled the economic potential of mixed-race persons and caused the majority to converge on urban centres where economic opportunities were better. Kingston and St Catherine thus had the largest free mixed-race population. Most of those who remained in the rural parishes raised provisions for markets. Only the wealthier ones, especially those who had inherited before the 1761 law or who successfully applied for privileges, could cultivate pimento and ginger or raise cattle. Benjamin Scott-Moncrieffe was arguably one of the most successful of these free mixed-race pen-keepers. He inherited Soho Pen from his father, John Moncrieffe, and also owned other properties including Thatch Hill Pen in St Ann. He was an outstanding horse-racer and used his winnings to supplement his income from livestock farms and his job as attorney for several estates.[37] Robert Hilton Anguin of St Ann, was also a mixed-race pen-keeper. His father was John Anguin and he inherited his pen from him.[38]

Pen-keepers were not all male. Women who owned land tended to be small-scale farmers, concentrating on coffee, pimento and livestock. Sheena Boa records that while few freed-women belonged to the planter class, only one being observed in 1762, a rather more substantial number owned pens. Anna Woodard, for example, the mulatto daughter of an enslaved woman and an Englishman, was the wealthiest free woman in 1762. She was the owner of Dirty Pit and Hoghole pens in St Catherine. British women also owned pens. The most notable was Catherine Buckeridge from Sonning, County Berks, in England. She was a widow and the proprietor of Salt Pond Hut Pen in St Catherine.[39]

Unlike the pen-keepers, most of the coffee planters, the other numerically significant group of non-sugar proprietors, were British. However, some free mixed-race persons were among this group.[40] Their entry into plantation agriculture was also primarily through the avenue of the legacies provided by their European fathers. For example, William Peart and John Morgan were both owners of considerable properties in Manchester. There were also William Alcock, owner of Seamones Garden in St David, and Thomas William Powell who owned Cassava River Mountain in St Thomas-in-the-Vale. Free mixed-race persons were also involved in the industry as superintendents and overseers. For example, Halberstadt coffee plantation in Port Royal was overseen by

Johann Casper Weisse, while Charly McNally of Manchester was reported to be 'doing duty on a coffee plantation', as was William Mortimer Taylor of St Elizabeth who worked as an overseer.[41]

However, the number of free mixed-race persons owning coffee plantations was probably lower than the number owning pen properties, and it must be stressed that the above-mentioned individuals were atypical of their class, as the majority of them in Jamaica were kept out of the plantation sector. This was mainly because the expansion of the industry occurred after the enactment of the Inheritance Law of 1762.[42]

Pen-keepers comprised creoles as well as those born in various parts of Britain. Among the creoles were John Blagrove, Benjamin Scott-Moncrieffe, Robert Hilton Anguin, J. Davis, Thomas Barnes and Mr Matthews of St Ann. The abolitionist writers Sturge and Harvey believed that enslavers born in the Caribbean were usually less severe than those born in Britain and some enslaved persons, apparently gave some pen-keepers 'high marks'. According to Sturge and Harvey:

> slave masters of European birth and education are accustomed to
> the active energy of free servants, while creoles, though familiar
> from infancy with despotic power, are more easily satisfied with
> the indolent langour and comparative inefficiency of slaves'.[43]

John Blagrove fits this description of 'creole masters'. His enslaved workers reportedly thought him 'kind' and 'generous' and, indeed, when he died he left the sterling equivalent of US$1 to each of them.[44] Similarly, the enslaved people on Matthews' Pen were said to have enjoyed a rather relaxed lifestyle. David Finlay of Ardoch was described by his overseer as the best man he had ever known and one who was 'exceedingly kind' to all of the enslaved. With no sense of irony, they, in turn, were said to have been 'truly happy and conducted themselves in the most orderly and respectful manner'.[45] At the other extreme, and more representative of Caribbean enslavers, was the 'busha' of Green Island Pen in Westmoreland, Benjamin Capon, who was 'constantly in the habit of striking, collaring and kicking the apprentices — men, women and children'.[46] He did not protect 'negro provision grounds' and wilfully allowed his cattle to destroy them.

Historians have, however, long disregarded this method of categorizing proprietors into 'cruel' and 'benevolent' rightly arguing that no act of 'kindness' could mitigate the effects of slavery. The differences in the characteristics of pen-keepers and planters may simply have been a function of their greater residency and the nature of their economic enterprise. Like the Cuban enslavers of the ranching areas in the eighteenth century, pen-keepers were thought to have had a better relationship with the enslaved who led a less regimented life on account of the nature of livestock industry.

The educational level of pen-keepers varied. Those who were primarily overseers tended not to be well-educated. The influential attorneys, particularly those who were the sons of planters or affluent pen-keepers, were usually sent to Britain to be educated. John Blagrove, for example, attended the prestigious Eton, and the equally impressive Oxford University.[47] Similarly, the Irishman, Hamilton Brown, sent his son Alexander Hamilton Brown, to be educated abroad. So did Scott-Moncrieffe whose son, Peter, trained as a lawyer. Francis Smyth's son William, was educated at Eton and Christchurch College, Oxford.[48] At the other end of the scale were men like Thomas Thistlewood who were privately tutored and did not go to university,[49] and J. Davis of Belmont Pen who, according to Blagrove, 'had never been off the country'.[50] Very few of the pen-keepers were from elite families. The genealogical information provided by N.B. Livingstone, for example, does not yield any information relating to pen-keepers other than the Rules and Ashleys of Rules and Ashley Pens in Clarendon, respectively.[51]

Another area of demographic diversity among pen-keepers relates to their marital status. It is impossible to divide the group quantitatively into those who were married and those who were single. Indeed, it was not until 1878 that compulsory registration of marriages was introduced into Jamaica. The parish registers are therefore of little help in this area. What fragmentary information is available relates to those married in the Anglican Church. From 1660, when civil government was introduced, the minister of the Church of England kept careful records. A few parishes kept records before 1878 but these were not sent in.

The returns sent in by the Anglican Church for St Ann, were nevertheless consulted, on the basis that it is safe to assume that the majority of Europeans and free mixed-race persons supported the Established Church. Very few pen-keepers were, however, identified as the information regarding marriage in the eighteenth and nineteenth centuries was not as detailed as it is today. These parish records could, however, be used along with wills. Those whose marital status was definitely established as married, from these sources, were John Baillie, Francis Smuth, Robert Hawthorne, James Kelly, William Parke, Joseph Hayne, Samuel Jefferies, James Ferguson, James Kerr, S.M. Barrett, Norwood Witter, Charles Graham, Hamilton Brown and John McGillevry.[52] Benjamin Scott-Moncrieffe referred in his will to his mother-in-law. He does not identify his wife in his will, and she may have predeceased him.[53]

It is quite possible, however, that the majority of pen-keepers were single. There was a shortage of European women in the colonies. This fact, combined with the 'taboo' against marriage to free mixed-race persons and Africans, would account for this. Contemporary comments about the sexual habits of attorneys and overseers who comprised the bulk of the pen-keepers, would seem to support this. In reply to his brother's inquiry about his marital status, Stephen Harmer, overseers on Old Hope Pen had replied: 'now the candid truth is I have got no wife and have never been married. It is not the fashion for overseers to be married in this Country Except over the Broom Stick'.[54] Harmer did, however, have four children. His children were mothered by an enslaved woman, as he hints, the more usual custom in the Caribbean.

This is supported by M'Mahon who explained the phenomenon of 'housekeepers'. According to him, the overseers in Jamaica usually kept one particular mistress 'called by themselves "housekeepers", but by the labourers, their "wives"'.[55] These women were always expected to yield to the sexual wishes of these overseers. It was the widespread practice of sexually abusing enslaved women under the pretext of property rights that resulted in the spectacular growth in the free mixed-race population. In 1789 there were 10,000 such persons in Jamaica. By 1825, this number had almost tripled.[56] The pen-keepers were responsible for a large number of these mixed-race children. Practically every one of the wills consulted showed this to be so; for like the planters, they often left their mistresses and children well provided for. Also, they clearly distinguished between their so-called legitimate and their 'illegitimate' children, at times giving the specific colour gradation (skin shade/pigment) of the latter.

John Anguin, for example, had lived with an enslaved woman, Sarah Tracey Williamson. She had three children for him and was catered for in his will with the usual proviso that she would forfeit this money if she had changed partners by the time he died. Similarly, James Kelly, Francis Graham, John Moncrieffe, Charles Stirling and Thomas Thistlewood all had mixed-race children by their 'housekeepers' who were provided for in their wills. Like John Anguin, Charles

Table 4.3
Sexual Activities of Thomas Thistlewood, Vineyard Pen, 1750–51

Female Slave	Nationality	Year	Frequency
Marina	African	1750	42*
Juba	Creole	1750	2
Betty	African	1750	3
Hago	Creole	1750	6
Sylvia	African	1750	1
Hago	Creole	1751	8
Peggy**	African	1751	1
Chrissy	African	1751	10
Cynthia	Creole	1751	1
Accubah	African	1751	2
Mary	African	1751	1
Betty	African	1751	2
Bella (Jussa)	African	1751	1

Notes: *Marina was Thistlewood's favourite bedmate in August and September 1750. By October he seemed to favour Hago. **She was actually from Fullerswood estate and had visited the Pen.
Source: Thistlewood's Journal, August 5, 1750–July 2, 1751, Mon. 31/1.

Stirling stipulated that his 'housekeeper', Rebecca Ash, would get £300 sterling and a £12 annuity 'as long as she remains single and does not begin to live with any man as housekeeper or mistress'.[57]

Others specifically requested that their 'housekeepers' be freed upon their death. In some cases, however, freedom would only be assured if the cost was at a certain rate. Thomas Thistlewood, for example, stipulated in his will that Phibbah's freedom should be purchased from John Cope, her owner, provided that her freedom did not cost more than £80. In that event, not only would she not be freed, but she would forfeit the land and house which she would have otherwise obtained from his executors.[58]

Thomas Thistlewood himself provides the best example of sexual exploitation of enslaved females by overseers and pen-keepers. While working for Mr Vassal on Vineyard Pen, and for Mr Cope on Egypt plantation, he had sex with practically every one of the adult enslaved females (see table 4.3). When he established his own pen in 1768, he continued his sexual exploits. While renting Phibbah from Mr Cope and

Table 4.4
Frequency of Thomas Thistlewood's Sexual Activities with Enslaved Females on Breadnut Island Pen, 1768

Name	Frequency
1. Phibbah	81 times
2. Sucky	2 times
3. Myrtilla	2 times
4. Sally	5 times
5. Nanny	4 times
6. Peggy	2 times
7. Frankie	2 times
8. Cubbah	1 time
9. Maria	1 time

Source: Thistlewood's Journal, 1768, Mon. 31/19.

living with her as his regular 'housekeeper', he also had sex with nine of the other 16 enslaved females. As he kept a detailed account in his journals of these cases, it is possible to accurately describe his sexual habits. Not only did he detail the frequency of his sexual contacts with these women (represented in table 4.4), but also the time, place and remuneration, when this was given. He usually slept with Phibbah at his house, but had the other women during the day at various places ranging from the 'negro' provision grounds to the road between Egypt and Breadnut Island Pen. Some enslaved women were given small sums of cash after he had them, usually at the rate of one bitt or 7½ d. per time. On rare occasions, he paid two bitts. After having Sucky 'in the large cove in the negro ground', for example, he records that he gave her two bitts. Only one other enslaved woman, Frankie, ever received two bitts from him.[59]

There was less diversity among the pen-keepers in the area of their religious persuasion. Whether British or creole, they all tended towards the Established Church. This is indicated by marriage and baptism records kept by the Church that showed that pen-keepers, like planters, were married by Anglican ministers and their children baptized in the Anglican Church. Robert Hawthorne, Charles Stirling, Alexander Kidston and William Park all had their children baptized in the Established Church.[60]

Some pen-keepers were prominent members of the Anglican-based

Colonial Church Union and openly opposed the proselytizing activities of the Baptists among the enslaved population. It was perhaps in an effort to counter the influence of the Baptists among the newly freed Africans and African-Jamaicans in St Ann that Robert Johnson of Annandale Pen in that parish in 1838 made available three acres of his pen land for the erection of a church. His stated rationale was, however, that 'from the extent of the parish of St Ann and the population thereof, it is necessary that some additional place of worship should be erected in the same parish for the performance of public worship according to the form of the Established Church'.[61] Johnson even obtained the material and provided the labour required for the building of the church at his own expense.[62]

Economic Status

Pen-keepers were unified in their economic interests but not necessarily in their economic status. Some were quite prosperous; others were only moderately prosperous in the period of slavery. This prosperity was early realized. Both Long and Gardner point to the profitability of the early pen-keepers in the Pedro's district of St Ann. One proprietor reportedly claimed to have made £1,200 per year by buying lean stock from the estates, fattening them on guinea grass, and selling them to the butcher.[63] Each head of fat stock fetched between £8 and £10 profit after disposal to the butcher or to the 'contractors for the king's shops'.[64] Another of these early proprietors allegedly cleared £2,000 profit annually as 'the charge and contingencies after a farm is once established are very trifling'.[65]

Long believed that even a lower profit level would have been quite acceptable. According to him, even if the 34 early settlers in the Pedro's district earned £500 per year, at an average, there would be an annual gain of £17,000. After all, the industry was at this time 'in its infant stage'; but if at this stage such profits could be realized, 'it is reasonable to expect they will every year become more considerable in proportion to the increase of improvements'.[66]

Later on in the eighteenth century, William Beckford also commented on the economic status of the Jamaican graziers. He noted in 1790 that

> the pen-keepers in Jamaica are generally found to be if not the
> most opulent, at least the most independent, of those who cultivate
> the soil. Their capitals indeed, are not so large as those possessed

of sugar plantations; but then, their risks are few, and their losses, except in building and provision grounds in consequence of storms, are very trifling.[67]

He remarked on the great degree of self-sufficiency enjoyed by these proprietors who had 'many subordinate comforts of life immediately within their reach'. Beckford stated: 'I do not believe that there are many people in the country of the same rank and capital that either do or can entertain with more abundance and hospitality'. Pens, in addition, earned between £12 and £20 each for steers and from £25 to £30 for mules, 'and when a pen can make such returns, it is more economically productive than a sugar estate'.[68]

These sentiments were reiterated by J.B. Moreton, writing in the same year as Beckford. He noted that 'a pen is a better property, and is attended with less trouble and expence than a sugar plantation'.[69] With a pen of just 300–500 acres, well-stocked and planted in guinea grass, a profit of £1,000 sterling per year could easily be realized.[70] The capital needed to establish such a pen in the late eigtheenth century was estimated at approximately £10,000 — just one-third of the estimated cost of developing a sugar estate in the same period.[71] In the seventeenth century, pen land was as low as £13 per acre. By 1792, such land was worth £60 an acre if planted in guinea grass and £40, if common grass.[72]

This optimism carried over into the nineteenth century as is demonstrated by the history of the pen-keeper, George Forbes, of Thatchfield Pen, St Elizabeth. Forbes had embarked on life as a pen-keeper around 1810. Writing to his brother in 1811, he expressed the feeling that the pen would pay and that he would easily clear £600 per annum after expenses. This projection he based on the fact that 'my expenses of living will be trifling — besides my supplies — indeed, I have everything that I want within myself'.[73] This referred to the self-sufficient nature of pens as far as meat and provisions were concerned.

By 1817, Forbes was still showing optimism. In that year, cattle sales were good and he expected to make £2,000 to £2,500. Furthermore, as he told Peter, 'in three years I shall be rich, at least according to my idea of wealth'.[74] To support the fact that pen-keeping was a paying business, he did an inventory of his possessions and sent the details to his brother. According to his calculations, in 1818, he was worth £15,400, excluding the value of the pen-land and enslaved labourers, including outstanding debts owed to him, household furniture, and stock. In fact, like all other prosperous pen-keepers, he was soon making plans to diversify and invest in a coffee plantation as well.[75]

Another very prosperous pen-keeper (who later invested in sugar) was Hamilton Brown. When he first came to Jamaica he obtained a job as attorney on Queenhithe sugar estate. He gradually secured similar jobs on several other properties in St Ann. With the money he accumulated, he bought lands in the parish including Minard, Retreat, the whole of the Browns Town and Buxton area, Antrim and Hilton Hill.[76]

One of the most reliable methods of ascertaining the wealth of pen-keepers is to examine the Probate Inventories in the Jamaica Archives. Unfortunately, not all pen-keepers' inventories have been found. Table 4.5, however, gives an idea of what some of the leading pen-keepers were worth at the time of their death. In a few cases, these inventories have been used in conjunction with their wills. That total usually excluded the value of the land, but included that of workers, stock and household and personal effects. Among the wealthiest were Francis Graham, Francis Smyth, Robert Hawthorne, Charles Graham, Samuel Queenborough and Samuel Barrett.

Although some of them were better off than coffee planters,[77] when compared to the bigger planters, most pen-keepers may only be said to have been in favourable circumstances with only a few of the larger planting attorney-pen-keepers approaching the economic position of the sugar planters. When John Tharp's properties were valued in 1792, for example, they totalled £821,530 (see table 4.6), with his livestock and enslaved workers being worth £221,854 or 27 per cent of that total.[78] Though not as wealthy as the Tharps or other equally rich planters, it was still felt in the eighteenth century that 'the life of a tolerably successful pen-keeper was ... the most enviable to be found in the colony'.[79] Cattle thrived well, pens required few labourers, were virtually self-sufficient in food, and once the pen was established, few extra charges were incurred.

As pens were subjected to the vagaries of climate and weather and depended on the continued profitability of the sugar industry, any changes in those conditions affected the profits of their proprietors. Despite Forbes's optimism in 1818, for example, a severe drought in the early 1820s practically wiped out his profits. This was compounded by the decline in the demand for stock on sugar estates which worsened after the abolition of slavery.[80]

Table 4.5
Value of the Possessions of Certain Pen-Keepers According to the Probate Inventories, 1739–1838

No.	Date	Name	Value			Remarks
			£	s.	d.	
1.	1739	David Moncrieffe	13,836	13	9¾	
2.	1762	Thomas Moncrieffe	2,650	18	9	
3.	1767	Norwood Witter	7,856	14	9	
4.	1788	Francis G. Smyth	41,300	3	2½	
5.	1790	James Donaldson	4,344	0	7½	
6.	1791	John Cunningham (1)	2,993	10	8¾	
7.	1795	Charles Sterling	12,032	10	0	
8.	1797	Robert Hawthorne	35,162	16	5	
9.	1803	Charles Graham	44,220	15	6¼	
10.	1808	John Cunningham (2)	15,063	0	0	
11.	1817	Samuel Queensborough	57,513	17	10½	
12.	1818	George Forbes	15,400	0	0	Incomplete
13.	1819	James McIntosh	15,373	17	7¾	
14.	1820	Francis Graham	36,525	5	5¼	
15.	1821	William Bennett	15,226	14	10	
16.	1821	Samuel Jefferies	6,333	8	10¼	
17.	1822	Caleb Dickinson	19,857	3	4	
18.	1822	Joseph Russell	29,088	6	8	
19.	1823	B.B. Nembhard	8,873	9	11¾	Excludes £15,000 in debts
20.	1823	James Rowe	815	0	0	Excludes slaves and stock
21.	1825	S.M. Barrett	61,249	0	0	
22.	1826	James Ferguson	9,674	10	3	
23.	1828	Roger Dobson	27,875	8	8	
24.	1829	Hon. J. Barnes	23,834	5	0½	
25.	1835	Robert H. Anguin	3,476	0	0	
26.	1838	S.M.B. Barrett	17,185	7	0	
27.	?	Jacob Graham	18,749	11	8	
28.	?	Benjamin Moncrieffe	9,644	4	7½	

Note: This is a random but representative list.
Source: JA, Inventories, IB/11/3/21-157, 1739-1838.

Another pen-keeper so affected was Hamilton Brown. According to Henry Blagrove, writing in the 1840s, Brown was once a prosperous man, 'but having met with reverses, is now heavily charged as to his estates'. Nevertheless, 'under his reverses, he bears the most cheerful countenance and state of mind I ever have seen — and exhibits it not only with reference to his own affairs but in regard to others'.[81]

The pen-keepers supplemented their earnings from horseracing. Breeders and graziers were prominent participants in the various meets and some were frequent winners. Among the most noted pen-keepers involved in horse-racing were J. W. Davis of Harmony Hall Pen and Benjamin Scott-Moncrieffe, the well-known mixed-race attorney and owner of Soho Pen. Several other pens were involved. The most prominent, judging from the list of the importers of stallions and blood mares, were Pepper, Agualta Vale, Goshen, Unity Valley, Sandy Gully, Friendship, Greenvale, Marlbro' and Gilnock. Of the 162 stallions imported by pens up to 1923, Pepper Pen received 26.[82] This pen was, indeed, noted for its thoroughbred English mares. Between 1824 and 1840, it is noted to have had the largest racing stud in the world (Lurcher) and also boasted 100 English mares and 7

Table 4.6
Valuation of the Properties Belonging to the Hon John Tharp, Esq., 1792

No.	Property	£ slaves
1	Covey	109,006
2	Good Hope	130,298
3	Lansquinet	92,453
4	Pantrepant	111,144
5	Potosi	80,679
6	Spring Castle in Polinck	30,850
7	Top Hill Pen	13,005
8	Wales	91,326
9	Wharf	10,000
10	Windsor Pen	152,769
	Total	821,530

Note: The above figures, unlike those in the previous table, include the value of lands and buildings. No figures seen for Chippenham Park and Merrywood.
Source: Cambridge County Record Office, Tharp Family Papers, R. 84/29.

sires.[83] The Blagroves of Cardiff Hall in St Ann, were also classed among the owners of the finest racing horses. The latter fetched the highest prices in the island and were the descendants of the blood horses they early imported from England.[84]

According to J.T. Palache, arguably one of the foremost authorities on the history of horseracing in Jamaica, this spot reached its zenith around 1840. There were meets in the parish of Trelawny, St James, St Catherine, Westmoreland, St Ann, Manchester, Clarendon, St Elizabeth, St Mary and Kingston. Races were also held at Old Harbour and Bath.[85] To encourage the importation of horses from Britain, the Assembly, in 1794, passed 'an Act for encouraging the importation of horses from Britain by granting a purse [the King's Purse] to be run for in each county'.[86] This Act functioned as an incentive for horse-racers as this purse was worth £133 6s. 8d.[87]

Despite the holding of meets in several parishes, it was the Kingston races that attracted most support. These were held over three days in December of each year. Breeders arrived from all over the island from late November to prepare for the meet. In addition to his entry fee, each breeder contributed a doubloon (£3. 4s.) to the fund. Breeders competed for the Queen's Purse, the Kingston Handicap, the Stand Cup, and several races of one mile. All but one race — the Pony Race — was reserved for breeders. The Kingston races usually ushered in the festivities for the Christmas season. According to DaCosta, 'it was the grand tableau to start Christmas, and provided a week's picnic for the masses of Kingston'. He also described the participants, the breeders, thus:

> One was always impressed with the appearance and general
> demeanour of the breeder on racings. He was invariably well-
> dressed and in a crowd of hundreds it was easy to discover that
> there was something different about this gentleman in comparison
> with other patrons of the Stand. Even though the men in the
> Stand were all well-dressed, far better than they are today, the
> stranger had no difficulty in spotting the breeder as somebody
> above the jolly crowd.[88]

One of the most successful winners at the Kingston and other meets was Benjamin Scott-Moncrieffe. He recorded particularly victories at the St Ann races, and his detailed racing accounts indicate that he won moderate amounts from such successes. Between 1828 and 1839, for example, he won £4,770 6s. 8d. at the various races held around the island. Though his racing expenses were high, he often recorded a profit. In 1833 when he earned £885, he spent £1438 12s. 11d. leaving a balance of £436 7s. 1d.[89]

The combination of attorneyships, pen-keeping and horseracing allowed some of the pen-keepers to maintain a fairly high standard of living, at times comparable to that of the sugar planter-class. This is evident from their inventories that detail the value of their household furniture. Items of furniture, cutlery, china and other wares were itemized in most cases. Francis Graham's inventory done in 1820, for example, reveals a rather lavish lifestyle. His house had ten rooms including the bedrooms, a dining room and a separate billiard room in which there was a large table and 12 chairs. In addition, there was a coach and harness room. He used wine, champagne and claret glasses, finger basins and cutlery of good quality. His furnishings included book cases and he had a grand piano. His household effects valued £3,096 0s. 10s. (see table 4.8).

Like the planter-class, the value of land, labourers, capital equipment and stock exceeded the value of household effects. Robert Hawthorne of

Table 4.7
Value of the Enslaved People and Stock on John Tharp's Estates and Other Properties, 1792

No.	Property	£ enslaved people	£ stock
1	Covey	33,930	2,656
2	Good Hope	35,530	2,768
3	Lansquinet	27,200	2,053
4	Pantrepant	23,775	3,729
5	Potosi	21,280	2,393
6	Spring Castle	3,850	-
7	Top Hill	1,460	1,605
8	Wales	27,440	4,486
9	Windsor	13,370	14,329
	Total	**187,835**	**34,019**

Source: Tharp Family Papers, R. 84/29.

Table 4.8
Value of Household and Personal Effects of Selected Pen-Keepers, 1739–1838

No.	Date	Pen-keeper	Value of possessions		
			£	s.	d.
I	1739	David Moncrieffe	1,658	9	7¾
2	1762	Thomas Moncrieffe	269	5	0
3	1767	Norwood Witter	7,856	14	9
4	1788	Francis Smyth	2,544	17	6
5	1790	James Donaldson	374	5	7½
6	1791	John Cunningham	243	17	4¾
7	1795	Charles Stirling	79	10	0
8	1797	Robert Hawthorne	872	9	5
9	1803	Charles Graham	671	10	0
10	1820	Francis Graham	3,849	11	10¾
11	1821	William Bennett	302	13	4
12	1822	Caleb Dickinson	56	5	10
13	1822	Joseph Russell	496	14	2
14	1823	James Rowe	825	5	9
15	1825	S.M. Barrett	140	0	0
16	1826	James Ferguson	108	0	0
17	1828	Roger Dobson	391	16	8
18	?	Jacob Graham	30	0	0
19	1838	S.B.M. Barrett	6,099	11	8

Source: Probate Inventories, JA, IB/11/3/21-157, 1739-1838.

Unity Valley Pen, for example, had household property valued at £374 5s. 7½d., compared to £3,387 for enslaved people and £582 15s. 0d. for livestock.[90] Table 4.9, relating to Peeke Fuller's estates and pens, serves as an example of the value of a planter's property.

The proprietors' houses at Chippenham Park Pen, Cardiff Hall and Harmony Hall were extravagantly proportioned and lavishly furnished by any standards. Cardiff Hall's proprietors' house was described as 'the finest in the island — very large and handsomely built'.[91] The floors were all of mahogany 'and the staircase, which is very fine also of solid mahogany.'[92]

Table 4.9
Inventory of Thetford Estate, Fuller's Rest and Thetford Hall Pen, St John

Property		Value in £		
		£	s.	d.
Thetford Estate	- Slaves	26,175	0	0
	- Stock	7,725	0	0
	- Household effects	*180	15	0
	Total	**34,080**	**15**	**0**
Fuller's Rest Estate	- Slaves	8,065	0	0
	- Stock	3,280	0	0
	- Household effects	10	0	0
	- Wain and boat	60	0	0
	Total	**11,415**	**0**	**0**
Thetford Hall Pen	- Slaves	11,645	5	0
	- Stock	3,895	0	0
	- Household effects	758	0	0
	Total	**16,298**	**5**	**0**
	Grand Total	****61,794**	**0**	**0**

Notes: *The value of household effects was lower where the proprietor was an absentee.
**This excludes the value of land and capital equipment.
Source: Bristol University Library, Special Collections Dept, DM 444.

Tenison's work on the Tharp estates reveals that Chippenham Park Pen was almost as lavishly furnished as the proprietor's house at Good Hope Estate.

As the next chapter will demonstrate, extravagant lifestyle, high economic or middle class status did not necessarily translate into high social and political status within a slave system that played the 'ranking game', assigning the highest social and political status to those directly involved in the sugar economy.

5

THE PEN-KEEPERS:
SOCIO-POLITICAL STATUS, IDEOLOGY RELATIONSHIPS AND THE 'RANKING GAME'

This chapter demonstrates that moderate to high economic status did not necessarily translate itself into high social status for the pen-keepers. It is true that Jamaican pen-keepers could not be regarded as the equivalent of the 'red legs'[1] of Barbados, or the poor whites of the Southern United States. Some of them could be compared to Southern yeomen who were socially headed by the livestock breeders in the blue grass region of Kentucky, in middle Tennessee and the river valleys of Missouri.[2] These would be at the lower end of the social ladder of the pen-keeping class, among those owning less than 30 enslaved workers. As non-sugar proprietors, however, pen-keepers were not ranked among the elite, even those who were European; a factor that made them discontented with their social status and led them to seek 're-ranking'. However, the dominant sugar sector exploited those dependent on it, thereby reinforcing its super-ordinate position.

This dominant-subordinate relation resulted from the fact that a central characteristic of eighteenth and nineteenth century Jamaica was the tendency to rank the inhabitants according to race, ethnicity, colour, place of birth or origin, gender, occupation, land use and class. This 'ranking game' was intensely practised in the age of modernity. In its simplest definition, 'ranking' is a metaphor for social ordering, social and cultural systems of hierarchy. But it should not be seen simply as a euphemism for the static social stratification model of sociologist M.G. Smith in which the racial, cultural and class categories are conflated into a simple social hierarchy.[3] Rather, 'ranking' represented the linguistic, oral and literary aspects of social culture that reflected the ritualized and politicized codes and consciousness of difference. 'Top ranking' went to those who were white-skinned, metropolitan born, the owners of large sugar plantations, able to live as absentee proprietors, or, if in the island, as members of the elite class of Europeans who controlled socioeconomic and political life and lived grandly in large houses staffed by an army of enslaved domestics. As we have seen from chapter four, this elite was usually Anglican, married, and adherent to the Western European culture, which it elevated above African, Euro-Creole and Afro-Creole culture.

The importance of place of birth as a factor affecting ranking was manifested in the discourses surrounding belonging, such discourses making it clear that during the period of slavery, Jamaican birth was sufficient reason for low ranking within the context of a society that elevated 'foreign birth' to a position of social importance. The only exception to this rule of devaluing local, creole birth applied to those of African descent who were born in the island and placed in a dialectical relationship with the devalorized African culture. As a consequence, African-Jamaicans were ranked above their continental African kin; and by the nineteenth century when planters granted them choice, they were given tasks suited to their alleged 'superior creole status' — for example, domestic, supervisory and artisan work.

Ethnicity and location within the island were also important to ranking; but this was mediated by class. Both Elsa Goveia and Kamau Brathwaite in their respective analyses of Caribbean society acknowledge that phenotype affinity did not seem to have been sufficient to guarantee elite status among Europeans because of the existence of class stratification and reinforced the fact that Euro-descended pen-keepers were clearly differentiated socially from the top echelons of sugar planter society, and, like coffee farmers, typically occupied an ambiguous position within the class configuration of the eighteenth and nineteenth centuries.[4] In his seminal work on the development of Creole Society in Jamaica, Kamau Brathwaite outlined the main social divisions within the society and differentiated between the several categories of settlers.[5] British pen-keepers along with 'minor staple' producers, who included the coffee planters, were grouped among those categorized as 'other whites'. More specifically, he referred to them as 'country whites' and 'small settlers', not numbered among the 'upper-class whites'.[6] The mixed-race pen-keepers and coffee planters were already regarded as socially inferior by European society. Even pen-keepers such as Robert Anguin and Benjamin Scott-Moncrieffe, whose economic position ranked them at the top of the mixed-race social ladder were marginal vis-à-vis British elites, as were other groups of 'unappropriated people'.[7] Similarly, M.G. Smith's account of White society does not list white pen-keepers among the elite or 'principal whites'. According to Smith, 'principal whites' formed a closed social class from which 'secondary whites', Coloureds and Blacks were vigorously excluded — with the possible exception of mistresses.[8]

Creole Economy and Creole Ideology

The complex relationship between the sugar sector and the pen-keeping sector during slavery can usefully illustrate the ways in which status mobility was attached to factors that did not include being 'native' or 'belonging' to Jamaica. Even those creoles, such as locally born pen-keepers whose livelihood depended on 'native' enterprises, maintained a colonial mentality that devalued their creole origins, rendering such pen-keepers 'creole colonials'.

So even though Jamaican society of the slavery period was described by Kamau Brathwaite as a Creole Society, (defined as a society in which a certain 'Jamaicanness' developed at the interstices between the cultures of Europe and Africa[9] and where the creolization process — a process of cultural interaction and synthesis, with its twin components of acculturation and inter-culturation — defined the process of cultural change and resulted in a tentative cultural norm),[10] such localization or 'indigenization' as occurred did not have unanimous support from the various classes and ethnic groups in the island's social structure. Indeed, even though Jamaican, like wider Caribbean identity, currently occurs within the discursive space of the creole, during slavery (and perhaps even now), 'Creole' was associated with 'inferior', 'local', and was always 'alternative' to the so-called 'pure' culture of the European elite or aspiring Euro-Creole elite. 'Creole' during slavery was placed in an antagonistic relationship with the symbolic capital of whiteness, in other words.

Social marginality was clearly linked to economic factors and elitism. From the early eighteenth century, pens were considered to be less prestigious properties and it was even usual to use the term 'pen' derogatively to apply to all small farms. J.B. Moreton emphasized that 'grass pens were considered as despicable objects for enterprising individuals to hunt after, nor would any man accept the management of one who had hopes of preferment on sugar plantations'.[11] Their differential rate of remuneration even made them unable to attract European workers. Moreton stressed that managers and overseers of sugar estates did not even like to associate with people in similar occupations on the pens. Furthermore, because pens were considered to be simply 'moderate-sized farms' their owners were more likely to be residents and less likely to join the elite group of absentees. Therefore, resident proprietors, particularly creoles, were regarded as socially inferior.[12] Relationships of superordination and subordination were also clearly discernible between 'principal' and 'secondary Whites' according to Smith's categorization.[13] This was because a significant number of Jamaican pen-keepers and coffee planters worked as attorneys and overseers of sugar estates. Dominant-subordinate relations were thus partly the result of the delegation of authority in the administration of estates.

Routes to Upward Social Mobility

As a result of the discriminatory social hierarchy, social status did not remain static or uncontested in colonial Jamaica. For example, their social status vis-à-vis the sugar elite caused pen-keepers, like coffee farmers, to seek to achieve upward social mobility and occupy the same social space as the sugar barons. Some were successful. Before examining the methods used to achieve upward mobility, the ideology of pen-keepers with respect to the society in which most were born — Creole Society — must be explained.

In his seminal work on Jamaica during the 50 years, 1770–1820, Kamau Brathwaite argued that 'the people, mainly from Britain and West Africa, who settled, lived, worked and were born in Jamaica, contributed to the formation of a society which developed ... its own distinctive character or culture'. In so far as this society was neither purely British nor West African, he characterized it as 'Creole'.[14] The dialectical relationship of colonial Jamaica and creole Jamaica and the dichotomy of two separate cultures which existed, however, frustrated, according to Brathwaite, the true development of Creole culture. Pen-keepers, for example, while contributing so much to the evolution of a Creole Economy, were less positive in their attempts to build Creole Society. They did not seem to have a greater commitment to Creole Society than did the British-born sugar planter-class, and did not appear to differ from them ideologically. Indeed, some could be classified as colonial reactionary elements, and as such, except in the economic arena (and part of this was purely economic necessity), impeded the development of a true Creole Society. This is revealed by their attitude to such issues as absenteeism, colour, class, slavery and abolition.

First of all, though largely resident, the ultimate aim of the majority of pen-keepers was to reside in Britain as soon as this was economically possible. Thus, George Forbes informed his brother in 1811 that he would return to live in Britain as soon as his financial circumstances permitted him to do so.[15] This attitude was not confined to white-skinned pen-keepers. Mixed-race pen-keepers such as Robert Hilton Anguin, also evinced a preference for life abroad. It was this which partially explains the absence of more wills and inventories in the local repositories which could have helped to fill out in more detail, the pattern of their lives.

Pen-keepers also adhered to the prevailing racial view of Africans. As a result, all mixed-race pen-keepers attempted to win acceptance into elite British society. According to Sheila Duncker, 'fundamental to all free-coloureds [mixed-race persons] was a desire to be measured by the same yardsticks as those used for people in similar economic positions who were White'.[16] Indeed, they often applied for the same privileges as the British. The privileged freedmen were required by law to marry into elite British society so that property could be passed to their offspring. Mixed-race persons adopted British values and rejected any association with the enslaved population or link with Africa. They aspired to be among the elite class in the island and were only impeded by prevailing British attitudes towards the relationship between colour and class. Their resident status and locally rooted economic activity, therefore, did not prevent them from reinforcing the norms and values of elite society.

An exception to the above observations relating to the attitudes of pen-keepers, has, however, been found. This was the St Ann pen-owner, Matthews, apparently white-skinned, who was totally anti-aristocracy and loathed the economic links that bound Jamaica to Britain. Wherever he could avoid it, he snubbed British goods including soap, candles, oil and salted provisions. Williams reported that 'he had neither tea, cider, porter, wines, fish, sauces, nor hams from England'.[17] His intention was to be as self-sufficient as possible in regard to food and manufactured goods from England. He manufactured his own plates on the pen and his clothes were locally made. His enslaved carpenters made all his furniture, his carriage was locally built and his mattress was stuffed with local silk cotton. Even pen tools such as machetes were made by his blacksmiths. For the defense of his pen, 'his own black-smiths have been known to make bows and arrows of the most diabolical invention that can be conceived'.[18]

Even Matthews, however, was at one with the majority of planters and pen-keepers with respect to slavery and abolition. Like other proprietors, he abhorred the Saints and particularly hated Wilberforce. He completely objected to the abolition fervour of the nineteenth century and though he was in other respects a 'paternalistic despot', he believed that his enslaved workers were totally unfit for freedom, 'and the entire disposal of their own time'.[19] According to Matthews, 'they must be kept in a state of pupilage under constant, though humane, restraint'.

Rivalling Matthews in his anti-abolition fervour, was Hamilton Brown. Like John Blagrove and other pen-keepers, he hated the Baptists for their presumptuous role in making the enslaved 'more aware' of their status as human beings. He accused them of inciting those enslaved to rebel and after the 1831/32 enslaved-led war or 'Baptist War', joined other members of the Colonial Church Union in burning the chapels of this denomination.[20] At one stage, the governor had to send the military to quell him. This was no easy task as Brown had armed retainers. Eventually, the military caught him at Minard Pen and entreated him to give up his sword. Instead of doing this, he broke it across his knee and threw it at the lieutenant, wounding him badly in his face.

Standing alone was David Barclay, who seemed to have been a departure from other pen-owners in his attitude to the enslaved. As a subsequent chapter will show, he described himself as a slave-owner, who, 'much dissatisfied with being so, determined to try the experiment of liberating my slaves'.[21] Consequently, in 1795, he freed those enslaved on Unity Valley Pen in St Ann. He then sold the pen, but only because he considered himself to be too old to run it. He had toyed with the idea of continuing livestock husbandry there, this time substituting British servants for enslaved labourers. He believed that they would cope in a climate such as St Ann's, had done well as labourers in Barbados, and were familiar with grazing practices in England. However, Barclay did not advocate immediate emancipation for all enslaved people in the Caribbean. He favoured gradual abolition, first starting with the abolition of the trade in captives. This, he felt, would result in an amelioration of the conditions of the enslaved and in time, their children would be fit for emancipation. By this time, 'their owners might, with security, have the heartfelt satisfaction of restoring human beings to their natural rights, as well as adding to society, many useful members'.[22]

A route to upward social mobility was direct investment in the sugar economy or even working on a plantation. There is evidence that those lower down the social scale sought jobs as overseers on sugar estates; for as has been shown, it was more prestigious to be employed on a sugar estate than on a pen.[23]

The mixed-race pen-keepers sought additional means of upward social mobility. They agitated vigorously for the removal of the restrictions imposed on them that ranked them below the British and excluded them from elite social life and also actively sought 'legal whiteness'. Between 1820 and 1830, a considerable number of mixed-race persons petitioned the Jamaican House of Assembly for the removal of these restrictions for equal privileges with white persons. This route was taken by both Anguin and Scott-Moncrieffe.[24] In 1827, both men petitioned the House of Assembly for white privileges for themselves and for their children. They claimed these on the basis that they were educated and had considerable property. Anguin further stated that he had 'obtained the good opinion of the most respectable inhabitants of the ... parish of St Ann'.[25] Both petitions were granted.

In an attempt to achieve upward social mobility some pen-keepers attempted to influence their children to marry 'upwards' instead of 'downwards'. To illustrate, the will of James Ferguson will be cited. He owned Rio Ho Pen in St Ann. Like other pen-keepers, he had mixed-race children. In his case, his two daughters, Suzannah and Mary, were quadroons. He stipulated that both girls were to get an annuity of £1,280.00. However, this was 'provided that they did not cohabit with, or had children for a negro man, or a mulatto man who was only one degree removed from a Negro',[26] that is, no Sambo. To increase their children's chances of upward social mobility, pen-keepers generally sent them to Britain to be educated. At least some of them, indeed, made favourable marital alliances. Joseph Barnes's daughter, Charlotte, married into the elite Trutch family of Somerset, and Ballard Nembhard's daughter Eliza, married Robert Dupre, son of Sir Alexander Dupre.[27]

In the absence of complete marriage records, it is impossible to quantify the extent to which pen-keepers themselves were marrying into the plantocracy in order to join the ranks of the elite. The degree to which their children succeeded in this venture cannot be ascertained either.

Social Interaction

Despite the fact that social differences separated sugar planters from pen-keepers and coffee planters, the necessity of trading links between economic sectors in the island determined that a certain level of interaction occurred.[28] Sugar planters or their representatives at times visited pens to select the stock for their estates. Pen-keepers similarly visited the sugar plantations to seek business and to see about the welfare of their 'jobbers'. Thus, even though sugar barons attempted to maintain social distance, economic dictates worked against their complete success and forced social interaction. The crucial question is: did such interaction extend beyond that dictated by economic necessity? There is no definitive answer. Caribbean social history highlights the social divisions between broad social groups but sheds very little light on the more complex subject of intra- and inter-class interaction within racial and colour groupings. Nevertheless, it can be safely assumed that interaction dictated by economic necessity did not result in complete egalitarianism.

Arguably, the best source of information on the extent and nature of the interaction among pen-keepers and others is Thistlewood's account of activities at Vineyard Pen, Egypt estate and Breadnut Island Pen. One year of his journal for Breadnut Island was selected for close examination. This property was selected because he was pen-keeper there while he was simply the overseer on the other units. What becomes clear from his diary of 1768 is that there were white visitors to his pen. Unfortunately, he does not always identify these people. Consequently, one is not always able to tell whether they were planters, overseers or attorneys. No independent check can be carried out because the In-Givings, a possible reliable method of doing so, only begin in 1816. Nevertheless, it is clear that at least one of his visitors, Mr Cope, was a sugar planter. The others — Hartnole, Oliphant, Hayward and March — seem to have been overseers.

Thistlewood himself visited surrounding properties for various reasons. Among these properties were Masemure, Cabarritta, Egypt, Moreland and Long Pond estates. These visits were not only for economic transactions. Some degree of socializing took place. On January 1, 1768, for example, Thistlewood rode to Egypt to see Mr Hartnole and dined with him on roasted bullock heart. Also, on several occasions, including March 25, 1768, he dined with Mr and Mrs Cope and on April 21, he had tea at Savanna-la-mar with Mr and Mrs Meyler.[29] Admittedly, economic forces shaped these social contacts, but nevertheless, such social relations between different social groups cannot be ignored.

The contacts and relationships were not always as amicable as those just described. Pen-keepers and planters conflicted over a number of issues, the most problematic being over pasturage, fencing and stray animals. Pen-keepers commonly sold stock sent to their pens for pasturage when they remained uncollected over the period originally contracted; for in such cases, pasturage fees remained unpaid. In order to recover such fees, the cattle, mules or horses concerned were sold. This created feelings of hostility and finally in 1849 Mr Justice McDougal ruled that it was illegal for pen-keepers to persist in this practice. The learned judge stated that although the pen-keeper had a lien on such stock, and could retain them until charges were paid, their sale by him was illegal.[30]

The matter of stray animals from pens posed a problem for neighbouring properties. In 1839, for example, the following advertisement appeared in the *Morning Journal:*

WILD CATTLE

Whereas great damage for a long period has been suffered by White Hall and Nonsuch Estates, from the trespass of stock in a wild state, said to belong to Harmony Hall Pen (in the possession of A.G. Fyffe, Esq.) which has been for years past, with regard to its stock, a nuisance to its neighbours, and with the damage now being committed to a ruinous extent, which it is impossible to prevent, as the cattle cannot be caught or impounded. These are therefore to give notice, that in future all such cattle so found trespassing shall be detroyed. Robert Fairweather, James Geddes, Walter Pollock.[31]

Needless to say, this brought an angry response from Fyffe. His advertisement, entitled *'Wild Men and Wild Cattle'*, was published the following week warning Fairweather and company that anyone found killing the stock of Harmony Hall 'shall be dealt with according to the law'. He accused them of faulty fencing, continuing,

the Attorneys of Nonsuch and White Hall, instead of making Line Fences, as they have often in vain been required to do, prefer, it appears, declaring hostilities against the stock of their neighbours. The Attorneys of Nonsuch will not, therefore, be surprised to learn (whatever may be the sentiments of the Proprietor) that three of his finest cows, which have been upwards of ten months on Harmony Hall, shall be forthwith killed - their carcasses sold, and the proceeds carried to the war credit of Nonsuch.[32]

The killing of the neighbour's stock was not always the solution adopted. In most cases, stray animals were sent to the pound where they were recoverable on payment of a fee. Advertisements relating to impounded stock appeared regularly in the various newspapers. At times, only cattle and horsekind were treated in this way, small stock being killed, as is indicated by the following example,

NOTICE

All cattle found trespassing on Friendship Pen in St Andrew's from this date (1 June 1839) will be sent to the Pound, and all hogs and goats found on the same, will be destroyed by persons in charge.[33]

Whereas the proprietors of pens and estates had set ways in which they dealt with stray animals, the enslaved workers often employed their own methods. On the morning of January 28, 1751, Thistlewood found that a sheep was missing from Vineyard Pen. He threatened the 'pen-keeper', old Sambo, because of his supposed negligence. The latter, in searching for the missing animal 'found a whole hog drest and hung up in the bushes to the back of Mingo's hut, against Fullerswood canes but in our pen'.[34] The Fullerswood watchman had presumably become fed up with Vineyard Pen's straying animals and the damage they did to the canes and took his own revenge. It was not only Fullerswood which suffered from Vineyard's straying animals caused by damaged fences. Salt Spring Estate was a constant victim. Countless hours were spent by Vineyard Pen's labourers in the frequent repairing of the fences.

The conflicts which developed did not only divide pen-keepers and sugar planters, but created internal dissension among the pen-keepers themselves. An explosive issue surrounding the price of fresh beef developed in 1821. In that year, Hay Hagart reduced the price of fresh beef from his pen from the prevailing 1s. 3d per pound to 10d. per pound. His reason was that the risk and expense of killing cattle in the rural area were small compared to what they were in urban centres, particularly Kingston.[35] This generated an angry response from his fellow graziers in St Ann who immediately called a meeting of all pen-keepers in the parish.[36] The decision was taken not to sell beef below the prevailing level.[37] The graziers of Westmoreland fully supported this position.[38] Furthermore, they resolved not to sell fat cattle below 1s. per pound. Despite the furore his action created islandwide, Hagart continued to sell his beef below the current price.[39]

The disagreements created a feeling of resentment by the larger public towards pen-keepers, however. One subscriber to the *Royal Gazette* expressed the view that pen-keepers were simply making a profit at the expense of all planters and consumers. The planters themselves, he felt, were partly to be blamed. In an attempt to make a profit on their old, meagre stock, they sold the latter at an inflated price to the pen-keeper. When fat, the pen-keeper sold the same stock to butchers at an equally exorbitant price. The result:

> The towns and the shipping, the prime consumers ... pay an extra 20 per cent for beef, purposely to enable him to get rid of his old stock, which have fairly earned their original price perhaps twice over, to wear out their teeth, and fret their guts with their tough, rigid and indigestible carcass.[40]

He angrily concluded:

> But, in regard to beef, the secret is out; the overgrown, wealthy
> planter must have a double return for his plantation stock — one,
> for work and labour performed, and the other from the butcher
> and consumer, who must be taxed 20 per cent extra to favour the
> joke — this is too much of a gull.[41]

Dissension among the pen-keepers was not the norm, though. They
usually banded together to protect their joint interests. One of the earliest
cases of such action was observed in 1755. On April 1 of that year, the
pen-keepers of St Dorothy, St John and St Thomas-in-the-Vale petitioned
the Assembly against the proposed removal of the Courts of Justice and
public offices to Kingston.[42]

In the post-slavery period, they collectively protested the attempt of
the Assembly to tax them unfairly. Where the parish vestry was planter-
dominated, the fight for fair taxation was even more protracted. In 1840,
for example, the pen-keepers of St Mary consistently petitioned the
Assembly to get the Vestry to remove the five shillings tax imposed on all
breeding stock. The Vestry had levied this charge with the explanation
that it was to offset the cost of road repair incurred in the parish in the
previous year. The pen-keepers objected on the grounds that in the past,
when money was raised for this purpose, little of it was actually correctly
applied. Rather, it was 'appropriated towards the disbursement of the
general accumulated debts of the parish'. They accused the vestry of using
this devious means of achieving its real purpose which was 'to evade a
recent law prohibiting Vestries from assessing any tax on stock for parochial
purposes, to an amount exceeding treble the amount per head, levied as a
public tax on stock'. The pen-keepers claimed that 'the nominal road tax
... is most unequal and oppressive in its operation and amount, falling on
a description of property which makes no use of the roads for the repairs of
which it is alleged to be imported'.[43]

Indeed, estates where the stock did use the roads had been assessed
only one-third of the sum levied on pens. On these units, breeding cattle
hardly ever left the property, the internal trade in stock involving primarily
working or fat animals. In 1843, other pen-keepers from various pen-
parishes added their voices to those of the St Mary protestors. They claimed

that the 'petitioners are heavier taxed than any other proprietors in the island'.

Two other issues which attracted the ire of the pen-keepers — in particular, those of St Catherine — were the proposed laying of railway lines and the planned diversification of the course of the Rio Cobre. The opposition to the diversion of the Rio Cobre was spearheaded by Mrs Catherine Buckeridge. The rationale for the attempt to change the course of the river was that it could no longer be allowed to run almost on the Ferry road. Buckeridge, however, protested on the grounds that pens in St Catherine in proximity to the Rio Cobre had always obtained water for pastures and cattle from it. More specifically,

> for some years past the said river in its present course hath afforded
> a constant supply of water to the grass pieces of petitioners' pen,
> and hath thereby fertilized them, and given the occupier the means
> of conveying grass to market.[44]

Similar petitions were sent in to the House of Assembly but, like the protest over the railway, were unsuccessful.

Finally, pen-keepers' political status must be considered as yet another area in which conflicts were manifested and marginalized status demonstrated.

Political Status

In the same way that economic prosperity did not guarantee the pen-keepers a high social status, it also did not necessarily give them great political power. In fact, Jamaican plantation society was politically dominated by the sugar planters by the late eighteenth and nineteenth centuries. It should be pointed out, however, that because of their economic status, white pen-keepers (and mixed-race, after 1830) participated fully in the political process in so far as voting was concerned. The owners of pens in St Catherine between 1757 and 1840 were among those applying for the franchise.

In 1757, for example, pen-owners formed 50 per cent of those agriculturalists who possessed the property rights entitling them to vote. Table 5.1 shows the basis on which they applied for the right to vote from 1760–1830.

Table 5.1

Number and Qualifications of Freeholders Applying for the Vote in St Catherine, at Five-Yearly Intervals, 1760–1840

Year		Number of Freeholders and property on which vote based								Total
	Houses only	Pen and Town Houses	House and Land	Sugar Plantation	Plan. Of Minor Staples	Land Only	Pen Only	Pen/House Plantation	Other	
1760	8	3	None	None	4	None	2	None	None	17
1765	10	None	20	None	None	2	9	None	None	41
1770	1	None	1	None	2	1	2	1	None	8
1775	13	None	9	None	2	1	9	1	2	37
1780	5	None	17	1	3	6	7	1	None	40
1785	4	None	1	None	None	2	None	None	None	7
1790	1	None	3	None	2	2	1	None	None	9
1795	1	None	7	None	None	2	2	None	None	12
1800	3	None	None	None	None	6	None	None	1	10
1805	2	None	2	None	None	6	3	None	None	13
1810	8	None	None	None	None	1	6	None	1	16
1815	3	None	None	None	None	None	None	None	None	3
1820	8	None	None	None	1	6	3	None	None	19
1825	4	None	None	None	1	6	1	None	None	12
1830	2	None	5	None	None	18	6	None	None	31
1835	7	None	13	None	None	19	11	None	None	50
1840	1	None	1	None	None	16	3	None	None	21

Source: St Catherine Vestry Minutes, JA, 2/2/27.

While most possessed the franchise, in general, specialized pen-keepers never occupied high political positions.[45] Up to 1845, none was noted in the Assembly or Legislative Council. Even in prominent pen parishes where pen-keepers managed to occupy public positions, these were usually low-status parochial positions (such as way-wardens and jurors).[46] To gain access to positions of political power meant that rural pen-keepers had to diversify into export-oriented economic activities, such as sugar or coffee production. Only those pen-keepers who joined the sugar planter class or combined pens with plantations eventually gained seats in the House of Assembly or were nominated to the Legislative Council. The successful ones were Joseph Barnes, Hamilton Brown, James Rule, John Blagrove who were all members of the Assembly at various periods in the eighteenth and nineteenth centuries. After 1830, mixed-race men did become members of the House of Assembly, but the only one who was remotely connected to pen-keeping, was Peter Moncrieffe, son of Benjamin Scott-Moncrieffe and heir to his father's pens in St Ann. Gad Heuman's seminal work on the mixed-race group only mentions that he was a barrister; however, he further points out that over one-third of the black and brown men in the Assembly between 1831 and 1866 were lawyers. Few of the remainder had any association with the land, being merchants, editors and public officials.[47]

Pen-keepers had more success, in terms of their political aspirations, at the parochial level. The best source of information for tracing their participation in local government is provided by the Vestry Minutes, arranged by parish.[48] There are drawbacks to relying on these records, however. In the first place, the occupation of those holding parochial positions was not always stated. Second, such occupations were not always correctly given. On jury lists before the 1870s, for example, it was customary to classify as 'planters' anyone remotely connected with agriculture. Thus, Benjamin Scott and Charles Stirling, well-known pen-keepers, were both labelled 'planters' in 1769.[49] John Baillie was classified similarly in the same list. In this period, however, it is more socially acceptable to be a planter than a pen-keeper. It is clear, therefore, that vestry records must be used in conjunction with other sources.

From the various sources consulted, it is obvious that the majority of pen-keepers qualified as jurors. Among these were Thomas Thistlewood, Edward Earl, [50] J.G. Jackson, Frederick Earl, John Reid, Henry Wray, John

Anguin, Benjamin Scott, Charles Stirling[51] and Hamilton Brown.[52] Even in St Ann, however, planters still dominated this post. On the jury list for 1769, for example, as far as can be established, only 12 out of the 89 names were those of pen-keepers.[53]

All property owners were likely to be waywardens who supervised enslaved labourers on the roads. As such, unless they were mixed-raced, before 1830, pen-keepers were among those occupying this position. All white St Ann pen-keepers, for example, were waywardens. The highest parochial positions were those of vestrymen, custodes, justices and church wardens. Again, planters dominated these offices. Some pen-keepers did become vestrymen, however. Among these were John Anguin, John Baillie, John Blagrove, James Ferguson, William Grier, William Voce, John Tracey, Hamilton Brown, Peter Forbes, James Donaldson and Joseph Geohagen.[54] Only Joseph Barnes of Cumberland and Half-Way-Tree pens and Duncan Robertson of Gilnock, St Elizabeth, seem to have been Custodes. Both also held other positions. Barnes was a member of the House of Assembly, mayor of Kingston and treasurer of the Jamaica district committee for promoting christian knowledge.[55] Robertson was major-general of the St Elizabeth militia.[56]

Military positions were held by other pen-keepers. John Cunninghame was at one time major-general of the militia and colonel of the St James militia,[57] and Peter Forbes was an officer attached to the grenadiers of the St Elizabeth regiment of the militia.[58]

Those who became justices included Thomas Thistlewood, John Baillie and Hamilton Brown. Church-wardens included James Ferguson, Hamilton Brown and John Moore.[59]

In the end, what did participation in the Creole economy and contributing to an indigenous system of production mean socially and ideologically? Participation in the local economy as a signal of a commitment to Creole Society was doubtful. Admittedly, in their various petitions to the House of Assembly in the 1770s, pen-keepers claimed that they had employed much time, labour and money in establishing pens and that their efforts had contributed to the development of the interior of the island and the opening up of new roads and lines of communication.[60] Such pronouncements were really designed to help their cause to get preferential tax laws passed in the legislature to protect the local cattle industry from external competitors. Those who patronized them equally seemed to have reacted to materialist concerns. It is true that pen keeping was encouraged by the colonial government during and after the American War of Independence as a strategy to offset the shortfall in the import trade with North America for plantation supplies. In anticipation of a disruption in trade with North America, members of the House of Assembly had established a sub-committee in 1775 to investigate the possibility of producing local supplies of grain, staves, lumber and food. Several Resolutions and Acts of the Assembly passed between 1775 and the early 1800s provided for the encouragement of local production of plantation supplies; the expansion of the coffee industry; the removal of the restrictions on new (European) settlement in the interior; the encouragement of immigration and settlement of loyalists from North America, the Bay of Honduras and the Mosquito Shore; and for new experiments in sugar and other industries.

But these were short-term measures. As soon as the crisis was over, it was business as usual, with trade resuming with external suppliers and sugar planters refusing to support any effort on the part of the pen-keepers to protect the local industry from external competition. This led planter-historian Edward Long (himself only a pragmatic supporter of Creole Economy), to accuse them of a lack of creole consciousness and of being prejudiced against local goods.[61] Disputes over the cattle taxes and to a lesser extent the price and quality of local beef[62] attest to the lack of planter support for the local economy. We have seen that the issue of taxes caused prolonged debates in the island's legislature, notably in Manchester and St Elizabeth.

During slavery, the pen-keepers were not sufficiently numerous in the House of Assembly to be able to operate as a solid political bloc within the colonial government and protect their economic interests directly. Admittedly, as early as 1757, 50 per cent of pen-keepers had the property qualification to vote; and many held lower-level parochial and military positions (see table 5.1). But the House of Assembly was the bastion of elite, sugar-planter power and remained so even as some pen-keepers became materially well off to become members of the Assembly at various periods in the eighteenth and nineteenth centuries. Sugar barons protected their own interests and marginalized those of the pen-keepers. This is why

Brathwaite concluded that 'at every step ... the creatively Creole elements of the society were being rendered ineffective by the more reactionary colonial.'[63]

Of course, this suggestion of a dialectical relationship between colonial and creole is problematic; one reason being that it masks the heterogeneity of non-sugar producers. Class, colour, gender, educational level, place of birth and ideology, for example, differentiated the pen-keepers, internally.

It was also clear that because of the high percentage of pen-keepers who were born, and continued to reside in Jamaica, with inferior social status accorded those who could not afford to live abroad,[64] relations of superordination and subordination defined the relations between colonials and creoles.[65] The absentee sugar planters had global ranking. They sat in the British Parliament, they had knighthoods and London offices and they lived in grandeur among the British elite. Pen-keepers, not surprisingly, aspired to re-ranking through the medium of absenteeism. In a letter to his brother Peter in 1811, George Forbes of Thatchfield Pen in St Elizabeth stated that as soon as his financial circumstances permitted, he would return to live in Britain.[66] Even free mixed-race pen-keepers shared this preference for metropolitan residence, Robert Hilton Anguin expressing a similar desire to live in Britain.[67]

Despite their lower social ranking and general lack of political power, the pen-keepers maintained an ideology that closely paralleled that of the sugar planters. The free mixed-race, creole pen-keepers were as colonial in their mentality as those who were white. While the Whites tried to transform the enslaved Africans into social creoles, therefore, ascribing a higher social status to enslaved people born in Jamaica or to Africans who showed evidence of 'creolization', free mixed-race people themselves looked down on those of their ethnicity who were born in Jamaica, and affirmed a Euro-creole worldview. There was thus a class and ethnic difference in how creole was constructed and assigned meaning in the Jamaican slave system. Distance from the idealized European phenotype and from Europe's cultural practices determined and defined the creole's position in the social hierarchy.

The foregoing analysis thus brings into question Brathwaite's suggestion that there was a dialectical relationship between creole and colonial, since pen-keepers, even mixed-race creoles, were as colonial in their ideological orientation as the sugar planters. There was no necessary dichotomy. Jamaican slave systems encouraged the coexistence, though not always peaceful, of colonial creoles and creole colonials. The ideal among Europeans and free mixed-race people of all classes was not to belong to Jamaica. Those who were forced by economic circumstances to remain as small-farmers, involved primarily in the Creole Economy, developed a symbiotic economic relationship with the sugar economy; and they did their best to lobby for the protection of their economic enterprise. But their conflicts with the dominant sugar sector over laws and taxes must be interpreted more as necessary strategies to protect their economic activities rather than a demonstration of commitment to Creole Society. They may have contributed to the development of a Creole Economy, but their attitude to living in Jamaica, to colour, class, slavery and abolition made them colonial reactionary elements rather than a group interested in the development of a true Creole Society.

6

THE ENSLAVED ON PENS:
DEMOGRAPHIC PROFILE AND WORK CULTURE

One of the results of the historiographical revolution of the 1960s and 1970s was the pluralization of the discourse on slave systems in the Caribbean, with scholars paying ever-increasing attention to issues relating to class, colour, ethnicity, gender and occupation. Of these five analytical categories, it is perhaps that of gender that has received most attention. As Hilary Beckles has observed, the radical character of the anti-colonial discourse, strengthened and supported by ideological imperatives of black redemption, worker empowerment and by feminist activism, also had the effect of targeting the androcentric nature of the colonial historiography that served to disarticulate the subaltern as woman.[1] Academic feminists, critical of the hegemonic male representation of the nationalist project and spurred on by the emergence and expansion of 'women's history', directed their research efforts towards a recuperation of the voice and experience of Caribbean women, in particular, those of the enslaved black woman. The florescence of social history and the popularity of the 'history from below' approach were particularly amenable to an exploration of the implications of gender in Caribbean history. The scholarship which resulted, attempting to compensate for past discursive shortsightedness, emphasized that there was no homogeneous experience among the enslaved and that analyses of their conditions, and, indeed, of slave systems, had to take gender differentiation into consideration.

As part of this project of differentiation, historians like Kamau Brathwaite, Lucille Mathurin-Mair, Hilary Beckles, Barbara Bush, Barry Higman, Marrietta Morrissey,[2] among others, have been engaged in research on the family of the enslaved and on reproduction, as well as on the gender differences in work regimes, access to 'privileges', enslaver-enslaved relations, representation and agency. The conclusions from these researchers have been instructive. They emphasize that slavery as a social system of oppression had a differential impact on enslaved women, forcing aspects of their opposition to their enslavement to assume gender-specific forms. The modern historiography of Caribbean slavery also reinforces the multifaceted importance of enslaved women and the contradictory productive, reproductive and sexual roles they were called upon to play.

The project of studying differentiation in slave systems is not complete, however, and one reason is that while scholars have subjected enslaved people's experiences to rigorous caste, class, colour, gender and ethnic analyses, such investigations of the plurality of experiences has tended to be located within the context of the sugar plantation, with occupational diversity being given less attention. Of course, it is undeniable that the majority of the enslaved in the British-colonized region, experienced slavery on the sugar estates where they were the backbone of the first and second gangs, which did the most arduous work in the fields on the estates, producing for the export market. Indeed, in all the British-colonized territories, which produced exportable quantities of sugar, with the exception of Jamaica, over 80 per cent of the enslaved workers, were on sugar estates by the nineteenth century. In fact, as Barry Higman's quantitative work has demonstrated, the percentage of the enslaved engaged in sugar ranged from 60–90 per cent in the British-colonized Caribbean. In St Kitts, Nevis, Antigua and Montserrat, few enslaved people were occupied other than in sugar cultivation.[3]

Nevertheless, despite the persistence of the plantation economy model which stresses the role of the sugar plantation with its elite sugar planters in structuring Caribbean society along a rigid enslaver-enslaved dichotomy, diversification was a significant feature of Caribbean economy. Thus, European colonialism did not succeed completely in introducing structural discontinuities by appropriating the land resources of the region for its monopolistic sugar plantation designs.

This chapter attempts to recuperate, even partially, the experiences of the enslaved who, while engaged in agriculture, did not labour on the sugar plantation. The objective is to interrupt and subvert the other process of homogenization that has occurred in slavery studies and to emphasize the multiple economic environments in which enslaved people's productive capacities were revealed, at times even within the same territory. Of course, as chapter seven will show, despite the differences in the work culture, the conditions of enslavement were such that, whether on sugar estates or not, the enslaved people's passion to resist remained similar, even if their strategies demonstrated variations. In other words, the contest over terrain, however defined, also characterized the relationship between pen-keepers and those they enslaved. For example, while Caribbean slavery launched a direct assault on traditional gender orders from those West African societies where agricultural labour was considered 'women's work' by placing large numbers of men in the fields, women still outnumbered men in all field gangs, though not in higher status skilled and supervisory positions. And, pro-slavery ideology, manifested in slave control mechanisms, demonstrated a striking unifying tendency, regardless of the economic context of slavery and the class position or economic status of the enslaver. Similarly, anti-slavery activities were as marked on non-sugar units as on sugar estates, exploding the myth that material conditions and differences in slave regimes bore a relationship to enslaved people's passion to resist.

Sources of Supply

As was the case on the sugar estates, up to 1808, the majority of labourers located on Jamaica's pens were enslaved and transported to the island directly from West Africa. It was the Iberians who pioneered the Trans-Atlantic trade in enslaved African captives with other nations following suit (but with Portugal controlling a large share up to the nineteenth century). Britain, of course, later surpassed most nations in the eighteenth century in terms of her market share in the trade in African captives. In discussing the recent quantitative findings based on the CD-ROM database on the Transatlantic slave trade, David Eltis notes that 'the British (including British colonials) and the Portuguese account for seven out of ten transatlantic slaving voyages, and carried nearly three-quarters of all slaves who embarked in Africa'.[4] The Portuguese seemed to have been dominant before 1640 and after 1807, with the British displacing them in the intervening period, but both participated in the forced transportation of millions of African captives to the Americas. There is still no agreement on a single figure as scholars continue to debate the so-called 'numbers game';

but there is some belief that somewhere around 20 million Africans reached the Americas, with millions more dying in the process of capture and shipment.[5] Jamaica and Barbados received the majority of captives transported to the British-colonized territories. Eltis has shown that for the period 1519–1867, Jamaica and Barbados received 11.2 per cent and 5.1 per cent of the trade respectively, compared to 4.2 per cent for the Guianas and 3.2 per cent for the British Windward Islands and Trinidad combined.[6] The majority of these enslaved Africans were male. Scholars of the Trans-Atlantic trade in enslaved Africans have shown that, despite regional variations (with a significantly high proportion of women exported from the Bight of Biafra or present day south-east Nigeria), overall less than 40 per cent of enslaved African captives were female (compared to over 60 per cent in the trade to Muslim areas), though women came to be over-represented in field labour assignment in all importing territories.[7] Eltis notes that in their search for labour in West Africa, Europeans 'carried their perception of women's role in society with them'.[8] Thus, it was no surprise that 'the Royal African Company's standard orders to its captains directed the latter to obtain at least two males for every female'.[9] As planters and traders became more knowledgeable about African societies and the central role of women in agriculture, they bent their attitude and secured more women for enslavement,[10] especially in light of the greater numbers of African women in certain areas like the Bight of Biafra. Of course, traders always had to compete with the domestic African market and the Trans-Sahara trade both of which favoured women. Adjusting their attitude to gender roles in African culture was not a sufficient guarantee of securing larger numbers of women for the Trans-Atlantic trade, unless they were prepared to pay very high prices. The male dominance in the trade thus persisted. In the period 1658–1713, enslaved males made up 78.1 per cent of captives to Jamaica from Senegambia; 58 per cent from the Gold Coast; 61.7 per cent from the Bight of Benin; 51.2 per cent from the Bight of Biafra and 60.9 per cent from West Central Africa.[11]

But not all of those enslaved Africans located on Jamaica's pens were imported directly from West Africa, especially after the abolition of the import trade. There was a tendency for those dual pen/sugar plantation proprietors to allocate their workers in the most efficient way; and this meant that those deemed too old for the intensive labour regime on sugar estates were relocated to the 'lighter' labour regime on 'satellite' pens. Thus, the pens tended to display an enslaved population already largely 'creolized'. In fact, Barry Higman's quantitative analysis of the enslaved population in Jamaica reveals that in 1817, compared to the coffee parishes of Manchester and Port Royal where they represented a majority, Africans (as opposed to creoles) comprised about one-third in the pen and sugar parishes (for example, Hanover and Vere).[12] Of course, the larger the enslaved population was on particular properties, the more creoles there tended to be in that population. In the older age groups (for example, where the aged were sent from estates to pens), Africans may have been significantly represented in the enslaved population. It is unclear if the stereotypical association of creoles with 'accommodation' and Africans with rebelliousness dictated the pattern on pens where there were fewer supervisory Whites. If this were so, the pen-keepers miscalculated, judging by the instances of resistance on the island's pens.

The practice of internal relocation of enslaved African men and women was observed in the case of Golden Grove Estate and Batchelor's Hall Pen in St Thomas-in-the-East which were both owned by Chaloner Arcedeckne and for some years administered by Simon Taylor. In several letters to his employer, Taylor stressed the usefulness of the satellite pen, first for the seasoning of newly arrived Africans before they were located on Golden Grove Estate; second for encouraging higher fertility among enslaved women; and third for the recuperation of those suffering from diseases. He noted in correspondence with Chaloner Arcedeckne 'a Penn is certainly better calculated for Negroes to breed at than Estates for there is no light work on them [estates] for Negro women'.[13] On pens, by contrast, 'new Negroes' could be engaged in 'light tasks' such as weeding and cleaning pastures. He also wrote that he 'desired for the future that when any of them [from Golden Grove Estate] got the yaws, that they might be sent to Batchelor's Hall Penn which is a dryer situation than the estate'.[14] Even European workers seemed to have realized the advantages of pens. When the bookkeeper on Retirement Estate developed a fever, he was advised by his doctor to go to Bromley Pen in St Ann, which had a healthier physical location. John Cooper, reporting on the condition of the apprentices on Montrose and Burrowfield pens indicated that all the labourers were healthy and attributed this partly to the healthy location of the pens; and the

Tharp-owned sugar plantations and pens in the parishes of Trelawny and St Ann also practised this flexible method of using enslaved peoples.[15] Those enslaved on pens thus represented a mobile labour force, with dual sugar/pen owners using their pens for the seasoning of new arrivals and the recuperation of sick workers, removing them to the estates afterwards.

Pen-keepers did not immediately adopt a more pro-natalist policy than other enslavers. Augmenting the enslaved population by natural increase, to add to imports and internal re-allocation, was thus a post-1808 phenomenon. In St Ann, for example, where, according to W.J. Gardner, in 1833 upwards of one-quarter of the enslaved population in the parish was attached to pens,[16] out of 19 pens for which detailed returns are available, (the returns hardly identified the properties by type) for 1829–32, 11 showed an increase of births, and two had the same number of enslaved people in 1829 and 1832.[17]

Eight of these had also had positive increases for the 1817–23 period. Indeed, where decreases in the total population were observed, they were less the result of natural increase and more the result of sale, transfers to estates and manumission. Where deaths exceeded births, these were less those of infants and more those of old Africans. Some pens in St Elizabeth also showed an increase in their enslaved populations. The case of Pepper and Bonavista pens will serve to illustrate. In their case, according to table 6.1, only in 1833 did deaths exceed births and this was only by one. In Westmoreland, the other parish for which a systematic analysis of the returns was done, Higman's conclusion that deaths exceeded births on sugar estates was confirmed. In 1817, for example, only three of the 47 estates in the sample recorded an excess of births over deaths. By contrast, only one pen, Paradise, showed an increase of deaths over births.[18] A similar trend was observed in 1832. Only eleven pens had complete returns for 1817–32, and seven of these improved their position in all years.

The reasons for the tendency of some units in Jamaica to increase their enslaved population by natural means while others registered an alarmingly high rate of natural decrease have been well-documented by Barry Higman[19] and will only be rehearsed briefly here. The reason the pens were generally more successful than the sugar plantations in sustaining their labour force by natural increase had nothing to do with planter benevolence, however.

Table 6.1
Slave Demography, Pepper and Bonavista Pens, 1826–38

	January each year			Increase			Decrease				December		
Year	M	F	Total	Birth	Purchase	Total	Death	Freed	Shipped or sold	Total	M	F	Total
1826	134	144	278	8	None	8	7	None	None	7	131	148	279
1827	131	148	279	10	None	10	6	None	None	6	134	149	283
1828	134	149	283	3	None	3	6	None	None	6	135	145	280
1829	135	145	280	10	None	10	10	None	None	10	138	142	280
1830	138	142	280	10	None	10	3	2	2	5	139	148	287
1831	139	148	287	7	None	7	2	None	None	2	139	153	292
1832	139	153	292	15	None	15	4	None	None	4	143	160	303
1833	143	160	303	11	None	11	12	None	None	12	142	140	282
1834	142	160	302	4	None	4	0	None	None	51	122	133	255
1835	122	133	255	0	None	0	3	None	None	3	119	133	252
1836	119	133	252	0	None	0	3	None	None	6	116	130	246
1837	116	130	246	0	None	0	1	None	None	1	116	129	245
1838	116	129	245	0	None	0	4	None	None	5	114	126	240

Note: The birth figures for the apprenticeship period may simply not have been recorded as children up to six were then free.
Source: WIC, UWI Library, Papers relating to Pepper and Bonavista Pens, 1826–38.

Four factors seemed relevant: (1) the better disease environment, pens being located in drier areas (2) the better care of mothers and infants after 1808, with fresh meat and milk being more available to them (3) the less regimented labour regime and (4) fertility-enhancing internal demographic variables relating to age, sex ratio, African/Creole ratio and colour. Treatment is now ruled out as a variable. These factors operated in conjunction with each other rather than in isolation.

The effect of environment cannot be absolutely proven, but all contemporary writers stressed the fact that some pens were located in healthier (cooler and drier) areas than estates. But this choice of location was more accidental than deliberate.

According to Higman, the sex ratio was important as a variable which promoted natural increase because high sex ratios stimulated fertility, especially where in the most fertile age group, 20–44, there was a high level of masculinity. On sugar estates, characterized by low masculinity, and low sex ratios, fertility was depressed.[20] Indeed, on the 47 Westmoreland estates in the sample, males represented 47.6 per cent and females, 52.4 per cent and males exceeded females in only nine (19 per cent) cases. The male to female ratio on these units was 1:1.1. The sexes were even in numbers on four estates only.[21] By contrast, 42.85 per cent of pens represented those with favourable male to female ratios, females exceeding males on eight pens. Even in the case of the latter, the disparity was not as great as on estates.

The African to creole ratio is also seen as an important variable, except in fertile age groups where the percentage of Africans was high, the rate of natural increase was correspondingly high.[22] But as there was a tendency for Africans and males to be concentrated in smaller holdings, this worked to the advantage of units such as pens, rather than on estates with their large number of enslaved creoles. On the estates in the Westmoreland sample, creoles comprised 73.07 per cent of the total labour force.[23]

Enslaved mixed-race people were believed by historical demographers to have been a particularly fecund group.[24] However, as these were concentrated primarily in urban centres, this was a factor least likely to promote fertility on estates and pens. Added to this was the fact that miscegenation was less likely to occur on those pens run by their settled families. On the pens in the sample, only 10.16 per cent of the population was mixed-race. This was still a higher percentage than the eight per cent calculated for the 47 estates in the parish.

Table 6.2
Demographic Characteristics of the Enslaved on Pens in Westmoreland, 1817

Pen	M	F	Total	Nationality				Black		Colour								Total Coloureds
				African		Creole				Mulatto		Sambo		Mustee		Quadroon		
				M	F	M	F	M	F	M	F	M	F	M	F	M	F	
Darliston	50	56	106	16	21	34	35	48	56	2	-	-	-	-	-	-	-	2
Robins River	32	31	63	0	4	32	27	30	30	2	1	-	-	-	-	-	-	3
Old Shafston	43	55	98	7	13	36	42	36	50	3	3	4	2	-	-	-	-	12
Ackendown	52	77	129	-	-	52	77	31	48	6	12	10	14	-	-	5	3	50
Culloden	7	8	15	3	4	4	4	7	8	-	-	-	-	-	-	-	-	0
Mt Carmel	44	76	120	9	36	35	40	38	66	1	3	3	7	-	-	2	-	16
Sweet River	34	37	71	-	-	34	37	32	33	2	3	-	-	-	-	-	1	6
Forest	65	103	168	16	35	49	68	62	101	1	-	2	1	-	-	-	1	5
Whitehall	75	65	140	35	26	40	39	74	63	1	-	-	2	-	-	-	-	3
Argyle	76	65	141	33	25	43	40	70	62	3	2	2	-	-	-	-	1	9
Old Hope	113	96	209	20	25	93	71	91	75	6	8	15	13	-	-	-	-	43
Paradise	83	60	143	39	23	44	37	76	59	4	1	2	-	-	-	-	-	8
Mt Edgecombe	109	135	244	34	51	75	84	106	125	1	7	2	3	-	-	-	-	13
Middlesex	22	14	36	11	7	11	7	22	14	-	-	-	-	-	-	-	-	0

Source: London, (PRO), T 71/178, RRS, 1817.

Table 6.3
Age Profile on Selected Pens, Westmoreland, 1817

Pen	0 – 6		7 –14		15 – 19		20 – 44		45 – 60		60 and over		Total		Overall Total
	M	F	M	F	M	F	M	F	M	F	M	F	M	F	
1 Ackendown	10	9	7	10	5	9	25	28	5	13	0	8	52	77	129
2 Darliston	5	9	6	4	5	4	22	28	10	9	2	2	50	56	106
3 Forest	12	12	10	19	3	13	19	37	14	14	7	8	65	103	168
4 Mt Carmel	8	5	9	12	9	10	14	35	3	10	1	4	44	76	120
5 Old Shafston	11	11	6	8	8	9	13	22	5	4	0	1	43	55	98
6 Robin's River	5	6	5	6	–	2	15	7	6	6	1	4	32	31	63
7 Sweet River	3	3	7	9	4	6	14	13	6	3	0	3	34	37	71

M = male
F = female
Source: London, (PRO),T 71/178.

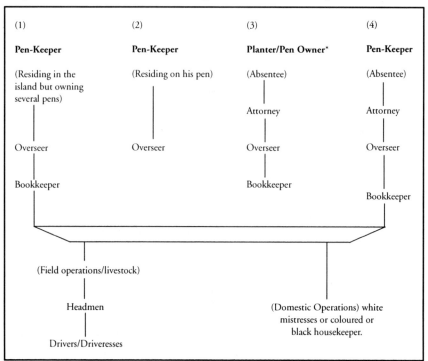

As table 6.2, which (along with table 6.3) illustrates the main demographic features of the pens in the sample further indicates, only on Ackendown and Old Hope pens were there significant numbers of enslaved mixed-race persons. These pens were administered by British overseers and bookkeepers in the absence of the proprietors. In such cases, miscegenation tended to be greater. However, as these enslaved mixed-race persons were mostly mulatto and sambo, they tended to remain in the enslaved population.

Finally, it was generally believed that where the enslaved were not engaged in the production of sugar, their chances of survival were greater.

Figure 6.1
Representation of the Management Hierarchy on Pens

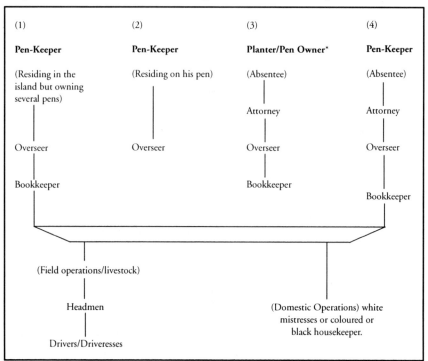

Note: If the planter/pen-owner resided in the island though not on the pen, the attorney was not employed.

Edward Long was one of the earliest writers to comment on this fact in the 1770s, although the characterization of the pen labour as 'easy' may have been an exaggeration. According to him, the enslaved workers were more likely to increase naturally where the labour was easiest.[25] This would seem to include livestock farms. Indeed, two contemporary writers commented on the difference between pen and estate labour. In his report on a tour of Jamaica published in 1826, Cynric Williams remarked of Mr Matthews's pen that 'if I had observed on other estates the bustle of sugar making I was no less struck with the tranquility that prevailed here'.[26] He continued, 'the negroes have a comparatively idle life, being engaged in cleaning the guinea grass or repairing the stone walls which divide the pastures'.[27] Similarly, Barclay, part owner of Unity Valley Pen in St Ann, observed that

> the labour on a pen is much lighter than on a sugar plantation, the employment of the former being only to look after cattle, horses and mules, etc. and to attend to them in the same manner as is practiced by graziers in England.[28]

A similar relationship between type of crop and intensity of the labour done was said to exist in Barbados. There, domestics, tradesmen and enslaved people belonging to the 'ten acre men' who owned cotton places were said to have lived a live of 'ease and plenty'.[29]

Characteristics of the Enslaved Labour Force: Ethnicity and Gender

While there is some evidence that African ethnicity was not totally irrelevant in property holders' choice of enslaved workers (as in the US South where Sierra Leonians were deliberately selected for rice plantations), there is little proof that enslavers in Jamaica selected enslaved peoples for the livestock farms according to their suitability for animal husbandry. The same applied to Spanish America where cattle-ranching was much more important than in Jamaica. Indeed, no particular African ethnic group seems to have been preferred or targeted for livestock rearing, regardless of their prior experiences in Africa; and in any case, the pastoral/savanna regions of West Africa were not the major sources of captives for the Trans-Atlantic trade.[30] Enslaved people on pens, like their counterparts on sugar and coffee plantations exhibited the same ethnic profile. That is, based on recent research, they would have been primarily Igbo, Akan/Aja, Ga, Coromantee and Congo with a sprinkling of other ethnic groups.[31] Indeed, around 75 per cent of enslaved Africans shipped to Jamaica in the seventeenth and eighteenth centuries originated in the Gold and (the disrespectfully named) 'Slave Coasts' and the Bight of Biafra. More specifically, between 1658 and 1713, the majority of enslaved peoples transported to Jamaica came from the Gold Coast (36 per cent), the Bight of Benin (26 per cent), West Central Africa (20.1 per cent) and the Bight of Biafra (11.5 per cent).[32] Gold Coast captives were displaced by the end of the eighteenth century. By 1776, for example, the Bight of Biafra had surpassed the Gold Coast as a supplier of African captives to Jamaica.[33] Curtin estimates that over the period of the trade to Jamaica, 1655–1807, the dominant sources of captives were (in order of numerical importance), the Bight of Biafra, the Gold Coast, Central Africa, the Bight of Benin, Sierra Leone and Senegambia,[34] reinforcing recent views that the Igbo presence in Jamaica became stronger after the seventeenth century. Indeed, in the years 1792–1807, an estimated 49 per cent of enslaved Africans imported into Jamaica comprised ethnic groups from the Bight of Biafra, with Central Africa (35 per cent) being the next significant.[35] In some years, the number of females from this area exceeded the number of males. In general, though, it would seem that rather than a focus on specialized occupational skills other than an overall ability to perform agricultural work, the factors affecting the composition of the trade in African captives tended to be forced 'availability', demand, gender, age, cost/price, with stereotypical national traits (industry, proneness to rebellion, honesty, faithfulness, physical suitability for field work) playing a more minor role than some scholars make out (especially in large markets like Jamaica).[36]

Size of the Enslaved Labour Force

Slaveholdings in Jamaica varied in size. Sugar estates tended to be more extensive and demanded a much larger enslaved population than pens. Whereas the average size of the estate enslaved population was 223 with a range up to 600.[37] Simon Taylor believed that for a pen with 600 head of cattle, a labour force of 50 workers was adequate.[38] The average size of the labour force on pens in Jamaica was somewhat higher than this, however, particularly in Trelawny, Hanover, Vere, St Catherine and

Westmoreland. This is because of the use of satellite pens by sugar planters for purposes unconnected with livestock husbandry. As satellite pens tended to have larger enslaved populations than the independent pens, this increased the average on pens taken islandwide. Higman's study of the 1834 Accounts Produce revealed an average of 98.73 on monocultural units and an island norm of 100 per unit.[39] An independent check in the Public Poll Tax Roll, which represented a larger sample of pens than the Accounts Produce, still revealed an average of 98.89 with a range up to 295. A small number of pens, such as Donnington, had no resident labour force, being worked entirely by jobbing gangs.[40]

Gender, Colour, Ethnicity and Productive Roles

The productive labour on the pens, like on the sugar estates, was unambiguously the terrain of African enslaved men and women whose labour time was appropriated by British and mixed-race men or women and deployed in a range of tasks. As on the sugar estates, it was black-skinned men and women who were the ones mostly engaged in field work and small stock rearing, with enslaved mixed-race women located in the house of the manager or owner.

Field work was also unambiguously the terrain of Black women. Material development in the colonial Caribbean, as in West Africa, was based upon agricultural activity; and production and productivity expansion eventually came to depend upon female labour, despite the under-representation of African women in the Trans-Atlantic trade in enslaved Africans and the late balancing out of the sex ratios and the achievement of an excess of females over males in the colonies. Whether in the field or in domestic labour, the numbers of enslaved women exceeded those of enslaved men. There is some debate over why this was so, with scholars disagreeing over the respective role of factors such as gender, ethnicity, age and colour. Barry Higman marginalizes the role of gender in task allocation, stressing materialist considerations and the primacy of age, colour and (health) 'condition'. In his view, considerations about gender roles in Africa, and European planters' perception of the traditional gender division of labour, had very little impact on task allocation in the field.[41] But Barbara Bush, Marrietta Morrissey and others show that while field work may have equalized the status of men and women on sugar and non-sugar properties, gender was important as a factor determining who held the skilled and supervisory positions. Plantation systems able to take advantage of economies of scale were most likely to exhibit a skill-based hierarchy in gender stratification. So, although planters reportedly professed a preference for enslaved men and though this supposedly influenced the sexual complexion of the trade in Africans, in the complex and hierarchical division of labour that existed on large plantations, men were valued for craftsmen skills or work in the semi-industrial processes of the sugar mill. While the majority of women worked in the fields, in the great houses as domestics and nursed the sick in the hot houses, men had a wider range of tasks.[42]

Richard Sheridan notes that on the Tharp estates in the early nineteenth century, by far the most medical attendants were female and were in poor physical condition and valued less than the average of all enslaved plantation workers. Enslaved men were the drivers, skilled artisans, messengers, watchmen, coopers, masons, enslaved male 'pen-keepers', and so on; and in many cases, only a minority of their total number worked in the fields.[43] By contrast to men, Higman found that only about seven per cent of tradespeople in the whole British Caribbean were women. The usual skilled occupations open to women were those of seamstress and cook.[44]

This gender-differentiated trend can be demonstrated quantitatively for both sugar and non-sugar properties in the Caribbean and was not unique to Jamaica. Michael Craton shows that in 1789 the Worthy Park Estate in Jamaica had an enslaved labour force of 339, 162 females and 177 males. A little more than 43 per cent of the women worked in a field gang, while just over 16 per cent of the men did so. In 1793, 44 per cent of the women were field labourers on the same plantation.[45] Richard Sheridan records that on Roaring River Estate in 1756, 70 of the 92 women were in the field; but of 84 men, only 28 were in the field.[46] In Barbados in the late 1700s, the Codrington Estates employed two thirds of the women in fields compared to half of the men.[47] Halse Estate in Clarendon in 1802 had 37 per cent of the total males and 56 per cent of the total females in the field.[48]

Enslaved women on non-sugar properties like coffee estates and livestock pens and in territories like Belize which relied on forest industries, were just as likely to be over represented in field labour and under-represented in the skilled and supervisory positions. In Belize, only the men were involved in logging; so that women and girls along with those males, who were incapable of arduous work, were concentrated in domestic occupations and food production.[49] On livestock farms, only men worked with large

Table 6.4
List of those Enslaved on St Jago and Paisley Pens, January 1, 1827

Names	Colour	Country	Age	Occupation	Condition
Males					
William Knight	Black	Creole	35	Driver	Subject to yaws
Quaco	Black	Creole	44	Pen-keeper	Sickly
Quashie	Black	Creole	30	Pen-keeper	Ruptured
Allick	Mulatto	Creole	11	Pen-keeper	Healthy
James Knight	Black	Creole	14	Pen-keeper	Healthy
Gabriel	Black	Creole	35	Waggoner	Weakly
Edward James	Black	Creole	18	Waggoner	Healthy
Scrub	Black	African	30	Watchman	Weakly
Quamin	Black	Creole	8	Houseboy	Healthy
Quamin	Black	Creole	40	Invalid	Blind
Tom	Black	African	60	Invalid	Infirm
Glasgow	Black	Creole	35	Runaway since	1826
Sandy	Black	African	60	Runaway since	1824
Matthias	Black	Creole	25	Field	Able
Tom Allison	Black	Creole	41	Field	Able
Cuffee	Black	Creole	21	Field	Able
Tom	Black	Creole	22	Field	Able
Daniel Knight	Black	Creole	16	Field	Healthy
George	Black	Creole	6	Unserviceable	Healthy
Henry	Sambo	Creole	4	Unserviceable	Healthy
Jamaica	Black	Creole	4	Unserviceable	Healthy
Cudjoe	Black	Creole	2	Unserviceable	Healthy
Cumberland	Black	Creole	1	Unserviceable	Healthy
Tom	Mulatto	Creole	1	Unserviceable	Healthy
Females					
Sucky	Black	African	75	Invalid	Inform
Phoebe	Black	Creole	45	Field nurse	Diseased
Margaret Scott	Mulatto	Creole	20	Housewoman	Able
Ann Donaldson	Sambo	Creole	42	Washerwoman	Able
Elizabeth Reid	Black	Creole	50	Field cook	Able
Janet Goulding	Black	Creole	40	Field	Diseased
Margaret Baron	Sambo	Creole	35	Field	Able
Auralia Knight	Sambo	Creole	40	Field	Able
Eve	Black	Creole	30	Field	Able
Nancy Goulding	Black	Creole	22	Field	Able
Ann Jones	Black	Creole	36	Field	Able
Sarah James	Black	Creole	30	Field	Able
Yabba	Black	Creole	35	Field	Able
Judy	Black	Creole	20	Field	Able
Bell	Black	Creole	14	Field	Healthy
Abba	Black	Creole	10	Field	Healthy
Katie Scott	Black	Creole	11	Field	Healthy
Sarah	Black	Creole	3	Unserviceable	Yaws
Olive	Black	Creole	2	Unserviceable	Healthy
Katie	Sambo	Creole	2	Unserviceable	Healthy

Source: Exeter University Library, Exeter, Gale/Morant Collection, 4/b/4.

stock, making it more likely that an even higher percentage of pen women would be in fieldwork producing food mostly. On Prospect Pen in 1784, 18 males laboured in the field compared to 40 women. In 1827 on St Jago and Paisly pens, as table 6.4 shows, 76 per cent of the women performed field labour. On Pepper and Bonavista pens, 57 per cent of the adult females were in the fields compared to 39 per cent of the adult men. On Mickleton Pen in 1836, 72 per cent of the females worked in the fields.[50] On William Hewitt's coffee plantation in the parish of Clarendon in Jamaica in 1812, 20 of the 55 adult and teenaged males were in the fields, compared to 39 of the 55 adults and teenaged females.[51]

Field tasks themselves were not always differentiated by gender, though there is some evidence that on cotton estates the more strenuous operation of constructing the ridges on which cotton was sown was entrusted to males while the removal of weeds, light littage after ridging and reaping were done by women. On cocoa estates, men picked the pods, which grew high in the trees, while women gathered and transported them to the processing area. Both men and women participated in the extraction of the beans and pulp, though men mostly did the cutting open of the pods and passed them on to the women for extraction. Women did the grinding of the parched beans.

Quantitative data also support the over-representation of men in supervisory and skilled positions; and gender specific realms were just as significant in the higher occupational levels on non-sugar properties as on estates. Livestock pens in Jamaica provide a good example, despite the fact that pens really had few artisans, the pen-keeper hiring when the need arose (see tables 6.4 and 6.5). On Prospect Pen in 1784, 25 men were in non-field occupations compared to 12 women. Windsor Pen in 1818 had a total enslaved population of 216, 109 males and 107 females. Only 29 men worked in the fields; but only seven enslaved women were in occupations that were described as skilled. On Top Hill Pen in the same year, of a total enslaved population of 68, there were 26 males of which only 6 were field labourers. The others were involved in a range of other jobs. By contrast, of the 42 females, 28 of them adults and 6 girls old enough to be given tasks, 20 were in the field and 5 were in ancillary and skilled positions. Similarly on Chippenham Park Pen, another of the Tharp properties, in 1818, there were 54 males and 52 females. Fifteen females

Table 6.5
The Division of Labour on Vineyard Pen, 1750

Slaves	Sex	Occupation
Dick	Male	Mulatto driver
Adam	Male	Gardner
Coffee	Male	Assistant to Phibbah
Toney	Male	Watchman
Mingo	Male	Watchman
Cesar	Male	Watchman
Roger	Male	Watchman
Sambo	Male	Goatherd
Joe	Male	Shepherd
Cudjoe	Male	Shepherd
Barho	Male	Negro Pen-keepers
Simon	Male	Negro Pen-keepers
Julius	Male	Negro Pen-keepers
Scipio	Male	Negro Pen-keepers
Guy	Male	Field [?]
Charles	Male	Field [?]
Titus	Male	Field [?]
Robin	Male	Run away
Port Royal	Male	Field [?]
Quashie	Male	Field [?]
Chessa	Male	Field [?]
Safrox	Male	Field [?]
George	Male	Field [?]
Phibbah	Female	Housemaid
Mimba	Female	Shepherdess
Quasheba	Female	Shepherdess
Joan	Female	Washerwoman
Bimba	Female	Water carrier
Wanninno	Female	Field [?]
Silvia	Female	Field [?]
Dinah	Female	Field [?]
Betty	Female	Field [?]
Mary	Female	Field [?]
Hager	Female	Field [?]
Marina	Female	Field [?]
Cynthia	Female	Field [?]
Chrissie	Female	Field [?]
Jenny	Female	Field [?]
Deborah	Female	Field [?]

Source: Journal of Thomas Thistlewood, Monson 31.1, 1750, fol. 318.

were too young to be employed. Of the other 37, 27 were in the field and 6 in ancillary and skilled activities. Of the 30 adult males, 10 worked in the fields. The others worked at a range of other tasks.[52]

Enslaved men thus dominated the 'slave elite'. As a result of the dominance of men in non-field occupations, they were more likely than women to accumulate cash for their services; for at times the enslaved received small sums from enslavers, or received incentives in kind, which boosted their economic and social status.

The Work Regime

There were identifiable differences in the work regimes of those enslaved on sugar and non-sugar properties. First of all, their labour routines involved no intense periods of work comparable to harvest time on the sugar estates, no peaks and troughs, no long night hours like those which the enslaved on the sugar estates had to endure during the manufacturing period. The records of two pens, Vineyard and Breadnut Island indicate that with the exception of the planting of guinea grass and corn, the other tasks had no clear annual cycle. Ground provisions and vegetables were planted, mostly by the women, between September and March. Men worked with large animals, women with small stock. For the most part, all work was completed by sundown, although women worked later when corn had to be shelled.

Even the supervision of those enslaved on pens appeared to have been less rigid than on sugar estates. On sugar estates, the attorney and overseer system made for close oversight of all tasks. On modest-sized pens, with their resident owners, smaller European populations, and closer relationships between the resident owner and the enslaved, supervision tended to be less rigid and close. Pens were legally required to maintain a White presence in the ratio of one to every 30 enslaved persons and 150 head of livestock. Given the average size of the labouring and livestock populations on the pens, at least three whites ought to have resided on each pen. This was rarely the case. On Vineyard Pen in St Elizabeth in 1750, for example, there were 40 enslaved Africans and one white overseer who, on occasions, left the enslaved under the supervision of an enslaved male driver while he overnighted elsewhere. Despite the legal requirement, most pens experienced difficulties, especially in the eighteenth century, in attracting white men, and they often had to pay the deficiency tax levied on non-compliance. In addition, though there was some supervision of field gangs whether by the overseer or the driver, there was little supervision of the more varied, individualistic tasks.[53]

While most owners of pens encountered difficulties in hiring white overseers, those owned by women (white or non-white) and by mixed-race (men or women) had the greatest difficulties in attracting Whites. The reports of Stipendiary Magistrates in the post-slavery period indicate that such pens were characterized by 'indiscipline and lax control'. Apparently, sugar planters recognized the potentially disruptive effects on their enslaved labourers, which labourers from the 'freer lifestyle' of the island's pens could have, and sought to restrict mixture. White-owned pens had problems in hiring too, chiefly because of the low salaries they offered and the low social status ascribed to pens and pen-keepers in this sugar-dominated society (see chapter five). The demographic implications of this varied work regime (higher fertility, lower mortality, greater racial mixing and therefore a higher percentage of mixed-race people) have already been explored by Barry Higman.[54]

Colour, Gender and Domestics

Domestic labour was an integral part of the slavery experience on both sugar and non-sugar units. The number of domestics varied according to the size of the colony and the total enslaved population, the economic status of the enslavers and the presence of resident planters, who maintained large homes. Jamaica had a higher degree of absenteeism than territories like Barbados and the French colonies. In Barbados in 1780, there were probably 15,529 domestics making up 25 per cent of the enslaved population. On some Jamaican sugar estates, about 10 per cent of the enslaved population worked as domestic servants. There was a gender bias in the allocation of domestic jobs. Enslaved women formed the majority of household labourers in the British colonized territories. Barry Higman found that 70 per cent of all domestics in plantation households were female. There was a gender division of labour among enslaved domestics, men working as grooms, butlers, valets and gardeners, women concentrated in childcare, sewing, cooking and laundering.

Enslaved domestics, whether on sugar estates or non-sugar units, were usually creole and mixed-race. The mixed-race domestics, because they were phenotypically closer to white-skinned Europeans, were considered delicate for field labour. The preference for creoles (as for colour), was linked to racist stereotypes. According to Thomas Attwood in his 1791 account of slavery in Dominica:

> the Creole Negroes ... having been brought up among white people, and paid some attention from their infancy, lose much of that uncommon stupidity so conspicuous in their new negro parents; and are in general tolerably sensible, sharp and sagacious.[55]

Historians have indicated that, unlike the present view of domestic labour, during slavery, those who worked in the enslavers' households enjoyed a higher status than field workers and that a common form of punishment was the sending of domestics back to the field. The female domestic was not considered skilled and was no more highly valued than a field hand; but the linking of domestic work to status seemed to have been related to the privileges, which usually accrued, particularly to women. To reinforce, Barry Higman has pointed out in a 1993 paper that:

> Historically, the low status attributed to the domestic worker in Jamaica must be dated to about 1930. Before that time the 'houseservant' was said to rank high in the social scale, with a relative advantage in material terms throughout the period of slavery and down to about 1850. Deterioration in the social status of the servant occurred when domestic service became the most common form of employment for women (replacing agriculture), when the women employed became predominantly black rather than coloured, and when the material living standards associated with the occupation declined sharply compared to other forms of employment.[56]

Certainly, some domestics like Thistlewood's Phibbah, and Old Doll of the Newton Estate in Barbados had high status.[57] Indeed, those categorized within the slavery culture as 'slave housekeepers' were part of an elite within the plantation household. Along with other mixed-race female domestics, they were sometimes able to negotiate freedom. Still, the percentage of those who either paid for or received gratuitous manumission was never high.

On smaller units this strict occupational differentiation between house/domestics and field slaves could not always be strictly maintained and slaves shifted from one to the other as the need arose.

Independent Production: The Economy of the Enslaved

As Douglas Hall, Sidney Mintz, Dale Tomich and others have argued, quite convincingly, during slavery, enslaved Africans and other racially marginalized groups, demanded room for themselves. Various strategies were used by the enslaved to carve out an economic niche for themselves within the confines of slavery. Tomich notes that while a large part of the enslaveds' existence entailed the appropriation of their labour time on the part of their enslavers (for the owner's economy pre-dominated), the exploitation entailed in the appropriation of the slaves' labour provides only the barest outlines of the lives they lived. The work of the enslaved was divided into what was done for the enslaver and what was done for themselves. Slave systems thus involved two inter-related economies: the production of export commodities for the enslavers and the independent production of the enslaveds' for themselves.[58]

The enslaved pursued the right to be autonomous economic agents, as part of the legitimate use of their 'leisure' time, in various ways. Like the workers on sugar estates, those on pens marketed crops from their provision grounds. There is also some evidence to suggest that where they kept cattle, poultry and hogs, this was done less for their own nutritional needs and more for their monetary and exchange value. The enslaved on Vineyard Pen, for example, exchanged pork for rum. Some sugar estate and pen personnel also bought pork from their enslaved workers for their white staff instead of buying the more expensive fresh beef. Mt Plenty Pen, for example, regularly purchased fresh pork from the slaves for the white staff.[59] Where fresh fish was available to the enslaved, this was also sold. Williams records, for example, that where, as on Mr Matthews's pen, the enslaved had a superabundance of fish, they sold the product rather than consume it. According to him, 'some they hung to dry, some they salted. These were then taken into the interior and exchanged for jerked hog'.[60]

As in recent years, archaelogical evidence points to a fairly high degree of meat consumption by Jamaican enslaved workers, it would not be inaccurate to state that the enslaved on pens marketed their surplus meat and provisions rather than deprive themselves totally of their benefits. The culture of marketing emerged among Africans as a common expression, and material and social conditions on the plantations as well as in the towns made it particularly attractive. Marketing allowed those enslaved to improve the quality and quantity of their diets in a context of general malnutrition, to own and possess property in a system that also defined them as property, and offered them time to travel, and to attempt to 'normalize' their social lives as much as possible under generally restrictive circumstances. These benefits, however, had to be militantly pursued, as Mary Turner demonstrates; and it is here that women in particular displayed great tenacity. Marketing symbolized a spirit of independence and was central to the process of non-violent protest and resistance, which characterized day-to-day anti-slavery behaviour.[61]

The enslaved people on pens had greater opportunities to participate in the informal economy than those on sugar estates. In Jamaica, for example, where the 1792 Consolidated Slave Act provided that each proprietor was to provide provision grounds for the enslaved in the ratio of one acre for every ten of them, it appears that the Act was more nearly put into practice on pens than on sugar estates. In addition to these individual plots, enslavers were required to set aside and have planted on each property at least one acre of land for every ten enslaved 'which lands should be kept up in a planter like condition, under the penalty of fifty pounds'. Clause 3 of the Act stipulated that where properties had no lands suitable for provision grounds, alternative provisions for food should be made to the value of 2s. 6d. per week per enslaved worker.[62] In addition to the allocation of provision grounds, the pens themselves set aside land for the cultivation of food for the labourers. This was to offset any deficiency in the efforts of the enslaved. Thistlewood noted in 1751 that 'Vineyard Pen's plantain walk has 1,800 trees and I imagine the negroes in their ground, new and old, may have as many'.[63] A return of the number of acres of compulsory provision grounds kept by estates and pens sent in to the Jamaican Assembly in the late eighteenth century reveals that, at least on paper, adequate land was, in fact, set aside. The returns from St David's pens, for example, reveal that on Monkland's Pen, 30 acres were planted in plantains, four acres in yams and cocos, and 15 acres in corn.[64] On Cow Bay Park

Pen, which in 1790 had 106 enslaved people, 100 acres were said to be allocated to 'negro grounds'.[65] In addition to ground provisions, pen labourers kept gardens in which they grew a variety of vegetables and fruits. They also kept poultry, hogs and some, even cattle. Where they lived near to ponds, rivers or the sea, fish supplemented their diet. On his visit to Mr. Matthews's pen in St Ann, Cynric Williams observed that 'the Negroes here are allowed to have as many hogs as they please, a privilege they cannot enjoy on sugar estates, where the canes would tempt them into destruction'.[66] Matthews's enslaved workers were also well supplied with fresh fish because of the pen's proximity to the sea. Fishing was reportedly done in the early morning and after the pen-keeper selected the supply for his family, 'the negroes came in a body and took away as much fish as they pleased, not less than a bushel a piece, and yet left many on the shore'.[67]

The comparatively smaller size of the pens meant that enslaved workers on pens travelled less distance to reach their grounds. Furthermore, the work day on pens was probably shorter than on the sugar estates, except during periods when women had to shell corn to make flour. Finally, as much of the labour on pens was not done in gangs, those enslaved on pens no doubt had more time to attend to their grounds, and consequently more opportunity to grow their own food. They also seemed to have had a wider range of possibilities to earn money in exchange for their labour and to keep their own animals. Of course, men on pens had more stock than the women as the keeping of large stock seemed to have been a privilege for the Black, usually male, driver. By 1837, for example, Whitehall Ellis of Farm Pen in St Catherine had 20 head of cattle, 70 sheep and lived in a large comfortable house.[68] There were other ways to earn money. On Vineyard Pen, Phibbah earned six bitts for each shirt and two bitts for each pair of trousers she sewed. She received one bitt for each garment mended. On Breadnut Island Pen, Phibbah earned enough cash to be able to lend Thistlewood £9.15.0 in May 1768 and £2.7.6 in June of the same year. She used money earned and saved to acquire land and livestock. Enslaved men on pens had even greater opportunities to earn extra cash.[69] 'Raceboys' and other enslaved men who accompanied their owners to the races were given money with which to bet on the horses, although their degree of success is unknown. Enslaved men who drove animals to and from estate markets were also given small financial rewards or incentives as planters and pen-keepers tried to ensure the good treatment of livestock.

In addition to what they obtained from their provision grounds and other supplementary means, the enslaved on pens were issued with rations of salted cod, pickled herrings, shad, pilchards and mackerel. These supplies were imported twice yearly and issued on a weekly or daily basis.[70] On Vineyard Pen, both methods were employed. While Thistlewood's usual practice was to issue rations each Sunday, he sometimes (and especially to 'new negroes') issued rations daily. Each enslaved worker obtained six herrings weekly. Those newly imported obtained quantities of flour in addition.[71] Enslaved workers on the pens received other items of food. Salt beef and salt pork were issued infrequently. These items were imported primarily for the Europeans. Had they been intended for the enslaved, they would have been imported in much larger quantities. The Accounts Current show that whereas some pens imported up to 1,800 pounds of codfish annually, in addition to several barrels of herrings and mackerel, only a couple barrels of beef and pork were brought in.

7

CONTESTING SLAVERY:
NEGOTIATIONS FOR FREEDOM IN A SLAVE SYSTEM

According to Franklin Knight, 'without African slaves and the transatlantic slave trade, the potential economic value of the Americas could never have been realized'.[1] Yet, despite the dependence of the North Atlantic on the South Atlantic for labour and commodities, the cultural experiences and interaction of Africans and Europeans did not determine the creation of a Creole vision that ultimately became the symbol of an Atlantic identity. On the contrary, deep division, inequality and instability characterized the 'Atlantic World.' One reason for the instability was that inhabitants of the Atlantic World were not all committed to the same ideals. Obviously those who coined the term 'Atlantic World' did so because they discerned common threads that seemed to have given a recognizable pattern and sense of community to the civilizations that developed and maintained intercontinental interconnections. As professor of history, City University of New York (CUNY), Michael Kraus, observed in, arguably, one of the earliest works to conceptualize what he termed at the time the 'Atlantic Civilization', 'out of the play of influences crossing the sea westward and eastward emerged a sense of community sufficiently distinctive to be called the Atlantic Civilization'. This 'civilization', he said, embraced 'the whole Western Hemisphere and much of Europe (and even African Negro culture)'.[2] The connections began in the age of modernity; for it was European colonialism and imperialism that ensured the transfer of metropolitan cultures to the South Atlantic zone. The linkages facilitated by colonialism, imperialism, trade, slavery and migration also facilitated the transfer and exchange of political systems, ideologies, religions, mentalities and social culture. Despite differences of location, imperial economic and political zone, origin, class, ethnicity, colour and status (bonded vs. free), common ideologies, loyalties and institutions developed in various parts of the Atlantic World.

But critics maintain that very little apart from transnational trade and finance and perhaps common imperial relationships and experiences held this world together — albeit loosely. There was no such designation as an 'Atlantic World citizen'; for each imperial power tried to carve out its own sphere of influence — to which not even its inhabitants were loyal. As early as 1957, Kraus had admitted that 'the areas most vigorously committed to [the] ideals [of the Atlantic World] are North America and western Europe', implying that the South Atlantic civilization was less committed to North Atlantic ideals.

Walter Rodney has also interrogated the conceptual foundation of the Atlantic World showing that there was no egalitarianism among its constituent parts; that Europe became the dominant section of the worldwide trading system and that the result of this was development in the core and underdevelopment in the periphery. Development and underdevelopment, he argued, are not only comparative terms but also have a dialectical relationship as the two help to produce the other through interaction. Western Europe and Africa, for example, while notionally a part of the Atlantic civilization in the age of modernity, 'had a relationship that ensured the transfer of wealth from Africa to Europe'.[3] The European segment of the Atlantic World formed only shifting alliances in times of war, whether against each other or against the exploited segment of the Atlantic World; and those who formed the contested Black Atlantic,[4] the argument goes, developed not only a different identity from the 'White Atlantic', but evolved an early sense of pan-Africanism and a revolutionary ideology that saw them supporting liberation struggles in the North and South Atlantic systems that contributed further to the destabilization of the Atlantic World.

The basis of this inequality and instability of what could, borrowing Benedict Anderson's formulation, be termed an 'imagined community',[5] were numerous and have been investigated by several scholars apart from Rodney. Eric Williams, author of the path-breaking *Capitalism and Slavery*, (and later supported by C.L.R James), argued that capital from the Caribbean periphery developed Europe; and George Beckford, who in *Persistent Poverty*, fingered that instrument of economic and political colonization, the plantation system, as a prime cause of Caribbean underdevelopment as it expropriated the resources of colonies, transferred wealth from the periphery to the core, and privileged the export production of staple commodities over the development of a domestic economy and intra-regional trade.[6]

Other factors apart from the exploitation of Africa and the Caribbean and the existence of slave relations of production in the Americas, were that there existed dominant/subordinate relations between the (essentially white) North and the (essentially black) South Atlantic systems; that racism, ethnocentrism, the denial of rights to non-Whites in European colonies in the Americas and Africa, and the tyranny of the 'pigmentocracy' that emerged in colonial settings were all potentially divisive.

The implications of the situation in which enslaved people were not incorporated into the Atlantic World as citizens with equal rights, but as chattel enslaved and as the inferior 'Other' were clear in Jamaica. There, as in other slave systems, the anti-slavery struggles (and later decolonization movement) — the battle for actual and metaphorical space — would illustrate the lack of consensus even within discrete economic zones like the British Empire.

The Same Passion for Freedom

In a 1995 article, David Blight, using the autobiography of Frederick Douglass, emphasized the complex nature of the world inhabited by the enslaved, showing how slavery and the response of enslaved people to their bonded status could vary even within the same geographical location.[7] The multi-dimensionality of enslaved people's work culture and their response to their enslavement was demonstrated with great clarity in Jamaica where the island's diversified economy facilitated the existence of slavery in different contexts — under the rigid regime of the sugar plantation, as well as under alternative regimes on non-sugar properties. But the history of Jamaica also demonstrates that from the inception of the slave mode of production, whether on sugar estates or on non-sugar properties, resistance to enslavement and the development of anti-slavery politics were endemic.

Slavery was the antithesis of freedom; therefore, the enslaved in Jamaica as elsewhere, launched an opposing struggle for liberation. Regardless of their location, enslaved men and women struggled to reclaim their natural right to liberty and to create the intellectual basis of the culture of resistance. This was the ultimate contest over terrain and social space that only ended with full legal freedom for enslaved people in the British-colonized Caribbean in 1838.

Therefore, at the same time that pen-keepers were seeking to carve out an economic niche for themselves and contesting the dominance of the sugar barons, their enslaved workers, essential to their economic and social project, were themselves engaged in struggles for freedom with enslaver pen-keepers. Of course, they were by no means willing collaborators in the pen-keepers' socioeconomic and political project and had the same aspirations for freedom as their counterparts on sugar estates. Furthermore, control was not designed to favour them over the enslaved on sugar estates, even though their work regime might have been less regimented.

Control and Supervision

The resistance of enslaved peoples in Jamaica occurred despite the control mechanisms instituted by the enslavers. These control mechanisms were legal, economic, social, political and psychological. They also included 'sexploitation'. Thomas Thistlewood's sexual abuse of enslaved women both on pens and plantations demonstrates that pro-slavery ideology was entrenched despite the economic context of slavery and that neither punishment strategies nor resistance were confined to the sugar estates where there was a brutalizing work and social regime. Thistlewood's and Robert Wedderburn's accounts indicate that while domestic women were open to the most frequent sexual abuse, field women were not immune. 'Housewomen' were however, particularly vulnerable, some being kept as 'mistresses'. Wedderburn underscores the abuse of enslaved domestic women owned by his father, the Jamaican planter, James Wedderburn, in the following way:

> My father's house was full of female slaves, all objects of his lust; amongst whom he Strutted like Solomon in his grand seraglio or like a bantam cock upon his own dunghill.... By him my mother [Rossanna] was made the object of his brutal lust .... My father

147

ranged through the whole of his household for his own lewd purposes; for they being his personal property, cost nothing extra [for sexual favors]....In short, among his own slaves my father was a perfect parish bull; and his pleasure was the greater, because he at the same time increased his profits [when enslaved women became pregnant].[8]

He also confirmed the practice of organized prostitution, noting that: 'a planter letting out his prettiest female slaves for purposes of lust, is by no means uncommon'.[9]

Thomas Thistlewood, who came to Jamaica in 1750 from Tupholme, Lincolnshire, England at 29 years old and who died in 1786, kept a detailed journal which reveals his activities in the island. It is clear that he accepted the social stratification and the system of European dominance in a slave society. He also accepted that the use of force was the way to control the slave societies; and was not at all averse to perpetrating the use of brutal force on enslaved male and female alike. He was very quick to understand the customs in Jamaica with respect to the sexual behaviour of Europeans with enslaved women. Thistlewood did not make many explicit negative statements about the physical character and attributes of women. He did on occasion comment that some enslaved women were incorrigible liars and he did claim that enslaved women were sensual. Nevertheless, his physical and sexual abuse of enslaved women leaves no doubt about his attitude towards them. He learnt from very early after his arrival that living openly with enslaved women or free mixed-race women brought no social condemnation; in fact it was acceptable behaviour. Thistlewood, like most other European men in Caribbean slave society, seemed to have believed that one advantage of coming to Jamaica was the chance of sexually exploiting African women. While working for Mr Vassell on Vineyard Pen in Westmoreland and Mr Cope on Egypt plantation, he sexually abused practically every enslaved female. His sexual contact expanded from five enslaved women (Marina, Juba, Betty, Hago, Sylvia) in 1750, to 11 enslaved women by 1751. In his first six months at Vineyard Pen, he slept with these enslaved women on a total of 20 different occasions. At Vineyard Pen from 1750–51, he had 42 sexual encounters with Marina who seems to have been his regular bedmate in the first part of 1750 before his attentions to Chrissey and Hago with whom he had 80 sexual encounters during 1750–55. In his first year at Egypt Sugar Plantation, he slept with 11 women on 53 occasions. By 1760 he had a steady relationship with Phibbah (but did not remain faithful to her). When he established his own property, Breadnut Island Pen in 1768, he continued with this habit.

Thistlewood abused enslaved women anywhere he pleased, even interrupting their work. For example:

'cum Flora in the canes(sept. 10, 1751). She had been going to collect water cress by the stream on the estate.'
'Sept. 11, 1751: in the early morning, cum negro in the east parlor on the floor at north bed foot'.

His Latin phrases give an indication of where he had the women and girls:

sup lect = on the bed
sup terr = on the floor
in silva = in the woods
in mag dom = in the great house
in parv dom = in the small house

When his encounters did not please him, he noted: 'sed non bene' (but not well). He only became less sexually active in 1786 when he was quite ill. He died in that year. In his edited work on the journals, Douglas Hall reveals that Thistlewood made the following entries: 'January, 5 times (twice with Phibbah, twice with Bess and once with Phoebe). In Feby. not at all. In March twice (Peggy and Phibbah). Now in April twice with Phibbah and Phoebe'.[10]

Like most overseers, Thistlewood kept an enslaved woman, Phibbah, as his concubine, but showed no loyalty at all to her in terms of his sexual behaviour, having had sexual relations with 9 of the 16 enslaved females on his own property, Breadnut Island Pen.[11] He also evinced no interest in marriage. In fact, few single European men in the Caribbean saw the need to marry, preferring to sexually exploit enslaved women. In response to his brother's query about his marital status, Stephen Harmer, overseer on Old Hope pen, said: 'Now the candid truth is that I have got no wife and have never been married. It is not the fashion for overseers to be married in this country except over the broomstick'.[12] Harmer, however, had four children by an enslaved woman. These enslaved 'partners' were euphemistically called 'housekeepers' in the Caribbean. As M'Mahon explained in *Jamaica Plantership*, 'the overseers in Jamaica usually kept one particular mistress called by themselves housekeepers but by the laborers their wives'. He further added that these 'housekeepers were expected to yield to the sexual demands of these overseers'.[13]

The attitudes and behaviour of Thomas Thistlewood and Stephen Harmer were consistent with the belief in European superiority and African inferiority, demonstrated in the physical abuse of the African male and the physical and sexual abuse of African women. 'Sexploitation' indicated that control was often gender specific. Such exploitation and sexual abuse, collapsed into the term (s)exploitation, must have added impetus to resistance, which was manifested in a variety of ways, some equally gender-specific.[14]

Historians indicate that the supervision of the enslaved on pens appeared to have been less rigid than on sugar estates. On sugar estates, the attorney and overseer system made for close oversight of all tasks. On modest-sized pens in Jamaica, with their resident owners, smaller British populations, and closer relationships between the resident owner and the enslaved, supervision tended to be less rigid and close.[15]

In the end though, the material conditions and varied demographic profiles of those enslaved and the rigid or lax control to which they were subjected had very little impact on their passion to resist. Indeed, as Craton remarked, resistance was just as likely to result from indulgence and rising expectations as from brutalizing treatment. Comparative data from properties in the Southern United States where the enslaved lived in small communities in close contact with owners reveal that most revolts occurred in areas of diversified agriculture where the slave regime was 'more indulgent' than in the plantations of the 'Cotton Kingdom'.[16]

Rather than viewing pens as oases of social stability, sugar planters and legislators regarded them as 'storm centers of radical ideas, racial mixing and rapid change' and tried to isolate enslaved people from them.[17] They could not, of course, prevent the mixing of slaves from different units. Pens and estates often shared boundaries; and as adjuncts of the sugar economy, as chapter three demonstrated, pens were essential for the supply of goods and services vital to the sugar estates. This necessitated frequent contacts between pen and estate and their enslaved workers often formed close social ties. Enslaved pen-workers who were involved in jobbing and in the marketing of the produce of the farms had a greater degree of mobility than those enslaved on estates. They could, indeed, have used the legitimate movements allowed them by marketing tasks to plan or spearhead revolts.

The main focus of Caribbean resistance studies now, however, is not on whether enslaved people were contented or discontented with their lot, but on how they resisted. The specific evidence relating to the response of the enslaved on pens to their servile conditions is fragmentary. They left few records of their intentions and traditional works have generalized about resistance, showing little or no property differentiation. From the few surviving accounts, though, (mainly court records, newspaper reports and the journals of Thomas Thistlewood), it is clear that the enslaved on pens employed a variety of means to subvert the system of slavery, overthrow it, facilitate their own escape from it through marronage or manumission, sabotage it or regularize their conditions within it. They used these resistant strategies independently or in collusion with others (at times with those from sugar estates).

The majority of the enslaved did not resort to armed revolt but negotiated their daily lives under slavery in various ways, including pressing for greater economic autonomy and day-to-day strategies of non-violent resistance. For others, freedom was purchased or gratuitously conferred. The routes to freedom were usually pursued at high personal costs to the enslaved, judging by the level of punishment meted out to the 'transgressors'; for enslavers hardly heeded James Grainger's cautionary note that in the punishment of the enslaved 'leniency should always temper justice'.[18]

Routes to Freedom: Negotiation for Economic Autonomy and Manumission

One response to slavery by those enslaved on pens was to participate in the informal economy and seek to maintain customary rights and privileges under slavery. A previous chapter has already shown that to reduce their cost of production and their expenditure on imported food, enslavers in the Americas shifted part of the burden of enslaved people provisioning onto the shoulders of the enslaved themselves. Neither plantations nor pens relied on the ration system exclusively. The 1792 Consolidated Slave Act that provided that each proprietor allowed the enslaved person access to provision grounds appears, in fact, to have been more closely put into practice on pens than on sugar estates. The comparatively smaller size of the pens meant that those enslaved on a pen travelled shorter distances to reach their grounds. Furthermore, the work day on pens was shorter than on the estates — at least for men. Finally, as much of the labour on pens was not done in gangs, the enslaved on pens no doubt had more time to attend to their grounds, and consequently more opportunity to grow their own food. The enslaved rigorously guarded their access to provision grounds and resisted all attempts to reduce time for their informal economic activities and marketing. Wise enslavers allowed the enslaved people to engage in their own economic activities to improve their conditions under slavery and stem the tide of violent revolts.

The enslaved used the money they accumulated from their independent activities in a number of ways. While some no doubt contributed to their churches, others purchased their freedom, improved their diet, bought property and fineries that served to improve their status among their fellow enslaved.

The extent to which those enslaved on pens battled with their owners for social space through negotiating a price for their freedom cannot be definitively ascertained from the manumission records. These records, which begin in 1747, though tantalizing, are of limited value to the researcher of pens. This is because, except for the Apprenticeship period, these records do not distinguish between those enslaved on pens and those enslaved on other units.[19] There is no reason to doubt, though, that those enslaved on pens, like those on sugar estates, bought their freedom from accumulated savings, despite the high prices set by the enslavers. The numbers could not have been high, though; freedom was contested terrain and the enslavers did not surrender this terrain that they dominated easily nor willingly.

Gratuitous manumission was also conferred. Some pen-keepers' wills indicate that in some cases, provisions were made for the freeing of 'special slaves' after their owners' death. These wishes were not always followed. When Gilbert Caddell died, he left instructions that two of his 'brown children' employed on Bushy Park Pen should be manumitted if Mitchell, the owner of the pen, did not object. The attorney objected strongly, expressing the opinion that 'for my own part I do think that these children are much better where they are now as there is no provision made for them after their freedom is obtained'.[20] He went on to comment that poverty always accompanied such methods of freedom, 'and as an instance of the poverty that often follows freedom the woman named Bessy that you manumized some years back from Phoenix Park Pen, and her Sambo son lately manumized, and a negro put in his room, would with much pleasure return to your service'.[21]

Arguably, the best account of the manumission on pens is provided by the records of Unity Valley Pen, St Ann. In 1795, all the enslaved people on that property were freed, an action which was totally frowned upon in the island at that time.[22] The proprietor, David Barclay, gave as his reason the fact that

> much dissatisfied in being a slave owner, I determined to try the experiment of liberating my slaves; firmly convinced, that the retaining of my fellow creatures in bondage was not only irreconcilable with the precepts of christianity, but subversive of the rights of human nature.[23]

Having arrived at this decision, David Barclay communicated his intention to his agent, Alexander McLeod of Spanish Town, who, though he applauded the principle, declined to 'execute a measure which would be very unpopular in the island.'[24] He consented to freeing only two of those enslaved whom he thought most likely to be able to provide for themselves by working on the pen and receiving wages at the rate of £17 per annum with certain 'fringe benefits'.[25] Accordingly, he manumitted a man named Hamlet who was 30 years old, and an enslaved female, Prudence, of the same age. After a year of freedom, however, McLeod accused these freed workers of having 'relaxed in their labour', and, consequently, dismissed them. He believed that their example would be 'very disadvantageous to the owners of the estate'.[26] McLeod agreed to give the two freed people £3 11s. sterling per annum for life (£5 Jamaican currency) 'agreeable to the existing law of the island upon the emancipation of a slave'. Hamlet subsequently set himself up in business as a horse-breeder and Prudence as a laundress 'in which occupations they maintained themselves with good reputation'.[27]

When his brother, John, died, however, David Barclay, who inherited the whole property, decided to free the remaining enslaved population and remove them to Philadelphia in the United States of America. For this purpose, he engaged William Holden to proceed to Jamaica and carry out his orders. Holden was to deliver the labourers to John Ashley, Barclay's agent in Philadelphia, who would turn the newly emancipated over to the care of The Society for Improving the Conditions of Free Blacks.

Holden arrived in Jamaica in March 1795 to carry out Barclay's wishes. He was accompanied to Unity Valley by McLeod. On arrival, they ordered all the enslaved people to assemble for inspection. Holden, after inspecting them, explained to them the purpose of his visit. Apart from two he felt too old and infirm to make the journey, he provided all the others with clothes and provisions, and, 'upon the strength of their unanimous consent to accept the offer of freedom I engaged a vessel to convey them to Philadelphia'.[28] Arrangements were then made to convey the enslaved workers to Kingston from where they would embark for Philadelphia. On arrival in Kingston, however, the Africans refused to embark, saying they had changed their minds. One of their numbers, John, described as 'one of the most sensible and intelligent', managed to persuade the others to get on the ship, which eventually sailed for Philadelphia, arriving there July 22, 1795.

In Philadelphia, the Africans and African-Jamaicans were at first temporarily accommodated in a meeting house procured from the African Methodists. They were afterwards put in the care of the 'Committee of the Pennsylvania Abolition Society for Improving the Conditions of Free Blacks'.[29] The members of this Committee arranged for the children to be sent to school and for the adults to be apprenticed to various members of the Society. The social status of these formerly enslaved people in the United States of America was no different from that of their counterparts in Jamaica after their eventual emancipation. Like the latter, those in Philadelphia also served a period of apprenticeship. Both groups earned minimal wages during this period. Though provision was made for their education in Philadelphia, the understanding was 'that they be taught mechanic trades in preference to any other business'.[30] Those bonded to members of the Abolition Society were also taught servile trades — carpentry, nailing, chair-making or domestic service.[31] Africans in Jamaica and enslaved people transported to the United States of America eventually settled into a society warped by the evils of racism.

The experiences of those freed did not deter others from trying every means possible to win their freedom. Day-to-day-resistance and armed revolt were two strategies employed.

Day-to-Day Resistance: Evidence from the Thistlewood Journals

Surviving evidence [mostly from the daily journals of Thomas Thistlewood], indicates the wide range of day-to-day strategies adopted by the enslaved peoples on pens to undermine the system of slavery. When he was overseer on Vineyard Pen from 1750–51, Thistlewood recorded that the enslaved stole animals, ran away, malingered, lied, feigned illness, deliberately opened old sores and destroyed or abused property (particularly animals). He seemed particularly disturbed about the extent to which the enslaved on Vineyard Pen stole goods, at times as part of the activities of runaways, and described them as 'a nest of thieves and villains'.[32] Thistlewood also recorded the ways in which those enslaved were punished for acts of resistance, some of which were deemed 'crime'. On Vineyard and Breadnut Island pens, those enslaved were punished severely by whipping, having faeces rubbed over their faces or put in their mouths, denied privileges, were put 'in the bilboes' and in chains and collars. What could be considered rape was also used as punishment.

The abuse and stealing of animals was a common means of sabotage used by those enslaved who worked closely with animals. In the Old South, Eugene Genovese claims that:

> slaves seem to have taken the greatest delight in abusing the horses, oxen and mules that were so essential to the day-to-day work of the plantations. If the hogs were not attended to, pork could be purchased but there was no substitute for work animals.[33]

As the enslaved on pens worked more closely with animals than those on sugar plantations, this act of resistance was predictably quite marked. Thomas Thistlewood constantly punished enslaved men for abusing horses and cattle and enslaved women for losing small stock. He punished Old Sambo when he brought him 'the bones of a missing goat, pretending that he found them in a hole'.[34] Thistlewood did not believe Old Sambo's story, but 'as there was no certain proof to me what was become of the flesh, had him given 100 lashes to make him more careful for the pasture'.[35] Cuffee and Joe were whipped for 'catching the old horse and keeping him tied up all day.'[36] Mimba and her children on Vineyard Pen, whose job was to watch small stock, were punished for neglecting the animals and for losing an ewe. Mimba received 50 lashes. At a trial held in St Elizabeth in 1815, Prosper from Hounslow Pen was sentenced to two months in gaol for 'stealing and killing a bull ... and for having upwards of 20 lbs. of beef in his possession.'[37] He received 39 lashes on first going to prison and was to get another 39 on his release.[38] Three men from Haughton Pen were tried for stealing goats but were acquitted.[39] Despite the severe punishment attached, it appears as if horse stealing was common among the enslaved men on pens.

Stealing, lying and malingering were also strategies of day-to-day resistance. Thomas Thistlewood tied up Mimba and gave her 50 lashes for stealing corns; he beat Titus for allowing the runaway, Robin, to raid the storehouse on Vineyard Pen. Mimba, Juba, Cynthia, Jenny and Deborah were all punished for theft of pen supplies. Juba was whipped for both these 'crimes' and was described by Thistlewood as an 'incorrigible liar ... there is no taking any notice of what she says'.[40] Malingering was a common strategy of resistance and the enslaved people were punished accordingly. Old Titus received 50 lashes for malingering on another occasion.[41] On April 8, 1751, he gave Scipio 50 lashes for 'delaying his time coming home from Westmoreland'.[42]

Thistlewood also punished those whom he accused of laziness and negligence. For example, he recorded that Dick, a mulatto boy was tied to an orange tree in the garden and 'whipped to some purpose' (300 lashes) for 'his many crimes and naughtiness'. He was so severely beaten that he could not report for work until nine days later.[43]

As table 7.1 indicates, marronage was a constant plague for Thistlewood. The enslaved people seemed to have engaged more in small scale and temporary marronage rather than permanent flight. This may have been explained by the existence of the British Treaty with the Maroons made in 1739. One of the provisions of the Treaty was that Maroons should return runaways. Whether they always did or not, cannot be proven with certainty. 'Incorrigible' runaways, on Vineyard Pen included Robin, Bank, Charles, Chelsea, George, Joan, Juba, Simon, Sussex and Old Titus. The punishment for marronage (depending on the length of absence) ranged from whipping

Table 7.1
Summary of Runaways, Vineyard Pen

Runaways	Occupation	Time Away	Month	How Taken	Why	Punishment
Bank	Pen-keeper	2 days	July	VR	n/s	Sent from estate
Charles	Courier	4 days	October	C	n/s	100 lashes/field
Chelsea	Cattleboy	½ day	October	VR	n/s	whipped
George	Cattleboy	2 days	October	C	n/s	Confined
		1 day	October	C	n/s	100 lashes
		1 day	October	C	n/s	n/s
		1 day	November	C	n/s	n/s
		2 days	November	C	n/s	Sent from estate
Joan	Washerwoman	2 weeks	August	VR	n/s	Sent from estate
Juba	House	1 day	November	VR	n/s	Whipped/field
Robin	Cattleboy	1 month+	June/July	C	n/s	Sent from estate
Simon	Pen-keeper	7 days	March	VR	Guilty of?	n/s
Sussex	House/field	2 days	March	C	Lame	Field
		1 week+	April	C	Lame	Whipped
		"long"	May	C	n/s	n/s
Titus	Odd jobs man	1 month	August	VR	"Tomasse"?	n/s

VR = voluntary return; C = 'taken up'; n/s = not stated/suggested
Source: D.G. Hall, 'Runaways in Jamaica in the Mid-eighteenth Century: One Man's Record', (Post-graduate Seminar Paper, Department of History, Mona, 1984), 42.

and confinement, to being sent away from the estate (sale or transportation) out of the island. Whipping of from 50–300 lashes was usual for absences of a few days or months; where runaways stayed away for six months or over, necessitating advertisements in the press, punishment was more severe. Such marronage was interpreted as political resistance, an attempt to undermine the productivity of the property. George, whom he gave 100 lashes for some misdemeanour and who he sent back to work almost immediately, ran away shortly after. He was said to have returned and raided the pen. Charles also ran away; and after he had accused Juba of lying and had severely whipped her, she also ran away. Other enslaved on the pen obviously collaborated with the runaways.[44]

George and Gubby of Cornwall Pen were transported out of the island for life for marronage in 1809 and 1810 respectively. A similar fate befell Oxford of Friendship Pen in St Elizabeth in 1815. Female runaways seemed not to have been transported to the same degree. They were whipped and imprisoned for three months or more, depending on the time away.[45]

When Thistlewood established his own property of 144 acres in 1767, the 27 enslaved men and women behaved in much the same way as those he had supervised on Vineyard Pen. As on other properties, he recorded that they stole, deliberately walked through his corn piece, ill-treated the animals, malingered, loitered, lied, stole, engaged in marronage, and were generally lazy and negligent. He used various forms of punishment to keep those enslaved on Breadnut Island Pen in line, including flogging, branding, putting them in chains, collars and in the 'bilboes'. In early January 1768, he flogged the fisherman Chub for 'neglect and roguery'.[46] In the same month, he recorded that he 'flogged ... field negroes for laziness'.[47] Cudjoe, Nanny and Coobah were flogged for 'misdemeanours'.[48] Sally, who seemed to have put up great resistance to his constant insistence on sex, ran away frequently. He punished her severely each time she returned. On August 22, 1768 he 'put a collar and chain about Sally's neck; also branded her TT on her right cheek'.[49] Resistance continued into the 1770s. In 1770, several enslaved people were punished for marronage and day-to-day acts of resistance. Coobah ran away frequently and each time she was caught and returned, she was severely punished. She was also accused of malingering and (like another field women, Franke), feigning illness to escape field labour. Between 1770 and 1774, when she was sold, she ran away four times.[50] She was flogged, branded in her face, chained and collared, and even had faeces rubbed over her face. In September 1774, he 'flogged Solon for neglect in bringing fish'.[51] He also flogged Solon for leaving the canoe so that other enslaved people could steal it; and for running away, supposedly to escape the punishment meted out to him for his various offences. Thistlewood also recorded that enslaved females deliberately tried to abort their pregnancies by drinking various herbs. Even if some of these actions on the part of the enslaved fall into the category of non-violent non-resistance in Sidney Mintz's model,[52] their frequency and the punishment they attracted are indications that they had the result of inconveniencing the pen-keeper and undermining the order and efficiency of production on the pen. Some of these acts were deliberate acts on the part of the enslaved and must be deemed resistance.

Armed Revolt

The enslaved on pens also participated in armed revolt though the evidence of their participation is more abundant for the nineteenth century than for earlier centuries. They were involved, for example in the 1824 plan of rebellion made in the parish of Hanover in the western end of the island. In June 1824 the planters in that parish reported that they had discovered rebellious conspiracy of 'a very alarming nature' involving the enslaved on the parish's sugar estates as well as on Argyle, Ramble, Burnt Ground, Silver Grove and Knockalva pens.[53] The plan had been for the enslaved to set fire to the properties in the parish and to kill any British people who attempted to put out the blaze. William Roach of Argyle Pen allegedly revealed the plot and prevented the revolt. Those implicated as leaders were hanged.[54]

Those enslaved on pens also played an active role in the 1831/32 emancipation war. This war, variously known in Caribbean history as the 'Christmas Rebellion', the 'Baptist War' or the 'Sam Sharpe Rebellion', was significant as it represented the last of a long period of enslaved workers' opposition to the oppressive and repressive system of slavery in Jamaica. Enslaved radicalism was immanent on plantations, pens, other rural properties and urban locations in the British-colonized Caribbean from the inception of the slave mode of production in the seventeenth century to the abolition of slavery in 1834. The magnitude of the 1831/32 war in Jamaica was reflected in the petitions and speeches of several inhabitants of the island at the time. For example, a petition of 'certain magistrates, &c of St. George's' presented to the Jamaica House of Assembly in 1832 described the war as one 'unparalleled in the history of the colony, whether for depth of design or the extent of misery and ruin which it has entailed on the inhabitants'.[55] Indeed, it was one of the two great enslaved-led wars that occurred in the Caribbean in the eighteenth and nineteenth centuries; the other was the Saint Domingue revolt of 1791 that led to the overthrow of the plantation system and the subsequent independence of Haiti in 1804.

The significance of such anti-slavery activism in ending the system of slavery is now widely acknowledged within the historiography. From the perspective of most scholars of resistance studies, the enslaved people played a fundamental role in effecting their own liberation from the brutal, European-imposed slave system in the Caribbean.[56] Within this context, the 1831/32 emancipation war in Jamaica is regarded as the event that forced the legislative machinery in Britain to call a halt to the system of slavery. The economic damage and social instability caused by the anti-slavery actions of the enslaved, combined with the humanitarian struggle and the impact of the free trade lobby within the context of a declining Caribbean plantation economy and an industrializing Britain, are now acknowledged as powerful factors in the passing of the Emancipation Act by the British government in 1833. The enslaved in Jamaica sent a final signal in 1831/32 that if emancipation would not come from above, it would come from below. The British government responded to this signal.[57]

Therefore, even though some historians like Mary Turner refer to the 1831/32 emancipation war in Jamaica as 'unsuccessful' and a 'failure',[58] perhaps because it did not achieve the specific and short-term objectives of the participants, it can still be said to have achieved some level of success as it had an impact on the economics of slavery in Jamaica and hastened emancipation. With an estimated 1,000 enslaved men and women killed during and after the war, the island lost a large number of valuable labourers. This was at a time when natural increase of the enslaved population was minimal and further importations illegal. With a declining labour force and the threat of more social instability if slavery were not abolished, the war represented a warning to British legislators that they would fail to act at their peril. Linton, an enslaved man involved in the war, had warned from his prison cell in Savanna-la-mar:

> I tell you again, if the gentlemen do not keep a good look out, the Negroes will begin this business in three or four years, for they think the Lord and the King have given them the gift, and because those who were joined in this business [the rebellion] were all sworn.[59]

Several scholars have already devoted their research efforts to the detailed study of the causes, course and consequences of the 1831/32 emancipation war in Jamaica and this chapter does not intend to repeat those ample studies.[60] But briefly, this emancipation war has come to be intimately associated with one of its outstanding leaders, Sam Sharpe. The testimonies of many of those who were tried or who gave evidence at the trial of those identified by the state as ringleaders, confirmed Sharpe's fundamental role, although several also gave prominence to George Taylor and others. The so-called 'confession' of John Davis, imprisoned in the

Savanna-la-mar goal, which was taken down and signed by Samuel Spence, Magistrate and Thomas Stewart, Rector, on February 1, 1832 illustrates:

> I know George Taylor. He lives at Montego-Bay. He is a head ruler. Whatever he sees or hears at Montego-Bay he sends and tells [Robert] Gardiner directly. Gardiner then sends the orders to M'Cail, M'Cail to Morrice, and Morrice to Frederick Gray, and Faithluck, who belongs to Retirement. There is another leader under George Taylor. He belongs to Burnt-Ground. George Taylor set on Gardiner and others to fight for freedom. I heard George Taylor say to Gardiner, "I am the head man; I shall look to you to see you begin in the mountains, and then I shall begin at the Bay". I heard George Taylor, who afterwards came to Greenwich, say there to Angus M'Cail the same thing. Angus M'Cail then came up to our quarter to tell us. The people in our quarter said they would not believe him unless Gardiner, who was the head man under Taylor, came himself and told them. Gardiner then came and told us.
>
> George Guthrie told me to go and ask Gardiner if he had received the canisters of powder and a few arms which daddy Taylor had mustered at Montego-Bay and had sent up. When I asked Gardiner, he told me that the ammunition and arms did not get further than Hazelymph to daddy ruler Tharp, but that it was not much. Daddy ruler Sharp is another great man in this business, but not greater than daddy ruler Taylor.
>
> Daddy ruler Sharp and Taylor, Gardiner, Dove, and all the other head people in the rebellion went to the Baptist church, Montego-Bay, in the Christmas. At the church one of them said they had better put off the war until after Christmas. Daddy Sharp and Taylor said no, and very nearly knocked the man down for so saying. They further said, if we put it off until after Christmas the white people will overcome us; let us do it now before any guards are put on, and then we will get the arms belonging to the different houses and estates easily.[61]

Robert Morris went even further, not assigning any leadership role to

Sharpe at all but fingering George Taylor:

> As I am now certain that I am going to die I am determined that
> those who led me to this shall be known. If I die, George Taylor
> must die also. He is a saddler at Montego-Bay, and belongs to
> Boyd, the saddler there. The white people must send to the
> governor, and immediately lay hold of George Taylor. He is a
> greater man than Gardiner, Dove, and McCail. He recommended
> "the thing," fighting for freedom, and he saw about the arms at
> Montego-Bay. The head of the whole of this bad business began
> from Montego-Bay, and Taylor is the head amongst them. I know,
> and so do all the rest, that he set on Gardiner; Gardiner is under
> him. The white people must at once lay hold of him. James Fray
> can, if he likes, tell about Taylor after I am dead. I declare, as I am
> going to give up my life this day, that what I have just said is
> true.[62]

The 1831 war erupted in the western parish of St James. The main
cause of the outbreak was the enslaved peoples' belief that they were to be
freed at Christmas, 'and that their freedom order had actually come out
from England but was being withheld and that they only had to strike *en
masse*, and they should gain their object'.[63] The enslaved people from the
parishes of Trelawny and St James had apparently agreed that any attempt
to force them back to work after the Christmas holidays was to be met by
setting fire to the properties, (though not their huts or provision grounds).[64]
They had even numbered the properties in the order in which they were
to be burned in this eventuality. Kensington Pen was numbered 'One'.
Blue Hole was number two, and Leogan, number three. This war is thus
important for the history of pens for two reasons. First, it was obviously
the enslaved on pens who gave the signal for the start of the war and
second, pens proved to be important revictualing centres for the roving
bands of rebels. Kensington Pen (referred to as an estate in other published
accounts) [65] was the first to be set on fire as a beacon to other properties to
activate the plans for the war. Its strategic location on an elevation (like
most pens), made it ideal for this important function. After reports were
heard that the enslavers were attempting to break the strike on Salt Spring
Estate, the enslaved man John Dunbar (oral history says an enslaved

woman) set fire to the proprietor's house on Kensington. He (or she) ordered the other enslaved people to plunder the house of all its furniture and shared it among them. Once the fires on Kensington were seen, the enslaved on Leogan and other properties started similar fires. Blue Hole's workers were unable to respond because of the successful defence of the property by the overseer and a small party.[66]

In the days that followed, pen after pen, estate after estate joined the war. The extent of pen involvement only became clear at the trials of enslaved people and the accounts of the war that followed. Although some of those enslaved on pens were reluctant to join the war, others were active leaders and agitators. Richard Trail from Shettlewood Pen, for example, with activists gathered from Ramble, Alexandria and 'nearly the whole of Silver Grove negro men',[67] went to Haughton Pen with a gun and forced those working in the pastures to take the oath of war. This oath, 'to fight against the white people as long as there was one of them left in the country' was executed on a bible which Trail's assistant, Thomas Haughton, headman at Shettlewood Pen, reportedly passed along the lines of those he had mustered. An enslaved man, Daniel Malcolm of Ramble Pen, testified that Trail accompanied Haughton along the line 'with his musket cocked, and swore that if any man refused to take the oath, he would blow his brains out'.[68] A section of Malcolm's deposition given at the trials in March 1832 follows:

> When we were sworn in at Haughton Grove gate pasture, Richard Trail was there from Shettlewood; he had a gun, and said if we did not take the oath he would shoot us; Thomas Haughton, belonging to Shettlewood, was there, and had a large bible, both acted as headmen; Andrew Llewellin, from Silver Grove, was there, and John Martin also, both had guns.[69]

Richard Lewis of Ramble Pen confirmed Malcolm's evidence and Trail's involvement:

> Richard Trail and Thomas Haughton, slaves belonging to Shuttlewood, mustered a large body of negroes by Haughton Grove cattle-pen; a good many negroes form Ramble pen, all men; a great many from Alexandria, all men; nearly the whole of Silver-Grove, negro men; Richard Trail had a gun and Thomas Haughton

a large bible; the negroes were drawn up in a line, which extended from Haughton Grove cattle-pen to the Farm; Thomas Haughton administered an oath to each man on the bible, that they would fight against the white people as long as there was one of them left in the country; Richard Trail accompanied Haughton along the line with his musket cocked, and swore that it any man refused to take the oath he would blow his brains out.[70]

The enslaved male, Bob Peterkin, was said to have led the other enslaved people on Springvale Pen in revolt. Along with Richard Grey, he broke into the proprietor's house, declared themselves the pen-keepers and demanded freedom and a share of the cattle on the pen. Similarly James Bernard of Bandon Pen set fire to the house of the British residents, armed himself and joined the war; and John Dunbar of Kensington was the one said by most accounts, who set the pen-keeper's house alight.[71] He ordered the other enslaved people to plunder the house of all its furniture, which they later shared among themselves.

The activities of some of those enslaved on pens during the course of this war demonstrate how essential these units were for bands of rebels unable to effectively fight while on the run with bulky food items. The activists (and even the British troops for the same reasons) often stopped at pens and used them as revictualling centres. With their large livestock populations, large quantities of provisions and small supervisory populations, pens were, in fact, ideal targets for the slave 'captains' and their 'armies'. Some pen workers had to be forced to provide these food supplies; others willingly slaughtered animals to feed the activists and still others carried provisions to the rebel camps.[72] When in the early stages of the war 'captains' Dehany and Duncan invaded Vaughansfield and Bandon pens respectively, with their bands of followers, some of the enslaved people on those properties stole cattle which they killed and cooked for their sustenance.

In his evidence against James Bernard of Bandon Pen who was said to have been 'captain' of the 'fort' at the pen, an eyewitness stated that it was Bernard who helped to organize dinner for 'Captain' McLennan's party when the latter invaded Bandon. When the enslaved workers had brought the yam 'he said he had nothing fresh and ordered two men to shoot two cows.'[73] The British troops also took over pens as their revictualling centres. In the evidence against Thomas Grey of Springvale Pen in Trelawny, two

Table 7.2
Properties attacked by the Anti-slavery Activists in the 1831/32 Emancipation War in Jamaica

Parish	Properties Destroyed	Pens Destroyed
St. Elizabeth	7	2
Westmoreland	53	11
Hanover	66	14
St. James	161	15
Total	*287	42

*Including wharves, settlements, mountains, residences and ca. 70 sugar estates.
Source: Morris, Cunningham and Woolredge, Map of the ...Properties Destroyed in the Late Rebellion, 1832.

enslaved men confessed that Grey had planned to catch a steer to carry to the rebel camp at Great Hill. Grey later pleaded not guilty, but was nevertheless found guilty and sentenced to two years in the workhouse and 300 lashes. The others mentioned above as ringleaders were all sentenced to death.

When it was over, more than 200 enslaved people [including 13 from 6 of the pens in Hanover and St James] had been killed by the militia.[74] A total of 287 non-pen properties and 42 pens in the parishes of St James, Hanover, Westmoreland and St Elizabeth suffered losses due to arson and the commandeering of provisions and cattle for the troops and activists.[75]

In Hanover alone, 10 pens, 31 settlements and 21 sugar estates suffered damage estimated at £429,922.15.0d. The total losses to the enslavers on pens —Burnt Ground, Prosper, Shettlewood, Coventry, Cacoon Castle, Ramble, Friendship Grove, Knockalva, Brae and Haughton — was estimated at £38,231 (see table 7.3).

Losses of the enslavers in other western parishes were also high. From an incomplete account of the losses sustained by properties in Westmoreland, it is clear that the total exceeded £29,000. Losses in Portland, St Thomas-in-the-East and in-the-Vale were less severe as fewer enslaved people and properties were involved. The state never attempted to compute the losses to enslaved Africans from the destruction of their houses and provision grounds.[76]

Accounts vary, but it has been estimated that close to 1,000 enslaved

Table 7.3
Losses Suffered by Enslavers in Hanover in the 1831/32 Emancipation War

Pen	Losses £
Burnt Ground Pen	9,180
Prosper Pen	1,370
Shettlewood P en	5,186
Coventry Pen	5,300
Cacoon Castle Pen	3,919
Ramble Pen	4,036
Friendship Grove Pen	550
Knockalva Pen	3,040
Brae Pen	4,300
Haughton Grove Pen	1,350
Total	**£38,321**

Source: Jamaica House of Assembly Votes, 1832, Appendix 18, p. 349.

people from nine parishes were tried in Civil (Slave) Courts and Courts Martial in 1832. As far as can be ascertained (for the records do not always state the type of property), 46 of those tried in Civil Courts were from pens. The majority were convicted and punished brutally. For example, Henry James (Burnt Ground); Charles James (Beverly); and Robert, alias Sam Griffith (Summer Hill), were all sentenced to death and duly executed. These were among the ringleaders and the most identified active participants. The breakdown of trials by type and parish, as indicated by the punishment records (see table 7.4).

The majority of the participants from the pens were from among the male slave elite, the most privileged on the property: the coloured, creole artisans; about 13 were enslaved praedials, one a newly imported African. Comparatively fewer females were involved; and those implicated often got lighter sentences or were acquitted.

Eugene Genovese is thus basically correct when he asserts that: 'enslavement in any form has figured as the antithesis of that individual autonomy considered the essence of freedom.'[77] The revolt against slavery emerged as the basic assertion of human dignity, and, clearly, resistance was just as likely to result from rising expectations and indulgence as from

Table 7.4
Summary of the Majority of Trials, 1831/32 Emancipation War

Parish	Court Type	No. Tried
Hanover	(Court Martial)	58
	(Civil Court)	82
Manchester	(Court Martial)	15
	(Civil Court)	16
Portland	(Court Martial)	23
	(Civil Court)	5
St. Elizabeth	(Court Martial)	73
St. James	(Court Martial)	100
	(Civil Court)	81
St. Thomas-in-the- East	(Court Martial)	11
	(Civil Court)	5
St. Thomas-in-the-Vale	(Court Martial)	9
Trelawny	(Court Martial)	70
Westmoreland	(Court Martial)	26
	(Civil Court)	52
Total		626

brutal treatment and poor material conditions. The involvement of enslaved people from Cascade and Cacoon Castle Pens in Hanover owned by Mrs Griffiths, testified to the fact that whether enslavers were male or female, those they owned objected to their enslavement. Additionally, the punishment list from the parish of Manchester, a parish with no sugar estates during slavery but with many pens, coffee estates and combined pen/coffee units, demonstrates that slavery in any form was contested.

Neither the abolition of the transatlantic trade in enslaved Africans in 1807/08 nor subsequent attempts to ameliorate the conditions of those enslaved could stem the tide of protest and battle for social freedom. Furthermore, the pro-natalist policies that were central to the success of the Amelioration plan could only work if women were taken out of the back-breaking field tasks. Women, however, *were* the backbone of the field aspect of pens and plantations; to take them out of the field so that they could more fruitfully multiply and ensure the survival of the labour force would affect production. To keep them in the field and subject them to harsh conditions of enslavement would defeat the pro-natalist strategies, fuel women's resistance and provide more ammunition for the humanitarians who centred enslaved women's conditions in their anti-slavery campaign.[78] From a gender perspective, then slavery was doomed to end sooner or later as long as women were so essential to production, reproduction, and the anti-slavery movement after 1808.

More importantly, by their participation in the 1831/32 emancipation war, those enslaved on pens helped to end the slave system in Jamaica and the wider Caribbean. While some historians like Reginald Coupland and Seymour Drescher argue that humanitarian forces were crucial factors in the abolition of the system of African enslavement,[79] others like Kamau Brathwaite insist that the resistant activities of the enslaved played an even more crucial role; that the nature of the 1831/32 war in Jamaica demonstrated clearly to Britain that emacipation was a must.[80] The implications of the war in Jamaica for anti-slavery activities in other parts of the British-colonized Caribbean, and the prospect of a black-controlled Jamaican society, impelled Britain to pass the Emancipation Act in 1833. Eric Williams and those who support the materialist explanation for abolition argue, however, that while resistance cannot be ignored as a factor in emancipation, it must be analysed alongside economic factors. Part of his thesis of abolitionism is that the free trade lobby triumphed over the protectionists, spurred on by the need to find wider markets for the products of an industrializing Britain. The Caribbean and the slave system were seen as impediments to that project and had to be abolished. The increasing political influence of the industrial class in the British Parliament acted as a further impetus for abolition as by 1832, they had more votes than the

West India/planter interest and defeated the latter when the matter was put to the vote.[81]

The coming of emancipation did not, of course, end systems of domination in Jamaica. Consequently, the post-slavery period was as plagued with battles over terrain as the preceding period had been; for the former owners seemed intent on recreating slave relations of production in a free society. Land once more became highly contested terrain as the former owners attempted to defeat the land claims of the formerly enslaved and impede the development and expansion of the peasantry and the reconstitution of the proto-peasantry of the slavery period.

Table 7.5
Sample of Enslaved Pen Anti-Slavery Activists Punished for their Role in the 1831/32 Emancipation War

Parish	Names	Pen	Sentence
St. James	James Bernard	Bandon	Death/Executed
	Charles James	Beverly	Death/Executed
	Henry James	Burnt Ground	Death/Executed
	Robert (alias Sam Griffith)	Summer Hill	Death/Executed
Trelawny	Henry Grey	Vaughansfield	300 lashes + Life Imprisonment
	Richard Allen	Springvale	100 lashes + 12 months in prison
	Richard Grey	Springvale	Death
	Thomas Grey	Springvale	300 lashes + 2 years in prison
	James Pertersgill	Springvale	Death
	Bob Peterkin	Springvale	Death
	Louis Vassell	Springvale	100 lashes + 12 months in prison
	Edward Dickson	Windsor	100 lashes + 3 months in prison
	Richard McThery	Greenvale	Acquitted
	William Palmer	Greenvale	200 lashes + 3 months in prison
Hanover	Henry Cowan	Argyle	Death
	James Malcolm	Knockalva	Death
	William Miller	Shettlewood	Death
	Robert Rose	Shettlewood	Death
	Richard Trail	Shettlewood	Death
	George Spence	Cacoon Castle	Death
	Samuel Wright	Cascade	100 lashes + 3 months in prison
	John Allen	Shettlewood	100 lashes
	Catherine Brown	Cascade	50 lashes + 3 months in prison
	John Campbell	Knockalva	Death, commuted to 3 months in prison
	James Cochrane	Ramble	75 lashes
	Esther Comba	Cascade	50 lashes + 3 months in prison
	James Davidson	Knockalva	Death
	Angus Forbes	Ramble	Death
	David Grant	Haughton Grove	Death
	James Grant	Haughton Grove	100 lashes
	John Grant	Haughton Grove	Death
	James Griffith	Cascade	100 lashes + 3 months in prison
	James Malcolm	Knockalva	Death
	William Miller	Shettlewood	Death
	Robert Rose	Shettlewood	Death
	Richard Trail	Shettlewood	Death
	George Spence	Cacoon Castle	Death
	Samuel Wright	Cascade	100 lashes + 3 months in prison
	John Allen	Shettlewood	100 lashes

Table 7.5 (Cont)
Sample of Enslaved Pen Anti-Slavery Activists Punished for their Role in the 1831/32 Emancipation War

Parish	Names	Pen	Sentence
	Catherine Brown	Cascade	50 lashes + 3 months in prison
	John Campbell	Knockalva	Death, commuted to 3 months in prison
	James Cochrane	Ramble	75 lashes
	Esther Comba	Cascade	50 lashes + 3 months in prison
	James Davidson	Knockalva	Death
	Angus Forbes	Ramble	Death
	David Grant	Haughton Grove	Death
	James Grant	Haughton Grove	100 lashes
	John Grant	Haughton Grove	Death
	James Griffith	Cascade	100 lashes + 3 months in prison
Hanover	Thomas Haughton	Shettlewood	Death
	Edward Heaven	Ramble	Death
	Charles James	Cacoon Castle	200 lashes, 3 months in prison & 50 lashes on discharge
	Christine James	Cascade	50 lashes + 3 months in prison
	Robert James	Cascade	100 lashes + 3 months in prison
	Robert Johnson	Cascade	100 lashes + 3 months in prison
	Samuel Kettle	Ramble	100 lashes

Source: UK National Archives, CO 137/185.

Table 7.6
Punishment List, Parish of Manchester 1831/32

Nos Nos.	Names Name	Age	Creole	African	Occupation or Trade	Plantation or Estate to which he belonged	Crime	Sentence	Remarks
1.	Andrew ?	?	Creole	-	Field Negro	Wickham	Rebellion	200 lashes	Inflicted
2.	Robert Brown	42	-	African	Field Negro	Spur Tree	Rebellion	Death	Executed
3.	Sam Boucher	50	-	African	Cooper	Malbro Mount	Rebellion	Death	Executed
4.	William Campbell	40	-	African	Head Driver	Green Vale	Rebellion	200 lashes 1 year imprisonment 200 lashes	Inflicted
5.	Thomas Cole	29	Creole	African	Carpenter	Bullhead	Rebellion	Death	Executed
6.	Henry Dwyer	38	-	African	Head Driver	Greenmount	Rebellion	Transportation	-
7.	Ellick	50	-	African	Head Driver	Glenhead	Rebellion	Death	Executed
8.	William French	35	Creole	-	Carpenter	Skiddaw	Rebellion	Death	Executed
9.	Harry	23	Creole	-	Field Negro	Keynsham	Rebellion	6 mths imprisonment 100 lashes, 100 more when discharged.	Inflicted
10.	Jacob	40	-	African	Field Negro	Marlbro Mount	Rebellion	Transportation	Died in gaol
11.	James King	40	-	African	Head Driver	Isle	Rebellion	Transportation	-
12.	Thomas Lamb	45	-	African	Hothouse doctor	Moreland	Rebellion	Death	Executed

Nos Nos.	Names Name	Age	Creole	African	Occupation or Trade	Plantation or Estate to which he belonged	Crime	Sentence	Remarks
13.	Richard Lewis	20	-	African	?	Berry Hill	Rebellion	Death	Executed
14.	John Lirie					Richard Boucher	Rebellion	140 lashes	-
15.	Joseph Melville	30	Creole	-	Cartman	Content	Rebellion	Death	No number of evidence are forwarded in these cases, none having been received.
16.	William Merrick	44	-	African	Cooper	Keynsham	Rebellion	Death	Executed
17.	James Miller	35	Creole	-	Head Driver	Hopeton	Rebellion	Death	Executed
18.	Thomas Mitchell	47	-	African	Field Negro	Keynsham	Rebellion	100 lashes	Inflicted
19.	William Mitchell	48	-	African	Field Negro	Keynsham	Rebellion	100 lashes	Inflicted
20.	Abraham Peart	30	Creole	African	Cartman	Spice Grove	Rebellion	Death	Executed
21.	Pompey	32	Creole	-	Cooper	Keynsham	Rebellion	Death	Executed
22.	William Proudlove	42	Creole	-	Carpenter	Bullhead	Rebellion	Death	Executed
23.	Richard	30	Creole	-	Field Negro	Spice Grove	Rebellion	Death	Executed
24.	John Ricketts	40	Creole	-	Head Driver	Kingsland	Rebellion	Death	Executed
25.	Edward	40	-	African	2nd Driver	Spice Grove	Rebellion	Death	Executed

Nos. Nos.	Names Name	Age	Creole	African	Occupation or Trade	Plantation or Estate to which he belonged	Crime	Sentence	Remarks
26.	William Sterling	28	Creole	-	Field Negro	Bullhead	Rebellion	Death	No number of evidence are forwarded in these cases, none having been received.
27.	John Thomson	24	Creole	-	Field Negro	New Forest	Rebellion	50 lashes, 3 months imprisonment.	Inflicted
28.	Thomas Webb	30	Creole	-	Pen Keeper	Keynsham	Rebellion	6 mths imprisonment 100 lashes, 100 more when discharged.	Inflicted
29.	Wellington	35	Creole	-	Head Driver	New Forest	Rebellion	Death	No number of evidence are forwarded in these cases, none having been received.
30.	William Wilson	36	Creole	-	Head Driver	Wickham	Rebellion	Death	Executed
31.	James Young	40	-	African	Head Driver	Goory	Rebellion	Death	Executed

Source: UK National Archives, CO 137/185.

174

8

POST-SLAVERY ADJUSTMENTS

On the first of August 1834, slavery was legally ended in the British-colonized Caribbean with the passage of 'An Act For The Abolition of Slavery Throughout The British Colonies; For Promoting The Industry Of The Manumitted Slaves; And For Compensating The Persons Hitherto Entitled To The Services Of Such Slaves'.[1] Before the complete abolition of African enslavement, however, the enslaved people first had to serve a period of apprenticeship of between four and six years, depending on their occupational status. All freed people above the age of six were to be classified as either agricultural or domestic servants on the basis of the type of labour which they had performed for the 12 months preceding the passage of the Abolition Act. For praedials (agricultural labourers) apprenticeship was to be for six years ending in 1840; but non- praedials (domestics) would be fully free in 1838 after a four-year Apprenticeship. apprentices, if they so desired and could afford it, could purchase their freedom before the legal termination of their apprenticeship. The amount of that payment was to be determined by an impartial appraisal of the labour value of the apprentices concerned.

The proprietors were to continue to provide food, clothing and other customary indulgencies, and in exchange, apprentices were compelled to give 40½ hours of unpaid labour per week. Children under six years old were, however, exempted from this transitional period, being entrusted to the care of their mothers unless they were unable to provide such care. In that event, the children would have to serve indentureship until the age of 21.[2]

The apprenticeship and post-apprenticeship periods did not go entirely smoothly on the island's pens. Unstable labour relations, the trek from the

Table 8.1
Valuation of Pen Apprentices, January to June 1836

No.	Quarter	Parish	Pen	Sex	Category	Value £	Value s.	Value d.	Paid or Unpaid
1	Jan.–Mar. 1836	St. Elizabeth	Salt Spring	F	Non-Praedial	30	0	0	Paid
2		St. Elizabeth	Malvern Hill	M	Praedial	46	11	8	Paid
3		St. Elizabeth	Luana	F	Praedial	32	0	0	Paid
4		St. Elizabeth	Newell	F	Non-Praedial	30	0	0	Paid
5		St Elizabeth	Salt Spring	M	Praedial	60	0	0	Paid
6		Trelawny	Epsom	F	Praedial	34	0	0	Paid
7		Trelawny	Litchfield	F	Non-Praedial	13	6	8	Paid
8		Trelawny	Hampshire	F	Non-Praedial	30	0	0	Paid
9		St. Thomas-in-the-East	Grange Hill	M	Praedial	73	12	3	Not Paid
10		St. Thomas-in-the-East	Friendship	F	Non-Praedial	13	0	0	Paid
11		St. Thomas-in-the-Vale	Rio Magno	F	Praedial	83	15	7½	Not Paid
12		St. Thomas-in-the-Vale	Rio Magno	F	Praedial	92	8	11	Not Paid
13		St.Thomas-in-the-Vale	Rio Magno	F	Praedial	55	7	1	Not Paid
14		St. Thomas-in-the-Vale	Rio Magno	M	Praedial	92	8	11	Not Paid
15		St. Thomas-in-the-Vale	Rio Magno	M	Praedial	77	12	9	Not Paid
16		St. Thomas-in-the-Vale	Rio Magno	M	Praedial	69	16	3	Not Paid
17		St. Thomas-in-the-Vale	Rio Magno	F	Praedial	92	8	11	Not Paid
18		St. Thomas-in-the-Vale	Rio Magno	F	Praedial	15	0	11	Not Paid
19	April–June 1836	St. Elizabeth	Look-Out	F	Non-Praedial	16	0	0	Paid

Table 8.1 (Cont.)

20	Clarendon	Sheckles	M	Praedial	25	0	0	Paid
21	Clarendon	Cotes	F	Praedial	35	0	0	Paid
22	Clarendon	Cotes	M	Domestic	22	10	0	Paid
23	St. Mary	Claremont	F	Praedial	40	13	4	Not Paid
24	St. Mary	Claremont	F	Praedial	26	13	4	Not Paid
25	St. Mary	Claremont	M	Praedial	53	6	8	Not Paid
26	St. George	Fort George	F	Non Praedial	26	0	0	Paid
27	St. Catherine	Farm	F	Praedial	12	0	0	Paid
28	St. Catherine	Spencer's	M	Non-Praedial	21	7	10	Paid
29	Westmoreland	Haddo	M	Non-Praedial	7	10	0	Paid
30	Westmoreland	Haddo	M	Non-Praedial	3	0	0	Paid
31	Westmoreland	Haddo	M	Non-Praedial	14	5	0	Paid
32	Westmoreland	Haddo	F	Non-Praedial	15	10	0	Paid
33	Westmoreland	Chilton	F	Praedial	54	2	8	Not Paid
34	Westmoreland	Chilton	M	Praedial	37	17	4	Not Paid
35	Westmoreland	Petersville	M	Praedial Carpenter	62	18	4	Paid
36	Westmoreland	Clifdeen	M	Praedial Apprentice Carpenter	55	10	0	Paid
37	St. Ann	Faith	M	Praedial	63	5	0	Paid

Table 8.1 (Cont.)

38	St. Ann	Faith	M	Praedial	63	5	0	Paid
39	St. Ann	Faith	F	Praedial	49	10	0	Paid
40	St. Ann	Faith	F	Praedial	49	10	0	Paid
41	St. Ann	Faith	M	Praedial	49	10	0	Paid
42	St. Ann	Faith	F	Praedial	49	10	0	Not Paid
43	St. Ann	Union	F	Non-Praedial	36	8	11	Not Paid
44	St. Thomas-in-the-East	Prospect	M	Praedial	36	0	0	Paid
45	St. Thomas-in-the-East	Prospect	M	Praedial	17	0	0	Paid
46	Trelawny	Seafield	F	Non-Praedial	17	0	0	Paid
47	St. Mary	Goshen	M	Praedial	100	0	0	Not Paid
48	St. Elizabeth	Hermitage	F	Praedial	37	0	0	Not Paid
49	St. Elizabeth	Newell	M	Praedial	52	0	0	Paid
50	St. Elizabeth	Newell	M	Praedial	72	0	0	Paid
51	St. Elizabeth	Salt Spring	F	Praedial	38	0	0	Paid

Sources: Sligo to Glenelg, April 17, 1836, Enclosure 19, Despatch No. 422, London, PRO, C.O.137/210; Sligo to Glenelg, July 25, 1836, Enclosure in Despatch No. 534, CO 137/211.

Table 8.2
Return of the Number of Enslaved People and Estimated Value Thereof, in Each Class, in Possession of Hamilton Brown, Owner on the 1st Day of August, 1834
Name of Estate or Domicile of Labourers, Grier Park Pen
Total Number of Workers –141

Divisions	No.	Classes	Male	Female	No.	Value in Sterling		
Praedial Attached	1	Head People	4	-	4	320	0	0
	2	Tradesmen	3	-	3	240	0	0
	3	Inferior Tradesmen						
	4	Field Labourers	30	54	84	5,580	0	0
	5	Inferior Field Labourers	5	5	10	300	0	0
Praedial Unattached	1	Head People	-	-	-		-	
	2	Tradesmen	-	-	-		-	
	3	Inferior Tradesmen	-	-	-		-	
	4	Field Labourers	-	-	-		-	
	5	Inferior Field Labourers	-	-	-		-	
Non Praedial	1	Head Tradesmen	-	-	-		-	
	2	Inferior Tradesmen	-	-	-		-	
	3	Head People employed on wharves, shipping and other avocations	-	-	-		-	
	4	Inferior People of the same description	-	-	-		-	
	5	Head Domestic Servants	1	1	2	160	0	0
	6	Inferior Domestics	2	4	6	360	0	0
Children under six years of age on 1st August 1834			15	14	29	435	0	0
Aged, diseased, or otherwise non-effective			-	3	3	30	0	0
Total					141	7,425	0	0

Source: London, PRO, C.O.T. 71/693.

pens — at times to sugar estates — and the heavy reliance of the units on the estate market for the disposal of output, had severe implications for their economies. These problems were not immediately apparent in the period 1834–36 which represented the start of the Apprenticeship System. For the majority of pens, the first years of this transitional period passed without major crises for the owners. As on sugar and coffee plantations, there had been the initial protests by the freed people over the denial of complete freedom in 1834,[3] but by late 1834 and 1835, reports from the pen districts indicated that work was regular, apprentices 'disciplined' and the demand for planters' stock high. The following extract from a letter to John Tharp from the Attorney for the Tharps' estates and pens in the island, typified the situation on livestock farms. According to him,

> it affords me great pleasure ... to inform you that the negroes are behaving themselves remarkably well and performing their labour with great cheerfulness on your properties. Rumours were prevalent throughout the island that a strike of workers would take place amongst the Apprentices on the 1st August, I apprehend nothing of the kind whatever, and as I anticipated the time has just passed over quite satisfactorily.[4]

Reports emanating from the pen districts of St Elizabeth, Manchester, St Ann and Westmoreland were similarly optimistic. Stipendiary Magistrate Alley, of the Mile Gully district of St Elizabeth, in his report of December 30, 1835, observed, for example, that 'in this district there are large coffee estates and extensive pens in good cultivation.... The negro population behave well, and are generally disposed to industry'.[5] He added that the Christmas holidays had passed peacefully and that all the apprentices had turned out to work after the holidays.

With regard to the economic state of pens, Stipendiary Magistrate Davies's reports for St Elizabeth are particularly insightful; for this parish was second only to St Ann in the number of pens it contained. In his quarterly report of December 1835, he wrote as follows:

> the pens ... have suffered very little by the dimunition of the hours of labour under the present system; most of them at least are in a very creditable condition, fences well kept up and pastures tolerably clean. It is an encouraging circumstance for this kind of property

that some descriptions of stock, particularly mules and horses, are realizing an improved price and are much in request. With respect to steers, if the price is low the demand is brisk.... One of the principal pen-keepers in this neighbourhood has assured me that he had not for many years known a larger demand.[6]

Towards the middle of 1836, both the demand and the price of 'steers' (oxen) had, however, improved. One Stipendiary Magistrate attributed this to the failure of the prediction that 'sugar estates must of necessity go down under the new system of labour'.[7] A few plantations had initially believed this prediction and had neglected to replenish their supply of stock. John Daughtrey's report stressed that

now, however, that these delusions (the offspring of prejudice) have been pretty generally dissipated, efforts are being made which must, of necessity, lead to a large demand for working stock and thereby improve the value and prospects of pen properties.[38]

There was another factor explaining the optimism on pens in the early years of the Apprenticeship System. This was the fact that pens had an advantage over sugar estates in the way their labour force was deployed. Sugar estates demanded continuous labour particularly during crop season. As a result, the 40½ hours of compulsory labour instituted by the Act of Emancipation were considered inadequate for the cultivation and manufacture of the crop. On pens, however, this time was adequate for livestock husbandry; so that unlike sugar estates, most pens did not need to employ apprentices to do extra labour and thus incur high wage bills. This was emphasized by Stipendiary Magistrate Laidlaw, of St Ann who pointed out that 'there has ... been very little need in the pen areas for extra labour, the time allowed by law being generally amply sufficient for the species of cultivation required'.[9] Laidlaw's views were generally replicated by the other Stipendiary Magistrates. Daughtrey, reporting on the pens of the Mile Gully and Santa Cruz districts of St Elizabeth indicated that on these units, the nine-hour work day was usual and that work was completed within this time.[10]

For all these reasons, up to 1836, as indicated by the Accounts Current, the majority of pens still seem to have been recording a profit in their internal transactions. Towards the end of 1836 and increasingly thereafter, however, the somewhat rosy picture on pens began to change. Indications of such change were first given in the half-yearly reports of the Stipendiary Magistrates. These reports clearly showed that several aggravating circumstances involved pen apprentices and that the attitude of those apprentices towards both the transitional system and their employers was different from that displayed earlier. Pen apprentices were bent on displaying their opposition to the continuation of the Apprenticeship System; but, predictably, such opposition was deemed 'intransigence' by proprietors and officials. Therefore, Stipendiary Magistrates complained increasingly of indolence, disaffection and a 'lack of respect to masters' on the part of the apprentices. In a letter to the governor, Robert Thompson, who reported that with one exception, his district of Black River comprised principally pens, wrote:

> I am sorry to say that the apprentices of this district are not so respectful to their masters as those of my last district were; they are much more indolent in their habits and if they can get the slightest opportunity to evade labour, they embrace it.[11]

One comparison which was repeatedly made by the magistrates was that such 'disrespectful' behaviour on the part of the apprentices was worse on pens and small settlements than on large estates. The explanation given was that, from the days of slavery on sugar estates, discipline was greater and the labour force more controlled, whereas on smaller properties with few British and a smaller African population, control was not so great. According to Thompson: 'I am sorry to say that they are very much disposed to use unbecoming and saucy language to their masters and more especially to those among the small settlers'.[12] Thompson's views were supported by Daniel Kelly, operating out of Westmoreland, who had only four sugar estates under his jurisdiction. The majority of properties he supervised were pens and small settlements. He said that with the exception of the small settlements, there appeared to be a good feeling existing between the employer and the apprentice.[13] Gurley, who had had jurisdiction over the Black River district in 1835, had already made a similar observation in a report to Governor Sligo. He had stressed that on large estates, good understanding existed between apprentices and employers, but 'I have to observe that my district comprises pens and settlements on which I do not think the discipline is so rigid as on sugar plantations'.[14]

The situation was said to be worse on the smaller properties managed or owned by women and mixed-race proprietors. Furthermore, where overseers were not strict and where employer-apprentice disputes were adjudicated by mixed-race Stipendiary Magistrates, similar problems were observed. This was clearly brought out in John Cooper's report on the labouring population on the late Simon Taylor's property of Haughton Grove Pen in Hanover in 1835. According to Cooper, 'the negroes are in a rather unsettled state which can be easily accounted for; they have an easy, stupid overseer who overlooks their faults'.[15] He went on to state that to compound matters, the pen was at a great distance from a magistrate and that even the nearest one, Mr Norcutt from Montego Bay, was accused of being too lenient with the apprentices. Cooper's explanation for this was that Norcutt was a Coloured man, held in high repute by Africans but disliked by the British. Once when an apprentice from an adjoining property was caught by the Haughton Grove Pen apprentices stealing their provisions, they took him to a Stipendiary Magistrate in Lucea, rather than to Norcutt. Their explanation was that 'Mr. Norcutt no good man to go to when Nagar tief from Nagar, only when Nagar tief from Buckra'.[16]

This changing attitude of the apprentices was said to have manifested itself in two other ways. One was the increase in their abuse and ill-treatment of animals and the other was the neglect of the pastures. On the other hand, from all reports the apprentices wisely ensured that their grounds did not suffer any similar neglect. Writing from Leinster Pen in St Mary, Stipendiary Magistrate Lambert, reported that the 'negro grounds are equally well-cultivated as previous to 1st August 1834'.[17]

The fortunes of pens began to change by 1836. First of all, those pens which had traditionally relied on hired labour for certain tasks, suffered from a shortage of such labour. This was emphasized by Stipendiary Magistrate Bell. He remarked that 'pimento and coffee properties and ginger are doing well, as also are pens wherever they worked with their own strength, and did not pay jobbing, which has become scarce'.[18] For the traditional work on the pen, the regular labour force was still adequate because of the guarantee offered by the Apprenticeship System. However, the shortage of jobbers now made it necessary for the pen proprietors to require their labourers to perform task work in their 'free time'. On many pens, apprentices refused to perform such extra labour. Such refusal was observed on Mt Pleasant Pen in St Elizabeth. Other cases were reported in the various replies of the Stipendiary Magistrates to the governor's request for such information.

Where apprentices did agree to work for wages in their spare time, they insisted on task work and received payment ranging from 1s. 8d. to 2s. 6d. per task; but task work was still not general on pens in the hours of compulsory labour. Laidlaw had explained in 1837 that 'the various sorts of labour required on pens renders it difficult to resort to task work, and it is not therefore generally practised in this district'.[19] Labour relations deteriorated further towards the expected termination of the Apprenticeship System for non-praedials (non-agricultural labourers, mainly domestics). On Worcester Park Pen in St Catherine, for example, a complaint was lodged by John Gray, the overseer, against the great and second gangs. The substance of his complaint was that the apprentices in both gangs had been guilty of disobeying orders and absenting themselves for two days without leave. Gray also accused them of turning up late when they eventually returned to work. The chief witness in the case was John McGlashan, the plantation constable, who said that he had ordered the apprentices to turn out for work the day after New Year's Day. They did not obey this order, instead, they reported for work the following day. The very next week, the two gangs again took a day off without permission. Furthermore, it was alleged that when these gangs did work, they were habitually late and the relations on the pen between the constable, overseer and apprentices were generally poor. The magistrate ordered the gangs involved to work extra hours to compensate for the time lost.

On Epping Pen, St Mary, Will Parker, the pen-keeper, brought a case against an apprentice, William Wilson, a praedial (agricultural) apprentice, for 'general neglect of duty and loss of labour'.[20] Four cases of neglect involving four days' work were cited by the pen-keeper. On the first day, Wilson had been sent to cut 'stuccadoes' (stakes). He cut three for the entire day. On the second day, he took the 'stuccadoes' from the woods to the house which was just 200 yards away. On the third day he cut six 'stuccadoes', and the following day, he brought those home. In addition, when sent to cut grass, he was said to cut very few bundles 'in comparison to the two old women with whom he works'. In his defence, Wilson said that the place where Parker sent him to cut wood was not Parker's property, that the property had a vigilant watchman and he was only able to cut 'stuccadoes' when there was a lapse in the watchman's vigilance. After hearing Wilson's evidence, the Stipendiary Magistrate dismissed the case against him.[21]

Three other cases of poor relations between apprentices and employers by 1837 were related by Joseph Sturge and Thomas Harvey after their visits to Jamaican properties in that year. Sturge and Harvey were members of the anti-slavery body referred to as 'Saints', who assiduously studied accounts of the working of Apprenticeship in the colonies and publicly attacked this despised system. In October 1836, four anti-slavery leaders — Sturge, John Scoble, William Lloyd and Harvey — sailed for the Caribbean to secure first-hand evidence on the operation of the apprenticeship system. Scoble and Lloyd visited colonial Guyana; Sturge and Harvey travelled among the Lesser Antilles and Jamaica. On their return to Britain, Sturge and Harvey published a detailed book condemning the apprenticeship system. Pens visited by Sturge and Harvey in Jamaica included Prosper, Pitfore and Green Island. The first case investigated on Prosper Pen, in St James, involved Richard Sheppie. His complaint was that he and his sister had two working 'steers', two young 'steers', two cows and one bull calf on the pen; for the head workers on many of these properties, and on sugar estates, had usually been allowed to raise cattle, mules and horses for themselves, and instances of the possession of livestock by apprentices were frequently met with by the two investigators. In 1837 the attorney, a Mr Grant, who was also a judge of the Assize Court, ordered Sheppie to sell the stock as he would no longer be allowed to keep them on the pen. Furthermore, Sheppie was ordered to sell the stock to Prosper Pen and was forced to brand them with the pen's own mark. Grant offered the apprentice £16 for the two working 'steers', and £16 for the rest combined. They refused on the basis that the market value of the 'steers' was £18 each; and the cows, £16 each. However, Sheppie and his sister were overruled.[22] The editor of the *Falmouth Post* felt that Grant may have, after buying Sheppie's stock for such a low price, made his own profit by reselling them to the pen or to his butcher brother in Lucea, at an inflated price. Sturge and Harvey saw this case as 'an example of the insecurity of such property, which depends at all times on the caprice of the overseers or the owners'.[23]

On Pitfore Pen in St James, the apprentices' complaint was that task work had been set for them without prior consultation. They complained further that such tasks were onerous, often causing them to work from 6:00 a.m.–6:00 p.m., and missing out on breakfast and dinner time. Also, unlike the situation under slavery, even a woman with a child only four months old was required to do the same amount of work as the other apprentices. On Green Island Pen in Westmoreland, the pen-keeper, Benjamin Capon, was accused of physically abusing the apprentices. The apprentices told Sturge and Harvey that they never 'got any right' in these matters. Further complaints were that their extra days were often taken away, their grounds destroyed by cattle, and that hospital care was sadly lacking. The latest incident related to a young girl whom the proprietor had ordered to be beaten and locked up for the night. When her mother, Oriana Webster, protested by saying 'Hi! this picaninny work so hard, no dinner time, and you go lock her up'.[24] Capon collared her and ordered that she be fastened in the dungeon.

Other aggravating elements of the Apprenticeship System soured labour relations even further. One such problem concerned the valuation of apprentices who wished to purchase the remaining term of their apprenticeship. Such requests for valuation, particularly on the part of female pen apprentices, were on the increase by 1837. Very often, pen-keepers, like planters, over-valued the apprentices to deter them from purchasing their freedom. The case of Sally Carter, a praedial-attached apprentice on a St Elizabeth pen under the jurisdiction of Stipendiary Magistrate Gurley, serves to illustrate this point. In 1836, Sally, aged 35, and said to be in good health, applied to be valued, and was appraised at £41 10s. 0d. This valuation was protested by Gurley who believed it was highly inflated. Sally had five children and at the time of valuation was expecting a sixth. She was in the second gang and was felt to be worth £10.[25] Yet, the Abolition Act had entitled apprentices to buy their freedom at a 'fair valuation'. Planters and pen-keepers, however, commonly obstructed this procedure by fixing exorbitant appraisements upon apprentices. As appraisement tribunals normally comprised the nearest Stipendiary Magistrate, a planter justice nominated by the employer, and a third planter justice agreeable to the Stipendiary Magistrate and the employer's nominee, biased decisions were regularly made. Value was determined by the labourer's age, strength, skills and 'general worth'. Strong, accomplished, reliable apprentices, the people most likely to seek appraisement, were said to have been valued more highly than their so-called 'idle, unproductive counterparts', and the inflated valuations which planters placed upon them bore no relation to the wages they were paid for the extra work done. Consequently, on pens, as on sugar estates, the number of apprentices appealing for valuation was relatively low; those actually paying for their freedom once valued, was even lower.[26]

Arguably the most aggravating problem facing the labourers on pens during the apprenticeship period was that surrounding their classification by the pen-keepers. The Emancipation Act of 1833 had stipulated that the occupation of the labourer prior to August 1834 was the criterion by which apprentices were to be classified as praedials and non-praedials. Pen-keepers objected to this method of classification on the grounds that, unlike on sugar estates, such a clear-cut distinction could never be observed on pens where occupations often overlapped. The labour force on these properties was generally smaller than on estates with the result that domestics and skilled labourers also did field labour on occasions. The shifting occupational roles of domestics was clearly illustrated in Thomas Thistlewood's Journals in which he noted the daily allocation of work on Vineyard Pen. The enslaved females Hago, Joan, Silvia, Diana and Juba, usually domestics, were also sent to work in the fields and pastures. The tendency among the pen-keepers was to classify domestics, tradesmen and 'race boys' (boys attending to race horses) as praedials instead of non-praedials.

There was some official opposition to this attempt to defy the principles of the Emancipation Act. The Attorney General D. O'Reilley, for example, refused to agree to a distinction between domestics on sugar estates and those on pens despite the fact that agricultural work was also performed by those on the latter. Pen domestics he deemed 'non-praedial apprenticed labourers'.[27]

Pen-keepers, like sugar planters, continued to classify tradespeople as praedials. This practice was clearly indicated in the Valuers' Returns of Claims for Compensation in the late 1830s. An examination of the 929 returns for St Ann revealed that no labourers except domestics were classified as non-praedials.[28] To legalize this practice, Jamaican proprietors passed a new 'Act for the Classification of Apprentices' in 1837 by which they sought to change the criterion for classification from occupation to the new criteria of hours of work and indulgences given.[29]

There was much opposition to this Act. Governor Sligo disputed the classification of tradespeople as praedials as this rendered the two-tiered system of abolition valueless. The rationale for stipulating that non-praedials were to be freed in 1838 and not 1840 was that proprietors needed their services at all times. This meant that such labourers would have little time available to attend to provision grounds and would continue to receive rations from employers. To classify them as praedials would mean that proprietors could not demand more than 40½ hours of work from them — a situation which, in Sligo's views, would create hardships for the employers. Pen-keepers disagreed. In their view, the nature of work on pens was such that all workers could complete their schedule within the stipulated 40½ hours per week. Furthermore, in this way labour would be guaranteed until 1840.[30]

The status of race boys or stable boys remained problematic. O'Reilley felt that 'as race boys continually and at all hours are obliged to attend to their horses, they are non-praedials'. Pen-keepers, again, maintained that they ought to be considered as praedials; a position supported by Sligo who claimed that 'stable boys or boys sent with racers, who have the weekly indulgences of apprentices literally employed in cultivating the soil are, I think, to all intents, praedials or persons attached to the pen' the Colonial Office, however, refused to sanction the Jamaican Act of 1837 and pen-keepers anticipated increased hardships when race boys, domestics and tradesmen — legally deemed non-praedials by the Colonial Office — were freed in 1838.[31]

By the time that the matter of classification was settled, the Apprenticeship System had come under so much criticism that a Select Committee to enquire into the working of the system had already been formed. The evidence collected, combined with the revelations of Sturge and Harvey, led to the ending of the system in August 1838. By the latter date, from all reports, the poor proprietor-apprentice relations on pens and estates had severely affected their economic state, and the optimism of pen-keepers between 1834 and 1836 had disappeared. Unfortunately, there are very few quantitative data to support the impression of economic decline conveyed in the magistrates' reports. However, the Accounts Current available indicate that pens such as Great Salt Pond which had been profitable up to 1835, had to be sold by 1837 because of poor economic performance. Similarly, Lapland, Mickleton, Spring Garden, Smallwood, Mahogany Hall, Whitheall, New Shafston and Up Park pens were all showing debit balances by 1838. In the case of Mahogany Hall Pen, the debit balance was not alarming, being £115 14s. 4½d., and perhaps would rally under the system of free labour depending on the extent to which sugar estates revived.[32]

When the Apprenticeship System finally ended, however, neither Stipendiary Magistrates, planters, nor pen-keepers held out much hope for the economic survival of their properties after 1838; for they all anticipated a further fall-off in labour — an important factor of production — on all properties. Indeed, as early as 1834, some apprentices on Col Grignon's pen in Westmoreland had indicated to him that they would not continue as field workers after Apprenticeship came to an end, 'but offered to be employed by me if I could put them to some domestic occupation'.[33] In 1839, Ricketts sent a similar report on the state of St Elizabeth parish. According to him, 'the labourers on pens having been formerly unattached praedials, cannot be expected to return for some time to come to labour on sugar properties, their lot having been one of peculiar hardship during the Apprenticeship'.[34] Clearly sugar plantations could not look to ex-pen labourers to boost their labour force — at least not immediately.

Predictably, one of the first complaints of pen-keepers after the end of the Apprenticeship System was that they had a shortage of labour, termed by them the 'labour problem'; and all indications are that most pens experienced a fall-off in the number of labourers after 1838. Salt Pond Pen in St Catherine had 45 apprentices up to 1838, but by 1840, the pen's regular, full-time labour force numbered 15. The labourers were described as 'unsteady' and significant numbers had refused outrightly to do any work. Similar drastic reductions occurred on other pens. In St Dorothy, on Retreat, Bannister and Ann Castle pens, the total black population during 1834–38 was 280. The average turnout then had been 60 in the great gang and 25 in the second gang. Between August 1834 and August 1838, the average attendance for both gangs was 60, but from August 1 to December 31, 1838, there had been a dramatic reduction in the turnout to an average of 25 on each pen. From August to December 1838, the average attendance for both first and second gangs was 25 on each pen. Furthermore, no work was performed in the weeks between January 1 and 18, 1839 and the pen had been unable to hire jobbers to fill the gap. The Stipendiary Magistrate for the area complained that 'the present state of the grass pieces are completely in bush and the stone walls are broken down, and the cattle are gone into a wild state'.[35] In addition, the overseer accused the labourers of refusing to plant corn and provisions as in former years. They had even stolen whatever he himself had planted. In Vere on Sandy Gully Pen, the complaint was similar. As on Salt Pond, the workers were said to be 'idle' and gave their labour irregularly. The reports from the pen area of lower Clarendon, for example, from Folly Pen also contained reports concerning the shortage of labour.[36] The reports from the overseers of Spring Garden, Thetford Hall, Hayes, St Helens, Industry, Labour, Bodles and Ythamside pens in the parish reflected a similar picture. In addition, they specifically mentioned the problematic issue of weekend employment. Livestock needed to be tended every day of the week, and during slavery pen labourers had been rotated in order to comply with the law relating to the enslaved's 'free' time, while at the same time, ensuring that animals were constantly tended. After slavery, however, workers were extremely reluctant to give up Saturdays and Sundays.

Envy Valley Pen also reported 'labour problems'. While also experiencing a labour shortage with the remaining workers demanding high wages, this pen had, in addition, to contend with what Grant, the overseer, referred to as 'the refractory state of the settlers in the neighbourhood'.[37] The latter reportedly stole, shot or otherwise destroyed cattle 'without the possibility of detection' and Grant despaired of ever checking these 'lawless acts' which threatened the viability of this breeding farm. Furthermore, settlers squatted on the pen's mountain lands which were located at a considerable distance from the farm.[38]

Perhaps the most accurate account of the effect of emancipation on the labour supply of pens is given in the journals of Fort George Pen, the property of Charles Ellis. Joseph Gordon, the overseer in the 1840s, kept detailed records of attendance, rents, wages and the progress of ejectment. Fort George Pen, located in the parish of St George, had had an enslaved population of about 200 at the time of emancipation, and this labour force had been regular during the apprenticeship period. In January 1843, however, just over 150 labourers worked on the pen. Judging from the list of those who were clearly tenants, only 64 of them actually resided on the pen, the residents being employed as daily jobbers. However, not all of the residents worked continuously as some work was seasonal. In January 1843, for example, only the head cattlemen, the head field labourer, the pen superintendent and the watchman worked 20 days or more. The majority of workers gave under ten days' labour, 26 of them giving from one to five days for the whole month. This pattern was typical of the remainder of the year. In March, for example, only the watchman worked for the whole month. Furthermore, the total number of labourers had been reduced from over 100 to just about 88; and by December, only 58 workers resided on the pen.[39]

The factors which determined the movement of labourers from the various properties after 1838 have been keenly debated by scholars. At the centre of the debate is whether push or pull factors should be accorded primacy in explaining this movement. While the pull theory, as advanced by planters and pen-keepers, had been the staple of the historiographical tradition and was linked by modern writers of the 'pull' school to land availability or scarcity, the 'push' school as articulated by Douglas Hall, O. Nigel Bolland, Swithin Wilmot, Michel Rolph Trouillot, Woodville Marshall and Thomas Holt has been steadily gaining ground, being supported by firmer empirical base. Scholars like Hall argue further that there was initially no large-scale exodus of labourers. Rather, the movement was gradual as evidenced by the gradual reduction in the wage bill each year. However, while the journals of the manager of Fort George Pen in the parish of St George on which Hall bases his analysis bears testimony to this notion of gradual withdrawal, other statistical evidence indicates that on some pens, the withdrawal was more immediate and drastic. None of the records tell us definitively the reasons for the gradual or immediate withdrawal of labourers, but the overwhelming complaints and records of planter coercion and poor labour relations (over wages, tools, hours, rents, estate residence, task work and so on), would seem to give credence to the argument that 'push' rather than 'pull' factors determined the labour movement. On the other hand, both can be said to have acted together.

While the reasons for the movement of labourers from their former work places are largely speculative, certain clear trends can be discerned. A clear factor hastening the movement of pen workers was the continued failure of the majority of pen-keepers to adopt the system of task work, long reverted to on sugar plantations. Pen-keepers continued to argue that pen labour was more suited to the daily rather than the task system, and up to August 1838 very few of them employed any task workers.[40] The reasons for the reluctance to adopt task work was summed up by Stipendary Magistrate Laidlaw who noted that 'the various sorts of labour required on pens renders it difficult to resort to task work, and it is not therefore genuinely practiced'. After the end of the Apprenticeship System, more pen-keepers succumbed to the pressure exerted by the freed people for task work, but most continued to engage resident labourers on a daily basis. Even those that adopted the task system, however, used it only for work unconnected with direct livestock husbandry. Pimento and coffee picking, road work, fencing and cleaning pastures were the common jobs subjected to task work.

Where the failure or inability of pens to employ freedpeople on a task basis occurred, there was a tendency for such labourers to register their protest by leaving and seeking alternative employment. Eventually, some sought such jobs on sugar estates. This drift to sugar estates was most notable from the 1840s, and was particularly encouraged by the seasonal nature of tasks on such properties rather than any appreciable higher wage rates.[41]

Evidence that it was the terms of employment and not the prospect of higher wages which attracted these freed people to sugar estates is provided by reports on comparative wage rates. These show that a remarkable uniformity existed in the wages paid on both types of properties. On the 79 St James sugar estates reviewed, first-class labourers received between 1s. 8d. and 2s. 6d; second-class labourers from 1s. 3d. to 1s. 4d. and third-class labourers, 10d. The same rates were observed on the nine St James pen examined. As St James was a foremost sugar parish, there is a fair chance that these wages were typical of those paid on sugar estates islandwide. An examination of the records relating to the remuneration of other pen labourers in the island reveals that they were very similar to wages paid on pens and sugar estates in St James. On Fort George Pen, for example, resident workers earned an average of 1s. 8d. and jobbers received wages commensurate with the nature of the tasks set. The cleaning of the pastures, for example, was carried out at 2s. 6d. an acre. The only exceptions were in the case of headmen, rangers and tradesmen whose wages were slightly higher, as pens attempted to retain their most skilled workers. In some cases, these were employed on an annual basis.[42]

In an effort to solve this growing labour shortage, pen-keepers adopted a number of strategies. One of the earliest was an experiment with European immigrant labourers, carried out essentially on pens in St Ann. Among these were Rose Hill and Phoenix Park. Phoenix Park began to import English and German immigrants in 1835, but this experiment was largely unsuccessful. By August 1835, the attorney began to accuse the labourers of recalcitrant behaviour. In a letter to his employers, the attorney stated that 'the English labourers from ... Phoenix Park are beginning to give some trouble'.[43] Some of them deserted the pen and travelled all the way to Spanish Town to complain to the Stipendiary Magistrate there. They seem to have been unhappy with the overseer, Braham. By November, more had departed, and the attorney was again writing: 'I am sorry to say that Phoenix Park immigrants have been behaving badly, indeed, they lately all quit the property'.[44] Even though some were apprehended and sent back to St Ann under police escort, others refused to return to work on the pen.

The cases of pens utilizing immigrant labourers up to 1845 were, however, extremely rare. It is true that indentured immigrant labourers would have been ideal for pens. After all, they were contracted for daily, as opposed to task labour. Furthermore, they received lower wages and their mobility was restricted by the proprietor or attorney. But the economic crisis faced by pens in this period made such properties least able to afford the high cost of immigration.

The failure of immigration led pen-keepers to adopt other coercive tactics. One was the tying of rents to wages. Basically, this meant that labourers were allowed to reside on the pen only on the understanding that in lieu of the payment of their rent in cash, they would work out such rent in labour for the pen. In other cases, pen-keepers compelled residents to work for the pen, and deducted rents from wages at the end of each week. Such tactics were employed on Bodles Pen and on Roden Hall Pen in St Ann in 1840. On Roden Hall the equivalent of £164 3s. 4d. for rent was worked out on the pen.[45]

Far from keeping labourers on the pens, the charging of rents and the controversy over wages only served as further aggravations and hastened the flight from these properties. The general practice adopted by the pen-keepers was to levy rents on labourers' houses, gardens and provision grounds. They also charged for the pasturage of labourers' stock on the pens' lands.

On William Jackson's pens in St Dorothy, each person was charged 3s. 4d. per week for his/her house and grounds. For families, only one house rent was imposed, but each occupant was individually charged for the use of provision grounds. On Spring Garden Pen in the same parish, cattlemen and domestics were exempted from the provision grounds rent, and in addition, received free medical care.[46] This situation does not appear to have been typical and indeed, pens in parishes such as Clarendon tended more towards the practice employed by Jackson.

The Fort George Pen Journals provide one of the most comprehensive accounts of the rates of rents and wages and the response of labourers to these charges. They indicate that the rates imposed by Jackson were not general on all pens. On his pens, labourers paid out in rent almost 45 per cent of their weekly wages, assuming that they worked every day at an average of 1s. 6d. per day. On Fort George Pen, where the average wage was also 1s. 6d., labourers paid under 25 per cent of their income in rents. The rates paid varied from labourer to labourer, depending on the facilities rented. With the exception of Robert Wilcock, the head superintendent, John Cargill, the field superintendent, and William Davidson, the head cattleman, all others residing on Fort George were charged rents for houses and provision grounds. The rent depended on whether workers rented only their houses, or both houses and grounds. Judging from the rent rolls, the average rent levied on houses was 5s. per month. Where both houses and grounds were rented, the cost was 8s. per month. Because of the exorbitant rents, some labourers were constantly in arrears. Some remained regardless, others simply left, and others were evicted. Eviction and voluntary 'resignation' accounted for the annual decline in the resident labour force on the pen, which by 1846 reached a low of 28. In 1843, 22 of the 64 labourers were in arrears. Six of them voluntarily left the pen by the end of that year, one had been ejected and eight others were stated to have given up either houses or grounds or both. The number in arrears in

Table 8.3
Accounts of Rents and Wages, Fort George Pen, 1843

Month	Received in rent by the Pen			Paid out in wages		
	£	s.	d.	£	s.	d.
January[1]	13	2	0	24	14	1
February	14	15	0	27	3	6
March[2]	15	14	0	66	6	8½
April	17	5	0	56	8	5½
May	14	0	0	16	4	7½
June	16	9	0	76	6	1
July	11	7	0	22	1	0
August	16	9	0	26	15	9
September	11	17	0	28	11	2
October	13	4	0	65	6	7
November	12	17	0	73	16	8
December	12	2	0	78	16	2½
Total	169	1	0[4]	562	10	10

Notes: 1. Incomplete: records partly damaged.
2. Incomplete.
3. Including jobbers working in coffee pieces.
4. Total is not reliable because of incomplete records. Another set of records reveal the correct total as £176 12s. 3d.

Source: NLJ, Fort George Pen Journal, 1843, MS 274b.

1843 was only slightly less than it had been in 1842. In the latter year, 26 workers had not paid their rent and five of them were consequently evicted. This situation continued into the 1850s.[47] By 1852, the overseer continued to complain that there had been 'no great improvement among the Tenants who are as usual very reluctant to pay up their rents'.[48]

Labourers also resisted payment on properties charging higher rates. On Haddo Pen in St Ann, for example, workers refused to pay their rents on the basis that the wages they received were lower than the rents levied. Similarly, labourers on Bromley and Greenfield in the same parish refused to pay for their houses and grounds. Whereas on Fort George some disgruntled labourers simply left the pen in protest over the rent issue, on some other farms labourers went on strike, at times for as long as three months.[49]

One obvious solution to the labourers' complaint that rents were exorbitant and wages low would have been for pen-keepers to increase the level of remuneration. But such an act of conciliation was not adopted. Instead, proprietors persisted in their claim that the wages demanded were already high and were out of all proportion with what they collected in rents. An attempt was made to test this claim by matching the Accounts Produce of the 1840s with the Accounts Current for the same years, but as the latter were so few, this task proved futile. From the accounts available, however, it is quite clear that the wage bill was a significant item of expenditure, exceeding rent collected in all cases. In 1842–43, for example, New Shafston Pen collected £72 2s. 10d. in rents and paid out £297 15s. 9½d. in wages. In that year, the wage bill was the largest item of expenditure. Similarly, the wage bill for Rowington Park Pen in 1843–44 represented 82.27 per cent of its earnings, and 62.34 per cent of its expenditure.[50]

Fort George Pen Journals reveal a similar trend. In 1843, the pen collected £169 1s. 0d. in rent and paid £562 10s. 10d. in wages. Yet, even these figures must be interpreted with caution. The wage bill represented remuneration paid to both residents and non-residents while the figure relating to rents applied only to the former. Also, the fact that these accounts list the total wage bill does not mean that such wages were willingly or promptly paid. The accounts naturally mask the controversy over wages which soured labour relations. According to Bill Riviere, in many cases continuous labour depended on the prompt payment of wages, but proprietors often reneged on their responsibilities.[51]

Pen-keepers and planters also blamed the labourers' 'quasi trade unions' — the missionaries — for much of the conflict over wages. Proprietors and missionaries were long-standing enemies. During slavery, missionary attempts to educate those enslaved and to teach them Christian principles had met with resistance. William Knibb's and James Phillippo's encouragement of the independent peasantry since 1835 had been equally resented. Now, in the 1840s, missionaries were encouraging workers in their demand for higher wages. For example, Henry Blagrove blamed missionaries for the labour conditions on Orange Valley Pen. He described them as 'fanatics who assiduously wormed themselves into the minds and practices of the negroes'. More specifically, he stated:

these men have told them the blacks time after time, that they are of themselves to set a price upon their labour, that any endeavour of the planter to grind them down, or lessen the rates of price; is contrary to the Spirit and character of Freedom — that in listening to them they stand their [sic] as their champions of their liberty and to watch narrowly any attempt that they may be made upon that liberty.[52]

As a result of the actions of these men, 'of low and grovelling minds', according to Blagrove, 'have the negroes caused all the trouble and annoyance as well as distress that has nigh sent this paradise to utter ruin'. Blagrove was particularly disparaging in his criticisms of William Knibb. He was equally critical of Knibb's brother whom he described as 'a Liverpool shop-keeper now come to Jamaica to keep a store and setting out to fleece the Negroes'.[53]

Despite clear evidence that poor labour relations as manifested in the examples given above should be elevated to a prominent position in freed people's reluctance to return to pens, overseers and pen-keepers persisted in giving 'laziness' as the primary reason. This is despite strong counter evidence represented by the contribution of enslaved peoples to the export and local economies in the eighteenth and nineteenth centuries and free workers' vigorous efforts to establish a viable peasantry. This tendency to characterize freedpeople as 'lazy' was clearly illustrated in the correspondence between Stephen Harmer, the overseer of Hope Pen in Manchester, and his relatives in England. In one of his letters, Stephen informed his brother,

> I regret to say that this once fine country is Goeing fast to destruction through the want of continuous labour ... One half of the Negroes have scarcely done anything since they were made free and them that do work demand very high wages from 4/- to 5/- per day and then they will not do even half a day's work for that.[54]

Continuing in this pessimistic tone and in a manner reflective of a later Carlylian stlye, Harmer attributed the disinclination of freedpeople to give continuous labour to the fact that they had few wants and were thus easily satisfied, so 'will lay down under their plantain trees and sleep sounder than work for fair wages'.[55]

However, in direct contrast to Harmer's unflattering and racist comments about Hope Pen's workers was a report on Cumberland Pen in St Catherine published in the *Morning Journal*. The editor stated that on the termination of Apprenticeship, the labourers on this pen had behaved themselves in an exemplary manner, because 'they had most handsomely come forward and voluntarily given upwards of one week's labour without hire fee or reward, to their late master'. This labour had been 'cheerfully tendered by a grateful and well-disposed people to their late master, as a testimonial to their good feeling and kindly disposition towards those who have hitherto had control over them'. In his view, Cumberland Pen's workers displayed the ideal attitude and he thus lamented the fact that other former owners had not generally been the recipients of similar 'gratitude and esteem'.[56] However, it was statements like Harmer's 'lament' rather than the *Morning Journal's* more positive representation that came to typify the post-slavery characterization of the black labouring population.

In addition to conflicts over labour, pen-keepers increasingly complained of their declining economic condition. The evidence of economic decline on pens came from several parishes. From St Mary came early complaints that fat 'steers' and cows were remaining on pens for a considerable time as market could not be found for them.[57] The *Morning Journal* carried an article in 1838 that endorsed these early complaints, emphasizing that pen-keepers had abundant stock that they were unable to sell.[58] In 1839 reports came from St Elizabeth that 'there are no demands for cattle on the pens and the labourers employ themselves in planting provision grounds in the hills'.[59] The accounts from the Stipendiary Magistrates who worked in St Ann also contain references pertaining to what they called the deplorable state of pen-keeping in that parish. The reports were similar in 1845. In that year, the attorney of Thatchfield Pen in St Elizabeth was complaining that 'the death of Pen-keeping seems to have made a great impression against the place'. He was unable to dispose of the cattle at a reasonable price, and eventually attempted to find a tenant for the place with a view to renting it. This was no easy task, and eventually the overseer, McTaggart, was paid £40 per annum to run the place.[60]

One contributory factor to the economic decline was obviously the reduction in the demand for livestock, linked to the decline of the sugar and coffee industries and technological changes in mill power.

Emancipation had been accompanied by a dramatic change in the pattern of agricultural output. The 1830s and 1840s saw a widespread abandonment of estates. In addition, those estates which survived began increasingly to experiment with steam power.[61]

Governor Charles Grey observed in 1849 that

> the estates in the high ground grounds which are called Pens and are laid out almost entirely in pasture, have been intended mainly for the raising of horned cattle, horses and mules for the use of the sugar and coffee estates. These are suffering due to the diminished demand for working animals on sugar and coffee estates which are in decline.[62]

The supply of 'planters stock' to the estates for use in the animal mills had, of course, been one of the factors responsible for the expansion of pen-keeping in eighteenth-century Jamaica. In 1763 there had been 34 wind, 150 water and 382 'cattle' mills in the island, indicating a large market for livestock on the estates.[63] By 1804, the number of cattle mills had increased to 656 or 61 per cent of the total number of mills.[64] In the post-slavery period, by contrast, those estates which remained in operation increasingly switched to steam mills. The use of steam power had commenced in the island around 1768 but had never been general. Only about one tenth of Jamaica's estates were equipped with steam engines in the three decades before abolition, but they were rapidly installed thereafter. By 1906, only one sugar estate in the island was still using a cattle mill.[65]

The decline in their main markets for livestock also caused the pen-keepers to sell animals to the butchers, often at a reduced price. Indeed, it was the anticipated expansion of the consumer market for fresh beef after 1838, which had acted as an incentive for some pen-keepers to remain in operation. The hope was that the large free population would now buy fresh beef instead of the old 'slave food'; but this hope was not realized as not only did the peasantry keep their own small stock which supplied them with meat, but they continued to buy the cheaper salted and pickled fish.

Pen accounts support the complaints of falling prices for both fresh beef and working stock. In 1840, for example, the average price of a mule was £28 7s. 0d.; of 'steers' £18; of spayed heifers £17; of bulls £42, and of fat stock for the butchers, £10 each. In 1845, however, these prices had fallen to the following average levels: 'Steer' £12 0s. 0d. each, Heifer £10 0s. 0d. each, Bull £24 0s. 0d. each, Mule £10 10s. 0d. each, Fat stock £9. 0s. 0d. each.[66]

Faced with these problems, pens were forced to restructure their economy. The smaller pens seem to have changed the emphasis of their operations from mainly livestock husbandry to the cultivation of minor crops or logwood. Thatchfield Pen in St Elizabeth, for example, attempted such a shift after an unsuccessful attempt to rent the pen. This shift caused some to eventually earn more from non-livestock products. The Accounts Current for the pens indicate clearly this trend among the surviving pens to earn more from the sale of products other than livestock. Whereas 19 of the 38 pens belonging to absentee owners which indicated the value of goods sold in 1860 collected more money from the sale of livestock than from other goods and services, only 11 of the 30 returned in 1880 still earned most from the sale of livestock. Of the 21 accounts for 1900, eight collected more from livestock sales than from any other product.[67] The accounts produce also indicate that fewer and fewer transactions were carried out between the pens and the estates. So, that both types of properties clearly became less and less dependent on each other.

A comparative analysis of the Accounts Produce for 1842 and 1845, representing one-third of the island's pens, confirms the reduction in the income derived from the sale of livestock, although there was still a significant degree of inter-property transactions. Table 8.4, based on a random sample of 25 per cent of the pens represented for each of these years, shows that only two pens, Sandy Gully and Up Park, did not experience a decrease in sales.

In order to get an idea of the degree to which earnings were adequate to meet expenses, it is necessary to consult the Accounts Current. Unfortunately, only the accounts of 14 pens exist for 1840–45. Furthermore, as not all of these are represented in each year, it is impossible to conduct a systematic analysis. Only Lapland and New Shafston pens have complete records. Their accounts, and those of three other pens represented both in 1840 and 1845, will first be discussed briefly. Lapland Pen began to record a debit balance in 1835. This situation continued down to 1842, when it was rented to Rev. Atkinson. Thereafter, the receipts were derived solely from Atkinson's rent. New Shafston was also showing a deficit by 1840. In that year, it was indebted to the amount of £410 12s.

Table 8.4
Comparative Earnings on Selected Pens, 1840 and 1845

Pen	Parish	1840			1845		
		£	s.	d.	£	s.	d.
1. Knockalva	Hanover	4,460	11	6	1,955	0	0
2. Phoenix Park	St. Ann	2,023	0	0¼	1,319	0	6
3. Hopewell	St. Ann	1,350	4	10	346	11	4½
4. Retreat	St. Ann	1,808	0	0	1,201	17	7
5. Haddon	St. Ann	2,848	2	6	566	6	0
6. Luana	St. Elizabeth	2,569	4	3	2,074	11	8
7. Spring Garden	St. Dorothy	2,790	15	9½	510	16	5
8. Hodges	St. Elizabeth	5,344	16	8	2,245	14	0
9. Sandy Gully	Vere	1,944	1	8	2,001	6	0
10. Penny's	St. Ann	1,923	19	2	843	19	6½
11. Haddo	Westmoreland	1,050	17	10	555	5	10
12. Soho	St. Ann	425	0	0	105	0	0
13. Hays	St. Dorothy	518	10	0	130	0	0
14. Retreat	St. Dorothy	984	0	0	808	9	8
15. Bannister	St. Dorothy	550	15	5			
16. Farm	St. Catherine				1,551	18	0
17. Cow Park	St. Catherine	5,847	3	0			
18. White River	St. George*	1,595	16	3¼	347	7	0
19. Tobolski	St. Ann	1,327	1	1½	742	11	0
20. Batchelor's Hall	St. Thomas-in-the-East	1,894	10	10	1,721	6	6
21. Mammee Gully	Clarendon	1,023	15	10	417	12	0
22. Bodles	St. Dorothy	1,411	0	0	417	12	0
23. St Jago	Clarendon	2,056	8	11	963	10	0
24. Silver Grove	Trelawny	941	12	1	166	2	6
25. Thetford Hall	St. Dorothy	1,650	0	6	922	13	0
26. Rio Magno	St. Thomas-in-the-Vale	2,791	17	11	977	7	0
27. Two Mile Wood	St. Catherine	2,273	16	2	817	17	9
28. Lillyfield	St. Ann	547	8	4	411	12	8
29. Fullerswood	St. Elizabeth	1,083	4	0	1,040	13	7
30. Old Hope	Westmoreland	4,226	6	0	1,646	12	5
31. Agualta Vale	St. Mary	2,865	18	10	2,319	19	2
32. Forest	Westmoreland	1,954	3	7	1,174	7	6
33. Up Park Camp	St. Mary	1,560	14	7½	1,974	3	3
34. Crawle	St. Catherine	3,083	6	11¼	516	5	9
35. Phantillands	St. Elizabeth	1,142	2	4	598	19	0
36. Haughton Grove	Hanover	2,232	13	2	1,371	8	0

*Metcalfe – Formed 1842.
Sources: JA, AP, 1840, IB/11/4/84-5 and AP, 1845, IB/11/4/90.

8d. By 1843, this had increased to £910 17s. 0d. Though the deficit was reduced to £460 15s. 5½d. by 1845, the economic decline was still very much evident. Up Park, Bannister and Retreat pens had mixed fortunes in this period. Up Park Pen recorded small profits compared to the period of slavery. While in 1833 its credit balance had between £1,499, in 1841 it was £3. 0s.11d. With the exception of Cornwall, all the remaining pens in the sample had debit balances. Even in the case of Cornwall Pen, the credit balance was £100 less than 1809.[68]

Clearly, the shift into non-livestock commodities did not always restore profitability. Even after the change to logwood production, Thatchfield Pen remained unprofitable and the overseer was soon complaining that 'the quantity of logwood sold off the property did not even pay the taxes far less the Ranger's and my salary'.[69] The pen was subsequently put up for sale by public auction, but the highest bid was a paltry £500.[70]

Other pens which were poor in financial circumstances were also advertised for sale. Indeed, such advertisements increased in the 1840s, judging from the newspapers of the day. These pens included Coxheath and Mt Lebanon in Trelawny, and Pepper and Bonavista pens in St Elizabeth. The first pens to suffer sale seem to have been the satellite holdings as sugar estates attempted to scale down their operations. Thus, Worthy Park estate sold its satellite pens of Mickleton and Spring Garden.[71] Some pen-keepers simply abandoned their pens while some rented them to sugar estates which had survived the post-emancipation crises. Other pens reduced their acreage in order to become more efficient in this period. As such reduction was usually made by renting or selling small plots of land to freed people, this was also a means of courting the black labour force.

One method of ascertaining the extent of land disposal to workers is to search through the thousands of maps in the National Library of Jamaica. These records suggest that the sale (or rent) of lands to workers was more marked in the post-1845 period — perhaps a function of the effects of the Sugar Duties Act of 1846. During the period 1838–45, only 19 cases of pens being rented or land sold to workers were found. These were in the parishes of St Mary, St Catherine, Trelawny, St Ann, St Thomas-in-the-East, St David and St Elizabeth. In the majority of cases, unfortunately, the maps are incomplete in their reference tables, so that one is unable to get an accurate idea of the proportion of land disposed of.

Those which give complete information indicate that the land sold, relative to the total acreage of the pen, was small. Belmont Pen in St Ann had a total of 1,068 acres, 6 roods and 3 perches. In 1838, it rented only 20 acres to small settlers.[72] Lloyd's Pen in St David which comprised 433 acres, sold 63 acres 3 roods to 15 small settlers and Kelsal's Pen in St Catherine rented 38 acres 2 roods of its 206 acres 2 roods 29 perches.[73] A minority of pens, such as Bonny Pen, St Mary, sold virtually their entire acreage. Some maps, such as that of Malven Park Pen in St Ann, simply show the part of the pen sold, so that no comparative statements can be made (see figures. 8.1, 8.2, 8.3).

Apart from these records, only isolated cases of pens rented or land sold to workers have come to light from other sources. A plan of Dorothy Pen, St Ann, was found among the Tweedie papers. It shows that 255 acres of pen land, renamed John's Hall Village, were sold to small settlers in the early 1840s. Also seen is a plan of Rooksby Park Pen in the same parish, which shows that eight small settlers bought 24 acres and 28 perches of the pen's land.[74]

This economic decline did not continue unabated. Research into the post-1848 period indicates that pens showed signs of economic recovery. There was a restructuring of the pen-keeping industry as enterprising individuals expanded their existing acreage and diversified their activities to include meat and dairy production. Abandoned sugar estates were increasingly converted into pens and with the development of the plantation economies in the Hispanic Caribbean and the horse-racing industry in parts of the British Caribbean, the pen-keeping industry once more assumed an export dimension formerly observed in the early sixteenth century. As an indication of their improved status, in 1864, on the eve of the Morant Bay Rebellion, the pen-keepers were being classified among the landed interest. In his dispatch to Secretary of State Cardwell of that year, Governor Edward Eyre noted that

> the sugar growers, coffee growers and proprietors of stock farms, or pens as they are here called, represent the landed interest and constitute the aristocracy of the country; but they [sugar planters and coffee farmers] are sadly fallen from the proud and wealthy position formerly occupied by the West India proprietors.[75]

While there have been disagreements among historians from L.J Ragatz and Eric Williams to William Green, J.R. Ward and Seymour Drescher over whether the decline of the sugar plantations set in around the 1750s,

1770s or later towards 1834,[76] there seems to be little controversy over this claim that after the 1840s and 1850s, the sugar plantation as a dominant economic and social unit was on its way out in Jamaica. The decline of the sugar industry affected the market for locally-produced animals; but at the same time, this decline allowed the pen-keeping industry to restructure and diversify its markets. Other non-sugar producers also capitalized on the decline of the sugar plantations, buying abandoned estates for the development of the banana industry, for example.

Figure 8.1
Plan of Lloyd's Pen, St David

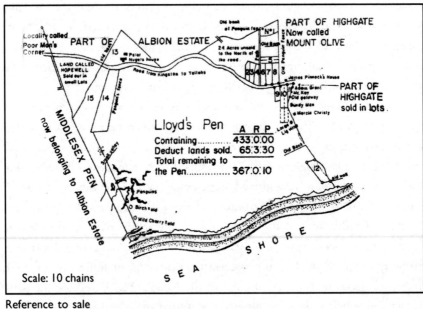

Reference to sale

1.	Sold to Francois Cassop......	1:0:30
2.	D° Ja Mc.Donald..............	0:2:30
3.	D° John Fisher.................	0:2:13
4.	D° W. Gordon.................	0:3:22
5.	D° A. Davidson} John Burnett}	1:0:00
6.	D° W. Moody.................	1:0:00
7.	D° W. Fisher.................	1:0:00
8.	D° John Mc.Dermot.........	1:0:00
9.	D° Joseph Hamilton.........	1:0:00
10.	D° David Lamont..............	2:0:00
11.	D° Betsy Green..............	1:0:00
12.	D° John Mc.Dermot.........	2:0:00
13.	D° M. Noel...................	12:2:16
14.	D° Rich & Renny...........	10:0:00
15.	D° Benjamin.................	30:0:00
	Total Sold	65:3:00

Figure 8.2
Plan of Bonny Pen, St Mary 1843/44

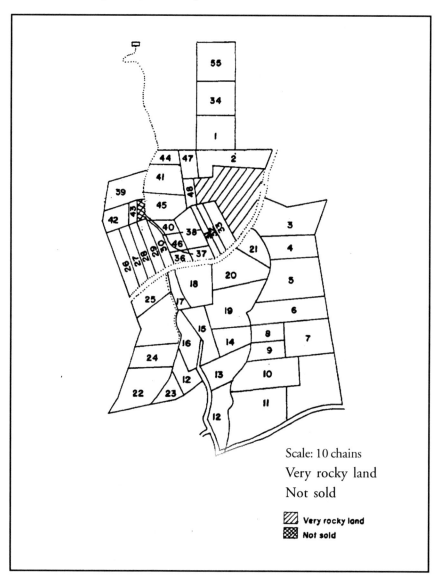

Scale: 10 chains
Very rocky land
Not sold

Very rocky land
Not sold

Figure 8.3
Plans of Malvern Park, St Ann

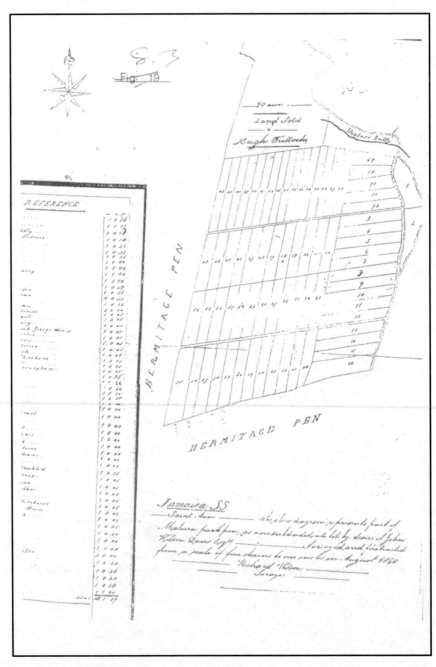

Table 8.5
Accounts of Rents, Fort George Pen, 1840–45

Year	Rent Paid £	s.	d.	Range of Rents	No. of Labourers
1840	Not stated			4s. to 9s. per month	85
1841	Not stated			4s. to 9s. per month	85
1842	223	17	6	4s. to 8s. per month	86
1843	176	12	3	4s. to 13s. per month	64
1844	124	19	0	5s. to 10s. per month	50
1845	82	4	3	Not stated	40
Total	607	13	0		

Source: NLJ, Rent roll, Fort George Pen, 1840–49, MS 274c.

In 1849, Governor Charles Grey of Jamaica was still maintaining that sugar was 'the produce which is raised for exportation [and that sugar] is beyond all comparison the chief object of the agriculture of Jamaica'.[77] By 1854, however, Governor Barkly was arguing oppositely to Grey, noting in his correspondence to the Duke of Newcastle that 'successful sugar cultivation may be said to be confined to three or four districts of limited area possessed of peculiar advantage. Elsewhere it would seem to be at its lowest ebb'; [78] and by 1860, William Sewell was observing that 'the [sugar] plantocracy of Jamaica is a thing of the past'.[79]

Qualitative statements by governors and visitors to the island relating to the decline of the sugar plantations and other agricultural units, are supported by quantitative data which show that whereas there had been 670 sugar estates in the island in 1830, between 1846 and 1869, 432 estates were abandoned. By 1882, the island had 188 sugar estates and by the 1890s, sugar was important only in the parishes of St James, Hanover and Westmoreland.[80] An 1884–85 agricultural report from a previously important sugar parish, St Thomas, is particularly insightful and was reflective of the general situation in the sugar parishes by this date. The report stated that: 'the area from the Plantain Garden River District to Port Antonio was once covered with flourishing sugar estates but is now utilized as grazing pens. Fifteen large sugar estates only are in operation'.[81]

Islandwide, the area under sugar cane had been reduced from 47,440 acres in 1869 to 26,121 in 1900.[82] Furthermore, whereas in 1770 sugar accounted for 76 per cent of the island's exports, with rum and molasses accounting for 13 per cent (making 89 per cent from sugar and its by-products), by 1870, sugar contributed 44.5 per cent to the value of total agricultural exports. By 1900, it contributed 11 per cent. By contrast, crops other than sugar were contributing an ever increasing percentage of the total exports, especially after 1880. The exception was coffee which declined as an estate crop in the immediate post-slavery period. Indeed, by 1865, 75 per cent of the coffee estates had been abandoned and by 1879, the rest had declined in output, value and exports.[83] In 1770, agricultural exports other than sugar had contributed only 11 per cent to the total value of exports. But by the second half of the nineteenth century their performance had improved.

The increasing importance of the non-sugar producers had been noted from 1854. In that year, Governor Barkly, after detailing the decline of sugar, coffee and livestock farms, which had dominated the agricultural landscape during slavery, observed that while the large plantations and the pens were in trouble, small settlers producing a variety of other commodities were doing better.[84] Indeed, by 1883 as the following table illustrates, rum, coffee, fruit, pimento and a variety of woods contributed 49.66 per cent.

It was the expanded livestock industry and the banana industry more than any other rural economic activity, which eventually controlled much of the former sugar lands. The *Handbooks of Jamaica* show that there were over 450 banana planters and penkeepers by the early twentieth century;[85] emerging as the new agro-elite.

Table 8.6
Share of Exports of Major Products, 1883

Product	Amount	Value (£ Sterling)	Share of Exports (%)
Sugar	33,392 hhds.	614,283	39.65
Rum	22, 742 puns.	295,645	19.09
Coffee	66,238 cwt.	133,535	8.62
Fruit	?	124,269	8.02
Pimento	76,022 cwt.	112,817	7.28
Dyewood etc	34,532 tons	103,034	6.65

Source: Handbook of Jamaica, 1883, p. 363.

The New Class of Non-Sugar Producers: The New Pen-Keepers and the Banana Barons

It was from the 1870s that concerted attempts were made to revive the pen-keeping industry in Jamaica and by 1900, there were some 307 pens, each with over 100 head of livestock.[86] The increased possibilities for the development of the meat and dairy industries and for the export of cattle and horses to Cuba and the Eastern Caribbean were incentives for this trend. Some pens were also occasionally exporting animals to the United Kingdom, the United States, Italy, France, Gibraltar, and South America.[87]

There were four main trends in the efforts to re-establish the pen-keeping industry in postslavery Jamaica. First, existing pen-keepers expanded their acreage, buying additional lands. Second, new investors bought up abandoned sugar estates and turned them over to cattle-rearing. As an indication of this tendency, the governor's agricultural report of 1884 pointed out that: 'the area from the Plantain Garden River District to Port Antonio was once covered with flourishing sugar estates but is now utilized as grazing pens. Fifteen large sugar estates only are now in operation'.[88]

Third, but least noted, sugar planters turned their land over to pasture, and fourth, pen-keepers who had switched to other enterprises such as logwood in the immediate post-slavery period, now switched back to livestock farming. This was the case of pen-keepers in St Elizabeth — like George Forbes — in the face of declining reserves of logwood in the late nineteenth century. The manager of Forbes's pen, Thatchfield, advised his employer in 1871 that the pen should once more be stocked with animals (which they had sold a few years back) because 'cattle is what will pay [on Thatchfield pen] for it has the expectation of being the best fattening pen in the parish'.[89] Montpelier's transformation from sugar estate to pen after its abandonment of sugar cultivation in 1855 has been well-documented by Barry Higman.[90]

By 1893, unlike in the period of slavery, the majority of animals were located on the pens. In that year, the pens had a total of 78,951 head of cattle and 18,912 horses and mules, compared to the estates' 24,612 and 4,361 respectively.[91]

The increase in grass cultivation islandwide was also phenomenal, the acreage in guinea grass moving from 110,705 in 1869 to 124,193 in

1900. The land in common pasture also increased from 222,790 acres in 1869 to 353,588 in 1900. Compared to sugar cane cultivation which engrossed 29,182 acres and banana cultivation which occupied 62, 685 acres in 1908, grazing lands comprised 615, 685 acres.

As the discussion of the banana farmers will show later, the majority of the members of what may be termed the 'penocracy', were not simply re-organized former sugar planters. In any case because the old 'sugarocracy' traditionally associated pen-keeping with a lower social position, this activity would not have been acceptable socially to some of them. That is not to say such a shift in activity by sugar planters never took place; for there had been an interplay of cattle and cane from the days of slavery. But this had not been a widespread occurrence. During slavery, some sugar planters had also invested in pen-keeping, but not as their primary income-generating activity. The newly established pens seemed to have been on average larger than the banana plantations. In 1908, those with over 100 head of livestock had an average of 615 acres, though not all of this land was always in pasture.[92]

Male pen owners were in the majority with females comprising just nine per cent of the group by the turn of the twentieth century. While the male members of the new group of pen-keepers were primarily resident on their properties, the female members were primarily absentees. Female pen-keepers may now have been freed from the stigma of owning livestock farms, but continued to be affected by other social factors which barred them from being integrally a part of the island's government. Male pen-keepers, on the other hand, became more and more visible in local and central government in the late nineteenth and early twentieth centuries. Before the 1870s, the list of jurors and vestry men rarely identified the occupation of office holders as pen-keepers. They would identify them as 'planters' even though independent checks on the names in these lists (for example in wills and inventories) reveal that some of those listed as planters were really pen-keepers. By the end of the nineteenth century and into the twentieth century, such lists identified occupations more correctly listing those who were pen-keepers or 'planter/pen-keepers'.

On the St Elizabeth Jury List of 1883 and 1884, 17 men were actually identified as 'pen-keepers'. This list contained the names of 110 planters, 17 pen-keepers, 55 store or shopkeepers and 122 professionals. In 1885, 22 pen-keepers were identified as jurors and in 1891, 32.[93] The *Blue Books of Jamaica*, *Votes of the House of Assembly* and the *Legislative Council Minutes* all reveal that pen-keepers were more visible as office holders in the post-slavery period. They held such positions as parish custos, attorney general, receiver general, member of the House of Assembly, speaker of the House of Assembly, clerk and deputy clerk of the Supreme Court and member of the Executive Committee. They were active in local and central government and held positions in both the lower and upper houses.[94]

Banana

The history of the rise of the banana barons, the other significant group of non-sugar proprietors in post-slavery Jamaica, represents an interesting parallel to that of the reconstituted pen-keepers and will be discussed by way of comparison. Before the 1870s, banana cultivation had been confined to the peasantry who contributed much to its widespread use as a fruit and as food (cooked when green). In fact in 1879, there was only one large banana plantation in the island. By 1900, however, the large banana plantation had become a dominant feature of the rural agricultural landscape.[95] Small banana farmers did not entirely disappear, but most of the good banana lands were by then in the hands of large-scale producers. Many banana plantations were established on former sugar lands and there seems to have been a direct relationship between the abandonment of sugar estates and the increase in the number of banana estates in north-eastern Jamaica. In 1900, close to 190 former sugar estates had been turned over to banana, and the number of banana plantations had increased from 113 in 1893 to 435 by 1910. There was also a dramatic increase in the number of stems being exported. In 1873, 38,689 stems had been exported. In 1880 this increased to 440,642 stems. By 1884, 1 million stems were being exported; by 1900, 11 million stems and by 1930, over 24 million stems valued at nearly £2 million.[96]

Banana estates first proliferated in parishes which had experienced the most drastic decline of the sugar industry — the parishes of St Mary, Portland and St Thomas. By 1890, not one large sugar estate was still in operation in Portland. Many St Mary planters had also long abandoned sugar cultivation. By 1910, the process of conversion of sugar estates into banana plantations had extended beyond these parishes to St Ann, St Catherine, and parts of Trelawny, St James, Hanover, St Elizabeth and Clarendon where the natural conditions for growing banana were less

Table 8.7
Contribution of Major Staples to Total Agricultural Exports 1870-1900

Crop/Export	1870	1880	1884	1890	1895	1900
Sugar	44.5	30.5	26.1	13.1	12.9	10.8
Rum	19.3	15.7	19.8	11.0	10.1	7.2
Coffee	15.1	20.9	11.1	15.7	19.3	7.8
Logwood	?	11.9	13.2	21.3	20.4	4.8
Banana	0.06	1.95	11.01	24.57	17.36	25.6
Pimento	?	8.0	4.3	4.5	5.1	9.7
Other (Minor) crops	21.04	11.05	14.49	9.83	14.84	24.1

Sources: Veront Satchell, *From Plots to Plantations*, (ISER, UWI, Mona, 1990), 46 and HBJ, Agricultural Reports, 1880–1900.

favourable but where they still brought higher returns than the sugar cane they replaced. Table 8.7 indicates that while sugar declined in its contribution to the share of exports, banana increased its share.

Table 8.8 gives an indication of the increase in the acreage under banana and the decrease in the land devoted to sugar cane cultivation.

There were many factors that attracted investors to the banana industry. In the first place, significant profits could be secured from banana

Table 8.8
Acres in Banana and Sugar Cane, 1891–1900

Year	Acres in Banana	Acres in Cane
1891	9,959	32,487
1892	14,860	32,486
1893	17,297	31,555
1894	18,528	31,284
1895	18,847	30,971
1896	19,227	30,036
1897	19,760	28,764
1898	23,405	27,123
1899	25,184	26,121
1900	27,543	25,616

Source: HBJ, 1906; G. Eisner, *Jamaica 1830–1930*, 206.

cultivation. Second, banana required a comparatively low capital outlay when compared to sugar. Capital could thus be in the form of re-invested profits from the professions and trades. This encouraged many Jewish merchants and professionals to invest in land. Only later did corporate channels from the United States, such as the United Fruit Company and the Boston Fruit Company, become heavy investors. A third factor was that land for the establishment of banana plantations could be bought at a much reduced cost. While abandoned estate lands were not made available to the black labouring class, they were sold relatively cheaply to the new investors, particularly as they were no longer being considered prime sugar lands. A fourth factor was that banana plantations required no capital equipment with most of the current expenses going into the payment of wages. The use by the banana barons of contract immigrant workers whom they paid extremely low wages further helped them to keep their production costs low. The importation of Asians took place within the context of an expanding labour force and a reduction in the plantations' demand for labourers. This effectively kept wages low and assured the planter class a steady nucleus of more 'controllable' workers.[97]

The banana barons — who along with the pen-keepers formed the new agro-elite in postslavery Jamaica — were distinct from the old 'sugarocracy'. In other words, they were not simply old sugar planters now investing in another crop, but were from a quite different section of the society. In fact not many of the old sugar plantocracy or their descendants were still connected with planting by the end of the nineteenth century. Those who remained in agriculture showed a strong disinclination to go into banana cultivation. They considered this a step down the social ladder, fruit growing being dismissed as 'a backwoods, nigger business'.[98] Those sugar planters who reluctantly made the shift to banana still devoted a part of their land to sugar cane, investing the profits from banana to keep the sugar industry going.

Many of the new land owners, such as the Jewish investors, had been engaged in commercial or professional activities not specifically linked to the sugar industry, and had not invested in landed property until banana offered a good investment opportunity. In fact Jews had only obtained their full civil rights in the nineteenth century. By the 1890s, the list of banana proprietors included several Portuguese Jewish names, one of the most notable of which was John Pringle who, according to the agricultural reports for the early twentieth century, invested also in livestock and cocoa.[99]

The typical banana baron tended to own smaller units than the earlier sugar planters. In 1893, the average size of a banana plantation was 75 acres. In 1920 it had increased to 123 acres, though of course some planters owned much larger individual units. Barry Higman's cartographic analysis indicates that large holdings of 1,000 acres and over had declined after the abolition of slavery. While in 1850 there had been 755 such holdings, in 1900 there were 456.[100]

The banana barons, unlike non-sugar producers in the period of slavery, were not at all marginal to the political process. They were active in local and central government and held offices previously associated with the 'sugarocracy.' John Pringle, for example, who was educated in Scotland at Aberdeen University, held several high offices in Jamaica. These included custos rotolorum for the parish of St Mary, chairman of the St Mary parochial board, justice of the peace for the parish, chairman of several boards, and member of the Privy and Legislative Councils of the island.[101]

Finally, the revival of pen-keeping and the transition of banana cultivation from an essentially small farming crop to an estate crop, had a negative impact on the labouring, specifically African-Jamaican, population. As Veront Satchell has shown, the tendency after 1880 was for the concentration of land into large holdings and as land was consolidated in the hands of large landholders, this affected the growth of the peasantry. This peasantry had been increasing rapidly since the 1840s; but the expansion of pen-keeping and the shift in banana cultivation from a peasant crop to an estate export crop, served to displace the peasantry from land they previously rented. Agricultural reports for 1897 show that the small banana cultivators were losing their land to the large land barons. In St Thomas for example, only 168 acres were in the hands of the small banana growers. The 20 large banana estates in that parish controlled some 12,000 acres of land. Similarly in Portland, in 1897, there were 35 large banana plantations and small farmers had only 735 acres of land. In St Mary, there were 41 large banana estates. There, the peasantry controlled 4,245 acres of banana land.[102] The re-emergence of the large plantations resulted in a reduction in the efforts of the Crown Colony government to increase landholding among the peasantry. The plantation sector, by re-asserting its hold on prime agricultural lands, contributed to the deterioration in the conditions of the African-Jamaicans and the ex-indentured Indian labourers. The re-emergence of an influential plantation sector resulted in a return to dependence on the estate for labour at subsistence wages. This dependence on the estate led to destitution and poverty because wages were constantly reduced in an attempt to rationalize production and keep command over the labour force.[103]

The solutions sought, emigration and rural to urban migration, were only partially successful in alleviating their condition. For those who returned to the estates, their positions were threatened by the importation of Indian indentured immigrants.

Contrary to the impression of homogeneity in the effects of apprenticeship and emancipation on Jamaican properties, conveyed in the existing literature, significant elements of property differentiation existed. In the first years of the implementation of the Apprenticeship System, both pens and plantations continued to experience fairly good labour relations. By 1836 labour relations had deteriorated. From all reports, the situation on pens became significantly worse. Pen-keepers attempted to classify all apprentices on pens as agricultural labourers, refused to implement task work and demanded work on weekends. As soon as slavery ended, these properties experienced a drastic reduction in their labour force. To counter the effects of this movement of labour some experimented unsuccessfully with immigrant labourers. Others employed alternative coercive tactics which simply hastened the trek from the pens. Sugar estates which had largely adopted the task system benefited from this movement of pen labourers. In addition to a reduction of labour, the dependence of pens on the sugar sector affected their economic conditions, for any reduction in the demand for working animals on the estates caused a predictable fall in the earnings of these properties. While some pens were abandoned outright, some sold parts of their acreage to small settlers and others shifted their orientation to other economic activities such as coffee, pimento or logwood.

Finally, the sugar planter class which had upheld and sustained this system of stratification was displaced by merchants and professionals turned banana planters, and livestock farmers. In the post-slavery period, then, while the sugar plantocracy declined in importance, it was those proprietors growing banana, cocoa and rearing livestock who came to dominate the agricultural economy and who formed the new agro-commercial elite. The continuation in the contest for space and economic power clearly continued long after the abolition of slavery.

CONCLUSION

J amaica's varied physical environment, combined with socioeconomic factors facilitated the emergence of a viable group of non-sugar producers in the island during the period of slavery and continuing into the post-slavery period. Thus, small-settler entrepreneurs who lacked the capital to invest in sugar were able to occupy and farm lands at first eminently suitable for the cane, after the switch to sugar, unsuitable for cane cultivation. By engaging in the production of livestock that found a ready market on the sugar estates, Jamaican pen-keepers created a niche for themselves in the sugar plantation society.

Theoretically, the sugar economy afforded a relatively substantial market capable of acting as a dynamic factor for the development of the island. This book has attempted to demonstrate, however, that such potential dynamism was not directed entirely towards the pen sector that in turn was unable to respond adequately to the market opportunities represented by the sugar economy.

Several factors seemed to have been responsible for this inability. Factors external to the independent pen-keepers included the production of livestock on estates' pasturelands and the establishment of satellite pens by sugar planters who were thus able to meet their own livestock needs. But even when the output of independent and satellite pens were combined, this was inadequate to meet the demand. The expansion of the sugar industry had, indeed, occurred at a time when the island had only a small number of pens. Furthermore, as the island experienced an initial and deliberate destruction of its livestock population formerly maintained by the Spanish settlers, by the invading English soldiers, the re-organization of the industry was predictably slow. The English settlers did make efforts to expand pen-keeping to meet the needs of the new sugar industry, but the general dislocation of coastal pens to facilitate the formation of sugar estates and the slow growth of interior pens established afterwards meant that some importation of animals was at first necessary. But as the sugar economy expanded and created competition among landholders in the island, pens were unable to maintain the required acreage of pasture and livestock population to supply the market. This dictated a continued dependence on imported supplies.

The precariousness of the sugar market in the nineteenth century was a further factor. Livestock farmers were heavily dependent on the sugar planters to purchase their animals. The section of the sugar estate market to which independent pen-keepers had access thus fluctuated according to the state of the market for sugar. This caused many livestock farmers to diversify their economic activities in an effort to cushion the effects of a low demand and thus a low price for working animals. This contributed to the comparatively low livestock density and drew off enslaved labourers for activities unconnected with livestock husbandry. The lack of a larger number of monocultural pens, therefore, had important implications for the supply of livestock in the island. Furthermore, the need to maintain a larger number of enslaved people than was usual for livestock husbandry (usually a ratio of one enslaved worker to 50 head of livestock was adequate but in Jamaica the ratio was higher) increased the production costs on the pens.

The socioeconomic and political marginality of the livestock farmers cannot be ignored as a contributing factor; for the lack of political power and of an effective lobby in the House of Assembly worked to their disadvantage. Indeed, the economic relations between planters and pen-keepers were not purely reciprocal but contained an exploitative element, generating tensions over 'contested terrain' at several junctures. The House of Assembly was dominated by sugar planters who, naturally, advanced their own interests. Planters, for example, did not acquiesce to the growing petitions of the graziers for an increase in the duty imposed on Spanish livestock. They argued that there was a great price differential in the horses, mules and cattle purchased from Spanish America, even after adding the profits of the middlemen merchants. Indeed, planters saw no need to pander to the wishes of the graziers. They blamed them for the high price of fresh beef and planters' stock and seemed not at all concerned about the economic viability of a domestic economic sector. While the dictates of mercantilism gave them little choice in the export market for their main staple, they exercised greater choice in the purchasing of plantation inputs and sought the cheapest markets when procuring these. Jamaica, like other plantation economies, therefore, maintained an import trade for plantation inputs. Nevertheless, as the degree of reliance was lower in that island, its divergence from the classic plantation model remained.

The existence of a domestic 'Creole' economy, (a phenomenon which might seem incompatible with a plantation system), had little impact on the level of absenteeism in Jamaica. It is true that pen-keepers and coffee planters were more resident than absentees; but it would seem that the availability of a local pool of prospective attorneys and overseers with vested interests in the economic viability of the sugar industry increased rather than decreased the trek of planters overseas. It has already been shown that the majority of pen-keepers were either old overseers or attorneys. Many of these had established pens from capital accumulated from their substantive posts. They relied on the estates for the profits of their pens and despite the charges of fraudulent practices by overseers/pen-keepers, surely had more to lose from an unprofitable estate than did independent overseers. The requirement after 1740 that all absentee proprietors be provided with annual accounts — the Accounts Produce — may also have served, in the case of Jamaica, to reduce the incidence of dishonest practices on the part of overseers. The combination of the existence of local units that would provide part of the plantations' input of working stock and proprietors with vested interests in the estates to manage them, may, arguably, have acted as a push factor for Jamaican sugar barons. The absence of these factors in places such as Barbados decreased rather than increased their level of absentee proprietors.

Finally, how different was Jamaica's plantation society from other plantation societies in the region as a result of its unique pen-keeping industry? The answer is that there was little qualitative deviance. The difference in the island's plantation economy was, admittedly very marked; but its society was similarly politically and culturally dominated by the planter class. European norms prevailed despite the significant role of the mixed-race pen-keepers. A Creole Society did develop, but resident proprietors such as coffee planters and pen-keepers aspired to the values of the British society. This was reflected in their lifestyle, the education of their children in the metropole and their trek to join the growing band of absentee proprietors as soon as their financial circumstances permitted. Thus, though their contribution was great in the evolution and maintenance of a Creole Economy, their role in Creole Society was less significant and Jamaica's plantation society remained remarkably similar to plantation societies elsewhere in the Caribbean.

The internal differences among the resident proprietors also served to reinforce the divisions in Creole Society. Kamau Brathwaite has duly noted that small settlers remained scattered, separate and without any consciousness of themselves as a group. He ascribes this primarily to their lack of political power and increasing marginalization to Creole Society.[1] However, the internal diversities even among particular groups of small settlers are other crucial factors. Pen-keepers, for example, comprised traditionally antagonistic sections — British and mixed-race, creole born and metropolitan born, small entrepreneurs and larger more profitable proprietors — among whom there was no common social goals outside of the context of their similar aspirations to the socioeconomic status of the sugar barons. Furthermore, resident sugar planters and resident pen-keepers were economically linked, yet socially separated. Consequently, the dichotomy between colonial and creole Jamaica which Brathwaite emphasized,[2] was evident despite the creole based pen-keeping class. Separation in the economic sphere only developed after the abolition of slavery; for as long as pens continued as adjuncts of the sugar economy, the fortunes of graziers and planters would continue to be inextricably linked. The decline of the plantations after 1776, for example, had had an impact on the pen-keepers. Admittedly, the transitional apprenticeship period had delayed the full economic effects of complete freedom; but technological changes in mill power, labour shortage and a reduced market for livestock in the late 1830s and 1840s caused pen-keepers to seek to regain their independent economic dynamic. A general restructuring of the industry occurred in the post-1845 period, which was characterized by the dramatic effects of the Sugar Duties Act. As a result the island had 604 pens by 1881 compared to 378 in 1844.[3]

It was the extension of pen-keeping to meet the expanding consumer market for meat and dairy products which accounted for the dramatic increase in the number of pens by the latter year and the development of what might well be termed the new 'penocracy' in the late nineteenth century. A factor in the expansion of pen-keeping was that many sugar estates were turned into cattle pens. This process was most marked in St Ann and Westmoreland.[5] Where existing pens were expanded this was usually carried out by sugar planters who were also converting their estates into cattle pens.[5]

Although the process of conversion of sugar estates into cattle pens had begun earlier, it was largely a phenomenon of the late nineteenth and early twentieth centuries.[6] By then, not only had the meat and dairy market expanded, but there also developed a demand for cattle in Cuba's sugar industry and for horses for the racing industry in other British Caribbean islands.[7] Jamaica's pen-keeping industry thus expanded to capitalize on this lucrative export trade. This expansion is indicated by the rise in the number of cattle in the island and the increase in the land under pasture. In 1880, there were 127,086 head of cattle in the island. By 1884, this had increased to 132,733 head.[8] Similarly, the acres in pasture in 1869 were 381,997 ½, and by 1891 this had risen to 422,535.[9]

This re-organized pen-keeping industry and the development of the new 'penocracy' are subjects which will have to be fully studied in the future in order to trace the cyclical history of pens in Jamaica. Moreover, the history of these non-sugar elite within a dominant sugar-based economy is crucial for an understanding of the difference in the structural composition of the ruling class in Jamaica's plantation society.

NOTES

Introduction

1. See Clinton Black, *The History of Jamaica* (London: Collins Clear-Type Press, 1958); Hilary Beckles and Verene Shepherd, *Liberties Lost: Caribbean Indigenous Societies and Slave Systems* (Cambridge: Cambridge University Press, 2004), chapter 1, and David Watts, *The West Indies: Patterns of Development, Culture and Environmental Change since 1492* (Cambridge: Cambridge University Press, 1987).

2. Beckles and Shepherd, *Liberties Lost*, chapter 1.

3. See Francisco Morales Padrón, *Spanish Jamaica*. Originally published 1952 (Kingston: Ian Randle Publishers, 2003), translated from the Spanish by Patrick E. Bryan in collaboration with Michael J. Gronow and Felix Oviedo Moral

4. W.J. Gardner, *A History of Jamaica from its Discovery by Christopher Columbus to the Present Time...including an Account of its Trade and Agriculture* (London: E. Stock, 1909).

5. B.W. Higman, *Slave Population and Economy in Jamaica, 1807–34.* (Cambridge: Cambridge University Press, 1976).

6. Hilary Beckles, *White Servitude and Black Slavery in Barbados, 1687–1715* (Knoxville: University of Tennessee Press, 1989).

7. See Philip Curtin, *The Atlantic Slave Trade: A Census* (Madison: University of Wisconsin Press, 1969) and David Eltis, *The Rise of African Slavery in the Americas* (Cambridge: Cambridge University Press, 2000).

8. E. (Kamau) Brathwaite, *The Development of Creole Society in Jamaica, 1770–1820.* (Oxford: Oxford University Press, 1971; Kingston: Ian Randle Publishers, 2005); Verene Shepherd and Hilary Beckles, eds., *Caribbean Slavery in the Atlantic World* (Kingston: Ian Randle Publishers, 2000).

9. Hilary Beckles and Verene Shepherd, eds., *Caribbean Freedom: Economy and Society from Emancipation to the Present.* (Kingston: Ian Randle Publishers, 1993).

10. Gad Heuman. *The Killing Time: The Morant Bay Rebellion in Jamaica.* (London: Macmillan, 1990).

11. *The Blackman Newspaper,* Kingston, Jamaica, 1929–31.

12. Beckles and Shepherd, eds., *Caribbean Freedom*; James Ferguson, *The Story of the Caribbean People* (Kingston: Ian Randle Publishers, 1999).

13. Brathwaite, *The Development of Creole Society in Jamaica.*

14. See Verene Shepherd, 'The Ranking Game: Discourses of Belonging in Jamaican History', Inaugural Lecture, University of the West Indies, Mona, April 2002.

15. B.W. Higman, 'The Internal Economy of Jamaican Pens', *Social and Economic Studies,* 38, no. 1 (1989): 61–86.

16. See Verene Shepherd, ed., *Slavery without Sugar: Diversity in Caribbean Economy and Society* (Gainesville: University Press of Florida, 2002).

17. See O. Nigel Bolland, *Struggles for Freedom: Essays on Slavery, Colonialism and Culture in the Caribbean and Central America.* (Belize City: Angelus Press, 1997).

18. Hilary Beckles, *A History of Barbados: From Amerindian Settlement to Nation-State* (Cambridge: Cambridge University Press, 1990), 74, and B.W. Higman, *Slave Populations of the British Caribbean, 1807–1834.* (Baltimore: Johns Hopkins University Press, 1984), 50–52.

19. See Herbert Klein, *African Slavery in Latin America and the Caribbean* (Oxford and New York: Oxford University Press, 1986), 93–96, and Watts, *The West Indies*, chapters 5,7,10.

20. Fernando Ortíz, *Contrapunteo cubano del tabaco y el azúcar.* (Habana: J. Montero, 1940).

21. B.J. Barickman, *A Bahian Counterpoint: Sugar, Tobacco, Cassava, and Slavery in the Recôncavo, 1780–1860* (Stanford: Stanford University Press, 1998); Stephen Bell, *Campanha Gaúcha: A Brazillian Ranching System, 1850–1920* (Stanford: Standford University Press, 1998). See reviews of these books by Allen Wells in *Plantation Society in the Americas* 6, no. 1 (Spring 1999): 95–106.

22. Higman, *Slave Population and Economy*, 12.

23. Higman, *Slave Populations of the British Caribbean,* 50, 52, and W. Dickson, *Letters on Slavery* (London: 1789), 6.

24. Yu Wu, 'Jamaican Trade, 1688–1769', PhD diss. The Johns Hopkins University, 1995. (University of Michigan's Microform Services, 1996).

25. See Gail Saunders, 'Slavery and Cotton Culture in the Bahamas', in V.A. Shepherd, ed *Slavery without Sugar: Diversity in Caribbean Economy and Society since the 17th Century.* Florida: University Press of Florida, 2002, p. 129-151; Michael Craton, 'Changing Patterns of Slave Families in the British West Indies', in Hilary Beckles and Verene Shepherd, eds., *Caribbean Slave Society and Economy,* (Kingston: Ian Randle Publishers, 1991), 228–49; Humphrey Lamur, 'Demographic Performance of Two Slave Populations of the Dutch-Speaking Caribbean', in Beckles and Shepherd, eds., *Caribbean Slave Society*, 209–20; A. Meredith John, *The Plantation Slaves of Trinidad, 1783–1816: A Mathematic and Demographic Enquiry.* (Cambridge: Cambridge University Press, 1988), and Jack Eblen, 'On the Natural Increase of Slave Populations: The Example of the Cuban Black Population', in S.L. Engerman and E. Genovese, eds., *Race and Slavery in the Western Hemisphere,* (Princeton: Princeton University Press, 1975), 211–47.

26. C.T. Onions, *The Oxford Dictionary of English Etymology* (Oxford: Oxford University Press, 1966), 663. According to W. Skeat, 'pennian' is of Latin origin. See W.W. Skeat, *An Etymological Dictionary of the English Language* (Oxford: Oxford University Press, 1910), 439. He also believes that the verb 'to pen' was connected to 'pindar', meaning a pound for cattle.

27. J. Wright, *The English Dialect Dictionary*, 6 vols. (London: Henry Frowde, 1903), IV, p. 464. See also E. Weekeley, *A Concise Etymological Dictionary of Modern English* (London: Secker & Werburg 1952 ed.), 303, and E. Partridge, Origins:

A Short Etymological Dictionary of Modern English (London; Greenwich House, 1966 edn.), 480. In old English, the word carried two 'ns', being spelt 'penns'. Such 'penns' or enclosures were known as 'fold' or 'fauld' in Scotland and Ireland, and 'faald' (ffauld?) in Cumbria. To 'fold' or to 'fauld', thus meant to pen or enclose. See Wright, *The English Dialect Dictionary*, II, p. 439; M. Robinson, ed., *The Concise Scots Dictionary* (Aberdeen: Aberdeen University Press, 1985), 189, and J.S. Otto and N.E. Anderson, 'Cattle Ranching in the Venezuelan Llanos and Florida Flatwoods: A Problem in Comparative History', *Comparative Studies in Society and History,* 28 (1986): 672–83.

28.   F.G. Cassidy & R.B. LePage, *Dictionary of Jamaican English* (Cambridge: Cambridge University Press, 1967), 345.

29.   Anthony Trollope, *The West Indies and the Spanish Main* (London, 1859), 42.

30.   Higman, 'The Internal Economy of Jamaican Pens,' 61–86.

31.   A list of enslaved people on Batchelor's Hall Pen, St Thomas in-the-East, in 1791, records the names of three 'pen-keepers' Yaw, Cudjoe, and Cuffie. Yaw was the 'head pen-keeper', Cudjoe, the 'second pen-keeper'and Cuffie the 'third pen-keeper'. (See Cambridge, Cambridge University Library, Vanneck, MSS, J.E.P., Slave List, 1791, box 2, bundle 27). Similarly, on St Jago and Paisley pens in Clarendon in 1827, four enslaved men were classified as 'pen-keepers'; (Exeter, Exeter University Library, Slave List 1827, Gale/Morant Collection, 4/B/4), and on Good Hope, Potosi and Lansquinet estates in Trelawny, a total of four 'pen-keepers' was listed. (J.A., John Tharp's inventory, 1805, 1B/11/3/104, fols. 3471). This type of occupational classification was typical of the period of slavery. Thus, 'field slaves'worked in the fields, 'hogboys' attended to the hogs and 'pen boys' assisted the adult male pen-keepers in the pens

32.   Lincoln, Lincolnshire Archives Office, Journal of Thomas Thistlewood, July 1, 1750, Mon. 31/1, fol. 320. Also, in a letter to the *Falmouth Post* of January 25, 1848, the writer who indicated that he was a 'pen-keeper' lauded a Mr. Edwards of Knockalva Pen in Hanover for the fine stock he bred there. He described Edwards as being 'among the finest pen-keepers in the island'. Edwards was, however, the overseer. He started working at Knockalva in 1843 as assistant manager, becoming manager in 1844. Pen overseers were, apparently, increasingly called 'managers' or 'superintendents' after emancipation.

33.   This is equivalent to the now obsolete 'penner', meaning the owner of a cattle pen. See Cassidy and LePage, *Dictionary of Jamaican English*, 345.

34.   Benjamin M'Mahon was an Irishman who had come to Jamaica in 1818. He claimed to have been 'eighteen years in the planting line', and considered himself an authority on Jamaica's affairs. See his *Jamaica Plantership* (London: E. Wilson, 1939), ii.

35.   The most notable of these planters who maintained their own pens were Simon Taylor, Chaloner Arcedeckne, Hon. John Tharp, John Wedderburn, Henry Dawkins, George Ellis and the Prices of Worthy Park.

36.   For an elaboration of the stated characteristics of the plantation economy, see Lloyd Best, 'The Outlines of the Model of a Pure Plantation Economy', *Social and Economic Studies,* 17 (1968): 238–326; George Beckford, *Persistent Poverty*:

Underdevelopment in Plantation Economies of the Third World (New York: Oxford University Press, 1972); F.L. Pryor, 'The Plantation Economy as an Economic System', *Journal of Comparative Economics,* 16 (1982): 288–317 and Alex Dupuy, 'Slavery and Underdevelopment in the Caribbean: A Critique of the "Plantation Economy" Perspective', *Dialectical Anthropology,* 17 (1983): 239.

37.   See Verene Shepherd, 'Pens and Penkeepers in a Plantation Society: Aspects of Jamaican Social and Economic History', PhD. diss, University of Cambridge, 1988 and Verene Shepherd, 'Liberation Struggles on Livestock Farms in Jamaica', in Shepherd and Beckles eds., *Caribbean Slavery in the Atlantic World,* 260–76; 896–904.

38.   Thomas Thistlewood, from Tupholme, Lincolnshire, lived in Jamaica from 1750–86. He worked initially as overseer on several properties in Western Jamaica before establishing his own pen. The edited journals can be read in Douglas Hall's *In Miserable Slavery: Thomas Thistlewood in Jamaica, 1750–1786* (London: Macmillan, 1989).

39.   Some historians are still reluctant to use the word 'rape' to refer to Thistlewood's sexual activities with enslaved women. Others ignore these sexual activities altogether. I was somewhat surprised to see Thistlewood's enslaved workers referred to only as his 'teachers and companions', in Philip Sherlock's and Hazel Bennett's book, *The Story of the Jamaican People* (Kingston: Ian Randle Publishers, 1997), 168.

40.   Immanuel Wallerstein, *The Modern World System* Vol. I (New York: Academic Press, 1974).

Chapter 1

1.   Philip Wright, ed., *Lady Nugent's Journal of her Residence in Jamaica 1801–1805* (Kingston: The Institute of Jamaica, 1966), 12.

2.   D. Mason, *Observations on the Present State of the Island of Jamaica* (London, 1837), 179.

3.   Bryan Edwards, *The History Civil and Commercial of the British Colonies in the West Indies,* vol. I (London, 1793), 149.

4.   Edward Long, *A History of Jamaica or, General Survey of the Ancient and Modern State of that Island: With Reflections on its Situations, Settlements, Inhabitants, Climate, Products, Commerce, Laws, and Government.* Add. Mss. 12,404, Long MSS, fols. 176 and 182, and Frank Cundall and Joseph L. Pieterz, *Jamaica Under the Spaniards.* (Kingston: Institute of Jamaica, 1919), 26.

5.   W.J. Gardner, *A History of Jamaica from its Discovery by Christopher Columbus to the Year 1872....including the Account of its Trade and Agriculture.* (London: E. Stock, 1909).

6.   Mason, *Observations.* See also P. Whittaker, 'The Spanish Contribution to American Agriculture', *Agricultural History,* 3 (1929): 2–3; and Peter Martyr, *History of the West Indies* (London, 1675), 11.

7.   C. Bishko, 'The Peninsular Background of Latin American Cattle Ranching', *Hispanic American Historical Review,* 32 (1952), 513.

8.   Noel Deerr, *The History of Sugar*, 1 (London: Chapman and Hall, 1949), 207.

9.   Ibid., 175.

10.   London, British Library, Department of Manuscripts, Sloane, MSS., 3,918, fols. 6–9; and Sir Hans Sloane , *A Voyage to the Islands*, I (London, 1707), lxxiv. See also Thomas Coke, *A History of the West Indies*, I (Liverpool, 1808), 246.

11.   Gardner, *History of Jamaica*, 13.

12.   Cundall and Pieterz, *Jamaica Under the Spaniards*, 35.

13.   Ibid., 50.

14.   Ibid. Around 1494, there were about 60,000 Tainos in Jamaica. By 1637, none was left. J.J. Wood, *Jamaica: Its History* (Kingston, 1844), 8.

15.   Ibid.

16.   G. Penn, *Memorials*, 11 (London, 1660), 1.

17.   *The Political Constitution of Jamaica* (London, 1844), 2.

18.   Gardner, *History of Jamaica,* 36.

19.   Ibid.

20.   Add. Mss. 12,404, ff. 190, 192.

21   Ibid.

22.   Add. Mss., 12,404, fol. 190. Coke had a religious explanation for the fate which befell the soldiers. According to him, 'the anger of Omnipotence appeared to frown upon them, and threatened to punish them with that famine which their own profligacy had occasioned'. T. Coke, *A History of the West Indies*, 251.

23.   J. Thirsk, *The Rural Economy of England* (London: Continuum, 1984), 139, 164, 170 and 204. See also F. Emery, 'The Farming Regions of Wales', in *The Agrarian History of England and Wales*, vol. IV, ed. J. Thirsk (Cambridge: Cambridge University Press, 1967), 137–42.

24.   D. Knight, *Gentlemen of Fortune: The Men Who Made Their Fortunes in Britain's Slave Colonies* (London: Frederick Muller, 1978), 36.

25.   Richard Sheridan, *Sugar and Slavery: An Economic History of the British West Indies* (Barbados: Caribbean Universities Press, 1974), 119.

26.   Edwards, *The History of the West Indies*, 245.

27.   C.O. 142/34–59, *Blue Books of Jamaica* [BBJ] 1811–1845.

28.   Charles Leslie, *A New History of Jamaica* (London, 1740), 167–68. *See also Laws of Jamaica*, 1681, Anno Caroli II, Cap. x, p.

29.   Michael Craton and James Walvin, *A Jamaican Plantation* (London: WH Allen, 1970), 30–42.

30.   Gardner, *A History of Jamaica*, 42.

31.   Long, *History of Jamaica*. Add. Mss. 12,405, f. 42.

32.   Gardner, *A History of Jamaica*, 79.

33.   J. Roby, *A History of St James* (London, 1849), 40.

34.   Ibid., 102.

35.   Long, *History of Jamaica*, Add. Mss. 12,404, f. 205.

36.   Sloane MSS, 3,918; H. Barham, *Account of Jamaica* (London, 1722), f. 56.

37.   Add. Mss., 12,404, f. 218.

38.   See Sheridan, *Sugar and Slavery*, 212.

39.   Ibid.

40.	The history of Cary Helyar is more fully explored in J.H. Bennett, 'Cary Helyar: Merchant and Planter in Seventeenth-Century Jamaica', *William and Mary Quarterly*, 21 (1964): 53–76.
41.	Ibid. Bybrook was in fact adjacent to Modyford's own plantation at Sixteen Mile Walk in St Catherine.
42.	Nuala Zahedieh, 'Trade, Plunder and Economic Development in Early English Jamaica, 1655–1689', The *Economic History Review*, 39 (1986): 205–22.
43.	Long, *History of Jamaica*, Add. Mss. 12,404, f. 223.
44.	Ibid., f. 224
45.	Ibid.
46.	Richard Dunn, *Sugar and Slaves: The Rise of the Planter-Class in the English West Indies, 1624–1713* (Chapel Hill: University of North Carolina Press, 1972), 5.
47.	T.W. Merrick and D.H. Graham, *Population and Economic Development in Brazil, 1800 to the Present* (Baltimore: John Hopkins University Press, 1979), and E.B. Burns, *A History of Brazil* (New York: Columbia University Press, 1980), 82–85.
48.	F.C. Innes, 'The Pre-Sugar Era of European Settlement in Barbados', *Journal of Caribbean History*, 1 (1970): 1–22. See Also Hilary Beckles, *A History of Barbados* (Cambridge: Cambridge University Press, 1990).
49.	Eric Williams, *History of the People of Trinidad and Tobago* (London: André Deutsch, 1964), 15–19.
50.	Lewis Gray, *History of Agriculture in the Southern United States to 1860*, vol. I (Washington DC: Carnegie Institute, 1933), 6–7.
51.	Ibid., 138.
52.	G. Dunbar, 'Colonial Carolina Cowpens', *Agricultural History*, 25 (1961):1.
53.	P. Kriedte, *Peasants, Landlords and Merchant Capitalists: Europe and the World Economy, 1500–1800* (Cambridge: Cambridge University Press, 1983), 109.

Chapter 2

1.	Richard Dunn, *Sugar and Slaves: The Rise of the Planter Class in English West Indies, 1624–1713* (Chapel Hill: The University of North Carolina Press, 1972), 169. This calculation was based on Bochart and Knollis, *A New and Exact Map of the Island of Jamaica c. 1684*, C.O. 7006. This figure probably also included a few hog crawles. Craskell and Simpson's map of 1763 grouped pens with 'non-sugar units', so that this makes it difficult to obtain an accurate idea of the number of livestock farms. See Craskell and Simpson, Map of Jamaica, 1763, C.O. 700/16
2.	W.J. Gardner, *A History of Jamaica from its Discovery by Christopher Columbus to the Present Time...* (London, 1873), 116.
3.	Noel Deerr, *The History of Sugar*, 2 vols. Vol. 1(London, 1949), 175.
4.	Richard Sheridan, *Sugar and Slavery: An Economic History of the British West Indies 1625–1775* (London: Caribbean Universities Press, 1974), 211–12.
5.	N. Sainsbury, ed., Calendar of State Papers: America and the West Indies, 1669–1674 1(London: Longman, Green and Roberts, 1964), 99-105.
6.	Dunn, *Sugar and Slaves*, 15–46.

7.   Ibid.

8.   Sheridan, *Sugar and Slavery*, 231.

9.   Bryan Edwards, *History, Civil and Commercial, of the British Colonies in the West Indies*. I, 2 vols. (London, 1793), II, p. 223.

10.   Ibid., 255.

11.   Edward Long, *History of Jamaica*, 3 vols., vol. 1, British Museum, Add. Mss. 12,404, 194.

12.   Ibid., f. 199.

13.   Instructions to Lord Windsor, March 31, 1661, C.O. 381, fol. 18, and Instructions to Colonel Modyford, 1664, C.O. 381, fols. 29–31.

14.   Long, *History of Jamaica*, I, Add. Mss. 12,404, fol. 218.

15.   Ibid., fol. 220.

16.   Dunn, *Sugar and Slaves*, 154.

17.   *Survey of Jamaica*, 1664, C.O. 381, ff. 617–34.

18.   Sainsbury, *Calendar of State Papers*, 1669-1674, ff. 99–106.

19.   'A list of landholders in the island of Jamaica together with the number of acres each person possesses, taken from the Quit Rent Books in 1754', C.O. 142/31, Enclosure to Governor Knowles' Despatch, 31 Dec. 1754. Admittedly, the use of the 1754 data represents a big jump from 1670, but accurate figures for the intervening years are unavailable.

20.   Long, *History of Jamaica* I, Add. Mss. 12,404, fol. 205.

21.   A.E. Smith, *Colonists in Bondage: White Servitude and Convict Labour in America, 1607–776* (Chapel Hill: University of North Carolina Press, 1947), 309–10 and David Galenson, *White Servitude in Colonial America: An Economic Analysis* (Cambridge: Cambridge University Press, 1981), 95, 218.

22.   Long, *History of Jamaica* I, Add. Mss. 12, 404, ff. 299–300.

23.   Phillip Curtin, *The Atlantic Slave Trade: A Census* (Madison: University of Wisconsin Press, 1969), 122. For additional reading on the African trade in Africans, see Michael Craton, *Sinews of Empire: A Short History of British Slavery* (London: Temple Press, 1974), 43-107; R. Anstey, 'The Volume and Profitability of the British Slave Trade, 1761–1807', in E. D. Genovese and S.L. Engerman, eds., *Race and Slavery in the Western Hemisphere: Quantitative Studies* (Princeton: Princeton University Press, 1975), 331; Phillip Curtin, 'Measuring the Atlantic Slave Trade', in Genovese and Engerman, eds., *Race and Slavery*, 107–28, and M. Craton, J. Walvin and D. Wright, *Slavery, Abolition and Emancipation: Black Slaves and the British Empire* (London: Longman, 1974), 43–107; David Eltis, *The Rise of African Slavery in the Americas* (Cambridge: Cambridge University Press, 2000).

24.   Curtin, 'Measuring the Atlantic Slave Trade', 212.

25.   Spanish Town, Jamaica Archives [J.A.], Accounts Produce [A.P.] 1740, 1B/11/41.

26.   Long estimates that there were 340 sugar estates in the island in 1740.

27.   See Sheridan, *Sugar and Slavery*, 212–14; Nuala Zahadieh, 'Trade, Plunder and Economic Development in Early English Jamaica, 1655-1689', *The Economic History Review*, 39 (1986): 221; Adam Smith, *An Enquiry into the Nature and*

Causes of the Wealth of Nations: (London, 1776), 587; J.H. Bennett, 'Cary Helyar, Merchant and Planter of Seventeenth Century Jamaica', *William and Mary Quarterly,* 3rd series, 21, (1964): 53–76, and Richard Pares, *Merchants and Planters* (Cambridge: Cambridge University Press, 1960).

28.   For example, H.A. Innes, *The Fur Trade in Canada: An Introduction to Canadian Economic History* (Toronto: University of Toronto Press, 1956).

29.   F.C. Batie, *A Comparative Economic History of the Spanish, French and English on the Caribbean Islands* (Michigan: University Microfilms, A Xerox Company, 1972), 152.

30.   The Earl of Balcarres to the Duke of Portland, May 25, 1800, C.O. 137/1-490. See also Deerr, *History of Sugar,* I, 176–207.

31.   Edwards, *History of the West Indies,* II, 247.

32.   Richard Sheridan, *The Development of the Plantations to* 1750: *An Era of West Indian Prosperity, 1750–1775.* (Barbados: Caribbean Universities Press, 1970), 40–47.

33.   J.M. Phillippo, *Jamaica: Its Past and Present State* (London, 1843), 85.

34.   Charles Leslie, *A New History of Jamaica* (London, 1740), 318 and Thomas Roughley, *The Jamaica Planter's Guide: Or a System of Planting and Managing a Sugar Estate in that Island and Throughout the British West Indies in General.* (London, 1823), 128.

35.   Randor Plantation Journal, 1826, N.L.J. MS 180.

36.   J.A, A.P., 1740–1840. Files 1B/11/41–48.

37.   Leslie, *A New History of Jamaica,* 318.

38.   Franklin Knight, *Slave Society in Cuba During the Nineteenth* Century (Madison: University of Wisconsin Press, 1970), 40.

39.   Anon., 'Extract from Blackwood's Magazine', *Jamaica Pamphlets* 22 no. 11 (1890): 781.

40.   Long, *History of Jamaica* I, Add. Mss. 12, 404, f. 220.

41.   Ibid., f. 308.

42.   Sheridan, *Sugar and Slavery,* 232.

43.   'Return of the Island Secretary Compiled from a Census of the Inhabitants of the Island'. Jamaica House of Assembly Votes, June 13, 1844. See also B.W. Higman, *The Jamaican Censuses of 1844 and 1861* (Social History Project, The University of the West Indies, Mona, 1980), 1. The Accounts Produce returned 20 pens in 1740. As the pens represented in these returns normally accounted for about 14 per cent of the island total in the eighteenth century, this figure is calculated on this assumption. This figure may still seem small when it is considered that 73 pens existed in 1684. However, at least some pens would have been swallowed up by sugar estates on the coast, to be later reestablished in the interior.

44.   Long, *History of Jamaica* I, Add. Mss., 12,404, ff. 391–92.

45.   James Knight, *The State of the Island of Jamaica* (London, 1726). See also F.W. Pitman, *The Development of the British West Indies 1700–1763* (New Haven: Yale University Press, 1917), 367–77.

46.   Pitman, *The Development of the BWI,* 367–77.

47.   Letter from the Attorneys to Messrs. W.R. & S. Mitchell, February 17, 1822. J.A., Attorneys' Letterbook, 1B/5/83/1.

48.   Ibid., Letter of December 30, 1822.

49. James Robertson, 'Maps of the Counties of Cornwall, Middlesex and Surrey' (Kingston, 1804). National Library of Jamaica.

50. Michael Craton, *Searching for the Invisible Man: Slaves and Plantation Life in Jamaica* (Cambridge, Mass.: Harvard University Press, 1978), 2.

51. Dunn, *Sugar and Slaves*, 28. See also Sir Hans Sloane, *A Voyage to the Islands*. 2 vols. vol. 1 (London, 1707), 33.

52. Sheridan, *Sugar and Slavery*, 144–46. For another perspective on planter attitude towards mill types and their relation to the extraction rate of cane juice, see W. Barrett, 'Caribbean Sugar Production Standards in the Seventeenth and Eighteenth Centuries', in J. Parker, ed., *Merchants and Scholars: Essays in the History of Exploration and Trade* (Minneapolis: The University of Minnesota Press, 1966), 147–70. See also David Watts, *The West Indies: Patterns of Development, Culture and Environmental Change since 1492* (Cambridge: Cambridge University Press, 1987), 194, 197.

53. N.L.J., St Andrew Estate Maps, St A. 1,134 and St A. 1,142. See also Bristol, Bristol Record Office, Elbridge Family Papers, AC/WO 16(2). A resurvey of the land done at the request of Captain Thomas French in 1745/6, revealed that the true extent of the land patented by Lewis was 931 acres. See N.L.J., St Andrew Estate Maps, St A. 446.

54. Edwards, *History of the West Indies*, II, 248–59.

55. N.L.J., Spring Plantation Accounts, 1784, MS. 1,058.

56. J.A., R.R.S., St Andrew, 1B/11/7/32.

57. See J.A., A.P., 1800, 1B/11/4/27–8 and A.P., 1832, 1B/11/4/73, and J.A., Spring Plantation, A.P., 1780–1800, 1B/11/4/9, 27–28.

58. Elbridge Family Papers, AC/WO 16(27), 1–11, September 7, 1749.

59. Hibbert and Jackson to Smyth, November 22, 1767, Elbridge Family Papers, AC/WO 16(27) 67c.

60. Elbridge Family Papers, 21–30, Watson & Company to Woolnough, June 25, 1757.

61. *Royal Gazette,* June 19–26, 1799, p. 55 and December 11–18, 1813.

62. N.L.J., Spring Plantation Accounts, 1784, MS 1,058.

63. Watson & Company to Woolnough, June 25,1757, Elbridge Family Papers, AC/WO 16(27) 21.

64. Hibbert & Jackson to Smyth, March 26, 1768, AC/WO 16(27) 68(b).

65. Ibid.

66. Hibbert & Company to Smyth, May 16, 1775, AC/WO 16(27) 91(a).

67. Stephens & Company to Smyth, December 8, 1783, AC/WO 16(27) 118(a).

68. See Verene Shepherd, 'Problems in the Supply of Livestock to Sugar Estates in the Period of Slavery: An Example From the History of Spring Sugar Plantation, St Andrew, Jamaica. c.1700–c.1800', (Postgraduate Seminar Paper, University of the West Indies, Mona, Jamaica, 1987).

69. See L.J. Symons, *Agricultural Geography* (London: Praeger Publisher, 1967), and J.T. Coppock, *An Agricultural Geography of Britain* (London: Bell, 1971).

70. B.W. Ilberry, *Agricultural Geography* (Oxford: Oxford University Press, 1985), 8–9.

71. J.A., A.P. 1B/1/4/11. An early map of the island confirms this southern concentration

of pens. It is Bochart & Knollis, *A New and Exact Mapp of the Island of Jamaica*, c. 1684. London, Public Record Office, C.O. 700/6. Simpson & Craskill's Map of Jamaica, 1763 (C.O. 700/16) shows the gradual spread of pens to western and northern parishes.

72.   J.A., A.P., 1800–1840. 1B/11/27–28, 54–56, 84–85.

73.   Jamaica Almanack, 1815, pp. 221–83. In-givings were really returns of proprietors, properties, enslaved people and stock for the purposes of taxation. In these returns, pens are easily recognizable by the ratio of enslaved people to stock. Pens had fewer enslaved workers than sugar plantations and a larger number of animals. In-givings were not always complete, but are still a fairly reliable check on the location of pens.

74.   See Rebecca Scott, *Slave Emancipation in Cuba: The Transition to Free Labour, 1860-1901* (New Jersey: Princeton University Press, 1984), 8–12 and E.B. Burns, *A History of Brazil* (New York: Columbia University Press, 1970 ed), 82–83.

75.   Other physical environmental factors were not as 'rigorously' applied. Higman found no significant correlation in 1832 between the distribution of sugar estates and altitude, slope, relative relief or rainfall. See Higman, *Slave Population and Economy in Jamaica*, 18.

76.   Edwards's *History of the West Indies*, II, 210.

77.   Douglas Hall, *Free Jamaica, 1835–1865:An Economic History* (London: Caribbean Universities Press, 1976), 14–17 and Higman, *Slave Population and Economy*, 18–25. See also J.M. Phillippo, *Jamaica: Its Past and Present State* (London, 1843), 88.

78.   See S. Jumper, T. Bell and K. Ralston, *Economic Growth and Disparities: A World View* (New Jersey: Prentice-Hall, 1980), 6.

79.   Long, *History of Jamaica*, I, Add. Mss. 12,404, fol. 335.

80.   Thomas Coke, *A History of the West Indies* 3 vols. (Liverpool, 1808), I, 373–74.

81.   Long, *History of Jamaica*, 1, Add. Mss. 12,404, fol. 335.

82.   Simon Taylor to Chaloner Arcedeckne, March 1, 1790, Cambridge, Cambridge University Library, Vanneck MSS J.E.P., box 2, bundle 16.

83.   Gardner, *History of Jamaica*, 326.

84.   Long, *History of Jamaica*, II, Add. Mss. 12,404, f. 48.

85.   Ibid.

86.   *Handbook of Jamaica* [HBJ], 1884–85, 242–43.

87.   G.W. Bridges, *Statistical History of Manchester* (Jamaica, 1824) and Higman, *Slave Population and Economy*, 21.

88.   Hall, *Free Jamaica*, 17 and B.W. Higman, 'The Internal Economy of Jamaican Pens, 1760–1890', *Social and Economic Studies*, 38, no. 1 (1989): 32, 65. Reprinted in Verene Shepherd, ed., *Slavery Without Sugar: Diversity in Caribbean Economy and Society* (Gainesville: University Press of Florida, 2002), 63–81.

89.   See William Dickinson to Thomas Salmon, September 2, 1792 and December 1, 1792, Taunton, Somerset Record Office, Dickinson Family Papers, DD/DN/468.

90.   Leslie, *A New History of Jamaica*, 23.

91.   Colin Clarke, *Kingston, Jamaica: Urban Development and Social Change* (Berkeley: University of California Press, 1975), 11.

92.   N.L.J., St Andrew Estate Maps, St A. 163 and 170; Hibbert and Jackson to John Hugh Smyth, 26 March 1768, Bristol Record Office, Elbridge Family Papers, AC/WO 16 (27) 68(b).

93.   Wilma Bailey, 'Kingston, 1692–1843: A Colonial City,' PhD diss., University of the West Indies, Mona, 1974, 150 and J. Stewart, *An Account of Jamaica* (London, 1808), 11–12.

94.   See Verene Shepherd, 'Livestock and Marginality in Jamaica Sugar Plantation Economy', *Social and Economic Studies*, Vol. 41, no. 2 (1992), 183–202.

Chapter 3

1.   Jamaica Archives [J.A.], *Accounts Produce* [A.P.] 1B/11/4/1.

2.   Ibid. 1B/11/4/9.

3.   Ibid., ff. 3–216.

4.   Ibid.

5.   Ibid., 1B/11 /4/27, 28.

6.   B.W. Higman, 'Slave Population and Economy in Jamaica at the time of Emancipation', PhD diss., University of the West Indies, Mona, 312–13.

7.   See Rebecca Scott, *Slave Emancipation in Cuba: The Transition to Free Labour 1860–99* (New Jersey: Princeton University Press, 1984), 11–12 and E.B. Burns, *A History of Brazil* (New York: Columbia University Press, 1980), 87.

8.   Bryan Edwards, *History of the West Indies*, 2 vols. (London, 1798), II: 259.

9.   Taylor to Arcedeckne, October 1782, Cambridge, Cambridge University Library, Vanneck MSS, JEP Box 2, Bundle 10.

10.   J.B. Moreton, *Manners and Customs in the West Indian Islands*, (London, 1790), 57.

11.   J.A., A.P. 1820, 1B/11/4/56.

12.   *St Jago de la Vega Gazette*, 1791–92: 4–11 and April 1801: 93.

13.   See James Stevenson to Mrs. Scarlett, April 8, 1800, Hull, Hull University, Brynmor Jones Library, Scarlett Family Collection, DDCA/41/17. Prices fluctuated according to prevailing market conditions. The chief factors influencing the market were drought, war and any consequent depression in the sugar trade. Drought could create an excess of demand over supply and cause and increase in the price of animals. This happened in 1804 when the price of mules moved from £130 to £140 each. The price of fresh beef also increased in times of drought. On the other hand, if production on estates suffered as a result of changes in the sugar market, pens could find themselves being unable to dispose of stock to their principal buyers. In such cases, they were forced to sell to the butchers at low prices. See correspondence between William Dickinson and John White, Dickinson Family Papers, DD/DN/471–4 and J.A. Attorneys' Letterbook, October 21, 1822, 1B/5/83/1.

14.   *Jamaica House of Assembly Votes* [J.H.A.V.], 1795–96: 282.

15.   *Royal Gazette*, 1780–1834, *St Jago de la Vega Gazette*, 1791–1831 and the *Falmouth Post*, 1791–1836.

16. Lincoln, Lincolnshire Archives Office, Thistlewood's Journal, Vineyard Pen, January 15, 1751, Mon. 31/2, fol. 8. Markham was a butcher from Black River.

17. Ibid., Mon. 31/1. fols. 342, 348.

18. Verene Shepherd, 'Problems in the Supply of Livestock to Sugar Estates in the Period of Slavery: An Example from the History of Spring Sugar Plantation, St Andrew, Jamaica, c.1700–c.1800'. Postgraduate Seminar Paper, Department of History, University of the West Indies, Mona, May 1987.

19. Thistlewood's Journal, Vineyard Pen, January 26, 1751, Mon. 31/2, fol. 14.

20. Ibid., April 10, 1751, fol. 58. It should be noted that Black River was five miles from Vineyard Pen.

21. Ibid., April 23, 1751, fol. 59.

22. Bristol, Bristol University Library, Special Collections, Thetford Hall Pen Accounts, 1807, DM 444.

23. Thistlewood's Journal, April 11, 1751, Mon. 31/2, fol. 25.

24. Accounts, Batchelor's Hall Pen, January–December 1833, Vanneck MSS, JEP box 2, bundle 60.

25. This included 140 sheep. The total figure ought to have been higher but some properties did not indicate the volume of livestock sold, though they indicated their value. However, as they tended to lump all types together as 'stock sold', it was impossible to apply prices and arrive at a figure.

26. J.A. Perkins, 'The Ox, the Horse and English Farming 1750–1850', Working Paper in Economic History, 3/1875, University of New South Wales, 2–15.

27. J.A., A.P. 1B/11/4/54-6 and 1B/11/4/9.

28. J.A., AP.. 1780, 1B/11/4/9.

29. Edward Long, *History of Jamaica*. 3 vols. (London, 1774), I. Add. Mss. 12,404, fols. 450–52.

30. Ibid., fol. 450.

31. A.P. 1820, 1B/11/4/54–6.

32. E. (Kamau).Brathwaite, *The Development of Creole Society in Jamaica, 1770–1820* (Oxford: Oxford University Press, 1971), 122.

33. A.P. Thornton, *West India Policy Under the Restoration* (Oxford: Oxford University Press, 1956), 1–2.

34. L.A. Harper, *The English Navigation Laws: A Seventeenth-Century Experiment in Social Engineering* (New York: Columbia University Press, 1939), 30–58.

35. Thornton, *West India Policy*, 78–80. See also, National Library of Jamaica [N.L.J.], 'Extension Treaty With Spain', MS 450 and 'Illicit Trade cl. 1740', MS 1,049.

36. F.G. Davenport ed., *European Treatises Bearing on the History of the United States and its Dependencies* , 4 vols. (Washington DC 1917–37, II, 1929, 1650–1697: 195.

37. Ibid. See also Nuala Zahadieh, 'The Merchants of Port Royal, Jamaica, and the Spanish Contraband Trade, 1655–1692', *William and Mary Quarterly*, 3rd series 43 (1986): 574 and W.A. Claypole and D.J. Buisserret, 'Trade Patterns in Early English Jamaica', *Journal of Caribbean History*, 15 (1972): 1–19.

38. Davenport, *European Treatises*, 195.

39. See F. Armytage, *The Free-Port System in the British West Indies: A Study in*

Commercial Policy, 1766–1822 (London, New York, Toronto: Longman, Green and Co.:, 1953), for an elaboration of the Free Port Act. See also Richard Sheridan, *Sugar and Slavery: An Economic History of the British West Indies, 1623–1775* (Barbados: Caribbean Universities Press, 1974), 42, 460.

40. Long, *History of Jamaica*, I, Add. Mss. 12,404, fol. 330.
41. J.H.A.V., 1815–25.
42. Long, *History of Jamaica*, I, Add. Mss. 12,404, fol. 330.
43. Ibid., fol. 329.
44. Ibid.
45. Ibid.
46. Ibid.
47. Ibid.
48. Letter of Petition to His Excellency, the Duke of Effingham from the Custos, Magistrates and Vestry of St Ann, June 29, 1790. JA, St Ann Vestry Minutes, 2/9/1.
49. Ibid.
50. Ibid.
51. Ibid.
52. Long, *History of Jamaica*, I, Add. Mss. 12,404, fol. 329.
53. Ibid., fol. 331.
54. Ibid., fol. 330.
55. Ibid.
56. J.H.A.V., 'Petition of the Stock Breeders and Graziers of St Elizabeth', November 27, 1816' and 'Petition of the Pen-keepers of Manchester', 1816.
57. Ibid. 'Petition of the Stock Breeders and Graziers of St Elizabeth', 114.
58. Ibid. 'Petition of the Pen-keepers of Manchester', 115.
59. J.H.A.V., 1817, 216.
60. B.B.J., 1832, London, P.R.O., C.O. 142/45.
61. B.B.J., 1837, C.O. 142/51.
62. *Falmouth Post*, November 29, 1837: 2–3.
63. J.H.A.V., November 29, 1843: 258.
64. See, for example, Governor Musgrave to Sir M. Hicks-Beach, August 28, 1878, Despatch No. 173, C.O. 137/487 and Musgrave to Hicks-Beach, June 16, 1879, Despatch 178, C.O. 137/490.
65. J.A., A.P. 1820 1B/11/4/53-5.
66. J.A., A.P., Paradise Pen, 1840 1B/11/4/85.
67. W.J. Gardner, *The History of Jamaica from its Discovery by Christopher Columbus to the Present ....* (London, 1873), 325.
68. *Royal Gazette*, 1799–1813, C.O. 141/1-3 and N.L.J., *Royal Gazette*, 1814–45.
69. See A. Lopez and J. Petras eds., *Puerto Rico and Puerto Ricans: Studies in History and Society* (New York: John Wiley and Sons, 1974), 20; F.A. Scarano, *Sugar and Slavery in Puerto Rico: The Plantation Economy of Ponce, 1800–1850* (Wisconsin: Madsion University Press, 1984), 4 and M.D. Clausner, *Rural Santo Domingo: Settled, Unsettled and Resettled* (Philadelphia: Temple University Press, 1973), 71.
70. Comment made at the Caribbean Societies Seminar, Institute of Commonwealth Studies, London, February 9, 1988, on the occasion of my presentation of a

paper entitled 'The Evolution and Expansion of the "Pen-keeping" Industry in Jamaica'.

71. Scarano, *Sugar and Slavery*, 4.

72. See Yu Wu, 'Jamaican Trade, 1688–1769', PhD diss., Johns Hopkins University, 1995 and University of Michigan Microform, 1996, p. 363. See also Armytage, (*The Free-Port System*, 51). He estimated that the number of vessels entering Jamaican free ports dropped by half in 1778. In 1778, only 35 vessels entered the free ports compared to 227 in 1775.

73. C.O. 137/104. Enclosure in the Earl of Balcarres' Despatch to the Duke of Portland, May 25, 1800.

74. Ibid. See also Armytage, *The Free-Port System*, 47, 51.

Chapter 4

1. W. Dickson, *Letters on Slavery* (London, 1789), 6.

2. London, British Library, Department of Manuscripts, Edward Long, *History of Jamaica,* 3 vols. (London, 1774), I, Add. Mss. 12,404, fol. 334.

3. Ibid., fol. 336.

4. Ibid.

5. Letter sent to His Excellency, Lord Effingham, Governor of Jamaica, from the Custos, Magistrates and Vestry Men of St Ann, June 29, 1790, Jamaica Archives [J.A.]. St Ann Vestry Minutes, 2/9/1.

6. Stephen Harmer to his father, April 3, 1840, National Library of Jamaica [N.L.J], MS 765.

7. 'Classification of the Inhabitants of St James Parish, 1773', Long MSS, Add. Mss. 12,435, fol. 3.

8. E. (Kamau) Brathwaite, *The Development of Creole Society in Jamaica 1770–1820* (Oxford: Clarendon Press, 1971), 135.

9. Thomas Roughley estimated that 7/8 of the landed interest comprised absentees. See Roughley, *The Jamaica Planter's Guide* (London, 1823), 4.

10. B. M'Mahon, *Jamaica Plantership* (London, 1835), 172.

11. Ibid., 65.

12. Ibid., 172.

13. Ibid.

14. Ibid., 174.

15. Ibid.

16. Ibid.

17. J.A., Gifts and Deposits, 7/177/8, April 18, 1835.

18. Ibid., 7/177/7. See also, Roughley, *The Jamaica Planter's Guide*, 11.

19. J.A., Returns of the registration of Slaves [R.R.S.], St Ann, 1817, 1B/11/7/24–9.

20. Brathwaite, *The Development of Creole Society,* 148–49.

21. J.A., Private Deposits, 4/110/12, Gunnis Papers, 1810.

22. Lincoln, Lincolnshire County Archives, Thistlewood Family History, 1675–1744, Mon. 31/83.

23. Thistlewood's Journal, Breadnut Island Pen, Mon. 31/19–37.

24.   R. Tomlinson, *Sociological Concepts and Research* (Washington: Random House, 1965), 10–12.

25.   Brathwaite, *The Development of Creole Society*, 138.

26.   J. Bigelow, *Jamaica in 1850* (London, 1851), 104.

27.   Ibid.

28.   M'Mahon, *Jamaica Plantership*, 172.

29.   J.A., A.P. 1740, 1B/11/4/1.

30.   Ibid.,1B/11/4/9 and 1B/11/4/76–7.

31.   Ibid.,1B/11/4/1, 1B/11/4/9 and 1B/11/4/54-6; Ibid.,1B/11/4/84–5. See table 4.2 for a breakdown of absentees by parish in 1820.

32.   Ibid.,1B/11/4/76-7.

33.   Kathleen E.A. Monteith. 'The Coffee Industry in Jamaica, 1790–1880', M.Phil diss. University of the West Indies, Mona, 1987, 82.

34.   J.A., AP., 1B/11/4/39-41; 1B/11/4/44, fol. 154; 1B/11/4/45, fols. 230–39; 1B/11/4/48, fols. 176–77; 1B/11/4/93-94.

35.   See Gad Heuman, *Between Black and White: Race, Politics and the Free-Coloureds in Jamaica, 1792–1865* (Connecticut: Greenwood Press, 1981), for a full discussion of these restrictions. See also, A.A. Sio, 'Marginality and Free Coloured Identity in the Caribbean Slave Society', *Slavery and Abolition*, 8 (1987): 166–82, and Mavid Campbell, *The Dynamics of Change in a Slave Society: A Socio-political History of the Free Coloureds of Jamaica, 1800–1865* (New Jersey: Fairleigh Dickinson University Press, 1976) for discussions on the role and status of the free coloureds in Jamaica.

36.   Heuman, *Between Black and White*, 6.

37.   Spanish Town, Island Record Office [IRO] District Court Wills, Liber 25, fol. 77. See also Journal of Benjamin Scott-Moncrieffe, 1828–40, J.A. Grand Court Records, 1a/5/26 and Journal of Henry Blagrove, May 25, 1842, J.A. Private Deposits, 4/4/1–2.

38.   I.R.O., District Court Wills, Liber 115, fol. 18.

39.   Sheena Boa, 'Freed Women's Economic Contributions to Jamaica, 1760–1834', (Postgraduate Seminar paper, UWI Mona, April 1985), 1; J.H.A.V., November 4, 1834, pp. 113–14 and Royal Gazette, January 1822.

40.   Brathwaite, *The Development of Creole Society*, 105, 172. See also Monteith, 'The Coffee Industry', 72–77.

41.   Monteith, 'The Coffee Industry', 74.

42.   Ibid., 74–75

43.   J. Sturge and T. Harvey, *The West Indies in 1837* (London, 1838), 159.

44.   N.L.J. Great Houses, File C.

45.   M'Mahon, *Jamaica Plantership*, 63.

46.   Sturge and Harvey, *The West Indies in 1837*, lix, Appendix.

47.   N.L.J. Great Houses, File C.

48.   P. Wright, *Monumental Inscriptions of Jamaica* (London: Society of Genealogists, 1966), 2.

49.   Thistlewood Family History, 1675–1744, Mon. 31/83.

50.   Journal of Henry Blagrove, 1841-2, J.A., Private Deposits, 4/4/1–2.

51. N.B. Livingstone, *Sketch Pedigrees* (Kingston, c.1670), 13.

52. J.A., St Ann, Register of Births, Baptisms and Burials, 1B/11/8/2

53. I.R.O., District Court Wills, Liber 25, fol. 77.

54. Stephen Harmer to Saul Harmer, June 21, 1842, N.L.J. MS 765.

55. M'Mahon, *Jamaica Plantership*, 18, 186. This phenomenon of coloured Mistress kept by overseers has been captured in novels as well as historical texts. See, for example, Cyrus Francis Perkins, *Busha's Mistress or Catherine the Fugitve: A Stirring Romance of the days of Slavery in Jamaica*, edited and introduced by Paul Lovejoy, Verene Shepherd and David Trotman (Kingston: Ian Randle Publishers, 2002). For other detailed discussions of this phenomenon, see Verene Shepherd, ed./ comp., *Women in Caribbean History* (Kingston: Ian Randle Publishers, 1999) and Hilary Beckles, *Centering Woman: Gender Discourses in Caribbean Slavery* (Kingston: Ian Randle Publishers, 1999).

56. Heuman, *Between Black and White*, xv.

57. I.R.O., Liber 55, fol. 114, 1789; Ibid., Liber 61, fol. 82.

58. Ibid., Liber 52, fols. 77–8, 1786.

59. Thistlewood's Journal, 1768, Mon. 31/19. For recent studies of Thistlewood and his relationship with Phibbah and other enslaved women, see Hilary Beckles, *Centering Woman*; Trevor Burnard, *Mastery, Tyranny and Desire: Thomas Thistlewood and His Slaves in the Anglo-Jamaican World* (Kingston: The University of the West Indies Press, 2004).

60. St Ann Parish Records, Register of Births and Baptisms, 1785–1814, J.A.,1B/11/8/ 1.

61. J.H.A.V., 1837–8, February 22, 1838.

62. Ibid.

63. W.J. Gardner, *The History of Jamaica from its Discovery by Christopher Columbus to the Present ...* (London, 1873) ,161.

64. Long, *History of Jamaica*, I, Add. Mss. 12,404, fol. 335.

65. Ibid., fol. 336.

66. Ibid., fol. 337.

67. W. Beckford, *A Descriptive Account of the Island of Jamaica*, (2 vols. London, 1790), II, 169.

68. Ibid.

69. J.B. Moreton, *Manners and Customs in the West Indies Islands* (London, 1790), 58.

70. Ibid., 59.

71. Ibid. and Bryan Edwards, *History of the West Indies*, 2 vols. (London, 1793), II, 248.

72. Josiah and George Heathcote to Charles Wilson, April 20, 1696, Kingston, UWI Library, W.I.C. Wilson Family Papers and Cambridge, Cambridge County Record Office, Tharp Family Papers, R. 84/39.

73. J.A., Private Deposits 4/110/12, Gunnis Papers, George Forbes to Peter Forbes, January 12, 1811, 4/110/17.

74. Ibid., George Forbes to Peter Forbes, June 11, 1817, 4/110/30.

75. Ibid., George Forbes to Peter Forbes, June 16, 1818, 4/110/37.

76. J.A., Tweedie Family Papers, Private Deposits, 4/45.

77. Brathwaite, *The Development of Creole Society*, 148–49.

78. Tharp Family Papers, R. 84/29.
79. Gardner, *A History of Jamaica*, 160.
80. J.A., Private Deposits, 4/110/40–6.
81. Journal of Henry Blagrove, May 31, 1842, JA Private Deposits, 4/4/1–2.
82. A.C.L. Martin and J.T. Palache, *The Jamaica Stud Book to 1923*, 2 vols. (Kingston, 1925), II, 2–23.
83. M. Beckwith, *Black Roadways: A Study of Jamaican Folk Life* (New York: New American Library, 1969 reprint), 37.
84. J.T. Palache, *The Jamaica Stud Book*, 2 vols. (Kingston, 1892), I, xvi–xvii. See also, John White to William Dickinson, November 17, 1802 and 29 August 29, 1804, Dickinson Family Papers, DD/DN/474.
85. Palache, *The Jamaica Stud Book*, I, xxi.
86. J.H.A.V., 1794–5, p. 10. The cost of imported stallions was high. An Arabian stallion cost Ackendown Pen £1300 in 1807. See J.A., Accounts Current [AC] 1807, 1B/11/5/2.
87. Grand Court Records, (Misc.), Journal of Benjamin Scott-Moncrieffe, 1828–40, J.A., Grand Court Records, 1A/5/26.
88. E. DaCosta. *Sixty Years of Horseracing in Jamaica* (Kingston: Stonyhurst, 1934), 8–11, .p. 15; p. 31.
89. Journal of Henry Blagrove, 1841–2, J.A., Private Deposits, 4/4/1–2 and Journal of Benjamin Scott-Moncrieffe, 1828–40, J..A., IA/5/26.
90. Inventories, J.A., 1B/11/3/134, fols. 1–5, 1820; 1B/11/3/74, fol. 10.
91. P.J. Tenison, *Good Hope: A Short History* (Jamaica, 1871), 9, N.L.J., Great House Files and Journal of Henry Blagrove, January 13, 1842, J.A., Private Deposits.
92. Journal of Henry Blagrove, January 13, 1842, J.A., Private Deposits 4/4/1–2.

Chapter 5

1. Jill Sheppard, *The 'Redlegs' of Barbados: Their Origins and History* (New York: Oxford University Press, 1977).
2. Lewis Gray, *History of Agriculture in the Southern United States to 1860*, 2 vols. (Washington: Peter Smith, 1933), I, 487, 489.
3. M.G. Smith, *The Plural Society in the British West Indies* (Berkeley: University of California Press, 1965).
4. Elsa Goveia, *Slave Society in the British Leeward Islands at the end of the 18th Century* (New Haven: Yale University Press, 1965), 314–15; E. [Kamau] Brathwaite, *The Development of Creole Society in Jamaica, 1770–1820* (Oxford: Oxford University Press, 1974).
5. Brathwaite, *The Development of Creole Society*, 105–50.
6. Ibid., 105–50; 135–48.
7. See Gad Heuman, *Between Black and White: Race, Colour and the Free Coloureds in Jamaica, 1792–1865* (Connecticut: Greenwood Press, 1981); Sheena Boa, 'Free Black and Colored Women in a White Man's Slave Society', MPhil diss., UWI, Mona, 1985, 64–69. Also, see D. Cohen, and J. Green, eds., *Neither Slave nor Free*, (Baltimore: John Hopkins University Press, 1972), and Jerome Handler, *The Unappropriated People* (Baltimore: John Hopkins University Press, 1973).

8.   M.G. Smith, 'Social Structure in the British Caribbean about 1820', *Social and Economic Studies* 1, no. 4 (1955): 55–59.

9.   Brathwaite, *The Development of Creole Society in Jamaica*.

10.   E. [Kamau] Brathwaite, '*Contradictory Omens: Cultural Diversity and Integration in the Caribbean*', *Savacou* (1974): 6.

11.   J.B. Moreton, *Manners and Customs in the West India Islands* (London, 1790), 58.

12.   J. Bigelow, *Jamaica in 1850* (London, 1851), 104; Verene Shepherd, 'Pens and Penkeepers in a Plantation Society', PhD diss., University of Cambridge, 1988, 100, 180.

13.   Smith, 'Social Structure', 55–59.

14.   Brathwaite, *The Development of Creole Society*, 101.

15.   George Forbes to Peter Forbes, January 12, 1811, Jamaica Archives [J.A.] Private Deposits, 4/110/17. Forbes was from Scotland, but indicated a preference to reside in England where it was warmer. See George Forbes to Peter Forbes, June 11, 1817, J.A. Private Deposits.

16.   Sheila Duncker, 'The Free-Coloured and Their Fight for Civil Rights in Jamaica, 1800–30', MA diss., London: University of London, 1960, 37.

17.   Cynric Williams, *A Tour Through the Island of Jamaica* (London, 1827).

18.   Ibid., 67–69.

19.   Ibid.

20.   J.A. Private Deposits, 4/45/36–9, Tweedie Papers.

21.   David Barclay, *An Account of the Emancipation of Slaves on Unity Valley Pen* (London, 1801), 4.

22.   Ibid., 6.

23.   The Crop Accounts and the Returns of the Registration of Slaves were usually made up by the overseers. Many of these overseers were pen owners.

24.   Petitions for Privileges, *Journal of the Jamaica House of Assembly* [J.H.A.V.], 1827: 87.

25.   Ibid., 71, 81.

26.   Island Record Office [I.R.O.], District Court Wills, liber 66, fol. 110, 1799.

27.   W.A. Feurtado, *Official and Other Personages of Jamaica* (Kingston, 1896), 110, 121.

28.   See B.W. Higman, *Slave Population and Economy in Jamaica, 1807–1832* (Cambridge: Cambridge University Press, 1976); B.W. Higman, *Slave Population of the British Caribbean, 1807–1834* (Baltimore: John Hopkins University Press, 1984), B.W. Higman, 'Slave Population and Economy in Jamaica at the Time of Emancipation', PhD diss., University of the West Indies, Mona, 1970 and Shepherd, 'Pens and Penkeepers', 135–50.

29.   Thistlewood's Journal, January 1, 1768–December 1768, Mon. 31/19.

30.   *Falmouth Post, Supplement*, October 20, 1849, p. 9. Matters seem to have come to a head in the case *Cushion v Codrington*, tried in the Surrey Assize Court.

31.   *Morning Journal*, April 13, 1839:3.

32.   Ibid., April 27, 1839, p. 3.

33.   Ibid., June 5, 1839:1.

34.   Thistlewood's Journal, 1751, Mon. 31/2, fol. 16.

35. *Royal Gazette*, January 13–20, 1821: 55.
36. Ibid, *Supplement*: 61.
37. Ibid., *Postscript*: 67 and *Royal Gazette*, January 27– February 3,1821: 122.
38. Ibid., January 13–30, *Postscrip*: 67.
39. *Royal Gazette*, January 27–February 3, 1821:122.
40. *Royal Gazette*, January 27–February 3, 1821; *Postscript*: 120.
41. Ibid.
42. Frank Cundall, *Historic Jamaica* (London, 1915), 86. A total of 472 signatures were appended to the petition. This figure comprised pen-keepers and provision farmers.
43. Petition of Certain Proprietors of St Mary, J.H.A.V., 1840.
44. Ibid., November 16, 1843; November 4, 1834: 113–14.
45. Shepherd, 'Pens and Penkeepers', 216.
46. Ibid., 218–20.
47. Heuman, G. *Between Black and White: Race Politics and the Free Coloured in Jamaica* (Connecticut: Greenwood Press, 1981) 61.
48. Local Government Records, J.A. 2/1–19.
49. St Ann Vestry Minutes, J.A. 2/9/1, 1769.
50. Thistlewood's Journal, March 12, 1768, Mon. 31/19.
51. *Falmouth Post*, 1837–38.
52. St Ann Vestry Minutes, J.A. 2/9/4, 1817–33.
53. Ibid., 2/9/1, 1769
54. Vestry Minutes, J.A. 2/9/1-5, and 1B/11/9/1–7, 2/7/11/2–5, 2/7/1/1–2. See also Private Deposits, 4/110/26, Gunnis Papers.
55. Capt. J. Archer, *Monumental Inscriptions* (London, 1875), 81. P. Wright, *Monumental Inscriptions* of Jamaica (London: Society of Genealogists 1966), 3 and *Medical Practitioners' Journal*, NLJ, MS 1,769, fols. 8, 101, 185.
56. W.A. Fuertado, *Important Personages of Jamaica* (Kingston, 1896), 39.
57. Wright, *Monumental Inscriptions*, 219.
58. J.A., Private Deposits, 4/110/26, Gunnis Papers, October 3,1814.
59. J.A., St Ann Vestry Minutes, 1769–1844.
60. J.H.A.V., vol. vi, November 1783, 21 & 609.
61. Edward Long, *History of Jamaica* (edited version), British Museum, Add, Mss, 12, 404, fol. 329.
62. *The Royal Gazette,* January 27 – February 3, 1821: 122.
63. Brathwaite, *The Development of Creole Society*, 100. See also Verene Shepherd, 'Questioning Creole', in Verene Shepherd and Glen Richards, eds., *Questioning Creole: Creolisation Discourses in Caribbean Culture* (Kingston: Ian Randle Publishers, 2002), 67–180.
64. With 90 per cent of them resident in Jamaica in 1800, only the coffee farmers had a higher residency status than the pen-keepers, about 70 per cent of whom were residents by 1834. See Verene Shepherd and Kathleen E.A. Monteith, 'Non-Sugar Proprietors in a Sugar Plantation Society', in *Plantation Society in the Americas,* vol. v: 2 & 3 (Fall 1998): 205–25.
65. Smith, *The Plural Society*.

66.   George Forbes to Peter Forbes, January 12, 1811, J.A., Private Deposits, 4/110/17.
67.   Shepherd, 'Pens and Pen-Keepers', chapter 5.

Chapter 6

1.   Hilary Beckles, *Centering Woman: Gender Discourses in Caribbean Slavery* (Kingston: Ian Randle Publishers, 1999), xiii.
2.   E. (Kamau) Brathwaite, *The Development of Creole Society in Jamaica, 1770–1820* (Oxford: The Clarendon Press, 1971); Lucille Mathurin-Mair, 'An Historical Study of Women in Jamaica', PhD diss, University of the West Indies, Mona, 1974; Hilary Beckles, *Natural Rebels: A Social History of Enslaved Black Women in Barbados* (New Brunswick: Rutgers University Press, 1989) and Beckles, *Centering Woman;* Barbara Bush, *Slave Women in Caribbean Society, 1650–1838* (Kingston: Ian Randle Publishers, Heinemann, 1990); B.W. Higman, *Slave Population and Economy in Jamaica, 1807–1832* (Cambridge: Cambridge University Press, 1976); Marietta Morrissey, *Slave Women in the New World: Gender Stratification in the Caribbean* (Lawrence: University Press of Kansas, 1989), Verene Shepherd, et al. (eds.), *Engendering History: Caribbean Women in Historical Perspective* (Kingston: Ian Randle Publishers, 1995), and Verene Shepherd, (ed./comp.), *Women in Caribbean History* (Kingston: Ian Randle Publishers, 1999).
3.   B.W. Higman, *Slave Populations of the British Caribbean, 1807–1832* (Baltimore: Johns Hopkins University Press, 1984), 46–71.
4.   David Eltis, *The Rise of African Slavery in the Americas* (Cambridge: Cambridge University Press, 2000), 4.
5.   For various perspectives on the numbers of Africans who were captured, shipped to the Americas and died before arrival in the Americas, see Philip Curtin, *The Atlantic Slave Trade: A Census* (Madison: The University of Wisconsin Press, 1969); Paul Lovejoy, 'The Volume of the Atlantic Slave Trade: A Synthesis', *Journal of African History,* 23 (1982): 473–501; Joseph Inikori and Stanley Engerman, 'Introduction: Gainers and Losers in the Atlantic Slave Trade', in Joseph Inikori and Stanley Engerman, eds., *The Atlantic Slave Trade: Effects on Economies, Societies and Peoples in Africa, the Americas and Europe,* (Durham: Duke University Press, 1992), 1–21; Joseph Inikori, *The Chaining of a Continent: Export Demand for Captives and the History of Africa South of the Sahara, 1450–1870* (Mona: University of the West Indies Press, 1992); Eltis, *The Rise of African Slavery in the Americas;* Eltis, 'The Volume and Structure of the Transatlantic Slave Trade: A Reassessment' (Paper presented at the Conference on Enslaving Connections: Africa and Brazil During the Era of the Slave Trade, York University, Toronto, October 12–15, 2000); David Eltis et al., *The Transatlantic Slave Trade: A Database on CD-ROM* (New York & Cambridge: Cambridge University Press, 1999), and Hilary Beckles and Verene Shepherd, *Slave Voyages* (Paris: UNESCO, 1999).
6.   Eltis, 'The Volume and Structure', Table 3, 36.
7.   Eltis, *The Rise of African Slavery*, 85–113; Eltis, 'The Volume and Structure', and Beckles and Shepherd, *Slave Voyages*, 42–44.

8. Eltis, *The Rise of African Slavery*, 100.
9. Ibid.
10. Ibid.
11. Ibid., 251.
12. Higman, *Slave Population and Economy in Jamaica*, 77.
13. Simon Taylor to Chaloner Arcedeckne, July 5, 1789. Vanneck Papers, Cambridge University Library.
14. Taylor to Arcedeckne, April 10, 1768.
15. See Verene Shepherd, 'Pens and Penkeepers in a Plantation Society', PhD diss., University of Cambridge, 1988. See also Philo Scotus, *Reminiscences of a Scottish Gentleman* (London, 1861), 217, and Jamaica Archives [J.A.], Gifts and Deposits, 7/177/1–2, 1835.
16. W.J. Gardner, *A History of Jamaica from its Discovery by Christopher Columbus to the Present Time....* (London, 1873), 106, 123.
17. Public Record Office [P.R.O.], London, T. 71/4350, Returns of the registration of Slaves [R.R.S.], 1817–32.
18. P.R.O., T 71/180, R.R..S., Westmoreland, 1823.
19. See Higman, *Slave Population and Economy*. For a comparison with other colonies in the Caribbean, see Higman, *Slave Populations of the British Caribbean 1807–1834*.
20. Higman, *Slave Population and Economy*, 117, 147.
21. P.R.O., T 71/178, R.R.S., Westmoreland, 1817.
22. Higman, *Slave Population and Economy*, 120.
23. P.R.O., T 71/178, R.R.S., Westmoreland, 1817.
24. Higman, *Slave Population and Economy*, 154.
25. Edward Long, *The History of Jamaica, 3 vols.*, vol. II (London, 1774) Add. Mss., 12,404, fol. 343; Higman, *Slave Population and Economy*, 123; Richard Dunn, 'A Tale of Two Plantations: Slave Life at Mesopotamia in Jamaica and Mount Airy in Virginia, 1799 to 1828', *William and Mary Quarterly*, 3rd series, 34 (1977): 32–65, and Michael Craton, 'Hobbesian or Panglossian?: The Two Extremes of Slave Conditions in the British Caribbean, 1783–1834', *William and Mary Quarterly*, 3rd series, 35 (1978), 324–56.
26. Cynric Williams, *A Tour Through the Island of Jamaica* (London, 1826).
27. Ibid.
28. David Barclay, *An Account of the Emancipation of Slaves on Unity Valley Pen, in Jamaica* (London, 1801), 19.
29. See W. Dickson, *Letters on Slavery* (1789; Westport, 1970), 6.
30. See Patrick Manning, *Slavery and African Life Occidental, Oriental, and African Slave Trades* (Cambridge: Cambridge University Press, 1990), 48–53 for an idea of the regional variations in the trade.
31. For a recent discussion of Igbo presence in the diaspora, see Douglas Chambers, 'Tracing Igbo into the Diaspora', in *Identity in the Shadow of Slavery*, ed. Paul E. Lovejoy (London: Allen & Unwin, 2000), 55–71.
32. Eltis, *The Rise of African Slavery in the* Americas, 245. See also Paul Lovejoy, *Transformations in Slavery: A History of Slavery in Africa* (Cambridge: Cambridge

University Press, 1983), 44–59.

33. Eltis, 'The Volume and Structure', Table 4, 38.

34. Curtin, *The Atlantic Slave Trade*, 144.

35. Ibid., 160 and Higman, *Slave Population and Economy*, 76.

36. Ibid., 154–162.

37. B.W. Higman, 'The Spatial Economy of Jamaican Sugar Plantations: Cartographic Evidence from the Eighteenth and Nineteenth Centuries', *Journal of Historical Geography*, 13 (1987) 24.

38. Taylor to Arcedeckne, September 3, 1787, Vanneck MSS, JEP Box 2, Bundle 13.

39. Higman, *Slave Population and Economy*, 14.

40. *Jamaica Almanack*, 1815, 221–83.

41. Higman, *Slave Population and Economy*, 190.

42. Bush, *Slave Women in Caribbean Society* and Morrissey, *Slave Women in the New World*.

43. Richard Sheridan, *Sugar and Slavery: An Economic History of the British West Indies, 1623–1775* (Barbados: Caribbean Universities Press, 1974) and Richard Sheridan, *Doctors and Slaves: A Medical and Demographic History of Slavery in the British West Indies, 1680–1834* (Cambridge: Cambridge University Press, 1985).

44. Higman, *Slave Populations of the British Caribbean*, 192.

45. Michael Craton, *Searching for the Invisible Man: Slaves and Plantation Life in Jamaica* (Cambridge: Cambridge University Press, 1977), 142.

46. Sheridan, *Sugar and Slavery*, 258.

47. Beckles, *Natural Rebels*, 35.

48. Shepherd, *Women in Caribbean History*, 52.

49. O. Nigel Bolland, *Struggles for Freedom: Essays on Slavery, Colonialism and Culture in the Caribbean and Central America* (Belize City: The Angelus Press, 1997).

50. Gale/Morant Papers, 4/b/4, Exeter University Library; Papers Relating to Pepper and Bonavista Pens, Mss. Collection, University of the West Indies Library; Jamaica Archives, Plantation Books, Private 4/23/12.

51. Shepherd, *Women in Caribbean History*, 48–51.

52. Papers of Pepper and Bonavista Pens; Gale/Morant Papers.

53. For recent works on plantation management, see Heather Cateau, 'Beyond Planters and Plantership', in Cateau and Rita Pemberton, eds., *Beyond Tradition: Reinterpreting the Caribbean Historical Experience* (Kingston: Ian Randle, 2006), 3-21 and B.W. Higman, *Plantation Jamaica, 1750–1850: Capital and Control in a Colonial Economy* (Kingston: The Press, University of the West Indies, 2006).

54. Higman, *Slave Populations of the British Caribbean*, 172–73, 191.

55. Thomas Atwood, *The History of Dominica* (London, 1791).

56. B.W. Higman, 'Long-Term Trends in Jamaican Domestic Service', (Paper presented at the Symposium, 'Engendering History', University of the West Indies, Mona, 1993), 8.

57. Beckles, *Centering Woman*, 38–58; 125–139.

58. See Sidney W. Mintz and Douglas Hall, *The Origins of the Jamaican Internal Marketing System* (New Haven: Yale University Press, 1960).

59. J.A., Accounts Current [AC] Mt. Plenty Pen, 1820, 1B/11/5/19.

60. Williams, *A Tour Through the Island*, 80.
61. Mary Turner, ed., *From Chattel Slaves to Wage Slaves: The Dynamics of Labour Bargaining in the Americas* (Kingston: Ian Randle Publishers, 1995).
62. Bryan Edwards, *The History, Civil and Commercial, of the British Colonies in the West Indies*, vol II (London, 1807), 153.
63. Lincoln, Lincolnshire Archives Office, Thistlewood's Journal, January 15, 1751, Mon. 31/2. fol. 9.
64. J.A., St David Vestry Minutes, 1B/119/1-7.
65. Ibid., 1B/11/9/1, 1788, f. 197.
66. Williams, *A Tour Trough the Island*, 61.
67. Ibid., 79–80. This pen consisted of 1,800 acres of land, 500 acres of which were woodland. It had 500 head of cattle in addition to other small and large stock. There were 130 enslaved people on the pen around 1823.
68. Joseph Sturge and Thomas Harvey, *The West Indies in 1837* (London, 1838), 185.
69. Thistlewood Journals, Vineyard Pen, December 25, 1750, Mon. 31/1–37, f. 531.
70. J.A., A.C. 1806-34, 1B/11/5/1–36.
71. Thistlewood's Journal, July 1, 1750, Mon. 31/1, f. 328 and 7 August 1750, f. 352.

Chapter 7

1. Franklin Knight, 'Slavery and Lagging Capitalism in the Spanish and Portuguese American Empires', in *Slavery and the Rise of the Atlantic System*, ed. Barbara Solow, (Cambridge: Cambridge University Press, 1991), 72.
2. Michael Kraus, *The North Atlantic Civilization* (Princeton: Princeton University Press, 1957), 11.
3. Walter Rodney, 'How Europe Became the Dominant Section of a World-Wide Trade System', in Verene Shepherd and Hilary Beckles, eds., *Caribbean Slavery in the Atlantic World*, (Kingston: Ian Randle Publishers, 2000), 2–10.
4. For a deeper discussion of the idea of the Black Atlantic, see Paul Gilroy, *The Black Atlantic* (London: Harvard University Press, 1993). For a later and somewhat different discussion, see James Walvin, *Making the Black Atlantic: Britain and the African Diaspora* (London: Cassell, 2000).
5. Benedict Anderson, *Imagined Communities: Reflections on the Origin and Spread of Nationalism* (London: Verso, 1991).
6. See Walter Rodney, *How Europe Underdeveloped Africa* (London: Bogle L'Ouverture, 1972); C.L.R. James, *The Black Jacobins* (New York: Vintage Press, 1963); Eric Williams, *Capitalism and Slavery* (Chapel Hill: University of North Carolina Press, 1944; Kingston: Ian Randle Publishers, 2005) and George Beckford, *Persistent Poverty* (New York: Oxford University Press, 1972). See also Barbara Solow and Stanley Engerman, eds., *British Capitalism and Caribbean Slavery: The Legacy of Eric Williams* (Cambridge: Cambridge University Press, 1987).
7. David Blight, 'Analyze the Sounds': Frederick Douglass's Invitation to Modern

Historians of Slavery', in Stephan Palmié, ed., *Slave Cultures and the Cultures of Slavery*, (Knoxville: University of Tennessee Press, 1995), 1–22.

8. Robert Wedderburn, *The Horrors of Slavery* (London, 1824), in Ian McCalman, ed., *The Horrors of Slavery and Other Writings by Robert Wedderburn* (New York: Mark Wiener, 1991), 46–47.

9. Ibid., 46.

10. Douglas Hall, *In Miserable Slavery: Thomas Thistlewood in Jamaica, 1750–1786* (London: Macmillan, 1989).

11. Thistlewood Journals, Lincolnshire County Archives, UK; Hilary Beckles, *Centering Woman: Gender Discourses in Caribbean Slavery* (Kingston: Ian Randle Publishers, 1999), 38–58, and Hall, *In Miserable Slavery*.

12. Manuscript 65, Harmer Letters, National Library of Jamaica [N.L.J.].

13. Benjamin M'Mahon, *Jamaica Plantership* (London, 1839).

14. For a discussion of the gender-specificity of resistance, see Hilary Beckles, *Natural Rebels* (New Brunswick: Rutgers University Press, 1989) and Beckles, *Centering Woman*.

15. Thistlewood Journals, Mon. 31/2, f. 382.

16. M.D. de B. Kilson, 'Towards Freedom: An Analysis of Slave Revolts in the United States', *Phylon* XXV (1964): 179–84, cited in G.M. Frederickson and C. Lasch, 'Resistance to Slavery', in *Civil War History*, 13 (1967): 316.

17. Michael Craton, *Sinews of Empire: A Short History of British Slavery* (New York: Anchor Press, 1974), 188.

18. James Grainger, 'An Essay on the Management and Diseases of Negroes', in Edward Hutson, James Grainger and William Wright, eds., *On the Treatment and Management of the More Common West India Diseases, 1750–1802*, (Kingston: University of the West Indies Press, 2005), 51.

19. Jamaica Archives [J.A.], Manumission Libers, 1B/11/6/5-70.

20. J.A., Attorneys' Letterbook, 1821–38, 1B/5/63/1–2, Letter of August 13, 1821, 1B/5/83/1.

21. Ibid., Attorney to W. Mitchell.

22. Unity Valley Pen was located about 40 miles from Kingston in the parish of St Mary. David and John Barclay, brothers of Walthamstow, Essex, came in possession of the pen 'in consequence of a debt owed to us by a correspondent in Jamaica'. See D. Barclay, *An Account of the Emancipation of the Slaves on Unity Valley Pen, in Jamaica* (London, 1801). The pen consisted of about 2,000 acres, 510 being in pasture. In 1795 it had 32 enslaved people. After they were sold, the pen was sold for £5,500 sterling.

23. Barclay, *An Account*, 5.

24. Ibid.

25. Ibid.

26. Ibid.

27. Ibid.

28. Ibid., 6. Holden to Barclay, March 7, 1801.

29. Ibid., 9. Extracts from the Minutes of the 'Committee… for Improving the Conditions of Free Blacks'.

30. Ibid., 9. Letter from Pemberton, Ashley and Parks to the Committee of the

Pennsylvania Abolition Society, July 24, 1795.

31.   Ibid., 17. 'Report of a Visit to the Liberated Africans'.

32.   Thistlewood Journals, Mon. 31/1, fol. 331.

33.   Eugene Genovese, *The Political Economy of Slavery: Studies in the Economy and Society of the Slave South* (New York: Pantheon Books, 1967), 112.

34.   Thistlewood Journals, Mon. 31/1, fol. 331

35.   Ibid.

36.   Ibid., fols. 338, 386.

37.   Public Record Office [P.R.O.], Colonial Office, [C.O.], 137/147. 'A Return of All Trials of Slaves Held in the Parish of St Elizabeth, July 1, 1814–30'. See also Verene Shepherd, 'Pens and Penkeepers in a Plantation Society' PhD diss.,University of Cambridge, 1988, 264.

38.   Ibid.

39.   Ibid.

40.   Mon. 31/1, f. 420.

41.   Mon. 31/2, f. 382.

42.   Ibid., f. 55.

43.   Mon. 31/1, f. 340.

44.   Ibid., f. 381.

45.   Shepherd, 'Pens and Penkeepers', 268.

46.   Mon. 31/19.

47.   Ibid., f. 123

48.   Ibid., February 9, 1768.

49.   Mon. 31/9.

50.   D.G. Hall, 'Runaways in Jamaica in the Mid-19th Century', (Staff/Postgraduate Seminar Paper, University of the West Indies, Mona), 191.

51.   Mon. 31/19, 1774.

52.   Sidney Mintz, 'Slave Life on Caribbean Sugar Plantations: Some Unanswered Questions', in Palmié, ed., *Slave Cultures and Cultures of Slavery*. (Knoxville: University of Tennessee Press, 1995), 12–22.

53.   Jamaica House of Assembly Votes [J.H.A.V.], 1824:164, 383–91.

54.   Ibid. The identified leaders in this revolt were hanged. See Slave Court, Lucea, Hanover, July 14, 1824, N.L.J., Manuscript 729.

55.   J.H.A.V., March 2, 1832, p. 15.

56.   See Michael Craton, *Testing the Chains: Resistance to Slavery in the British West Indies* (Ithaca: Cornell University Press, 1982); 'Proto-Peasant Revolts? The Late Slave Rebellions in the British West Indies, 1816–32', in *Past and Present* 85 (1979): 99–125, and 'Slave Culture, Resistance and the Achievement of Emancipation in the British West Indies, 1783–1838', in James Walvin, ed., *Slavery and British Society, 1776–1846* (London: Macmillan, 1982), 100–122. Hilary Beckles 'The 200 Years War: Slave Resistance in The British West Indies: An Overview of the Historiography', in *Jamaica Historical Review*, 12 (1982): 1–10; 'Caribbean Anti-Slavery: The Self-Liberation Ethos of Enslaved Blacks', in Shepherd and Beckles, eds., *Caribbean Slavery in the Atlantic World*, 869–78, and Hilary Beckles, 'Emancipation by War or Law? Wilberforce and the 1816

Barbados Slave Rebellion', in David Richardson, ed., *Abolition and its Aftermath: The Historical Context, 1790–1916* (London: Frank Cass, 1985), 80–105. Richard Hart, *Slaves Who Abolished Slavery: Vol. 1, Blacks in Bondage* (Kingston: Institute for Social and Economic Research, University of the West Indies, 1980) and Richard Hart, *Vol. 2, Blacks in Rebellion* (Kingston: Institute for Social and Economic Research, University of the West Indies, 1985).

57. See Williams, *Capitalism and Slavery*, 208.

58. Mary Turner, *Slaves and Missionaries: The Disintegration of Jamaican Slave Society, 1787–1834* (Kingston: University of the West Indies Press, 1998), 148.

59. CO 137/185, 'Voluntary Confession of Linton, a prisoner in Savanna-la-mar gaol, under sentence of death, March 1832'. Thomas Stewart, Rector of Westmoreland recorded the evidence.

60. These include Beckles 'The 200 Years War'; Craton, *Testing the Chains*; Hart, *Slaves Who Abolished Slavery* and Hart, *Blacks in Rebellion*; C.S. Reid, *Samuel Sharpe: From Slave to National Hero* (Kingston: Bustamante Institute for Public and International Affairs, 1988), Turner, *Slaves and Missionaries* and Kamau Brathwaite, *Wars of Respect: Nanny, Sam Sharpe and the Struggle for People's Liberation* (Kingston: Agency for Public Information, 1977).

61. C.O. 137/185, Confession to Thomas Stewart, February 1, 1832.

62. Ibid.

63. Viscount Goderich to the Governors of the West India Colonies, March 16, 1832, Enclosure in Despat ch No. 137, C.O. 137/181.

64. Ibid.

65. See for example, Turner, *Slaves and Missionaries,* map facing p. 1 and p. 148.

66. The pen-keeper at Kensington had actually been warned about the intention to burn his property. He had received a letter from one Benjamin Haughton Tharp advising him that his house would be burned that evening and his family destroyed. He applied immediately to Major Pennefeather of the 22nd Regiment for a small guard, but this request was refused and the pen-keeper dubbed an alarmist. Nevertheless, he took his family and fled to Montego Bay. His house was set on fire ten minutes after he left. See J.H.A.V., 1832, Appendix 18, p. 328.

67. Evidence of Daniel Malcolm, enslaved man of Ramble Pen, as reported by the manager of Shettlewood Pen, J.H.A.V., 1832, p. 231.

68. Ibid. Haughton Pen seemed to have been at the centre of the 'rebellious district' in 1831. See J.A., Gifts & Deposits, 7/177/7.

69. C.O. 137/185.

70. Ibid.

71. C.O. 137/138, Slave Trials, 1831/32, Trial of James Bernard, 31 July 1832. See also Verene Shepherd and Ahmed Reid, 'Rebel Voices: Confessions, Testimonies and Trial Transcripts from the 1831/32 Emancipation War in Jamaica', *Jamaica Journal* 28, nos. 2 & 3 (December 2004): 59–64; Verene Shepherd, 'To Be Hanged by the Neck Until He Be Dead: The King Against Samuel Sharpe, April 1832', *Jamaica Journal,* 29, nos. 1 & 2 (June–October, 2005), 54–59, and Shepherd, 'Monuments, Memorialisation and Decolonisation in Jamaica', *Jamaica Journal* 29, no. 3 (December 2005–April 2006): 34–43.

72. CO 137/138, Slave Trials, 1831/32. Evidence against the enslaved man Thomas Grey of Springvale Pen, Trelawny.

73. Ibid., January 31, 1832, evidence of Harry Hine. The action on Bandon Pen was replicated on several other pens including Worcester Pen in St James.

74. The data available (C.O. 137/185) do not allow for an exact calculation of the enslaved from pens who were killed as the property is not always identified.

75. Slave Trials, 1832. J.H.A.V., 1832.

76. See W.S. Grignon, *Vindication of the Conduct of Colonel Grignon and the Western Interior Regiment* (Kingston, 1833) and Hart, *Slaves Who Abolished Slavery*, 244–337.

77. Eugene Genovese, *From Rebellion to Revolution: Afro-American Slave Revolts in the Making of the Modern World* (Baton Rouge: Louisiana State University Press, 1979), xiii.

78. Claire Midgley, *Women Against Slavery: The British Campaigns, 1780–1870* (London: Routledge, 1992).

79. Reginald Coupland, *The British Antislavery Movement* (London: Oxford University Press, 1933); Seymour Drescher, *Capitalism and Antislavery: British Mobilization in Comparative Perspective* (New York: Oxford University Press, 1987).

80. See E (Kamau) Brathwaite, 'The Slave Rebellion in the Great River Valley of St James, 1831/32', *Jamaican Historical Review*, 13 (1982), 11-30; Beckles, 'The 200 Years War, and Beckles, *Natural Rebels*. For an idea of the recent debates over the causes of abolitionism in the British Caribbean, see section 17 of Shepherd and Beckles, eds., *Caribbean Slavery in the Atlantic World*, especially articles by Selwyn Carrington and Seymour Drescher. See also Robin Blackburn, *The Overthrow of Colonial Slavery* (London: Verso, 1988).

81. Williams, *Capitalism and Slavery*.

Chapter 8

1. K.N. Bell and W.P. Morrell, *Select Documents on British Colonial Policy 1830–1860* (Oxford: The Clarendon Press, 1968).

2. Public Record Office (P.R.O.), Colonial Office (C.O.) 137/222, Governor Smith to Lord Glenelg, March 13, 1837, Despatch No. 76. See also William Green, *British Slave Emancipation: The Sugar Colonies and the Great Experiment* (Oxford: The Clarendon Press, 1976).

3. For protest on sugar estates and coffee plantations, see Swithin Wilmot, 'Not "Full Free": The Ex-Slaves and the Apprenticeship System in Jamaica 1834–38', *Jamaica Journal* 17, no. 3 (1984): 2–10 and Wilmot 'Emancipation in Action: Workers and Wage Conflict in Jamaica 1838–1845', *Jamaica Journal* 19, no. 3 (1986): 55–61.

4. J.H. James to John Tharp, August 4, 1835, R. 55/7/128/j, Tharp Family Papers, Cambridge Record Office.

5. C.O. 137/214, Enclosure in Despatch 259, Governor Sligo to Glenelg, January 1, 1836.

6. Ibid. Report to Stipendiary Magistrate (hereafter S.M.) Davies.

7. C.O. 137/212, SM Daughtrey's report, Enclosure in Despatch 551, Sligo to Glenelg, July 28, 1836.

8. Ibid.
9. C.O. 137/219, Enclosure in Despatch 90, Governor Smith to Glenelg, April 4, 1837.
10. Ibid., Enclosure 33, January 10, 1837. Daughtrey himself was in favour of task work and wished to see it more widely used. See Bell and Morrell, Select Documents on British Colonial Policy 1, 395–99, SM Daughtrey's report, June 30, 1835.
11. C.O. 137/210, Enclosure in Despatch 401, Sligo to Glenelg, April 2, 1835.
12. Ibid.
13. Ibid. Kelly to Sligo, March 29, 1836.
14. C.O. 137/214, Enclosure in Despatch 48, Sligo to Glenelg, July 7, 1835.
15. C.O. 137/214, SM Davies' Report, Enclosure in Despatch 259, Sligo to Glenelg, January 1, 1836 and Jamaica Archives [J.A.], Gifts and Deposits (Phillips), 7/177/7, April 18,1836.
16. J.A., Gifts and Deposits (Phillips), 7/177/7, April 18, 1836.
17. C.O. 137/210, Agricultural Report, 1835–6, Enclosure in Despatch 401, Sligo to Glenelg, April 2, 1836, and Enclosure in Despatch 422, Sligo to Glenelg, April 17, 1836.
18. C.O. 137/214, Enclosure in Despatch 259, Sligo to Glenelg, January 1, 1836.
19. C.O. 137/219, I, Henry Laidlaw to Smith, January 9, 1837, Enclosure in Despatch 90, Smith to Glenelg, April 4, 1837. He referred to the Crescent Park district of St Ann.
20. C.O. 137/219, Despatch 111, Smith to Glenelg, May 11, 1837.
21. Ibid.
22. Joseph Sturge and Thomas Harvey, *The West Indies in 1837* (London, 1838), 347. See also *Falmouth Post*, March 21, 1838: 5.
23. Sturge and Harvey, *The West Indies in 1837*, 317.
24. Ibid., ix.
25. C.O. 137/211, Enclosure in Despatch 499, Sligo to Glenelg, June 23, 1836.
26. See J.A., 1B/11/6, Manumission Libers.
27. C.O. 137/205, Sligo to Glenelg, December 5, 1835.
28. P.R.O., T71/685-733, Valuers' Returns by parish, 1834.
29. C.O. 137/222, Enclosure in Despatch 76, Sligo to Glenelg, March 13, 1837.
30. C.O. 137/205, 259, Sligo to Glenelg, December 5, 1835.
31. C.O. 137/62, Despatch 289, Glenelg to Smith, June 1, 1838.
32. J.A. 1B/11/4, Liber 36, fols. 67–71, Libers 32–40.
33. C.O. 137/194, III, Extracts from the Examination of William Stamford Grignon before a Committee of the House of Assembly, Sligo to Glenelg, November 11, 1834.
34. British Parliamentary Papers [P.P.], Accounts and Papers (523) xxxvi, fol. 113, 1839.
35. P.P., (1958) xxxc, 1839, Report from John McClarty, overseer in *Correspondence Relating to the Negro Population of Jamaica,* Appendix E, 64.
36. British Library, Official Publications Library, P.P. (523) xxxvi, Accounts and Papers, 1839, 'Statement Exhibiting the Progress of Fieldwork', in Papers Relating to the Condition of the Labouring Population 1, West Indies, Pt. I, Jamaica.
37. J.H.A.V. 1, 1840, 187.

38.   Ibid., 188.

39.   National Library of Jamaica, [N.L.J.], MS. 274 a–c, Fort George Pen Journals, 1840–62. See also Douglas Hall, 'Fort George Pen, Jamaica: Slaves, Tenants, and Labourers' (Association of Caribbean Historians Conference Paper, Curaçao, April 1979).

40.   Ibid., 64–66 and J.H.A.V. 1, 'Petition of the Pen-keepers', November 16, 1843, 170.

41.   C.O. 137/232, VII, Despatch 189, Smith to Glenelg, November 1, 1838, and P.P. (523) xxxvi, Accounts and Papers, 1839, 'Statement Exhibiting the Progress of Field Labour'.

42.   N.L.J., MS. 274b, ii, Journal of Labour, Fort George, 1843.

43.   Letter from the attorney to W.R. and S. Mitchell, August 22, 1835, 1B/5/83/2, Attorneys' Letterbook, 1831–38, Jamaica Archives.

44.   Ibid., Attorney to W. Mitchell, November 18, 1835.

45.   J.A, 1B/11/4/84, Accounts Produce [A.P.], 1840.

46.   P.P., (158) xxxv, Correspondence Relative to the Negro Population of Jamaica, Appendix E, 63.

47.   N.L.J., MS. 247c, Rent Roll, Fort George Pen, 1843, 1840–49.

48.   N.L.J., MS. 274b, John Patridge's Report, March 31, 1852.

49.   J.A. 1B/11/5/39, Accounts Current [A.C.], New Shafston Pen, fols, 142–5, and Liber 43, Rowington Park Pen, fols. 61–3.

50.   W.E. Riviere, 'Labour Shortage in the British West Indies after Emancipation', *Journal of Caribbean History*, 14 (1972): 10. It is clear from the preceding discussion of the reasons apprentices left the pens that though there was no immediate mass exodus after 1838, where labourers eventually departed or were evicted, 'push' factors predominated. Thus Hall's argument in 'The flight from the Estates Reconsidered', *Journal of Caribbean History* 10 and 11 (1978): 7–24, is equally applicable to pens. For a debate over the reasons ex-slaves deserted their former residences, see O. Nigel Bolland, 'Systems of domination after slavery: the control of land and labour in the British West Indies after 1838', *Comparative Studies in Society and History* (*CSSH*) 1, no. 23 (1981): 591–619. In this article, Bolland rejects the primacy accorded by historians to the land/people ratio as a factor in the formation of the peasantry. He particularly criticizes Green's argument. For the latter's reaction, see W. Green, 'The perils of Comparative History: Belize and the British Sugar Colonies After Slavery', *CSSH* 1, no. 26 (1984): 117–19; and for Bolland's reply to Green, see *CSSH* 126 (1984): 120–25.

51.   J.A., Private Deposit 4/4/1–2, Journal of Henry Blagrove, July 2–11, 1842.

52.   Ibid.

53.   Ibid, January 11, 1842.

54.   N.L.J., MS. 765, Stephen Harmer to Henry Harmer, February 11, 1840.

55.   N.L.J., MS. 765, Stephen Harmer to Saul Harmer, March 16, 1842. Thomas Carlyle, *Occasional Discourse on the Nigger Question* (London, 1953). Carlyle similarly accused the freed people of idleness simply because they refused to work on the plantations on a full-time basis.

56.   *Morning Journal*, August 20, 1838, 2.

57.   J.A., Gifts and Deposits, 7/177/4, Report on Montrose Pen, St Mary, John Cooper,

1835.

58. C.O. 142/4, *Morning Journal* 1, April 24, 1838, 3.

59. P.P., (523) xxvi, S.M. Rickett's report on the state of agriculture in St Elizabeth, 1839, 111.

60. J.A, Private Deposit 4/100, Gunnis Papers. Anderson to McTaggart, November 11, 1856 See also P.P., (212), xxc. Half-yearly agricultural reports, 1840, 4–22; P.P., (344), iii, Accounts and Papers, Session 2, Papers Relative to Jamaica 1, 1841, 579, and P.P., (374), xxix, Agricultural reports, 1842, 41.

61. Gisela Eisner, *Jamaica 1830–1930: A Study of Economic Growth.* (Connecticut: Greenwood Press, 1974), 198–99. Despite this obvious decline in the sugar industry, Eisner, nevertheless claims that the shortage of labour on plantations forced them to use more animals to do work normally done by enslaved people and freed people. This increased the demand for stock and contributed to the expansion of pen-keeping. However, there is absolutely no evidence to support this claim. All sources point to the decline in the demand for livestock between 1838 and 1845. Her comments might be more applicable to the post-1848 period, as after the passing of the Sugar Duties Act the issue of labour became more acute and labour-saving devices were increasingly adopted.

62. C.O. 137/302, Enclosure in Despatch 31, Henry Barkly to Newcastle, December 31, 1853.

63. C.O. 700/16, Simpson's and Craskell's Map of Jamaica, 1763.

64. James Robertson, County Maps of Jamaica, 1804, Map Collection, National Library of Jamaica.

65. J.R. Ward, *British West Indian Slavery, 1750–1834: The Process of Amelioration* (Oxford: Oxford Press, 1988), 101 and Handbook of Jamaica [H.B.J.] 1908, 406–12.

66. J.A., 1B/11/4/90–1, A.P., 1845.

67. A.P., J.A, 1B/11/4/93-99, 1860–79 and New Series vols. 1 & 2, 1879–1927.

68. J.A., 1B/11/5/39–45, A.C., 1840–45.

69. J.A., Private Deposit, 4/110, Gunnis Papers, McTaggart to Anderson, December 1, 1856.

70. Ibid., Nath-Spines to F.G. Gunnis, December 26, 1888.

71. Michael Craton *Searching for the Invisible Man: Slaves and Plantation Life in Jamaica* (Cambridge: Cambridge University Press, 1977), 29–30.

72. N.L.J., uncatalogued estate maps, St Ann, 1838.

73. Ibid., St David. See also St C. 295, Kelsall Pen, St Catherine, 1843.

74. J.A, 4/45/27-27a, Tweedie Papers.

75. C.O. 137/1-490, Eyre to Cardwell, September 10, 1864.

76. Lowell J. Ragatz, *The Fall of the Planter Class in the British Caribbean, 1763–1833* (New York: The Century Co, 1928); Eric Williams, *Capitalism and Slavery* (Chapel Hill: University of North Carolina Press, 1944; Kingston: Ian Randle Publishers, 2005); William A. Green, 'The Planter Class and British West Indian Sugar Production before and after Emancipation', *Economic History Review* 26 (1973), 448–463; J.R. Ward, 'The Profitability of Sugar Planting in the British West Indies, 1650–1834', *Economic History Review* 31, no. 2 (1978):197-213

and Seymour Drescher, 'The Decline Thesis of British Slavery Since Econocide', *Slavery and Abolition* 7, no. 1 (1986): 1–24; For a summary of the various arguments presented by authors mentioned above, see Selwyn Carrington, 'The State of the Debate on the Role of Capitalism in the Ending of the Slave System', *The Journal of Caribbean History* 22, nos.1 & 2 (1988): 20–41. This article has been reprinted in Verene Shepherd & Hilary Beckles, eds., *Caribbean Slavery in the Atlantic World* (Kingston: Ian Randle Publishers, 2000), 1031–41.

77. C.O. 137/302, Charles Grey to Earl Grey, Jamaica Governor's Despatches # 31, September 3, 1849.

78. C.O. 137/322, Despatch 24, February 21, 1854.

79. William Sewell, *The Ordeal of Free Labour in the British West Indies* (London, 1868), 188.

80. The Blue Books of Jamaica [B.B.J], 1869, 43; 1882, x4–x6; 1885–86, x2–x4 and 1889–91, x4–x5.

81. H.B.J., 1884–85, 231.

82. B.B.J. 1870, 44–45; HBJ 1908, 398.

83. H.B.J. 1883, 363–65; Veront Satchell, *From Plots to Plantations: Land Transactions in Jamaica* (Kingston: Institute of Social and Economic Research, University of the West Indies, 1990), 46 and H.B.J. 1883, 364.

84. C.O. 137/322, Barkly to Newcastle, February 21, 1854.

85. N.L.J, MS. 65 'List of Planters and Penkeepers compiled from Mr. Espeut's List'. This list gives us an idea of the parishes in which these landowners lived. Only the initials and surnames appear on the list so that it is impossible to identify the female landowners.

86. H.B.J., 1908, 412–17.

87. Trade Statistics, B.B.J. 1885–86, u49–u115; B.B.J. 1887–8, u50–u107; B.B.J. 1888–89, u52–u110 and B.B.J. 1891–92, u61–62.

88. H.B.J. 1884–85, 231.

89. J.A., Private Deposit 4/110, Anderson to Forbes, March 30, 1871.

90. B.W. Higman, *Montpelier, Jamaica: A Plantation Community in Slavery and Freedom, 1739–1912* (Kingston: University of the West Indies Press, 1998), 65–74.

91. H.B.J. 1893, 289.

92. H.B.J. 1908, 412–17 & 413–19.

93. J.A., 2/10/1. Vestry Minutes and Municipal Board Minutes, 113, 1891, St Elizabeth.

94. B.B.J., 1840–62; J.H.A.V., 1859–65 and Legislative Council Minutes, 1880–92.

95. H.B.J. 1897, 413; H.B.J. 1902, 378 and Eisner, *Jamaica 1830–1930*, 256–57.

96. H.B.J. 1882–1902, Agricultural Reports, 1879–1900.

97. For a fuller discussion of Asian immigration and the deployment of immigrant labour, see Verene Shepherd, *Transients to Settlers: The Experience of Indians in Jamaica, 1845–1950* (Warwick/Leeds: Peepal Tree Press, 1994).

98. Eisner, *Jamaica 1830–1930*, 313.

99. H.B.J. 1908, 406–10.

100. B.W. Higman, *Jamaica Surveyed: Plantation Maps and Plans of the 18th and 19th*

Centuries (Kingston: Institute of Jamaica, 1988).

101. S.A. Hill. comp. *Who is Who in Jamaica* (Kingston: Stephen A. Hill, 1916), 116.
102. H.B.J. 1897, 412–13.
103. For an elaboration of this thesis, see Satchell, *From Plots to Plantations*, 55.

Conclusion

1. E. (Kamau) Brathwaite, *The Development of Creole Society in Jamaica, 1770–1820* (Oxford: The Clarendon Press, 1971; Kingston: Ian Randle Publishers, 2005), 146–50.
2. Ibid., 100–01.
3. A. Roxborough, 'Stock and Stock-raising in Jamaica', Institute of Jamaica Lecture Series', Lecture V, 19.
4. This is clearly evidenced in Thomas Harrison's 1890 map of the parish of Westmoreland. See also *Handbook of Jamaica [H.B.J.]*, 1880–89, 185.
5. Thus, Orange Valley Estate was converted to a pen and Orange Valley Pen expanded after emancipation. See J.A. Private Deposits, 4/4/1-2, Journal of Henry Blagrove, June 15, 1842. For a nineteenth-century list of some of these planters and pen-keepers, see National Library of Jamaica, [N.L.J] MS 65. This list, frustratingly for me, does not distinguish unambiguously between 'planters' and 'penkeepers'.
6. John Morant, for example, turned his estates into pens in 1894. See Winchester, Hampshire Record Office, 6M 80M/E/T261, 'Settlement of John Morant and Edward Eden of Hereditaments in the Island of Jamaica, 1894'. George Cunningham of Greenside Estate in Trelawny converted that estate into a pen in the 1850s. See Cyrus Francis Perkins, *Busha's Mistress, Or Catherine the Fugitive*, edited and introduced by Paul Lovejoy, Verene Shepherd and David Trotman (Kingston: Ian Randle Publishers, 2002). Another famous estate returned to a cattle pen was Worthy Park. See Michael Craton, *Searching for the Invisible Man: Slaves and Plantation Life in Jamaica* (Cambridge: Cambridge University Press, 1977), 19. Other such conversions were recorded in the Collector General's reports.
7. *Blue Books of Jamaica* [B.B.J.] 1865–92.
8. Collector General's Reports, Jamaica Annual Returns., 1880–1884.
9. B.B.J., 1869 and 1891. Veront Satchel recorded that these figures relate to guinea grass, but they in fact represent the total of land in guinea grass and common pasture. In 1869, the land in guinea grass was just about 100,000 acres and in 1891 it was 121,343 acres. See Satchell, 'Rural Land Transactions in Jamaica, 1866–1900', M.Phil. diss.,University of the West Indies, Mona, 1986, 99–101.

BIBLIOGRAPHY

MANUSCRIPTS

BRISTOL RECORD OFFICE
Elbridge Family Papers, Spring Plantation Accounts, 1744–1801. AC/WO 16(27) 1–178.

BRISTOL UNIVERSITY LIBRARY
Papers Relating to Thetford Estate and Thetford Hall Pen, St. John, 1795–1802. D.M 444.
Slave Lists, Fairhall and Hopewell Hall. DM 41/12/2.

BRITISH LIBRARY, DEPARTMENT OF MANUSCRIPTS
Barham, H. 'Account of Jamaica', 1772. Sloane MS 3,918.
Long, E. Classification of the Inhabitants of St. James's Parish, 1773. Add. MS 12,435.
———. *History of Jamaica* (with Long's editorial changes). 3 vols., 1774, Add. MSS 12,404–6.

CAMBRIDGE UNIVERSITY LIBRARY
Vanneck Manuscripts, Jamaican Estate Papers, 1765–1810, box 2, bundles 1–60.

CAMBRIDGESHIRE COUNTY RECORD OFFICE
Tharp Family Papers. Correspondence, Slave Lists and Accounts Relating to the Tharp Estates and Pens in Jamaica, 1745–1866. R. 55. 7/12133, R. 83/58, R. 83/58(pt.), R. 84/29.

EXETER UNIVERSITY LIBRARY
Gale/Morant Collection. General Correspondence and Accounts Relating to the Properties of William Gale and Edward MorantGale, Jamaica, 1731–1845. Sections 1–6.

ISLAND RECORD OFFICE, JAMAICA
District Court Wills, Libers 1–136.

JAMAICA ARCHIVES, SPANISH TOWN
Accounts Current, 1806–45. 1B/11/5/1–45.
Accounts Produce, Selected Volumes, 1740–1845. 1B/11/4/1–85.
Attorneys' Letterbook, 1821–38. 1B/5/83/1–2.
Harrson, T. Map of Westmoreland, 1890.
Jamaica House of Assembly Journals, 1740–95. 1B/11/5.
John Cooper's Report on Simon Taylor's Properties, 1835. Gifts and Deposits (Phillips), 7/177/1–8.

Journal of Benjamin ScottMoncrieffe, 1828–40. Grand Court Records, Misc., 1A/5/26.
List of Freeholders Qualified for the Franchise, St. Catherine, 1757–1840. 2/2/27.
Local Government Records, Vestry Minutes, 1759–1890. 2/1/1–19.
Manumission Records, 1747–1838. 1B/11/6/5–70.
Moravian Church Records, 1756–1890. 5/5.
Parish Registers, 1785–1845. 1B/11/8.
Private Deposits 4/4/12, Journal of Henry John Blagrove, 1841–42.
Private Deposits 4/33/4, Pantrepant Estate Journal, 1834–35.
Private Deposits 4/45/3664, Tweedie Family Papers, 1808–32.
Private Deposits 4/110, Gunnis Papers, 1801–45.
Probate Inventories, 1739–1838. 18/11/3/21–157.
Returns of the Registration of Slaves, 1817–32. 1B/11/7.
St. David Vestry Minutes, 1785–1829. 1B/11/9/1–7.

LINCOLNSHIRE COUNTY ARCHIVES OFFICE
Journals of Thomas Thistlewood, 1748–86. Monson 31/1–37.
Journals (Further), Accounts and Memoranda. Monson 31/83–92.
Thistlewood Family History. Monson 31/83.

NATIONAL LIBRARY OF JAMAICA
A List of Planters and Penkeepers in Jamaica. MS 65.
Estate Maps and Plans by Parish (largely uncatalogued).
Extension Treaty with Spain, 1667. MS 450.
Extract of a Letter from Simon Taylor, 20 May 1798. MS 624.
Five Letters from Stephen Harmer to His Family in England, 1830–42. MS 765.
Illicit Trade c. 1740. MS 1,049.
Indenture Between Richard Stratton and A.P. Collings, 1804. MS 1,555.
Journals of Fort George Pen, 1841–56. MSS 274a–c.
Letters from Thomas Hall, 1760–78. MS 1,069.
Medical Practitioner's Journal. MS 1,769.
Morris, Cunninghame and Woolredge. 'A Plan of the Parish of St. James Together with a Part of the Parishes of Hanover, Westmoreland and St. Elizabeth Showing the District and Properties Destroyed in the Late Rebellion', March 1832.
Radnor Plantation Journal, 1822–26. MS 180.
Robertson, J. Maps of the Counties of Cornwall, Middlesex and Surrey (Kingston, 1804).
Slave Court, Lucea, Hanover, 1824. MS 729.
Spring Plantation Accounts, 1783–84. MSS 1,055, 1,058.
Valuation of the Properties of John Wedderburn, 1808. MS 219.

PUBLIC RECORD OFFICE, LONDON
'A List of Landholders in the Island of Jamaica Together with the Num-ber of Acres Each Person Possesses, Taken from the Quit Rent Books in 1784'. Enclosure in Governor Knowles' Despatch, 31 Dec. 1754. CO /31.

Bochart and Knollis. A New and Exact Map of the Island of Jamaica c. 1684. CO 700/6.
Compensation Claims and the Returns of the Registration of Slaves, 1817–32. T 71.
Despatches or Original Correspondence between the Governors of Jamaica and the
Secretary of State for the Colonies, 1668–1879. CO 137/1–490.
Naval Office Shipping Lists for Jamaica, 1756-1788. C.O. 142/16–20.
Original Correspondence, 1660–1703. CO 138/1–10.
Simpson and Craskell. Map of Jamaica, 1763. CO 700/16.
Slave Trials, 1831/32. CO 137/138; C.O. 137/185

SOMERSET RECORD OFFICE
Dickinson Papers Relating to Appleton and Barton Isles Estates and Pepper, Bonavista
and Watchwell Pens, 1742–1849. DD/DN465–85.

UNIVERSITY OF HULL, BRYNMOR JONES LIBRARY
Scarlett Family Papers, Langdale Manuscripts, 1797–1867. Accounts and
Correspondence, DDLA/41/1–37.

UNIVERSITY OF THE WEST INDIES LIBRARY
Jamaican Estate Records, Carton Pen, 1818–25. MS 18/8.
Pepper and Bonavista Pens. MSS 1826–45.
Wilson Family Papers, 1692–1700.

WINCHESTER, HAMPSHIRE RECORD OFFICE
Deed Relating to Brokenhurst and Other Plantations and Pens in Jamaica, The Property
of John Morant, 1894. 6M80M/E/T261.

PRINTED PRIMARY SOURCES

OFFICIAL PUBLICATIONS AND NEWSPAPERS

Jamaica
(National Library of Jamaica)
Blue Books of Jamaica, 1838–92.
Claims for Compensation Filed with the Assistant Commissioners for Jamaica. Kingston,
n.d.
Collector General's Reports: Jamaica Annual Returns.
Cornwall Chronicle, 1813–20.
Correspondence Relative to the Negro Population, Jamaica. PP, (House of Commons) 1839
(158), XXXV, 7–79.
Falmouth Post, 1791–1849.
Great Houses, files a–z, NLJ.
HalfYearly Agricultural Reports of the Stipendiary Magistrates, *Papers Relative to the
Affairs of Jamaica*. PP, (Accounts and Papers) 1840 (212), XXXV, 7–71.
HalfYearly Agricultural Reports of the Stipendiary Magistrates, *Papers Relative to the*

Affairs of Jamaica, Session 2. PP, (Accounts and Papers) 1841 (344), 111, 325–579.

Handbooks of Jamaica, 1881–90.

Jamaica Annual Reports, 1880–92.

Jamaica Census, 1891, 1911.

Jamaica House of Assembly Votes, 1787–1845.

Jamaica Mercury, 1799–1800.

Laws of Jamaica, 1691–1759.

Report of the Cattle Industry Enquiry Board, 1952.

Royal Gazette, 1819–1845.

St. Jago de la Vega Gazette, 1791–1831.

The Blackman Newspaper, Kingston, Jamaica, 1929–31.

Hill, S.A. comp. *Who is Who in Jamaica.* Kingston: Stephen A. Hill, 1916.

London

(British Library)

British Parliamentary Papers (P.P.).

HalfYearly Agricultural Reports of the Stipendiary Magistrates. *Papers Relative to the Affairs of Jamaica.* PP, 1842 (374), XXIX, 22–41.

'List of all Persons Confined in the Different Gaols and Workhouses in Jamaica', PP, (House of Commons) 1830 (673), XXI, 197.

Papers on the Condition of the Labouring Population, West Indies. PP, (Accounts and Papers) 1839 (107), XXXV, 295.

Report from the Select Committee on West Indian Colonies Together with the Minutes of Evidence, Appendix and Index. PP, (Accounts and Papers) 1842 (479), XIII, 391–424.

'Statements Exhibiting the Progress of Field work', *Papers on the Con-dition of the Labouring Population, West Indies, Part I, Jamaica.* PP, 1839 (523), XXXVI, 73–113.

'Summary of Sugar Estates, Coffee Properties and Pens in Cultivation in the Island of Jamaica', PP, 1854 (848), XLIII, 79.

London

(Public Record Office)

Blue Books of Jamaica, 1821–45. CO. 142/3459.

Morning Journal, 1838–54. CO 142/412.

SECONDARY SOURCES

CONTEMPORARY WORKS (Pre-1900)

BOOKS

Archer, Capt. J. *Monumental Inscriptions*. London, 1875.

Atwood, T. *The History of Dominic*a. London, 1791.

Barclay, D. *An Account of the Emancipation of Slaves on Unity Valley Pen*. London, 1801.

Beckford, W. *A Descriptive Account of the Island of Jamaica*. 2 vols. London, 1790.

Bigelow, J. *Jamaica in 1850*. London, 1851.

Bridges, G. W. *The Statistical History of the Parish of Manchester*. Kingston, 1824.

Carlyle, T. *Occasional Discourse on the Nigger Question*. London, 1853.

Coke, T. *A History of the West Indies*. 3 vols. London, 1808–11.

Collins, Dr. *Practical Rules for the Management and Medical Treatment of Negro Slaves in the Sugar Colonies*. London, 1811.

Davy, J. *The West Indies Before and Since Slave Emancipation*. London, 1854.

Dickson, W. *Letters on Slavery*. London, 1789.

Edwards, B. *The History, Civil and Commercial, of the British Colonies in the West Indies*. 2 vols. London, 1793.

———. *History of the West Indies*, 2 vols. London, 1798.

Feurtado, W.A. *Official and other Personages of Jamaica*. Kingston, 1896.

Grignon, W.S. *Vindication of the Conduct of Colonel Grignon and the Western Interior Re*giment. Jamaica, Office of the St. Jago Gazette, 1833.

Hakewell, J. *A Picturesque Tour of the Island of Jamaica*. London, 1825.

Knight, J. *The State of the Island of Jamaica*. London, 1726.

Leslie, C. *A New History of Jamaica*. London, 1740.

Lewis, M.G. *Journal of a Residence Among the Neqroes in the West Indies*. London, 1845.

Livingstone, N.B. *Sketch Pedigrees*. Kingston, 1670.

Long, E. *The History of Jamaica*. 3 vols. London, 1774.

M'Mahon, B. *Jamaica Plantership*. London, 1839.

Martyr, P. *History of the West Indies*. London, 1675.

Mason, D. *Observations on the Present State of the Island of Jamaica*. London, 1837.

Moreton, J.B. *Manners and Customs in the West India Islands*. London, 1790.

Penn, G. *Memorials*. London, 1660.

Phillippo, J..M. *Jamaica: Its Past and Present State*. London, 1843.

Roby, J. *A History of St. James*. Kingston, 1849.

Roughley, T. *The Jamaica Planter's Guide: Or a System of Planting and Managing a Sugar Estate in that Island and Through-out the British West Indies in General*. London, 1823.

Roxborough, A. *Stock and Stockraising in Jamaica*. Kingston, 1881.

Scotus, P. *Reminiscences of a Scottish Gentleman*. London, 1861.

Senior, B. *Jamaica As It Was, As It Is, and As It May Be*. London, 1835.

Sewell, W. *The Ordeal of Free Labour in the British West Indies*. London, 1868.

Sloane, Sir H. *A Voyage to the Islands*. 2 vols. London, 1707, 1725.

Smith, A. *An Enquiry into the Nature and Causes of the Wealth of Nations*. London, 1776.

Stephen, J. *The Slavery of the British West Indian Colonies Delinea-ted*. 2 vols. London, 1824, 1830.

Stewart, J. *An Account of Jamaica and its Inhabitants*. London, 1808.

Sturge, J., and Harvey, T. *The West Indies in 1837*. London, 1838.

Tenison, P.J. *Good Hope: A Short History*. Jamaica, 1871.

Trollope, A. *The West Indies and the Spanish Main*. London, 1859.

Wedderburn, R. *The Horrors of Slavery*. London, 1824.

Williams, C. *A Tour Through the Island of Jamaica*. London, 1827.

Wood, J.J. *Jamaica: Its History*. Kingston, 1884.

ARTICLES

A Penkeeper, 'Pen-keeping or CattleFarming', *Handbook of Jamaica (HBJ)* (1882): 491.

Anon, 'Extract from Blackwood's Magazine', *Jamaica Pamphlets* 22, No.11 (1890): 778–90.

MODERN WORKS (Post-1900)

BOOKS

Anderson, B. *Imagined Communities: Reflections on the Origin and Spread of Nationalism*. London: Verso, 1991.

Anstey, R. *The Atlantic Slave Trade and British Abolition, 1760–1810*. New Jersey: Humanities Press, 1975.

Armytage, F. *The Freeport System in the British West Indies: A Study in Commercial Policy, 1766–1822*. London: Longmans, Green and Co., 1953.

Atkinson, L. *The Earliest Inhabitants: The Dynamics of the Jamaican Taino*. Kingston: The Press, University of the West Indies, 2006.

Augier, F.R., S.Gordon, D.G. Hall and M. Reckford. *The Making of the West Indies*. Trinidad and Jamaica: Longmans Caribbean, 1960.

Barickman, B.J. *A Bahian Counterpoint: Sugar, Tobacco, Cassava, and Slavery in the Recôncavo, 1780-1860*. Stanford: Stanford University Press, 1998.

Batie, F.C. *A Comparative Economic History of the Spanish, French and English on the Caribbean Islands*. Michigan: University Microfilms, A Xerox Company, 1972.

Beckford, G. *Persistent Poverty: Underdevelopment in Plantation Economies of the Third World*. New York: Oxford University Press, 1972.

Beckles, H. *Black Rebellion in Barbados: The Struggle Against Slavery, 1687–1838*. Barbados: Antilles Publications, 1984.

———. *A History of Barbados: From Amerindian Settlement to Nation-State*. Cambridge: Cambridge University Press, 1990.

————. *White Servitude and Black Slavery in Barbados, 1687-1715*. Knoxville: University of Tennessee Press, 1989.

————. *Great House Rules: Landless Emancipation and Workers' Protest in Barbados, 1838-1938*. Kingston: Ian Randle Publishers, 2004.

————. *Centering Woman: Gender Discourses in Caribbean Slavery*. Kingston: Ian Randle Publishers, 1999.

Beckles H. and V. Shepherd. *Liberties Lost: Caribbean Indigenous Societies and Slave Systems*. Cambridge: Cambridge University Press, 2004.

————. *Trading Souls: Europe's Transatlantic Trade in Africans*. Kingston: Ian Randle Publishers, 2007.

————. *Saving Souls: The Struggle to End the Transatlantic Trade in Enslaved Africans*. Kingston: Ian Randle Publishers, 2007.

————. *Freedoms Won: Caribbean Emancipations, Ethnicities and Nationhood*. Cambridge: Cambridge University Press, 2006.

Beckles, H. and V, Shepherd. eds. *Caribbean Freedom: Economy and Society From Emancipation to the Present*. Princeton, N.J.: Markus Wiener Publishers, Kingston: Ian Randle Publishers, 1993.

————. *Caribbean Slave Society and Economy*. Kingston: Ian Randle Publishers, 1991.

————. *Natural Rebels: A Social History of Enslaved Black Women in Barbados*. New Brunswick: Rutgers University Press, 1989.

————. *Slave Voyages*. Paris: UNESCO, 1999.

Beckwith, M. *Black Roadways: A Study of Jamaican Folk Life*. New York: New American Library, 1969.

Bell, K.N. and W.P. Morrell. *Select Documents on British Colonial Policy, 1830–60*. Oxford: The Clarendon Press, 1968.

Bell, S. *Campanha Gaúcha: A Brazilian Ranching System, 1850-1920*. Stanford: Stanford University Press, 1998.

Black, C. *The History of Jamaica*. London: Collins Clear-Type Press, 1958.

Blackburn, R. *The Overthrow of Colonial Slavery, 1776-1988*. London: Verso, 1988.

Bolland, O. Nigel. *Struggles for Freedom: Essays on Slavery, Colonialism and Culture in the Caribbean and Central America*. Belize City: Angelus Press, 1997.

Brathwaite, E. (Kamau). *The Development of Creole Society in Jamaica, 1770–1820*. Oxford: Oxford University Press, 1971; Kingston: Ian Randle Publishers, 2005.

————. *Wars of Respect: Nanny, Sam Sharpe and the Struggle for People's Liberation*. Kingston: Agency for Public Information, National Heritage Week Committee, 1977.

————. *Contradictory Omens: Cultural Diversity and Integration in the Caribbean*. Mona, Jamaica: Savacou Publications, 1974.

Burn, W.L. *Emancipation and Apprenticeship in the British West Indies*. London: Jonathon Cape, 1937.

Burnard, T. *Mastery, Tyranny & Desire: Thomas Thistlewood and His Slaves in the Anglo-Jamaican World*. Kingston: The Press, University of the West Indies, 2004.

Burns, E.B. *A History of Brazil*. New York: Columbia University Press, 1980.

Bush, B. *Slave Women in Caribbean Society, 1650-1838*. Kingston: Heinemann Caribbean, 1990.

Caldecott, A. *The Church in the West Indies*. London: Frank Cass, 1970.

Campbell, M. *The Dynamics of Change in a Slave Society: A Socio-political History of the FreeColoureds of Jamaica, 1800–1865*. New Jersey: Fairleigh Dickinson University Press, 1976.

Campbell, P.C. *Chinese Coolie Emigration to Countries within the British Empire*. London: P.S. King, 1923.

Caribbean Committee on Agriculture, Nutrition, Forestry and Fisheries. Washington: Crop Enquiry Series No. I, Washington, 1946.

Cassidy, F.G. and R.B. Le Page, eds. *Dictionary of Jamaican English*. Cambridge: Cambridge University Press, 1967.

Cateau, H and Pemberton, R., eds. *Beyond Tradition: Reinterpreting the Caribbean Historical Experience*. Kingston: Ian Randle Publishers, 2006.

Clarke, C. *Kingston, Jamaica: Urban Development and Social Change, 1692-1962*. Berkeley: University of California Press, 1975; Kingston: Ian Randle Publishers, 2006.

Clausner, M.D. *Rural Santo Domingo: Settled, Unsettled and Resettled*. Philadelphia: Temple University Press, 1973.

Cohen, D. and J. Green, eds. *Neither Slave nor Free: The Freedman of African Descent in the Slave Societies of the New World*. Baltimore: The Johns Hopkins University Press, 1972.

Coppock, J. T. *An Agricultural Geography of Britain*. London: Bell, 1971.

Coupland, R. *The British Anti Slavery Movement*. London: Frank Cass, 1933.

Courtenay, P. P. *Plantation Agriculture*. London: Praeger, 1965.

Craton, M. *Sinews of Empire: A Short History of British Slavery*. London: Temple Smith, 1974.

———. *Searching for the Invisible Man: Slaves and Plantation Life in Jamaica*. Cambridge, Mass: Harvard University Press, 1978.

———. ed. *Roots and Branches: Current Directions in Slave Studies*. Toronto: University of Waterloo Press, 1979.

———. *Testing the Chains: Resistance to Slavery in the British West Indies*. Ithaca: Cornell University Press, 1982.

———. and J. Walvin. *A Jamaican Plantation: The History of Worthy Park, 1670–1970*. London: W.H. Allen, 1970.

———. and J. Walvin and D. Wright. *Slavery, Abolition and Emancipation: Black Slaves and the British Empire*. London: Longman, 1976.

Cuban Economic Research Project. *A Study on Cuba*. Miami: University of Miami Press, 1965.

Cundall, F. *Historic Jamaica*. London: West India Committee, 1915.

Cundall, F. and J. Pieterz. *Jamaica under the Spaniards*. Kingston: Institute of Jamaica, 1919.

Curtin, P.D. *The Atlantic Slave Trade: A Census*. Madison: University of Winconsin Press, 1969.

————. *Two Jamaicas: The Role of Ideas in a Tropical Colony, 1830–1865.* Cambridge Mass: Atheneum, 1955.

DaCosta, E. *Sixty Years of HorseRacing in Jamaica.* Kingston: Stonyhurst, Glasgow: Robert Maclehouse & Co. Ltd, 1934.

Davenport, F.G., ed. *European Treaties Bearing on the History of the United States and its Dependencies.* 4 vols. Washington: Carnegie Institute, 1917–37.

Deerr, N. *The History of Sugar.* 2 vols. London: Chapman & Hall, 1949.

Dicken, P. *Location in Space: A Theoretical Approach to Economic Geography.* London: Harper & Row, 1977.

Dietz, J.L. *Economic History of Puerto Rico: Institutional Change and Capitalist Development.* New Jersey: Princeton University Press, 1986.

Douglass, F. *The Narrative of the Life of Frederick Douglass, an American Slave.* Harmondsworth: Penguin, 1960.

Drescher, S. *Econocide: British Slavery in the Era of Slavery.* Pittsburgh: University of Pittsburgh Press, 1977.

————. *Capitalism and Antislavery: British Mobilization in Comparative Perspective.* New York: Oxford University Press, 1987.

Dubois, L. *A Colony of Citizens: Revolution and Slave Emancipation in the French Caribbean, 1787-1804.* Kingston: Ian Randle Publishers, 2004.

Dunn, R. *Sugar and Slaves: The Rise of the PlanterClass in the English West Indies, 1624–1713.* Chapel Hill: University of North Carolina Press, 1972.

Eisner, G. *Jamaica, 1830–1930: A Study in Economic Growth.* Connecticut: Greenwood Press, 1974.

Eltis, D. *The Rise of African Slavery in the Americas.* Cambridge: Cambridge University Press, 2000.

————. Behrendt, S. D., H. S. Klein and P. D. Richardson. *The Transatlantic Slave Trade: A Database on CD-ROM.* Cambridge: Cambridge University Press, 1999.

Engerman, S.L. and R.W. Fogel. *Time on the Cross: The Economics of American Negro Slavery.* 2 vols. Boston: Little Brown, 1974.

Ferguson, J. *The Story of the Caribbean People.* Kingston: Ian Randle Publishers, 1999.

Galenson, D. *White Servitude in Colonial America: An Economic Analysis.* Cambridge: Cambridge University Press, 1981.

Gardner, W.J. *A History of Jamaica from its Discovery by Christopher Columbus to the year 1872... including an Account of its Trade and Agriculture.* London: E. Stock, 1909.

Geggus, D. *Slave Resistance Studies and the St. Dominque Slave Revolt: Some Preliminary Considerations.* Occasional Paper Series 4. Florida International University, Latin American and Caribbean Centre: Florida International University, 1983.

Genovese, E.D. *The Political Economy of Slavery: Studies in the Economy and Society of the Slave South.* New York: Pantheon Books, 1965.

————. *Roll, Jordon, Roll: The World the Slaves Made.* New York: Vintage, 1976.

————. *From Rebellion to Revolution: AfroAmerican Slave Revolts in the Making of the Modern World.* Baton Rouge: Louisiana State University Press, 1979.

Gilroy, P. *The Black Atlantic: Modernity and Double Consciousness.* Cambridge, Mass: Harvard University Press, 1993.

Goveia, E. *The West Indian Slave Laws of the Eighteenth Century.* Chap-ters in Caribbean History, 2. Barbados: Caribbean Universities Press, 1970.

———. *Slave Society in the British Leeward Islands at the end of the 18th Century.* New Haven: Yale University Press, 1965.

Gray, L. *History of Agriculture in the Southern United States to 1860.* 2 vols. Washington: Carnegie Institute, 1933.

Green, W. *British Slave Emancipation: The Sugar Colonies and the Great Experiment.* Oxford: The Clarendon Press, 1976.

Hall, D.G. *Free Jamaica: An Economic History, 1838–65.* London: Caribbean Universities Press, 1969.

———. *Planters, Farmers and Gardeners in Eighteenth Century Jamaica.* The 1987 Elsa Goveia Memorial Lecture. Depart-ment of History, University of the West Indies, Mona, 1988.

———. *In Miserable Slavery: Thomas Thistlewood in Jamaica, 1750-1786.* London: Macmillan, 1989.

Handler, J.S. *The Unappropriated People: Freedmen in the Slave Society of Barbados.* Baltimore: The Johns Hopkins University Press, 1973.

Harper, L.A. *The English Navigation Laws: A SeventeenthCentury Experiment in Social Engineering.* New York: Columbia University Press, 1939.

Hart, R. *Slaves who Abolished Slavery: Blacks in Rebellion.* 2 vols. Mona, Kingston: Institute for Social and Economic Research, University of the West Indies,1980,1985.

Heuman, G. *Between Black and White: Race, Politics and the Free Coloureds in Jamaica, 1792–1865.* Connecticut: Greenwood Press, 1981.

———. *The Killing Time: The Morant Bay Rebellion in Jamaica.* London: Macmillan, 1990.

Higman, B.W. *Slave Population and Economy in Jamaica, 1807–34.* Cambridge: Cambridge University Press, 1976.

———. *The Jamaica Censuses of 1844 and 1861.* Mona, Kingston: Social History Project, University of the West Indies, 1980.

———. *Slave Populations of the British Caribbean, 1807–34.* Baltimore: The Johns Hopkins University Press, 1984.

———. *Jamaica Surveyed: Plantation Maps and Plans of the Eighteenth and Nineteenth Centuries.* Kingston: Institute of Jamaica, 1988.

———. *Montpelier, Jamaica: A Plantation Community in Slavery and Freedom, 1739-1912.* Kingston: The Press, University of the West Indies, 1998.

———. *Plantation Jamaica, 1750-1850: Capital and Control in a Colonial Economy.* Kingston: The Press, University of the West Indies, 2006.

Hutson, J.E. *On the Treatment and Management of the More Common West India Diseases, 1750-1802.* Kingston: The Press, University of the West Indies, 2005.

Ilbery, B.W. *Agricultural Geography.* Oxford: Oxford University Press, 1985.

Inikori, J. The *Chaining of a Continent: Export Demand for Captives and the History of Africa South of the Sahara, 1450-1870*. Mona, Kingston: Institute of Social & Economic Research, University of the West Indies, 1992.

Inikori, J. and Engerman, S., eds. *The Atlantic Slave Trade: Effects on Economies, Societies and Peoples in Africa, the America and Europe*. Durham: Duke University Press, 1992.

James, C.L.R. *The Black Jacobins*. New York: Vintage Books, 1963.

John, M. *The Plantation Slaves of Trinidad, 1783-1816: A Mathematical and Demographic Enquiry*. Cambridge: Cambridge University Press, 1988.

Innes, H.A. *The Fur Trade in Canada: An Introduction to Canadian Economic History*. Toronto: University of Toronto Press, 1960.

Johnson, S. *A Dictionary of the English Language*. 2 vols. London: Longmans, 1967.

Jordon, T.G. *Trails to Texas: Southern Roots of Western Cattle Ranching*. Nebraska: University of Nebraska Press, 1981.

Jumper, S., T. Bell and K. Ralston. *Economic Growth and Disparities: A World View*. New Jersey: Prentice-Hall, 1980.

Kiple, K.K. *The Caribbean Slave: A Biological History*. Cambridge: Cambridge University Press, 1984.

Klein, H.S., *The Atlantic Slave Trade*. Cambridge: Cambridge University Press, 1999.

———. *African Slavery in Latin America and the Caribbean*. Oxford & New York: Oxford University Press, 1986.

Knight, D. *Gentlemen of Fortune: The Men who Made their Fortunes in Britain's Slave Colonies*. London: F. Muller, 1978.

Knight, F. *Slave Society in Cuba during the Nineteenth Century*. Madison: University of Wisconsin Press, 1970.

Kraus, M. *The North Atlantic Civilization*. Princeton and New Jersey: D. Van Nostrand Co. Inc., 1957.

Kriedte, P. *Peasants, Landlords and Merchant Capitalists: Europe and the World Economy, 1500–1800*: Cambridge: Cambridge University Press, 1983.

Lloyd, P. E. *Location in Space: A Theoretical Approach to Economic Geography*. London and New York: Harper and Lee, 1977.

Lopez, A. and J. Petras, eds. *Puerto Rico and Puerto Ricans: Studies in History and Society*. New York: John Wiley and Sons, 1974.

Lovejoy, P. *Transformations in Slavery: A History of Slavery in Africa*. Cambridge: Cambridge University Press, 1983.

Lovejoy, P. ed. *Identity in the Shadow of Slavery*. London: Allen and Unwin, 2000.

Perkins, C. F. *Busha's Mistress or Catherine the Fugitive: A Stirring Romance of the Days of Slavery in Jamaica*. P. Lovejoy, V. Shepherd and D. Trotman, eds. Kingston: Ian Randle Publishers, 2003.

Mandle, J.R. *The Plantation Economy: Population and Economic Change in Guyana, 1838–1960*. Philadelphia: Temple University Press, 1973.

Manning, P. *Slavery and African Life: Occidental, Oriental, and African Slave Trades*. Cambridge: Cambridge University Press, 1990.

Martin, A.C.L. *The Jamaica Stud Book to 1823*. Jamaica: Gardner & Co, 1925.

Mathieson, W.L. *British Slavery and its Abolition, 1823–1838*. New York: Octagon Books, 1967.

Mathurin-Mair, L. *A Historical Study of Women in Jamaica, 1655-1844*. (Edited & with an introduction by H. Beckles & V. Shepherd). Kingston: The Press, University of the West Indies, 2007.

Merrick, T.W. and D. H. Graham. *Population and Economic Development in Brazil, 1800 to the Present*. Baltimore: The Johns Hopkins University Press, 1979.

Midgley, C. *Women Against Slavery: The British Campaigns, 1780-1870*. London & New York: Routledge, 1992.

Morrissey, M. *Slave Women in the New World: Gender Stratification in the Caribbean*. Kansas: University of Kansas Press, 1989.

Onions, C.T. *The Oxford Dictionary of English Etymology*. Oxford : Oxford University Press, 1966.

Ortíz, F. *Contrapunteo Cubano del Tabaco y el Azúcar*. Havana: Jesus Montero, 1940.

Padrón, F. Morales. *Spanish Jamaica (Jamaica Española)*. Orig. Pub. Sevilla: Escuela de Estudious Hispano-Americanos de Sevilla, 1952. Trans. Patrick Bryan. Kingston: Ian Randle Publishers, 2003.

Palache, J.T and A.C.L.Martin. *The Jamaica Stud Book*. Kingston, 1925.

Pares, R. *Merchants and Planters*. Cambridge: Cambridge University Press, 1960.

Partridge, E. *Origins: A Short Etymological Dictionary of Modern English*. New York: Greenwich House, 1966.

Patterson, O. *The Sociology of Slavery: An Analysis of the Origins, Development and Structure of Negro Slave Society in Jamaica*. London: Grenada Publishing, 1973.

Pitman, F.W. *The Development of the British West Indies, 1700–1763*. New Haven: Yale University Press, 1917.

Ragatz, L.J. *The Fall of the Planter Class in the British Caribbean, 1763–1833*. New York: The Century Co, 1928.

Reid, C. S. *Samuel Sharpe: From Slave to National Hero*. Kingston: Bustamante Institute of Public and International Affairs. 1988.

Robinson, M., ed. *The Concise Scots Dictionary*. Aberdeen: Aberdeen University Press 1985.

Rodney, W. *How Europe Underdeveloped Africa*. London: Bogle L'Ouverture, 1972.

Sainsbury, N., ed. *Calendar of State Papers: America and the West Indies, 1669–1674*. London: Longman, Green & Roberts, 1964.

Satchell, V. *From Plots to Plantations: Land Transactions in Jamaica, 1866–1900*. Mona, Kingston: Institute of Social and Economic Research, University of the West Indies, 1990.

Scarano, F.A. *Sugar and Slavery in Puerto Rico: The Plantation Eco-nomy of Ponce, 1800–1850*. Wisconsin: University of Wisconsin Press, 1984.

Schuler, M. *Alas, Alas, Kongo: A Social History of Indentured African Immigration into Jamaica, 1841–1865*. Baltimore: The Johns Hopkins University Press, 1980.

Scott, R. *Slave Emancipation in Cuba: The Transition to Free Labour, 1860–1899*. New Jersey: Princeton University Press, 1984.

Shepherd, V. *Transients to Settlers: The Experience of Indians in Jamaica, 1845–1950.* Warwick/Leeds: Peepal Tree Press, 1994.

———. and Bridget Brereton, and Barbara Bailey, eds. *Engendering History: Caribbean Women in Historical Perspective.* Kingston: Ian Randle Publishers, 1995.

———. ed. and comp. *Women in Caribbean History.* Kingston: Ian Randle Publishers, 1999.

———. and H. Beckles. eds. *Caribbean Slavery in the Atlantic World.* Kingston: Ian Randle Publishers, 2000.

———. ed. *Slavery Without Sugar: Diversity in Caribbean Economy and Society.* Gainesville: University Press of Florida, 2002.

———. and G. Richards. eds. *Questioning Creole: Creolisation Discourses in Caribbean Culture.* Kingston: Ian Randle Publishers, 2002.

Sheppard, J. *The 'Redlegs' of Barbados: Their Origins and History.* New York: Oxford Press, 1977.

Sheridan, R.B. *The Development of the Plantations to 1750; An Era of West Indian Prosperity, 1750–1775.* Barbados: Caribbean Universities Press, 1970.

———. *Sugar and Slavery: An Economic History of the British West Indies, 1623–1775.* Barbados: Caribbean Universities Press, 1974.

———. *Doctors and Slaves: A Medical and Demographic History of Slavery in the British West Indies, 1680–1834.* Cambridge: Cambridge University Press, 1985.

Sherlock, P. and H. Bennett. *The Story of the Jamaican People.* Kingston: Ian Randle Publishers, 1997.

Skeat, W.W. *An Etymological Dictionary of the English Language.* Oxford: Oxford University Press, 1910.

Smith, A.E. *Colonists in Bondage: White Servitude and Convict Labour in America, 1607–1776.* Chapel Hill: University of North Carolina Press, 1947.

Smith, J.E. *Slavery and Rice Culture in Low Country Georgia, 1750–1860.* Knoxville: University of Tennessee Press, 1905.

Smith, M. G. *The Plural Society in the British West Indies.* Berkeley: University of California Press, 1965.

Solow, B. and S. L. Engerman. eds., *British Capitalism and Caribbean Slavery: The Legacy of Eric Williams.* Cambridge: Cambridge University Press, 1987.

Symons, L.J. *Agricultural Geography.* London: Praeger, 1967.

The Oxford English Dictionary. 8 vols. Oxford: Oxford University Press, 1933.

Thirsk, J. ed. *Agrarian History of England and Wales, 1500–1640.* 8 vols. Cambridge: Cambridge University Press, 1967.

———. *The Rural Economy of England.* London: Continuum, 1984.

Thompson, V.B. *The Making of the African Diaspora in the Americas, 1441–1900.* New York: Random House, 1987.

Thornton, A.P. *West India Policy under the Restoration.* Oxford: The Clarendon Press, 1956.

Tomlinson, R. *Sociological Concepts and Research.* New York: Random House, 1965.

Turner, M. *Slaves and Missionaries: The Disintegration of Jamaican Slave Society, 1787–1834.* Illinois: University of Illinois Press, 1982.

————. ed. From *Chattel Slaves to Wage Slaves: The Dynamics of Labour Bargaining in the Americas*. Bloomington: Indiana University Press, 1995.

Wallerstein, I. *The Modern World System*. New York: Academic Press, 1974.

Walvin, J. *Making the Black Atlantic: Britain and the African Diaspora*. London: Cassell, 2000.

Ward, J. R. *British West Indian Slavery, 1750–1834: The Process of Amelioration*. Oxford: Oxford University Press, 1988.

Watts, D. *The West Indies: Patterns of Development, Culture and Environmental Change since 1492*. Cambridge: Cambridge University Press, 1987.

Wedderburn, R. *The Horrors of Slavery and Other Writings by Robert Wedderburn*. Ian McCalman ed. New York: Mark Wiener, 1991.

Weekley, E. *A Concise Etymological Dictionary of Modern English*. London: Secker & Warburg, 1952.

White, D.G. *Ar'n't I a woman?: Female Slaves in the Plantation South*. New York: W.W. Norton, 1985.

Williams, E. *Capitalism and Slavery*. Chapel Hill: University of North Carolina Press, 1944; Kingston: Ian Randle Publishers, 2005.

————. *History of the People of Trinidad and Tobago*. London: Andre Deutsch, 1964.

Wood, B.C. *Slavery in Colonial Georgia, 1730–1775*. Athens: University of Georgia Press, 1984.

Wright, J. *The English Dialect Dictionary*. 6 vols. London: Henry Frowde, 1903.

Wright, P. *Monumental Inscriptions of Jamaica*. London: Society of Genealogists, 1966.

————. ed. *Lady Nugent's Journal of Her Residence in Jamaica from 1801-1805*. Kingston: Institute of Jamaica, 1966.

ARTICLES

Anstey, R. 'The Volume and Profitability of the British Slave Trade, 1761–1807', in S.L. Engerman and E.D. Genovese, eds., *Race and Slavery in the Western Hemisphere: Quantitative Studies*. Princeton: Princeton University Press, 1975: 3–32.

Barrett, W. 'Caribbean Sugar Production Standards in the Seventeenth and Eighteenth Centuries', in J. Parker, ed., *Merchants and Scholars: Essays in the History of Exploration and Trade*. Minneapolis: University of Minnesota Press, 1965: 145–70.

Beckles, H. 'The 200 Years War: Slave Resistance in The British West Indies: An Overview of the Historiography', *Jamaica Historical Review*, 12 (1982): 1–10.

————. 'Caribbean Anti-Slavery: The Self-Liberation Ethos of Enslaved Blacks', in H. Beckles and V. Shepherd, eds., *Caribbean Slavery in the Atlantic World*. Kingston: Ian Randle Publishers, 2000: 869–78.

————. 'Emancipation by War or Law? Wilberforce and the 1816 Barbados Slave Rebellion', in D. Richardson, ed., *Abolition and its Aftermath: The Historical Context, 1790–1916*. London: Frank Cass, 1985: 80–104.

Belding, R. 'A Test of the Von Thunen Locational Model', *Institute of British Geographers*, 6, (1981):176–87.

Bennett, J.H. 'Cary Helyar, Merchant and Planter of Seventeenth -Century Jamaica', *William and Mary Quarterly*, 3rd series, 21 (1964): 53–76.

Best, L. 'Outlines of the Model of a Pure Plantation Economy', *Social and Economic Studies*, 17(1968): 283–326.

Bishko, C. 'The Peninsular Background of Latin American Cattle Ranching', *Hispanic American Historical Review*, 32 (1952): 491–515.

Blight, D., 'Analyze the Sounds': Frederick Douglass's Invitation to Modern Historians of Slavery', in S. Palmie, ed., *Slave Cultures and the Cultures of Slavery*. Knoxville: University of Tennessee Press, 1995:1–11.

Bolland, O. Nigel. 'Systems of Domination After Slavery: The Control of Land and Labour in the British West Indies after 1838', *Comparative Studies in Society and History*, 23 (1981): 591–619.

———. 'Reply to William Green's: "The Perils of Comparative History"', *Comparative Studies in Society and History*, 26 (1984): 120–25.

Brathwaite, K. 'The Slave Rebellion in the Great River Valley of St. James, 1831/32', *Jamaican Historical Review*, 13 (1982): 11–30.

Bush, B. 'Towards Emancipation: Slave Women and Resistance to Coer-cive Labour Regimes in the British West Indian Colonies, 1790–1838', in D. Richardson, ed. *Abolition and its Aftermath: The Historical Context, 1790–1916*. London: Frank Cass, 1985: 27–54.

Chambers, D. 'Tracing Igbo into the Diaspora', in P. E. Lovejoy, ed., *Identity in the Shadow of Slavery*. London: Continuum International Publishing Group, 2000: 55–71.

Carrington, S. 'The State of the Debate on the Role of Capitalism in the Ending of the Slave System', *The Journal of Caribbean History*, 22, 1 & 2 (1988): 20–41.

Cateau, H. 'Beyond Planters and Plantership', in Cateau and Rita Pemberton, eds., *Beyond Tradition: Reinterpreting the Caribbean Historical Experience*. Kingston: Ian Randle, 2006: 3–21.

Claypole, W.A and D.J. Buisserret. 'Trade Patterns in Early English Jamaica', *Journal of Caribbean History*, 15 (1972): 1–19.

Craton, M. 'Jamaican Slave Mortality: Fresh Light from Worthy Park, Longville and the Tharp Estates', *Journal of Caribbean History*, 3 (1971): 1–27.

———. 'Hobbesian or Panglossian?: The Two Extremes of Slave Conditions in the British Caribbean, 1783–1834', *William and Mary Quarterly*, 3rd series, 35 (1978): 324–56.

———. 'The Historical Roots of the Plantation Model', *Slavery and Abolition*, 5 (1984): 189–221.

———. 'Proto-Peasant Revolts? The Late Slave Rebellions in the British West Indies, 1816–32', *Past and Present*, 85, (1979): 99–125.

———. 'Slave Culture, Resistance and the Achievement of Emancipation in the British West Indies, 1783–1838', in J. Walvin, ed., *Slavery and British Society, 1776–1846*. London: MacMillan, 1982: 100–122.

————. 'Changing Patterns of Slave Families in the British West Indies', in H. Beckles and V. Shepherd, eds., *Caribbean Slave Society and Economy*. Kingston: Ian Randle Publishers, 1991: 228–49.

Curtin, P.D. 'Measuring the Atlantic Slave Trade', in S.L. Engerman and E. D. Genovese, eds., *Race and Slavery in the Western Hemisphere*. Princeton: Princeton University, 1975: 107–28.

de Kilson, M.D., 'Towards Freedom: An Analysis of Slave Revolts in the United States', *Phylon*, 25 (1964): 179–84.

Drescher, S. 'The Decline Thesis of British Slavery Since Econocide', *Slavery and Abolition*, 7, 1 (1986): 1–24.

Dunbar, G. 'Colonial Carolina Cowpens', *Agricultural History*, 25 (1961):125–30.

Dunn, R. 'A Tale of Two Plantations: Slave Life at Mesopotamia in Jamaica and Mount Airy in Virginia, 1799–1828', *William and Mary Quarterly*, 3rd series, 34 (1977): 32–65.

————. '"Dreadful Idlers" in the Cane Fields: The Slave Labour Pattern on a Jamaican Sugar Estate, 1762–1831', *The Journal of Interdisciplinary History*, 17 (1987): 795–822.

Dupuy, A. 'Slavery and Underdevelopment in the Caribbean: A Critique of the "Plantation Economy" Perspective', *Dialectical Anthropology*, 7 (1983): 237–51.

Eblen, J.E. 'On the Natural Increase of Slave Populations: The Example of the Cuban Black Population, 1775–1900', in S.L. Engerman and E. D. Genovese, eds., *Race and Slavery in the Western Hemisphere*. Princeton: Princeton University Press, 1975: 211–47.

Emery, F. 'The Farming Regions of Wales', in J. Thirsk, ed., *The Agrarian History of the British West Indies*. Cambridge: Cambridge University Press, 4 (1967): 137–42.

Engerman, S.L. 'Some Economic and Demographic Comparisons of Slavery in the United States and the British West Indies', *Economic History Review*, 2nd series, 29 (1976): 258–75.

Farley, R. 'The Rise of the Peasantry in British Guiana', *Social and Economic Studies*, 2 (1954): 87–103.

Frederickson, G.M., and C. Lasch. 'Resistance to Slavery', *Civil War History*, 13 (1967): 315–29.

Genovese, E.D. 'Livestock in the Slave Economy', in E.D. Genovese, *The Political Economy of Slavery: Studies in the Economy and Society of the South*. New York: Pantheon, 1965: 106–123.

————. 'The Treatment of Slaves in Different Countries: Prob-lems in the Application of the Comparative Model', L. Foner and E.D. Genovese, eds., *Slavery in the New World: A Reader in Comparative History*. New Jersey: Prentice-Hall, 1969: 202–10.

Grainger, J. 'An Essay on the Management and Diseases of Negroes', in J. Edward Hutson, ed., *On the Treatment and Management of the More Common West India Diseases (1750–1802)*. Kingston: University of the West Indies Press, 2005: 9–54.

Green, W. 'The Perils of Comparative History: Belize and the British Sugar Colonies after Slavery', *Comparative Studies in Society and History*, 26 (1984): 112–19.

————. 'The Planter Class and British West Indian Sugar Production before and after Emancipation', *Economic History Review,* 26 (1973): 448–463.

Hall, D.G. 'The Flight from the Estates Reconsidered', *Journal of Caribbean History,* 10 and 11 (1978): 7–24.

Higman, B.W. 'The Slave Family and Household in the British West Indies, 1800–1834', *Journal of Interdisciplinary History,* 7 (1975): 261–67.

————. 'Methodological Problems in the Study of the Slave Family', in V. Rubin and A. Tuden, eds., *Comparative Perspectives on Slavery in New World Plantation Societies.* New York: New York Academy of Sciences, 1977: 591–96.

————. 'Domestic Service in Jamaica Since 1750', in B.W. Higman, ed., *Trade, Government and Society in Caribbean History, 1700–1920: Essays Presented to Douglas Hall.* Kingston: Heinemann Educational Books Caribbean, 1983: 117–38.

————. 'The Spatial Economy of Jamaican Sugar Plantations: Cartographic Evidence from the Eighteenth and Nine-teenth Centuries', *Journal of Historical Geography,* 13 (1987): 17–39.

————. 'The Internal Economy of Jamaican Pens', *Social and Economic Studies,* 38, no. 1 (1989): 61–86.

Inikori J., and Engerman, S. L. 'Introduction: Gains and Losers in the Atlantic Slave Trade', in Joseph Inikori & Stanley Engerman., eds., *The Atlantic Slave Trade: Effects on Economies, Societies and Peoples in Africa, the Americas and Europe.* Durham: Duke University Press, 1992: 1–24.

Innes, F.C. 'The Pre-Sugar Era of European Settlement in Barbados', *Journal of Caribbean History.* 1 (1970): 1–22.

Klein, H. S. and S.L. Engerman. 'Fertility Differentials between Slaves in the United States and the British West Indies: A Note on Lacta-tion Practices and their Possible Implications', *William and Mary Quarterly,* 3rd Series, 35(1978): 357–74.

Knight, F. 'Slavery and Lagging Capitalism in the Spanish and Portuguese American Empires', in B. Solow, ed., *Slavery and the Rise of the Atlantic System.* Cambridge: Cambridge University Press, 1991: 62–74.

Lamur, H. 'Demographic Performance of Two Slave Populations of the Dutch-Speaking Caribbean', in H. Beckles and V. Shepherd, eds., *Caribbean Slave Society and Economy.* Kingston: Ian Randle Publishers, 1991:209–20.

Lovejoy, P. E. 'The Volume of the Atlantic Slave Trade: A Synthesis', *Journal of African History,* 23,(1982): 473–501.

Mintz, S. 'Slave Life on Caribbean Sugar Plantations: Some Unanswered Questions', in S. Palmiè, ed., *Slave Cultures and the Cultures of Slavery.* Knoxville: University of Tennessee Press, 1995: 12–22.

————. 'The Origins of the Reconstituted Peasantries', in S. Mintz, *Caribbean Transformations.* Chicago: Aldine Publishing, 1974: 146–56.

————. 'Slavery and the Rise of Peasantries', in M. Craton, ed., *Roots and Branches: Current Directions in Slave Studies.* Toronto: Pergamon Press, 1979: 213–42.

Mintz, S. and D.G. Hall. 'The Origins of the Jamaican Internal Marketing System', *Yale University Publications in Anthropology,* no. 57, 1960: 3–26.

Morgan, P.D. 'Work and Culture: The Task System and the World of Low Country Blacks, 1700–1880', *William and Mary Quarterly*, 3rd series, 39 (1982): 563–99.

———. 'The Ownership of Property by Slaves in the Midnineteenth Century Low Country', *Journal of Southern History*, 49 (1983): 399–420.

Otto, J.S. 'Livestockraising in early South Carolina, 1670–1700: Prelude to the Rice Plantation Economy', *Agricultural History*, 61 (1987): 13–24.

Otto, J.S. and N.E. Anderson. 'Cattle ranching in the Venezuelan Llanos and Florida Flatwoods: A Problem in Comparative History', *Comparative Studies in Society and History*, 28 (1986): 672–83.

Paget, H. 'The Free Village System in Jamaica', *Caribbean Quarterly*, 1(1948): 7–19.

Perkins, J.A. '*The Ox, the Horse and English Patterns of Slave Families in the British West Indies,*' Working Paper in Economic History, 3/1875, University of New South Wales: 2–15.

Pryor, F. L. 'The Plantation Economy as an Economic System', *Journal of Comparative Economics,* 6 (1982): 288–317.

Riviere, W.E. 'Labour Shortage in the British West Indies after Eman-cipation', *Journal of Caribbean History*, 4 (1972): 1–30.

Rodney, W., 'How Europe Became the Dominant Section of a World-Wide Trade System', in H. Beckles and V. Shepherd, eds., *Caribbean Slavery in the Atlantic World*. Kingston: Ian Randle Publishers, 2000: 2–10.

Saunders, G. 'Slavery and Cotton Culture in the Bahamas,' in V.A. Shepherd, ed., *Slavery without Sugar: Diversity in Caribbean Economy and Society since the 17th Century.* Florida: University Press of Florida, 2002, pp. 129-151.

Senior, C. H. 'German Immigrants in Jamaica, 1834–1838', *Journal of Caribbean History*, 10 and 11(1978): 25–53.

Shepherd, V.A. 'Transients to Citizens', *Jamaica Journal*, 18 (1985): 17–26.

———. 'From Rural Plantations to Urban Slums: The Economic Status and Problems of East Indians in Kingston, Jamaica, in the Late Nineteenth and Early Twentieth Centuries', *Immigrants and Minorities,* 5 (1986): 129–44.

———. 'Economic Problems of Indians in Western Kingston (Jamaica) 1930–1950', *Jamaican Historical Review*, 15 (1986): 17–30.

———. 'Depression in the "Tin Roof Towns": Economic Problems of Urban Indians in Jamaica, 1930–1950', in D. Dabydeen and B. Samaroo, eds., *India in the Caribbean*. London: A Hansib/University of Warwick, Centre of Caribbean Studies Publication, 1987: 173–88.

———. 'Livestock and Marginality in Jamaica's Sugar Plantation Society: A tentative Analysis', *Social and Economic Studies*, 41, no. 2 (1992):183–202.

———.'Liberation Struggles on Livestock Farms in Jamaica', in H. Beckles and V. Shepherd, eds., *Caribbean Slavery in the Atlantic World*. Kingston: Ian Randle Publishers, 2000: 896–904.

———. 'Questioning Creole', in V. Shepherd and G. Richards, eds., *Questioning Creole: Creolisation Discourses in Caribbean Culture*. Kingston: Ian Randle Publishers, 2002: 67–80.

———. '"To Be Hanged by the Neck Until He Be Dead": The King Against Samuel Sharpe, April 1832', *Jamaica Journal,* 29, nos. 1 & 2 (June-October, 2005): 54–59.

———.'Monuments, Memorialisation and Decolonisation in Jamaica', *Jamaica Journal,* 29, no. 3 (Dec. 2005–April 2006): 34–43.

———.and K.E.A. Monteith. 'Non-Sugar Proprietors in a Sugar Plantation Society', *Plantation Society in the Americas,* 2 & 3 (Fall 1998): 205–25.

———. and Ahmed Reid. 'Rebel Voices: Confessions, Testimonies and Trial Transcripts from the 1831/32 Emancipation War in Jamaica', *Jamaica Journal,* 28, nos. 2&3 (December 2004): 59–64.

Sheridan, R.B. 'Simon Taylor: Sugar Tycoon of Jamaica, 1740–1815', *Agricultural History,* 45 (1971): 285–96.

———. 'Mortality and the Medical Treatment of Slaves in the British West Indies', in S. L. Engerman and E. D. Genovese eds., *Race and Slavery in the Western Hemisphere.* Princeton: Princeton University, 1975: 285–310.

Sio, A.A. 'Marginality and FreeColoured Identity in the Caribbean Slave Society', *Slavery and Abolition,* 8 (1987): 166–82.

Smith, M.G. 'Social Structure in the British Caribbean about 1820', *Social and Economic Studies,* 1, no. 4 (1955): 55–59.

Ward, J.R. 'The Profitability of Sugar Planting in the British West Indies, 1650–1834', *Economic History Review,* 31, 2 (1978): 197–213.

Wells, A. 'Review: A Bahian Counterpoint: Sugar, Tobacco, Cassava, and Slavery in the Recôncavo, 1780–1860' and 'Campanha Gaúcha: A Brazillian Ranching System, 1850–1920?', *Plantation Society in the Americas.* 6, 1 (1999): 95–106.

Whittaker, A.P. 'The Spanish Contribution to American Agriculture'. *Agricultural History* 3(1929): 1–14.

Wilmot, S. 'Not "Full Free": The Exslaves and the Apprenticeship System in Jamaica, 1834–1838', *Jamaica Journal,* 17 (1984): 2–10.

———. 'Emancipation in Action: Workers and Wage Conflict in Jamaica, 1838–1840', *Jamaica Journal,* 19 (1986): 55–61.

Wood, B.C. 'Some Aspects of Female Resistance to Chattel Slavery in Low Country Georgia', *The Historical Journal,* 30, no. 3 (1987): 603–22.

Wood, B.C. and T. R. Clayton. 'Slave Birth, Death and Disease on Golden Grove Estate, Jamaica, 1765–1810', *Slavery and Abolition,* 6 (1985): 99–121.

Zahadieh, N. 'Trade, Plunder and Economic Development in Early English Jamaica, 1655–1689', *The Economic History Review,* 39 (1986): 205–22.

———. 'The Merchants of Port Royal, Jamaica, and the Spanish Contraband Trade, 1655–1692', *William and Mary Quarterly,* 3rd series, 43 (1986): 570–93.

DISSERTATIONS

Bailey, W. 'Kingston, 1692–1843: A Colonial City'. PhD diss., University of the West Indies, Mona, Jamaica, 1974.

Duncker, S. 'The Free-Coloured and their Fight for Civil Rights in Jamaica, 1800-30'. M.A diss., London, 1960.

Higman, B.W. 'Slave Population and Economy in Jamaica at the Time of Emancipation'. PhD diss., University of the West Indies, Mona, Jamaica, 1970.

Mathurin-Mair, L. 'An Historical Study of Women in Jamaica'. PhD diss., University of the West Indies, Mona, Jamaica, 1974.

Montieth, K. 'The Coffee Industry in Jamaica, 1790-1880'. M. Phil diss., University of the West Indies, Mona, Jamaica, 1987.

Satchell, V. 'Rural Land Transactions in Jamaica, 1866–1900'. M. Phil diss., University of the West Indies, Mona, Jamaica, 1986.

Senior, C.H. 'Bountied European Immigration into Jamaica, 1834–42'. PhD diss., University of the West Indies, Mona, Jamaica, 1977.

Shepherd, V.A. 'Separation vs Integration: The Experiences of the Indian Group in the Creole Society of Jamaica, 1879–1945'. M. Phil diss., University of the West Indies, Mona, Jamaica, 1984.

———.'Pens and Penkeepers in a Plantation Society: Aspects of Jamaican Social and Economic History.' PhD diss., University of Cambridge, 1988.

Sohal, H. S. 'The East Indian Indentureship System in Jamaica, 1845–1917'. PhD diss., Waterloo, 1979.

Wu, Yu. 'Jamaican Trade: 1688-1769: A Quantitative Study'. PhD diss., Johns Hopkins University, 1995.

Zahadieh, N. 'Trade Plunder and Economic Development in Early English Jamaica, 1655–1689'. PhD diss., London, 1984.

PAMPHLETS/ PAPERS

Armstrong, D.V. 'The Slave Village at Seville, Jamaica: The First Phase of Archaeological Research'. Paper presented at the Twentieth Conference of the Association of Caribbean Historians, St. Thomas, US Virgin Islands, March 1988.

Beckles, H. 'Slaves and the Internal Market Economy of Barbados: A Perspective on NonViolent Resistance'. Paper presented at the Twentieth Conference of the Association of Caribbean Historians, St. Thomas, US Virgin Islands, March 1988.

Boa, S. 'Freed Women's Economic Contributions to Jamaica, 1760–1834'. Postgraduate Seminar Paper, Department of History, University of the West Indies, Mona, April 1985.

Eltis, D., 'The Volume and Structure of the Transatlantic Slave Trade: A Reassessment'. Paper presented at the Conference on Enslaving Connections: Africa and Brazil during the Era of the Slave Trade, York University, Toronto, October 2000.

Gaspar, B. 'Amelioration or Oppression?: Abolition of the Slaves' Sunday Markets in Antigua'. Paper presented at the Twentieth Conference of the Association of Caribbean Historians, St. Thomas, US Virgin Islands, March 1988.

Hall, D.G. 'Fort George Pen, Jamaica: Slaves, Tenants and Labourers'. Paper presented at the Eleventh Conference of the Asso-ciation of Caribbean Historians, Curaçao, April 1979.

————. 'Runaways in Jamaica in the Mideighteenth Century, One Man's Record: A Working Paper'. Postgraduate Seminar paper, Department of History, University of the West Indies, Mona, February 1984.

————. 'Long-Term Trends in Jamaican Domestic Service'. Paper presented at the Symposium: Engendering History, University of the West Indies, Mona, 1993.

Marshall, B. 'Slavery and the Plantation System in the British Windward Islands'. Paper presented at the Third Con-ference of the Association of Caribbean Historians, Guyana, April 1971.

Marshall, W. K. 'Provision Ground and Plantation Labour: Competition for Resources'. Paper presented at the Twentieth Con-ference of Caribbean Historians, St. Thomas, US Virgin Islands, March 1988.

Shepherd, V.A. 'Problems in the Supply of Livestock to Sugar Estates in the Period of Slavery: An Example from the History of Spring Sugar Plantation in the Parish of St. Andrew, Jamaica, c.1700–c.1800'. Postgraduate Seminar paper, Department of History, University of the West Indies, Mona, Jamaica, May 1987.

————. 'The Evolution and Expansion of the Penkeeping Indus-try in Jamaica'. Caribbean Societies Seminar paper, Institute of Commonwealth Studies, London, February 1988.

————. 'The Effects of Emancipation on Jamaican Pens, 1838–1845'. Paper presented at the Society for Caribbean Studies Conference, Herts., England, July 1988.

————. 'The Ranking Game: Discourses of Belonging in Jamaican History'. Inaugural Lecture, University of the West Indies, Mona, April 2002.

INDEX

Africans, enslaved: augmentation by natural increase, 124, 126, 130; control and supervision of, 147-151; ethnic profile of, on pens, 130-131; income earning activities on pens, 141-143; internal relocation of, 123; as labour force on plantations, 19-20; on pens, participation in armed revolt, 158-174; pursuit of economic independence, 140-143; resistance to Spanish occupation, xx; self-liberation ethos of, xxxv; size of labour force on pens, 131-132; sources of supply of, 121-130; struggle for freedom, 147; work regime of, on pens, 137-148

Africans: enslavement of, xxii

Agricultural decision-making: behavioural model, 37; models of, 37

Anguin, John, 88

Anguin, Robert Hilton, 85, 102, 104; petition for white privileges, 106

Apprenticeship: on pens, 175, 180-198

Armed revolt: participation of enslaved on pens in, 158-174

Asiento: negotiation of, by Britain, 20

Atlantic World: concept of, 144-146; instability of, xxix; interconnectedness of the, 48

Attorneys: becoming pen-keepers, 79, 80, 82

Banana: rise of, 211-215

Baptist War. *See* Emancipation War

Barbados: mills in, 30

Barclay, David: attitude to the enslaved, 105-106; manumission of enslaved Africans, 153-154

Belonging, xiv, xv

Black Power movement: in Jamaica, xxvii

Blagrove, John, 87

Blagrove family: in horseracing, 96

Border clashes, xiii, xvii

Brathwaite, Kamau: on categories of settlers in Jamaica, 101

Brazil: inter-property links in, 52-53; livestock industry in, 39

Brown, Hamilton, 82, 87, 93, 105

Cane: interplay of cattle and, 39

Cardiff Hall, 96, 98

Cattle: increase in, 26; interplay of cane and, 39

Cattle mills, 23, 25, 26, 27, 29. *See also* Mills

Chippenham Park Pen, 98, 99

Christmas Rebellion. *See* Emancipation War

Ciboney: struggle between Tainos and, xvii

Coffee: production of, xxi, 43

Coffee planters: racial composition of, 85-86

Columbus, Christopher: in Jamaica, xix

Consolidated Slave Act, 1792: in practice on pens, 141

Creole economy: and Creole ideology, 102-103

Creole ideology: and Creole society, 102-103

Creole society: pen-keepers in, xxviii-xxix, 220

Crop specialization: by geographic zone, 43

Cuba: cattle ranching in, 39; inter-property links in, 52-53

Davis, J.W., in horseracing, 95

Demographic studies: of Caribbean slavery, xxxi-xxxii

Domestics, enslaved: gendered division of labour among, 138; mixed race, 138-139; status of, 139

Economic diversification, xiv; in the Caribbean, 120; impact of, xxix
Elbridge, Aldworth, 32
Elbridge Papers, 33
Emancipation War, 1831/32, 160-168; enslaved Africans on pens in, 159; role of, in ending slavery, 159-160
English: capture of Jamaica, xx
Exports: cocoa, 9-10

Federation, West Indies, xxvi
Ferguson, James: will of, 106-107
Forbes, George, 82, 92-93, 104
Fort George Pen: labour supply after emancipation, 190-191
Freedom: routes to, 151-155; struggle of enslaved people for, 147

Garrisons, xvii
Garvey, Marcus, xxvi
Gender differentiation: in task allocation to enslaved Africans, 132-137
Graham, Francis: inventory of, 97
Graziers. See Pen-keepers
Guinea grass, 40

Harmer, Stephen, 149-150
Hatos: establishment of, under Spanish, xx
Haughton Court estate, Hanover, 81
Helyar, Cary, 10
Hibbert, Thomas, 34
Hides: export of, under Spanish Jamaica, 2
Higman, Barry: Slave Population of the British Caribbean, xxxi; Slave Population and Economy in Jamaica, 1807-1834, xxxi
Horseracing: as income earner for pen-

keepers, 95-97
Housekeepers, 88-89, 150
Hunt, Joseph, 32

Immigration, European: in post-emancipation period, 193
Indentureship, European: and conflict over terrain, xxi, xxii

Jamaica: context of development in pre-sugar era, 11-13; diversified economy in early settlement period, 1; independence for, xxvi; plantation economy model in, xiv; rise of pen-keeping in, 1-2
Jews: in banana business, 213
Jobbing, 53-54

Labour problems: immigration experiment to solve after Emancipation, 193; on pens, after Apprenticeship, 189-208
Land use: contests over, xiv; hierarchy in, xxvii
Landholdings: change in pattern of, 17-18
Lewis, John, 32
Livestock: demand for, in plantation economy, 22, 24, 25; duty on imported, 70-71; importation of, 65, 68-70; interplay of cane and, 39; types, 22-23; volume sold domestically, 57
Livestock, Sugar and Slavery: Contested Terrain in Colonial Jamaica: organization of, xxxvi-xxxvii; sources, xxxv-xxxvi
Livestock economy: stages of, 6-10
Livestock farmers. See Pen-keepers
Livestock farming, xiv, xxi; decline of, in Spanish Jamaica, 3-4; in England, 5-6; export dimension of, 49; in Jamaica, 1, 13; revival of, 1870s, 209;

revival of, under English, 5-6; role of, in pre-sugar Jamaica, 11; in rural economies, 1

Livestock trade: and development of internal economic links, 59

Lluidas Vale, 7

M'Mahon, Benjamin, xxxiii, 79-80, 224 n.34

Manumission: on pens, 152-154

Marketing: by enslaved Africans, 141

Maroons: resistance to Spanish occupation, xx

Matthews, pen-keeper, 104-105

Mills: animal, 23, 27, 30; in Barbados, 30; in Jamaica, 31; tide, 27; water, 26, 29; wind, 23, 29

Monoculture: of sugar, in the Caribbean, xxx-xxxi

Morant Bay Rebellion, xxv-xxvi

Navigation Acts, 65

Overseers: becoming pen-keepers, 79, 80, 82; sexual exploitation of enslaved women, 89

Pasturage, 54

Pedro District, St Ann: pens in, 40, 78, profitability of pens in, 91

Pen: meaning, xxxii-xxxiii

Pen-keepers, xiv; aspirations to elite society, 104; attorneys as, 79, 80, 82; character of, 78-79; collective action among, 111-112; contest between sugar planters and, xxvii; creole, 86; diversity among, 83-91; economic status of, 91-99; educational level, 87; female, 85; in horseracing, 95-97; ideology of, 117; interaction between sugar planters and, 107-112; investment in sugar industry, xxvii-xxviii, 46; labour problems after

Apprenticeship, 189-208; marital status, 87-90; meaning, xxxiii-xxxiv; of mixed race, 84-85; as new agro-elite in the 1880s, 208; overseers as, 79, 80; political status, 112-118; religious persuasion, 90-91; as resident proprietors, 83-84; role and status of, xiv, xxviii; routes to upward social mobility, 103-107; self-sufficiency among, 92; sexual exploitation of women, 89; as social inferiors, 103; visibility of males, 210

Pen-keeping: attempts to revive, 1870s, 209; restructuring of, post-1848, 203; rise of, in Jamaica, 1-2; settler population and, 8-9; sugar revolution and, 14-15

Pens: compared to plantations, xxxiv-xxxv; connections to sugar industry, xiv; creolized enslaved populations on, 123; distribution pattern of, 38-39, 40-43; economic decline in post emancipation period, 198-203; enslaved on, in Emancipation War, 1831/32, 162-166; enslaved labourers on, xiv; exports from, 49-52; grass, 44-46, 103; importation of livestock for, 65; increase in number, 14-15; in internal trade, 49, 52-64; labour problems on, after Apprenticeship, 183-189; in Pedro District, St Ann, 40, 78; satellite, 123; services provided by, 53, 54-55

Pepper Pen, 95-96

Phoenix Park: immigration experiment after emancipation, 193

Plantation economy model (PEM): and Jamaica's economic history, xxxiv

Plantations: compared to pens, xxxiv-xxxv; and demand for livestock, 22, 24, 25

Price, Francis, 7

Pringle, John, 214

Ranking: class and, 101; defined, 100-101; ethnicity and, 101; location and, 101; place of birth and, 101; top, 101

Ranking game: belonging and unbelonging, xv; Caribbean societies in the, xxviii; roots of, xiv, xv

Rastafarianism: development of, xxvii

Resistance: day-to-day strategies, 155-158; runaways, 156-157, 158; to slavery, xxiii, 150-151;

Royal African Company, 20

Rum: internal sale of, 54

Sam Sharpe Rebellion. *See* Emancipation War

Scott-Moncrieffe, Benjamin, 82, 85, 102; in horseracing, 95, 96-97; petition for white privileges, 106

Settler population: and growth of pen-keeping, 8-9

Sexploitation, 147

Sexual exploitation: of enslaved women, 89

Shepherd, Verene: *Livestock, Sugar and Slavery: Contested Terrain in Colonial Jamaica*, xxxv-xxxvi , xxxvi-xxxvii

Slave Population of the British Caribbean, xxxi; *Slave Population and Economy in Jamaica, 1807-1834*, Barry Higman, xxxi

Slavery, xxii-xxiii; complexity and diversity of, xxxiv; resistance to, xxiii

Social mobility: routes to, for pen-keepers, 103-107; through marriage, 106-107

Spanish America: trade with Jamaica, 65-69, 71-76

Spanish Jamaica: decline of, 3-4; economic activities in, 2-3; pen-keeping in, 2; sugar planters in, 3. *See also* Jamaica

Spring Plantation: case study, 32-36

St Ann: agricultural zones in, 40-41

Stray animals, 108-110

Sugar Duties Act, 220

Sugar estates: replaced by pens, 43-46

Sugar industry: connections with pens, xiv

Sugar planters: contest between pen-keepers and, xxvii; interaction between pen-keepers and, 107-112; in Spanish Jamaica, 3

Sugar revolution: impact on pen-keeping, 14-15; factors leading to, in Jamaica, 11, 15-22

Tainos: settlement in Jamaica, xviii-xix; struggle between Ciboney and, xvii;

Terrain: contest over, xiii, xvii, xix; ideological, xiii, xxvii; physical, xiii

Tharp, John, 93; value of enslaved people and stock of, 97

Thistlewood, Thomas, xxxiii, xxxv, 82-83, 87, 89; evidence of resistance, 155-158; sexual exploitation of enslaved women, 89-90, 147, 148-149; social relations of, 107-108, 225 n.38

Tidemills. *See* Mills

Trade: between Jamaica and Spanish America, 65-69, 71-76; external, 9-10, 49

Trade, internal, 9, 49; goods involved in, 53; services provided by pens, 53

Trading network: in the Atlantic World, 48; mercantilist model, 48

Turf: contest over, xvii

Unbelonging, xv

Unity Valley Pen: manumission of enslaved persons on, 153-154; 245 n.22

Vineyard Pen, 55

Watermills. *See* Mills
Wedderburn, James: sexual exploitation
    of enslaved women, 147-148
Wedderburn, Robert, 147
Williamson, Sarah Tracey, 88
Windmills. *See* Mills
Women: as pen-keepers, 85; sexual
    exploitation of enslaved, 89
Woodard, Anna, 85
Work regime: of enslaved persons on
    pens, 137-138
Worthy Park: formation of, 7

Lightning Source UK Ltd.
Milton Keynes UK
UKOW05f2109061014

239718UK00002B/195/P